After the War Was Over

PRINCETON MODERN GREEK STUDIES

This series is sponsored by the Princeton University Program in Hellenic Studies under the auspices of the Stanley J. Seeger Hellenic Fund.

After the War Was Over

RECONSTRUCTING THE
FAMILY, NATION, AND STATE
IN GREECE, 1943–1960

Mark Mazower, Editor

PRINCETON UNIVERSITY PRESS

PRINCETON AND OXFORD

Library of Congress Cataloging-in-Publication Data

After the war was over : reconstructing the family, nation, and state in Greece,
1943–1960 / Mark Mazower, editor.
    p. cm. — (Princeton modern Greek studies)
    Includes bibliographical references and index.
    ISBN 0-691-05841-5 (alk. paper) — ISBN 0-691-05842-3 (pbk. : alk. paper)
    1. Greece—History—Civil War, 1944–1949. 2. Reconstruction
(1939–1951)—Greece—Political aspects. 3. Greeks—Social conditions—1945–
I. Mazower, Mark. II. Series.

DF849.5.A48 2000
949.507′4—dc21   00-036680

This book is dedicated to the memory of

Nancy Crawshaw
and
Mando Dalianis

Contents

Abbreviations and Glossary of Terms

AGDNG *Archeio Genikis Doiikisis Voreio Ellada*
       Historical Archive of Macedonia, Archives of the General
         Directorate of Northern Greece
AGDWM *Archeio Genikis Doiikisis Dytikis Makedonias*
       Archive of the General Directorate of Western Macedonia
AJDC   American Joint Distribution Committee
ASKI   *Archeia Synchronis Koinonikis Istoria*
       Archive of Contemporary Social History, Athens
BA   *Bundesarchiv Koblenz*
       Federal Archives
BA/ZWA *Bundesarchiv-Zwischenarchiv Hengelar*
       Federal Archives, Hengelar Archive
BLO   British Liaison Officer
CJMCAG The Conference for Jewish Material Claims against
         Germany
DSE   *Dimokratikos Stratos Ellados*
       Democratic Army of Greece
EA   *Ethniki Allilengyi*
       National Solidarity
EAM   *Ethniko Apeleftherotiko Metopo*
       National Liberation Front
EASAD *Ethnikos Agrotikos Syndesmos Antikommounistikis*
       Draseos
       National Agrarian Federation of Anticommunist Action
EDA   *Eniaia Dimokratiki Aristera*
       United Democratic Left
EDES   *Ethnikos Dimokratikos Ellinikos Syndesmos*
       National Republican Greek league
ELAS   *Ethnikos Laikos Apeleftherotikos Stratos*
       National People's Liberation Army
EP   *Ehniki Politofylaki*
       Civil Guard (EAM)
EPON   *Eniaia Panelladiki Organosi Neon*
       United Panhellenic Organization of Youth

ESAG	*Eidiki Scholi Anamorfosi Gynaikon*
	Special School for the Reeduction of Women
FO	Public Record Office, London, Foreign Office Files
"Joint"	see *AJDC*
KEPP	*Kentriki Epitropi Peloponnisiakis Periferias*
	Central Committee for the Peloponnese Region
KKE	*Kommounistiko Kommo Ellados*
	Communist Party of Greece
OPLA	*Organosi Perifrourisi tou Laikou Agona*
	Organization for the Protection of the People's Struggle
OSS	Office of Strategic Services
PAAA	*Politisches Archiv des Auswärtigen Amtes,* Bonn
	Foreign Ministry, Political Archive
PASOK	*Panellinio Sosialistiko Komma*
	Panhellenic Socialist Movement
PEEA	*Politiki Epitropi Ethnikis Apeleftherosis*
	Political Committee for National Liberation
PEOPEF	*Panelliniki Enosi Oikogeneion Politikon Exoriston kai Fylakismenon*
	Panhellenic Union of Families of Political Exiles and Prisoners
PRO	Public Records Office, London
SB	Security Battalions
SNOF	*Slovenomakedonski Narodno Osloboditelen Front*
	Slav Macedonian Liberation Front
SOE	Special Operations Executive
USNA	United States National Archives, Washington, D.C.
WO	Public Record Office, London, War Office files

GLOSSARY OF TERMS

andarte	resistance fighter
archigos	political or military leader
Dekemvriana	December events (December 1944)
dilosi	declaration of repentance
dilosies	those who signed declarations of repentance
ethniki syneidisi	national consciousness
ethnikofrosini	national-mindedness
ipefthinos	village leader
kapetan	leader of a guerrilla band
laokratia	People's rule (EAM/ELAS slogan)

-Key-

- Original Greek Kingdom
- Ionian Islands ceded by Great Britain, 1864
- Thessaly, added 1881
- Macedonia, Crete and Islands added after the Balkan Wars, 1913
- Ceded by Treaty of Sèvres (not ratified) 1920
- Ceded by Treaty of Lausanne, 1923
- Dodecanese ceded by Italy, 1947

The Territorial Development
of the Greek Kingdom
1832-1947

Miles
0   50   100   150   200

Historical

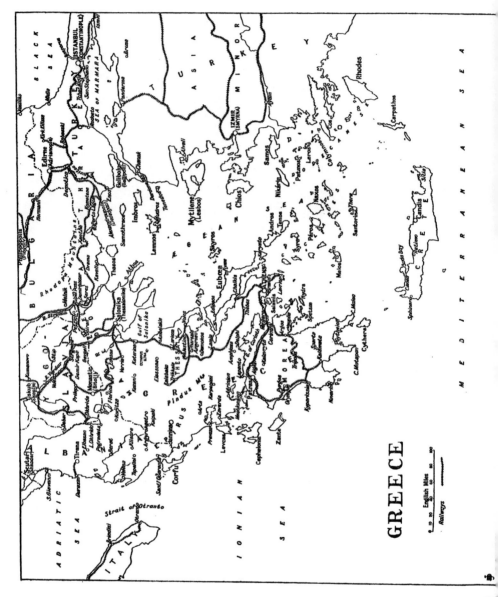

GREECE

English Miles

0 10 20 40 60 80 100

Railways -----------

After the War Was Over

Introduction

Mark Mazower

IN APRIL 1941, the German army swept into Greece, ushering in nearly a decade of social disintegration, political collapse, and mass violence unprecedented in degree and scale. The country's governmental system had been unstable before the war, but despite a volatile history of coups, military interventions, purges, and countercoups, it had never generated the intense hostility and bloodshed that were to follow. The interwar years had been a period of chronic crisis, as Greece's parliamentary democracy split apart in the "national schism" between republican Venizelists and royalist anti-Venizelists. A frail economy burdened by foreign indebtedness and the cost of fighting a decade of wars between 1912 and 1922 had also struggled to cope with the aftermath of that earlier era of conflict—the huge influx of refugees who fled the lands of the Ottoman empire and the Black Sea shoreline. Perhaps more than one and a half million newcomers entered a nation-state yet to absorb into the governmental machinery the large new territories it had won in the north—in Macedonia and Thrace—with their Slavic, Jewish, and Muslim minorities. Not surprisingly, the resultant strains—between Venizelists and royalists, between refugee newcomers and so-called autochthones, between the Greek majority and non-Greek minorities—presented obstacles that the country's political elite found it hard to overcome. The interwar economic depression brought about the downfall of the only politician of any stature: Venizelos himself. In 1936, parliamentary democracy was suspended and replaced by the right-wing dictatorship of General Ioannis Metaxas, a loyal royalist. Metaxas immediately set about destroying the Left, making lavish use of the anticommunist legislation passed by his predecessors. Communists real and suspected, as well as union organizers, were exiled or jailed by special tribunals. All this was repression on a scale not seen before in Greece; but it paled into insignificance compared with what was to follow.

In the spring of 1941, the country was split between three occupiers: the Italians held central Greece, Epiros, the Peloponnese, and the Cyclades; the Germans held most of the remaining points of strategic importance, including central Macedonia (with its capital, Salonika) and

Crete; the Bulgarians took over eastern Macedonia and western Thrace. Although a quisling government was set up in Athens under General Tsolakoglou, its rule over these three occupation zones was generally indirect and its hold precarious. Just how precarious was revealed almost immediately, as the food supply dwindled and starvation threatened the major cities and the islands. Soon it became clear that the Tsolakoglou regime was not powerful enough to collect the harvest from the farmers and deliver it to the towns. The tens of thousands of victims who died of hunger in the first winter of occupation testified to the political and administrative impotence of the Greek state machine in Athens. In effect, Greece barely existed as a political entity.

In this political vacuum, the efforts of most ordinary people to keep themselves alive and to secure access to food and security—basic citizenship rights that the Greek state could no longer guarantee—slowly assumed a political coloration. What one might call social resistance emerged alongside the pro-Allied intelligence and sabotage work in which some small groups had engaged almost from the moment the occupation began. In the summer and autumn of 1941 there were even sporadic attacks upon Axis troops: some were the acts of bands of Greek ex-servicemen, some represented the political initiative of Leftists. But when local communists organized an uprising against Bulgarian rule in the area of Drama, they unleashed a Bulgarian massacre of Greek civilians in retaliation, and thousands of frightened refugees fled the Bulgarian zone for Salonika. In October 1941, an attack on German soldiers in the Strymon valley was followed by Wehrmacht reprisals that led to the mass execution of more than two hundred villagers in Ano and Kato Kerzilion.

Hence in the winter of 1941, shocked by the vehemence of the Axis response, armed resistance died away. When opposition began again to emerge in a more sustained fashion, it was through urban mobilization. *Ethniki Allilengyi* (EA: National Solidarity) emerged as an underground movement to control access to food, prevent profiteering, and guarantee distribution; it was linked to another organization, the *Ethniko Apeleftherotiko Metopo* (EAM: National Liberation Front), which quickly became the leading resistance movement in Athens and beyond. Many of its growing number of members failed to realize that behind EAM lay the Greek Communist Party (KKE), which was turning out to be far more successful than any of its prewar political rivals in exploiting the massive resentment at Axis rule to its own ends. From the late spring of 1942, armed resistance organizations began to operate again on a small scale, chiefly in remote mountain areas. But in the course of that year, the KKE established its own military resistance wing, *Ethnikos Laikos Apeleftherotikos Stratos* (ELAS: Greek People's Liberation

Army), and this began to disband rival resistance bands, often by force. Unlike in France, for instance, communist policy in Greece was to monopolize the armed resistance and to insist upon enrollment in a single Popular Front movement dominated by the Party and its cadres.

Even before Stalingrad turned the tide of the war early in 1943, the outlines of Greece's longer-term political problem were clear. Metaxas had swept away the old political elite of the interwar parliamentary system, and there had been few who mourned its passing. But the Germans had swept away the dictatorship in its turn, and even fewer wished for a return of the prewar authoritarian Right. The monarchy had been discredited by these events, and the bulk of popular opinion in occupied Greece was unmistakably opposed to the king's return. Hence the course of events, combined with the Communist Party's adroit domination of the resistance movement and the general Leftward shift across wartime Europe, seemed to point to a new democratic postwar order in which the organized Left (and in Greece that meant nothing else but communism) would take the lead. But what, then, of Britain's traditional strategic interest in Greece, and in particular Churchill's highly emotional commitment to ensuring King George's return to Athens? When a British unit of SOE (Special Operations Executive) was parachuted into Greece in the autumn of 1942, its members found themselves, much to their own initial bewilderment, in the middle of a political minefield.

British military and political interests tugged different ways. The war effort dictated supporting EAM/ELAS as it was providing the most effective guerilla opposition to the Axis; but longer-range political concerns required some kind of anticommunist counterweight. Hence, while continuing to work with and supply EAM/ELAS, the British also financed another resistance group, EDES (*Ethnikos Dimokratikos Ellinikos Syndesmos*, National Republican Greek League), led by the notorious Napoleon Zervas. Zervas was forced by British officers to take to the hills and build up an armed organization, and then was persuaded to drop his initial republicanism and come out in favor of the monarchy. Efforts to get the two resistance organizations to cooperate were largely a failure, and fighting broke out between them from 1943 onward. At Liberation, in the late autumn of 1944, EAM/ELAS turned on EDES and drove it from its stronghold in Epiros to the island of Corfu. At the same time as they were shoring up EDES, the British also retained more informal links with officers in the Greek gendarmerie and other nationalist units, and were prepared to overlook the fact that they were collaborating with the Germans.

When the Germans withdrew from Greece in October 1944, there was little to prevent EAM/ELAS seizing power. It dominated the countryside and the towns. EDES was driven off the mainland. Collaborators were rounded up, besieged, and in some cases massacred before the British could intervene. The paltry British forces then in Greece were no match for the thousands of armed men under ELAS's control. But EAM/ELAS did not make a move against, and indeed welcomed the arrival of, the incoming prime minister, George Papandreou, in whose government it held several ministries. One reason for its stance was undoubtedly that Russia had made it clear to the Greek communist leadership that it did not support an armed seizure of power: Churchill's negotiations with Stalin had resulted in an agreement, unknown in Greece at the time, that consigned the country unambiguously to the British sphere of influence. The Soviet Union had bigger fish to fry elsewhere in eastern Europe.

Nevertheless, many members of EAM/ELAS, while not opposed to the British, could not understand why the leadership hesitated to take power. Behind the scenes, the mistrust and suspicion between the resistance and those ushered into power by British support reached almost unbearable levels. At the beginning of December 1944, barely two months after the Wehrmacht pulled out, the resistance ministers in the Papandreou government resigned over a critical issue: the composition of the new police force. Unable to agree upon who should control the means of armed force in the postwar state, the two sides broke apart; two days later, on 4 December, following a demonstration in central Athens in which police fired on and killed several demonstrators, fighting broke out throughout the capital. These were the Dekemvriana—the December Events—which ended up with ELAS units pinning down British soldiers round the Grande Bretagne Hotel, and British jets strafing resistance positions in the leftist suburbs of Athens.

To this day there is enormous disagreement over the origins and meaning of the Dekemvriana: were they the onset of a communist seizure of power, or a spontaneous response by the Left to right-wing violence and provocation? Were they the first, or indeed perhaps the second, stage in the civil war between Left and Right that would explode into full-scale war again between 1946 and 1949? These questions remain unresolved. What is not in dispute is that when the fighting ended, in January 1945, and peace terms were agreed upon at the seaside resort of Varkiza the following month, the balance of power in Greece as a whole swung suddenly and decisively against the Left for the first time since 1942. Purges now took place in the civil service, and later in the new gendarmerie, but these purges were not, as elsewhere in Europe, of suspected collaborators but rather of suspected leftists and *resistants*.

It is against this background of right-wing terror, in which many scores were settled with the Left and new crimes were committed, that

Greece's returning political elite, clinging desperately to British support, tried to consolidate its position. 1945 stands out, in retrospect, as a year when moderate centrist politics, combined with a serious effort to tackle the problems of economic stabilization and reconstruction, were tried and failed. When elections were held in March 1946, the Left abstained—against Soviet advice—and the royalist Right triumphed. Despite the fact that the new government was led by a liberal, power chiefly lay in the hands of anticommunists at the regional and village level: right-wing violence intensified to the point where the government itself scarcely controlled what was happening in the provinces. That autumn, a rigged plebiscite secured the return of the king. British counsels of moderation were ignored, and the political center ground vanished.

As leftists fled their homes and villages for self-protection, armed bands began re-forming in the mountain areas of the Peloponnese and central Greece. By late 1946 it was evident that the country was once again facing civil war. The Democratic Army of Greece (DSE: *Dimokratikos Stratos Ellados*) was, in effect, the postwar successor to ELAS, except that communist control was much tighter and the ideological stakes were less ambiguous. Initially it was highly successful against the newly reformed National Army. But British and later American materiel and assistance, combined with a policy of forcibly relocating tens of thousands of villages to starve out the guerillas and increasing Greek military sophistication, turned the tide. As the guerrilla struggle became something much closer to a conventional military conflict, the advantages enjoyed by the official army proved decisive. The Tito-Stalin split in 1948 was the last straw. Tito had been the main backer of the DSE; when the leadership of the latter opted for Stalin and loyalty to the Soviet Union, Tito's backing was withdrawn. The following year, the DSE was finally defeated. Thousands of refugees streamed home; others sought refuge across Greece's northern borders; thousands more were interned in island camps or imprisoned on the mainland. From 1950 onward, Greece was at peace, but it was a strange, strained peace, guarded by what was formally a democratic order but held in place by repression, persecution of the Left, and armed violence on the fringes of society. It was, arguably, not until the anticommunist Right was itself discredited with the fall of the junta in 1974 that the country could return to some semblance of tranquility.

The Greek civil war was Europe's bloodiest conflict between 1945 and the breakup of Yugoslavia, and a turning point in the Cold War. Even before 1945, as internecine fighting developed within the resistance, bitterly polarized interpretations of Greek domestic politics were circulating inside British wartime agencies. After the Truman Doctrine in 1947 — a dramatic shift in American foreign policy directly brought about by events in Greece — historians of the Right and the Left began to battle in print, attempting to settle the issue of who was responsible for the civil war. This was a debate that largely took place outside Greece (scholarly discussion of the subject inside the country was virtually impossible before the mid-1970s), and its contours followed those of the broader Cold War historiography.[1]

In the 1980s, at about the time that a kind of political reconciliation took place in Greece itself, a scholarly postrevisionist synthesis was also reached, exemplified by the series of volumes edited by John Iatrides. Around this synthesis — critical of both the Allies and the Left — quite substantial differences of emphasis were possible. While Iatrides underlined the KKE's commitment to revolution, David Close stressed the responsibility of the Right, and the emergence of an apparatus of terror and repression. Those who insisted upon the basic continuity of events between 1943 and 1947 — the "Three Rounds" — faced those who insisted upon the real possibility of other outcomes, for instance, after Liberation. Yet so long as the Soviet Union existed, the main debate was conducted essentially on Cold War terms: historians focused either on the Greek Communist Party or on British and American policy-makers, and sought to pin blame on one or the other group. The dominant vein was politics, the mode diplomatic history. Civil-war scholars tended to see the war as a question of political strategies and policy-making, determined chiefly by discussion in cabinets or central committees; issues of gender, of culture, of *Alltagsgeschichte*, or indeed of social history broadly conceived, scarcely made an appearance. Athens, London, and Washington provided the focus, not villages, valleys, or the provinces.[2]

With the ending of the Cold War, the bounds within which this entire debate took place have become more obvious. Underlying intellectual and political concerns have changed, and slowly the civil war is moving from the realm of politics into that of history, thereby acquiring a new significance as part of the longer-run story of the formation of the Greek nation-state. In this and other ways, it starts to look more and more like a part of a common European experience of those years.

Claudio Pavone's *Una guerra civile: Saggio sulla moralità nella Resistenza* (Turin, 1991), with its radical reassessment of the Italian resistance and its frank recognition of the internecine nature of the fighting in northern Italy in 1943–1945, has sparked off a growing tendency among historians to view the European crisis of the 1940s generally as a profound shock to nations and states, weakened by the humiliation of defeat and foreign occupation, riven by deep ideological and ethnic divisions over the shape of the political and social order. Pavone's work, alongside comparable work in French history, has led to a new interest in the social character of wartime resistance movements, but it has also focused attention on the *dopoliberazione*, the moment in which the violence of the resistance itself and the impotence of the traditional state, tainted by accusations of collaboration, became manifest. If the war years are seen as part of a broader continuum of conflict, it follows that the war cannot be seen as coming to an abrupt end with the German defeat. The immediate postwar years must also be brought into the picture: the whole issue of what Italians call the *dopoguerra* now forms a central concern of contemporary European historians, and the fighting in Greece can be seen as an extreme instance of a more general tension across Europe. It offers analogies with the violent resistance to Communist rule found in Poland, the Ukraine, and the Baltic states; it also acted as a warning and a deterrent in Italy.

Pavone's work stimulated a shift of geographical as well as temporal perspectives. If the mid-1940s constituted an unprecedented legitimacy crisis for the nation-state, then the depths of that crisis can be charted in the way power over territory slips from the control of the central state machine and, for greater or shorter periods, falls into the hand of occupying forces, partisans, or local elites. Much of the most interesting recent work on Italy and France in the 1940s has highlighted the limits to central power through an array of village and regional micro-histories. Of course, serious academic research into local history has long assumed an importance in French and Italian intellectual life that it lacks still in Greece. This volume represents an effort to apply these approaches to Greece as well.

One further factor behind the shift of scholarly concerns was Yugoslavia's experience in the 1990s, which cast a different light on civil wars generally. On the one hand, events there unquestionably accelerated the post–Cold War interest in nationalism and ethnicity, highlighting the whole ethnic dimension of the 1940s anew; on the other, they raised questions concerning the longer-term social and psychological repercussions of civil war. Civil wars come to an end: the question of how a society returns to some form of peace is no less intractable than that of why it was torn apart by conflict in the first place.

For all the above reasons, therefore, we are drawn back to the observations made by Nikos Svoronos on the need to search for the causes of the conflict of the 1940s in "the very structures of Greek society." Greece in the late 1940s unquestionably became a focus for global rivalries, yet a civil war by definition raises the problem of what happens when differing groups *within* the polity come to blows. Here our attention is very much on the domestic arena, and on the various ways in which internal conflict manifested itself and permeated society. In par-

Orphan children, a settlement outside Thessaloniki, October 1946. Reproduced by kind permission of the estate of Nancy Crawshaw.

ticular, the volume as a whole explores three crucial structural elements of the social order: the law, the family, and the nation.[3]

Across Europe, the ending of the Second World War and the defeat of fascism raised the question of the basis on which the postwar order would legitimize itself. Who would control the means of violence, and in the name of which political principles? The state apparatus had in most cases continued to function under foreign occupation, and thus itself faced an acute legitimacy crisis when the Germans pulled out; in Greece, the gendarmerie, for instance, had reportedly "lost the confidence of the people" at Liberation. This compromised state machine faced rival contenders—the resistance and returning exile governments — whose mutual relations were often laden with suspicion and mistrust.[4]

One way to look at the post-Liberation period, then, is in terms of a power vacuum in which different armed groups contested the right to impose their judicial and political norms upon all or part of the country while the state struggled to recover its monopoly of armed force. In Chapter One, I attempt to delineate what seem to have been the three most powerful and clearly defined rival versions of political justice: EAM/ELAS and its conception of "People's Justice," the nationalist conception of ethnic justice, and the liberal norms of the returning Greek political elite. This picture is of course simplified, because it takes little account of more local and less ambitious struggles. But it may help convey the enormity of the task that faced the returning Papandreou government and its successors, and the limits of their real power over much of Greece.[5]

Perhaps the chief reason for this outcome was that postwar governments lacked a loyal and disciplined police force and found themselves reliant upon a disparate conglomeration of anticommunist forces in their struggle with EAM/ELAS. In many ways, this new alignment came together under the pressure of the Dekemvriana and evolved uneasily in the following months. The new National Guard was dominated by right-wing officers, while British efforts to reconstruct the gendarmerie on professional lines failed. In reality it was neither the British nor the Greek political elite who called the tune, but rather officers in the security services and army. Between June 1945 and September 1946 the gendarmerie grew from 9,000 to 28,569 men and became increasingly militarized. Yet far from establishing itself with the Greek public, it was losing popularity. In mid-1946, its ineffectiveness led the government to empower the army to take over the task of restoring law and order.[6]

These developments underline the very limited extent to which politicians in postwar Athens managed to assert any greater control over the countryside than their occupation predecessors had done. In April 1945, it was reported from Volos that "purely local affairs still absorb the public mind and there is an apparent lack of knowledge [of] and even interest in events occurring elsewhere in Greece," while from rural Crete came reports that "law and order are absent . . . and a state bordering on anarchy is said to prevail." The prefect responsible for Karpenisi complained at the lack of government support, and said it was "impossible to get anything accomplished." The following month, Captain Pat Evans reported from Florina on "a general lack of confidence . . . a number of people have been remarking in cafes and other public places: 'There is no State.' 'The Communists did at any rate make things run, whatever else they may have done.' 'The present Government is useless!' "[7]

As 1945 wore on, this situation did not change very much, and the only significant alteration in Greek politics was that whereas formerly it had been the Left that ignored Athens with impunity in the provinces, now it was the Right. In March 1945 it was reported from the small Evia spa resort of Aidipsos that "the Mayor is reported to be a member of KKE and when asked by the Prefect to hand over to his predecessor, he simply ignored the order since there was no one to compel him." A few months later such an episode would have been unthinkable. That summer Woodhouse reported on the right-wing grip on the Peloponnese and recorded with astonishment that "in the village of Eva near Kalamata, the X organization have established a private government under a man called Stavreas, which controls several neighbouring villages and runs an armed civilian police force. . . . Eva lies on the main road from Kalamata to Meligala."[8]

The new government's weakness was not solely geographical. It also manifested itself in its inability to come to terms with the war through the kind of purging of the civil service and punishment of collaborators that public opinion desired, and that took place in most of Europe at this time. Eleni Haidia's study of the collaborators' courts in northern Greece (Chapter Two) makes it clear that despite a strong popular desire for collaborators to be punished, little happened in many cases. Greece's poor record in this respect was not only a consequence of the Dekemvriana; it was also a product of the extraordinary weakness of an unpopular political elite, which was unable to organize itself and was challenged by the proven and successful rival EAM/ELAS, which had become in terms of Greek politics the organization par excellence.[9]

As often in Greek affairs, national political weakness allowed intermediate groups and institutions to block state action and policy. The popular desire for purges of war criminals, collaborators, and even individuals closely associated with the Metaxas regime ran up against institutional resistance, as Procopis Papastratis shows in his study of higher education (Chapter Three). Here we have a striking illustration of what Pavone calls "the continuity of the state" in the face of sporadic but seriously intentioned political attempts, backed, it can be said, by the British, to intervene in its workings to dismiss collaborators. The highly conservative and politically compromised leadership of the University of Athens successfully appealed to the notion of academic freedom to ward off the Ministry of Education, while at the same time taking advantage of the new mood to rid the faculty of leftists *and* gain greater influence over its rival university in Thessaloniki.

The acute legitimacy crisis of the Greek state was reflected not only in its inability to assert new democratic institutional norms inside the judiciary, higher education, or the organs of public security, but also in the array of laws it passed to consolidate its position. As Nikos Alivizatos has pointed out, though the civil war never led to the collapse of Greek democracy, it did lead to the enactment of a body of legislation with obvious authoritarian consequences. This legislation built upon and extended the reach of various prewar laws, and forces us to compare the political uses of the law in Greek society before and after the Second World War.[10]

From the summer of 1945 onward, the Greek state attempted to control the Left with the aid of public security committees, originally set up in 1924, which allowed the government to outlaw persons considered dangerous to public security. Together with special military tribunals, these committees contributed to the mushrooming of special courts that lay outside the regular judicial system; as in Ireland during the war of 1919–1921, such a proliferation of judicial fora indicated the precariousness of the government's hold on power. In addition, the 1871 brigandage law was also restored, initially for a six-month term, and later extended. Political opposition was thus criminalized, and families as well as individuals became subject to punishment: article 2 of the 1871 law detailed which family members could be sent into internal exile. This was followed in September 1946 by another law punishing the families of army deserters, part of the right-wing fear of communist infiltration of the state itself that lay behind the purges of the Left and the vetting of bureaucracies that were a common feature of the early Cold War everywhere in the West.[11]

The extent of the increase in the scale and ambition of the state's use of the law can be gauged quantitively, and not just through the increased surveillance of its own servants that the fight against communism required. The gendarmerie alone more than doubled in size compared with the Metaxas period. Imprisonment for political crimes was also much more common. As the camps of the Metaxas era were being closed down, regular prisons were becoming dangerously overcrowded, and a new system of detention centers, islands of deportation, and camps was coming into existence, culminating in the creation of the Makronisos "re-education" center. Although we lack an overall study of this system as seen in the context of the longer run of Greek penal policy, the studies contained in this volume help gauge its internal dynamics and social impact.

It is true that the idea of incarcerating a large number of communists, "male and female of all ages," dated back to before the war — indeed, even to before the Metaxas dictatorship.[12] The ideological foundations of state anticommunism, involving the punishment of people for their ideas, were in place already by the 1930s. But the sheer number of those incarcerated was far larger than at any time in the past, and easily dwarfed even the thousands jailed or detained under Metaxas. The greater severity of the law was reflected in particular in the unprecedented number of women and even children who were officially detained, necessitating the founding of special women's camps. In 1934, for instance, there had been roughly 130 female inmates housed in the Averoff Women's Prison in Athens; a little more than a decade later, it housed nearly ten times as many. The strains upon the primitive infrastructure required to support such an expansion of the system of incarceration can be judged in the remarkable collection of photos taken by women inmates and recently published under the heading *Gynaikes exoristes sta stratopeda tou emfyliou*.[13]

The amount of violence used by the state was also greater than in the past. We lack a reliable study of the use of the death penalty in Greek history, but it is fairly clear that its use against the Left between 1945 and 1950 overshadowed that in all previous and subsequent periods. It is also striking that while governments in the immediate postwar period were reluctant to carry out death sentences against convicted collaborators and war criminals, such inhibitions were much less in evidence against the Left, especially after the 1946 elections. In general, it is possible to say that for Greece, as for most other European countries, society in the 1940s became familiar as never before or since with violent death.

The implications of this closeness to death are explored in Polymeris Voglis's research into political prisoners on death row (Chapter Four). The threat of death was part of the pressure exerted by the state upon the minds of its opponents to persuade them to recant and publicly rejoin the national community. In this respect, it was the expression of a bitterly polarized ideological struggle and the logical culmination of a series of laws aimed explicitly at punishing thoughts and beliefs rather than acts — most notably the 1929 *Idionymon*, but also those laws which punished ethnic minorities for their supposed lack of an *ethniki syneidisi* ("national consciousness").

The phenomenon of public recantation that Voglis scrutinizes is only now beginning to attract the attention it deserves. A source of shame and embarassment both to the Party and to those who succumbed, it is the great unspoken of postwar Leftist historiography, despite the fact that a majority of political detainees probably did sign repentances, which were widely and deliberately disseminated in magazines, newspapers, and radio broadcasts by the authorities in order to discredit communism. But as Voglis argues, those who repented found themselves trapped not only between the competing forces of Right and Left, but also between the competing realms of political and domestic responsibility.[14]

The KKE stigmatized those who repented as sinners and traitors, just as the government stigmatized those who refused to repent. Those on death row who held out saw themselves as heroes dying honorably for the sake of their beliefs; the letters they sent before execution expressed such views and transmitted them to their relatives. On the other hand, the families of prisoners often saw matters differently and urged inmates to repent so that they could be released and could care for their children. Mando Dalianis's research (Chapter Five), a fascinating complement to the piece by Voglis, shows that the children of political prisoners carried very mixed feelings about their parents for generations afterward. Interviewed in the 1980s, many of these children both admired their parents and criticized them for putting politics above their domestic responsibilities. Such criticisms did not reflect any indoctrination by the Right: one of the many fascinating aspects of Dalianis's research is that it shows how little influence the official anticommunist line peddled in schools and orphanages had upon the children educated there. None of them swallowed for very long the line that the king and queen were now their real parents. What many of these children really felt was that the ideological politics of the 1940s had demanded too much of their parents, and had ended up forcing them to choose between the Party and the family.

Two other contributors also explore facets of this dilemma. Tassoula Vervenioti traces how in Greece, as across Europe in the 1940s, women experienced the transition from war to peace as a more or less unwilling move from public action back into the domestic sphere (Chapter Six). In the Second World War, adherence to the left-wing resistance meant participation in social revolution at a time when the war had eroded the bonds of the traditional family; after 1945 it meant persecution and imprisonment at a time when older domestic and patriarchal values were reasserting themselves. Some women squared the circle: they reentered the world of politics as mothers of prisoners protesting to publicize their childrens' plight and secure their release. But many others found themselves up against the choice of Party or family: they fell in love, and resented the way the Party claimed the right to decide for them whether or not they could marry; they became aware of the male-dominated structure of authority in the Party itself, present even in the prisons and camps where many were held; or they simply found themselves dreaming of home.

Riki van Boeschoten's study of the "impossible return" to the mountain village of Ziakas (Chapter Seven) also analyzes the impact of the war on attitudes toward politics and community. Ziakas was a predominantly left-wing village, 90 percent of whose inhabitants fled during the civil war. As with the Jewish community of Salonika, if for different reasons, there could be no reestablishment of the prewar community, no return home. Yet a strong sense of community helped villagers through decades of separation and exile. Indeed, van Boeschoten argues that this sense of community was an important aid in helping villagers survive and cope with the catastrophe of the 1940s. This coincided with their growing alienation from the Party, increasingly seen not merely as complicit in their tragedy but as incapable of more than a bureaucratic and authoritarian response to the problems of exile itself. Party meetings turned into crude mechanisms of social control, and villagers resented the Party's intervention in matters of private life.[15]

The fate of the villagers of Ziakas should also prompt us to consider the impact of the 1940s on what we might call the political geography of Greece. The war itself saw mountain villages like Ziakas first cut off from the capital and the national government, and then briefly moving closer to the center of politics in the mountains of Free Greece. In the case of this village, the reestablishment of control from Athens resulted in the almost total destruction of its traditional society. Only a few villagers lived on there, awaiting the infrequent letters from abroad whose arrival signified the continuation of village life abroad and which they experienced as a kind of "resurrection." But the end of village life can be seen differently—as part of the urbanization and modernization of Greek life that took place from the 1950s on. According to van Boeschoten, the children who left Ziakas to go into exile behind the Iron Curtain, forming part of the highly debated *paidomazoma* (lit., "gathering of the children"), combined regret at having had to leave their homes with a sense of having escaped the world of limited opportunities for the educational chances offered by cities like Prague and Bucharest.

Perhaps, then, the 1940s were the last time Greece's political destiny would be played out in the countryside as much as in the cities. Yet this makes it all the more extraordinary that there have been virtually no scholarly historical analyses of that critical decade from the perspective of particular villages or regions. Rural Greece has remained until very recently fixed in the image of an unchanging, traditional, ahistorical world established by postwar social anthropology and reflected in the photographs that Meletzis, Papaioannou, and others took for the country's growing tourism industry. These studies and photographs make no reference to the catastrophic events that swept the face of the land. But in this volume, Stathis Kalyvas, John Sakkas and Lee Sarafis all offer accounts of the violence of the 1940s as seen from the countryside. Kalyvas's pioneering study of left-wing violence focuses upon the little-studied Argolid (Chapter Eight). Sakkas explores a group of villages near Karpenisi in central Greece, one of the most isolated parts of the mainland (Chapter Nine). Sarafis discusses the village of Deskati in Thessaly (Chapter Ten). This was perhaps less isolated, but not by much: after all, the main Athens-Larissa road was not fully reopened until 1949. Local perspectives serve to underscore the decisive importance of local politics and show how national political loyalties and struggles were filtered through a dense layer of village and regional concerns and interests.[16]

In all three chapters, the civil war stands out as a far more catastrophic experience than the Axis occupation. From 1943 onward, national political groupings needed to draw on unprecedented reserves of force and violence to compel or induce support and obedience. This went for EAM/ELAS as well as for a series of Athens-based regimes. It was the Left, according to Kalyvas's meticulously researched analysis of the spiral into violence around Argos, whose systematic assassination of political opponents triggered reprisals from Germans and Security Battalionists. The Argolid had shown almost no support for the Left before the war; preservation of EAM's swiftly acquired wartime power, especially when filtered through communist ideology, required high levels of killing, especially in that topographically intermediate zone between the mountains, where resistance control was easier, and in the plains, where it was almost impossible.

EAM may have been rather more popular in Deskati, as Sarafis describes (though her own family links to the village should be borne in mind), but around Karpenisi repression was vital in showing the peasants EAM's power. Aris Velouchiotis's brutality was one instance of the extreme violence the Left was capable of unleashing. Yet as Sakkas shows, the Right's power after Liberation was, if anything, more precariously based and more reliant upon an unsavory network of mercenaries and paramilitaries, who patrolled the outlying areas where the National Guard was afraid to go, targeting whole families when they could not find the suspects they wanted. When the civil war broke out in earnest, different villages responded very differently, some managing to contain the level of killing, others suffering massacre and terror. Once again, one returns to the possibility that the mass violence and political polarization of the civil war played an important part in destroying the older, more flexible forms of political allegiance that had been found in the villages before the war, and thus hastened the outflow of people from rural areas into the towns.[17]

North of Kastoria, in the region of the Prespa Lakes, lies a series of deserted villages. In this border zone, villages have multiple names:

Women and children homeless refugees in the ruins of Naoussa, after a rebel raid, 1949. Reproduced by kind permission of the estate of Nancy Crawshaw.

Gavdos, whose houses are collapsing into the overgrown fields, appears on the pre-1914 Austrian military maps as Gabres; Milionas, whose empty buildings now shelter passing Albanians on their way south, is shown as Metovo. These are the valleys where the civil war reached its climax in 1949, before the remnants of the Democratic Army fled across the border into nearby Albania. Many Slavic-speaking villagers fled at the same time, when they had not already left to escape the raids of the Greek air force. A few years later, the Greek government became worried at the depopulation of its vital border regions and resettled the villages with Vlachs from Thessaly and Epiros. But with time, most of these left, too.

Today the whole region bears testimony to the tangled and complex ethnic dimension of the civil war years. With the collapse of communism and the emergence of an independent Macedonia across Greece's northern border, scholars have become newly attentive to the ways the stresses of the 1940s revealed the faultlines in the Greek nation, and underlined the limitations of the nation-building project of the previous century. In northern Greece—the New Lands of the post-1912 conquests—the war decade massively altered the ethnic balance of rural and urban areas alike. The Greek nation was built up anew on the basis of a narrative of selected historical memories in which the experience of Jews, Slavs, and others found no place.

Anastasia Karakasidou's study of nation-building and patriotic celebrations in postwar Macedonia (Chapter Eleven) charts the careful way the Greek state constructed a cult of national pride through decrees and administrative regulations. One is tempted to see this intensive bureaucratic effort as a response to the sense of anxiety that both occupation and civil war provoked. The same anxiety expressed itself in the patriotic ceremonials surrounding the royal family, which was desperate to promote its place in Greek society after fleeing the country in 1941 and then being prevented from returning until the 1946 plebiscite allowed it back in.

Thessaloniki, which is the city at the heart of Karakasidou's analysis, also features prominently in Bea Lewkowicz's contribution (Chapter Twelve). The city's largest religious group at the turn of the century had been the Jews, a flourishing community almost totally destroyed by the Final Solution. Almost, but not entirely, and Lewkowicz discusses how the survivors slowly rebuilt both their own lives and their much-reduced community in the following decades. The contrast with Voglis's proud leftists is striking: for the Jewish survivors of the Holocaust, the heroization of suffering was rarely a compelling possibility; they seem to have turned inward far more decisively, to the family, children, and domesticity. Shaken by their experiences, they and their children avoided entry into a public realm that forced upon them unwelcome issues of national and ethnic self-definition. Only in the 1990s, with the rise of a new kind of identity politics more globally as well as the emergence of an international acceptance of Jewish wartime suffering, did it become possible to acknowledge more publicly the presence of Jews in Greek life. Even then, as the 1997 unveiling of the Holocaust memorial in Thessaloniki demonstrated, that acknowledgment remained highly conditional, above all in the erstwhile "mother of Israel" itself.

The burden of memory in the case of Greek suffering forms the subject of Xanthippi Kotzageorgi-Zymari and Tassos Hadjianastassiou's fascinating analysis of three generations of memory of the wartime Bulgarian occupation of northeastern Greece (Chapter Thirteen). Lands that were ruled by Bulgaria in both World Wars now form part of Greece. The members of the youngest generation have no personal memory of war, and a gulf seems to separate them from parents and grandparents who survived some of the harshest experiences of the entire occupation period. Teenagers who live today in the area investigated by Zymari appear scarcely interested in what happened half a century earlier. They also seem not to share the relatively harsh attitudes toward the Bulgarians that are more commonly and perhaps unsurprisingly found among their elders. Whether this shows the greater political maturity of the young or the benefits to be derived from historical amnesia is hard to say. But it is striking that the heroization of wartime suffering, the appeal of patriotic narratives of martyrs and sacrifices for the nation, appears more and more to leave Greek teenagers cold. Perhaps Greece is entering an era in which history and its public uses have less attraction than they once did. Or is it that public myth-making was never very attractive, and only imposed itself upon people's lives when the state devoted its resources to this end? In the mid-twentieth century, history was an essential weapon for the protagonists of the struggle of ideologies; at the century's end, it may no longer serve any obvious public function. A waning interest in the heroes and struggles of the past thus goes hand in hand with the more modest place of politics in daily life.

Finally, Susanne-Sophia Spiliotis's study of the politics of the Merten affair opens up the subject of the deliberate silence that enveloped discussion of wartime collaboration during the 1950s and 1960s. The nature of Greek wartime collaboration has in fact never been seriously researched. That it existed on a wide scale, in a variety of forms and for various motives, is unquestioned. The Merten scandal of the late 1950s, which erupted when a German war criminal was arrested in Greece, was not just the moment when it became clear how deeply the postwar Greek elite was implicated in unsavory wartime dealings. Thanks to Spiliotis's exploitation of recently released German archives, we can now see how the scandal itself affected Greco-German postwar diplomacy, and how the question of war crimes became enmeshed with issues of economic assistance and even the construction of the Common Market.

On the one hand, silence, denial, repudiation; on the other, the elaboration of ceremonies, parades, and myths. Destroyed, abandoned, or lost communities on the one side; constructed, reinforced, or reshaped communities on the other. This collection of essays has attempted to contribute to the mapping out of Greece in the 1940s in these directions, histories of a polity fragmented and reformed. The effort is based upon the searching out of new sources and testimonies, both oral and written, including many local archives and other collections that were not available for research two decades ago. Stimulated by this unveiling of materials, but also stimulating more discoveries in its turn, historical research into contemporary Greece is flourishing. Much more remains to be investigated: the social and political aspects of postwar urban growth, for example, or the functioning of the judiciary; above all, perhaps, the nature of conservative and parliamentary right-wing politics in the postwar years seen not simply as a front for extra-parliamentary fascisms but as a successful vehicle in its own right for Greece's social and economic transformation. This volume scarcely aspires to be comprehensive, let alone to offer the last word on its subject. It will have succeeded, however, if it makes available to the scholarly community some of the innovative and exciting work currently under way exploring how Greece recovered from the most prolonged and traumatic experience of its brief life as a nation-state.[18]

NOTES

1. Early accounts include C. M.Woodhouse, *The Apple of Discord: A Survey of Recent Greek Politics in Their International Setting* (London, 1948); E. C. Myers, *Greek Entanglement* (London, 1955); R. Leeper, *When Greek Meets Greek* (London, 1950); G. Chandler, *The Divided Land: An Anglo-Greek Tragedy* (London, 1959); D. G. Kousoulas, *Revolution and Defeat: The Story of the Greek Communist Party* (London, 1965); S. G. Xydis, *Greece and the Great Powers* (Thessaloniki, 1963). Scholarly accounts include J. O. Iatrides, *Revolt in Athens: The Greek Communist "Second Round"* (Princeton, 1972); J. Hondros, *Occupation and Resistance: The Greek Agony, 1941–1944* (New York, 1983); L. Wittner, *American Intervention in Greece, 1943–1949* (New York, 1982); P. Papastratis, *British Policy towards Greece during the Second World War, 1941–1944* (Cambridge, 1984).

2 John O. Iatrides, ed., *Greece in the 1940s: A Nation in Crisis* (Hanover and London, 1981); L. Baerentzen, J. O. Iatrides, and O. L. Smith, eds., *Studies in the History of the Greek Civil War* (Copenhagen, 1987); Iatrides and Linda Wrigley, eds., *Greece at the Crossroads: The Civil War and Its Legacy* (University Park, Pau 1995); David H. Close, *The Origins of the Greek Civil War, 1945–1949* (London, 1995).

3. N. Svoronos, "Greek History, 1940–1950: The Main Problems," in J Iatrides, ed., *Greece in the 1940s*, 2

4. Public Record Office, London, War Office files [henceforth WO] 204/9380, cited in M. Mazower, "Policing the Anti-Communist State in Greece, 1922–1974," in Mazower, ed., *The Policing of Politics in the Twentieth Cen-*

tury (Providence, R.I., and Oxford, 1997), 142. For the general problem, see C. Pavone, "The General Problem of the Continuity of the State and the Legacy of Fascism," unpublished ms.

5. On the uses of violence by local populations, see for instance G. Crainz, "'Guerra civile" e 'triangolo della morte'", *Meridiana* 13 (1992): 17–55; L. Alessandrini, "The Option of Violence: Partisan Violence in the Bologna Area, 1945–1948," unpublished ms. presented at the conference "After the War Was Over," University of Sussex, July 1996.

6. Close, *Origins*; Mazower, "Policing the Anti-Communist State."

7. Public Record Office, London, Foreign Office files [henceforth FO] 371/48270, Weekly Report, 15–21 Apr. 1945; FO 371/48272, Weekly Reports, 6–19 May 1945.

8. FO 371/48263, Weekly Reports, 4–10 Mar. 1945; FO 371/48279 R 14675, Caccia-Bevin, 25 Aug. 1945.

9. Note how even before the war, anticommunist modernizers feared the threat posed by communist organization to the disorganization of the Greek state. "The organization of communists, in Greece at least, is higher and broader than the organization of the state services charged with their prosecution and safe-keeping," comments S. Glykofrydi (*Fylakai*, vol. 2 [Athens, 1936], 83).

10. N. Alivizatos, *Oi politikoi thesmoi se krisi, 1922–1974: Opseis tis ellinikis empeirias* (Athens, 1995).

11. K. Oikonomopoulou, *Ektakta stratodikeia kai nomothesia aforousa tin dimosian taxin kai asfalian* (Athens, 1951), 89, 115.

12. See Glykofrydi, *Fylakai*, 2: 140 for an interwar prison expert's recommendation for a special prison for communists.

13. V. Theorodou, ed., *Gynaikes exoristes sta stratopeda tou emfyliou: Chios, Trikeri, Makronisos, Aï-Stratis, 1948–1954* (Athens, 1996). My thanks to Tasoula Vervenioti for drawing my attention to this book. Details of the 1930s can be found in Glykofrydi, *Fylakai* 2: 20.

14. See now S. Bournazos, "O anamorfotikos logos ton nikiton sti Makroniso," in N. Kotarides, ed., *To emfylio drama, Dokimes* 6, special edition (1997): 101–34

15. See also van Boeschoten's book, *Anapoda chronia: Syllogiki mnimi kai istoria sto Ziaka Grevenon (1900–1950)* (Athens, 1997).

16. Insofar as this approach has been adopted, it has been not by historians but by anthropologists. See van Boeschoten's comments in her "Geopolitiki tis ellinikis antistasis," in Kotarides, *To emfylio drama*, 8n.2.

17. One should not omit in this connection the enormous population movements, whether organized or spontaneous, which accompanied the conflict. See A. Laiou, "Population Movements in the Greek Countryside during the Civil War" in Baerentzen, Iatrides and Smith, eds., *Studies in the History of the Greek Civil War*, 55–105.

18. Many of the chapters in this volume were originally essays commissioned for the Contemporary History conference "After the War Was Over: Reconstructing Family, Nation and State in Southern Europe," held at the University of Sussex in 1996. Thanks are due to the following sponsors of the conference

for their support: the University of Sussex Research Development Fund and the Graduate Research Centre in the Humanities, the British Academy, the Elisabeth Barker Fund, Victoria Solomonidis and the Embassy of Greece, Edwige Girardin at the French Embassy, the Italian Cultural Institute, the Sternberg Foundation, the Royal Historical Society, the Hellenic Foundation, the Kessler Foundation, and the Economic History Society.

ONE

Three Forms of Political Justice: Greece, 1944–1945

Mark Mazower

NAZI OCCUPATION in Greece, as elsewhere in Europe, led to a complete breakdown of state and society. The civil war that followed was the culmination of numerous clashes between different groups, each with its own vision of social and political reconstruction. As World War II neared its end, the question of political justice assumed great urgency, but there was no single understanding of its implications. Instead, the contenders for power advanced widely diverging conceptions of political justice: the "People's Courts" of communist-controlled Free Greece, for example, rested on a wholly different understanding of the purpose and nature of justice from the courts established after Liberation by the British-backed state in Athens.

What complicates the picture still further, and perhaps gives it added fascination, is that alongside the legal norms evolved by nationally organized political forces, there were also numerous expressions of individual and local efforts to respond to the demands of justice. These "improvisations of authority," as de Gaulle termed their French equivalents, emerged during the war, erupted at Liberation, and continued for months, even years, against the background of civil war. Without losing sight of this important dimension of "popular justice," this chapter focuses on the three main forms of political justice that emerged in Greece around Liberation: collective revenge against the ethnic enemy; the judicial norms of the left-wing resistance, EAM/ELAS; and the judicial policies adopted by the official government from Liberation onward.

Of these three forms of political justice, perhaps the least important, at least as far as Greece was concerned, was the first. During the war, the Axis powers had attempted to stir up ethnic discord in Greece, but with relatively little success. The Italians had tried to promote a Vlach "Roman Legion" in Thessaly, the Bulgarians had encouraged Macedonian "autonomists" in the Kastoria area, and in Epiros, in northwestern Greece, both Italians and Germans had tried to build up a fifth column among the Muslim Albanians around Filiates. The Vlachs were highly hellenized, while the Macedonians were a numerous and considerable force in the isolated mountain regions where they were settled. As a result, neither group was targeted on a collective basis for the treachery of its collaborationist minority. But the 20,000 or so Muslim Albanians (known as Chams) occupying fertile land not far from the Albanian border were not so fortunate. The Greeks of Epiros were staunch nationalists, and the region was the stronghold of EDES, a resistance organization with irredentist and royalist inclinations. Events in 1944–1945, still passed over in silence in Greece today, show how EDES put into practice its conception (which undoubtedly closely mirrored that of the local Greek peasantry) of collective ethnic justice.

The roots of the antagonism between Greeks and Chams lay in the recent past. In this poverty-stricken region, the Chams possessed much of the most fertile land. Since Epiros had passed into Greek hands in 1913, the Muslim beys had lost the political weight they had had under the Ottomans; nevertheless, their economic influence persisted, to the anger of the local Greek population. Three decades of Greek rule had not seen any serious effort to encourage the assimilation of the Chams; on the contrary, a stream of complaints to Geneva bore witness to their sense of grievance.[1]

The war saw communal relations worsen quickly. In October 1940, the Greek authorities disarmed 1,800 Cham conscripts and put them to work on local roads; the following month they seized all Albanian males not called up and deported them to camps or to island exile. Not surprisingly, when the Italians finally took control of mainland Greece in 1941, they found Cham activists willing to call for unification of the region with Albania. Several hundred were conscripted into the anti-communist Bal Komitare to act as local gendarmes. From the autumn of 1943, these armed bands took part alongside the Wehrmacht in burning Greek villages. Such actions, it seems, were not supported by many of the local beys, nor by the Mufti. By the summer of 1944 it was obvious that a German withdrawal from Epiros was imminent. After the Cham bands turned down a demand from EDES to join it against the left-wing ELAS, EDES's leader Napoleon Zervas ordered a general attack on the Cham villages. Two attacks took place, in July and August, with the participation of the EDES Tenth Division and local Greek peasants, eager to gain revenge for the burning of their own homes: many of the Cham villages were burned, and the remaining inhabitants — some 18,000 — fled across the border into Albania.[2]

The whole operation had a military rationale, which was to enlarge the area of the vital coastal strip north of Parga under EDES (and hence British) control. But this bout of what we might now call "ethnic cleansing" was accompanied by much destruction and plundering. British onlookers described it as "a most disgraceful affair" involving "an orgy of revenge" with the local guerillas "looting and wantonly destroying everything." "The Bishop of Paramythia," reported a Foreign Office emissary, "joined in the searching of houses for booty and came out of one house to find his already heavily laden mule had been meanwhile stripped by some *andartes* [resistance fighters]." Afterward, EDES notables took over former Muslim lands and estates.[3]

Unlike EDES and the local Greek peasantry in Thesprotia, ELAS was opposed to the idea of collective punishment of the Cham community. Several hundred Chams had enlisted in its ranks, and it had fairly good relations with the communist-led resistance in Albania itself. As a result, when ELAS forces drove Zervas's men onto the island of Corfu at the end of 1944, the situation facing the Chams suddenly changed; in the first two months of 1945, while Epirus remained under ELAS control, some 4–5,000 refugees returned southward to their homes.

Their return was only temporary, however. Following the February 1945 Varkiza Agreement, which brought the fighting in Athens between ELAS and the British to an end, the balance of power in Epiros swung away from ELAS once again. In March, the embittered remnants of Zervas's EDES forces made the short crossing from Corfu to the mainland and enlisted in the newly formed National Guard. They were not slow to turn their attention back to the Chams. Led by Zervas's former officer, Col. Zotos, a loose paramilitary grouping of former guerillas and local men went on a rampage. In the worst massacre, at the town of Filiates on 13 March, some sixty to seventy Chams were killed. The rest fled back across into Albania, leaving just the few families encountered in grim circumstances by a British United Nations Relief and Rehabilitation Administration worker that summer.[4]

Thereafter, the fate of the Chams surfaced only rarely, usually in connection with Greek irredentist claims to "northern Epirus." Officially, the Greek position was that it had neither encouraged the Chams to flee nor opposed their return; it simply reserved the right to try alleged war criminals and collaborators for their crimes. In practice, there was little chance of the refugees coming back. For much of 1945, the writ of the Greek state scarcely ran in Thesprotia; armed gangs held sway, backed by the National Guard, which was overwhelmingly nationalist and anti-Muslim in complexion. Nor were the Chams likely to be reassured by the results of an official inquiry carried out by the Greek Army, which concluded that the massacre at Filiates never took place: at the time the inquiry took place, the perpetrator, Col. Zotos himself, just happened to be stationed at the Jannina headquarters of the Epiros High Command.[5]

EDES, as I have discussed elsewhere, was not weighed down by any ideological project for postwar Greece beyond the nationalist goal of an

ethnically homogeneous state extending as far as possible into the irre-
denta. Collective ethnic guilt thus expressed the chief form of political
justice as EDES understood it. With EAM/ELAS, the case was very different. Basically uninterested in the nationalist agenda, EAM/ELAS attached great importance to the reform of social institutions. In the vast
territories under its control at the end of the war—virtually the whole
of Greece with the exception of Athens, Crete, and parts of Epiros—
EAM/ELAS was already engaged in realizing "People's Rule." Observers had already noted the Manichaean quality of EAM's worldview:
"Anyone who was not on their side was naturally to be considered an
enemy," noted an American liaison officer. For all sorts of reasons,
therefore, the unmasking of traitors and collaborators became one of
the organizations's leading concerns. The evolution of "revolutionary
justice" required both new legal institutions and sweeping violence.[6]

The violence of the Left—directed not against the Germans but
against other Greeks—has been even less acknowledged or discussed in
Greece than it has been in France or Italy. For instance, the recent spate
of mostly hagiographic publications about Aris Velouchiotis has con-
spicuously failed to arouse any kind of debate about the violence of this
notorious partisan leader. Yet during the occupation itself, EAM had
killed not only real collaborators but also potential opponents. In some
areas, such as the Argolid, the activities of "death squads" (mostly the
Organosi Perifrourisi tou Laikou Agona, or OPLA—the EAM political
police) created a climate of terror. In the mountains around Delphi,
ELAS was arresting and executing people for assisting the British on the
grounds that such activity indicated they must be Gestapo agents.
"Throughout Attica and Boeotia there is a reign of terror," reported
another British officer in early September. He went on: "Over 500 have
been executed within the last few weeks. Owing to the stench of rot-
ting corpses, it is impossible to pass near a place by my camp. Lying
unburied on the ground are naked corpses with their heads severed.
Owing to strong reactionary elements among the people, [ELAS has]
picked on this area." The numerous mass graves dug up in 1945–
1946 testified to the severity of this repression; so, too, did the blacklists—some of which subsequently came to light, and which could not
all be written off as forgeries—of individuals whom EAM had targeted for execution, mostly royalists, nationalists, or simply wealthy
"bourgeois."[7]

From the summer of 1944, EAM's hold over "Free Greece" was con-
solidated with the creation of its own police force, the EP (Ethniki Politofylaki, or Civil Guard), which took over policing duties from the
andartes (resistance fighters) in ELAS. As British forces landed in the
Peloponnese, they found the EP keeping order in place of the old, discredited gendarmerie. Thus in Patras, for example, the EP patrolled the

town jointly with the British into November. As for the Salonika area, it was reported that "on the arrival of the District and Regional HQs into their respective areas EAM/KKE were in complete control and were backed by the armed forces of ELAS, ELAN and EP. There was no Police Force or Gendarmerie functioning and their duties were undertaken by the EP." It was the same story throughout most of the country.[8]

High on the list of the collaborationist groups targeted by EAM/ELAS were, of course, the gendarmerie and the paramilitary Security Battalions. Holed up in the Peloponnese as the Germans pulled out, these units feared massacre at the hands of ELAS. ELAS itself took the view that as these groups had been publicly proscribed by the Greek government, they had to be regarded as enemy formations. Aris himself crossed over into the Peloponnese to supervise operations against them. The British warned ELAS against taking the law into its own hands and insisted that Battalionists be treated as enemy prisoners-of-war; suspected collaborators were to be held until "proper civil courts were established by the Greek Government." It is worth noting that the Greek general staff in Italy commented at this stage that it would have preferred the Security Battalions to "remain armed in barrack areas."[9]

This exchange of views took place in the first half of September. But as it happened, the first attacks on besieged collaborators were occurring. Then on 18 September, it was reported that a massacre of Battalionists and other collaborators had taken place at Meligala and Kalamata in the southern Peloponnese: scores had been killed in Meligala after a gun battle, while the rest had been marched by Aris to Kalamata, where twelve had been hanged from lampposts and others beaten to death by an angry mob. This was a major embarrassment to the EAM leadership, which first denied the massacres had taken place, then denounced them. Alexandros Svolos and Stefanos Sarafis, moderates in the resistance elite, both insisted that EAM was following the orders of the Greek government. "Stop all executions," cabled Svolos. "All must await court sanctions under the . . . law now being drafted. If the arrest of traitors is absolutely necessary to calm public opinion, it should take place under responsible ELAS sections." From Kefalonia it was reported on 26 September that "leaders of ELAS have stated . . . they will not deal with any of their prisoners until proper courts are set up by the Greek Government."[10]

But while some elements in EAM/ELAS were affirming their solidarity with the Greek government, others were taking a more radical line. Thus on Kefalonia itself, for example, we can see the signs of a split between ELAS and the EP, which remained under tight communist control. Arrests of so-called traitors continued to be made by the EP, which insisted it was acting on orders from above. At the same time,

EAM announced that it was setting up a "popular self-government" in the island.[11]

In fact, despite the soft line pedaled by EAM delegates outside Greece, on the ground the organization was continuing to build up the institutions of "People's Rule." The public pressure to act against collaborators to which Svolos referred above was certainly there, and as around Liberation, many people were inclined to take the law into their own hands. Hence the "People's Courts" can be seen in part as an attempt by EAM to respond to the popular mood at a time when passions were running very high: "A shooting affray occurred outside the Ministry of War at 1415 hrs when Maj Pappadopoulos was entering the building. He was approached by a youth holding a pistol who accused him of being a collaborationist and that it was proposed to arrest him. When the civilian took him by the arm he fired three shots all of which hit his assailant. The youth fired twice, both shots missing. . . . The Major is under arrest."[12]

Such sudden incidents were occurring all the time, especially with gendarmerie or police officers. In addition, ELAS *andartes* were often tempted to settle old scores themselves, as could be seen in this incident in Athens in November:

> At approx. 1430 hrs an ELAS Offr posted ten ELAS tps round a Tavern opposite the Gendarmerie School. Inside the Tavern were in particular Lt. JOHN TRIPITSIS (Concerned in some way with the Security Bns) and EM-MANUEL KALLIGEROS, who are both Nationalists.
>
> When TRIPITSIS saw the ELAS sentries had been posted he tried to walk out of the door but was shot at. He returned the fire.
>
> A Gendarmerie sentry nearby tried to stop the firing verbally, when this failed he fired shots into the air to try to frighten off the ELAS. The ELAS then flung a hand grenade into the Tavern and departed. One woman was wounded in the forehead.[13]

But responding to popular outrage was only part of the story of the "People's Courts," and perhaps not the most important part at that. Popular justice had its own ideological value for the "Organization," too. The "People's Courts" had been a proud achievement of EAM from the first days of its emergence in the mountains of central Greece in early 1943: after all, they manifested the resistance's most important claim — to have created an alternative state. After Liberation, these "courts" continued to function.

In Salonika, for instance, "cases of a penal nature were tried by EAM's own 'People's Courts' or ELAS Courts Martial." Even after the Papandreou government established itself in Athens in October and issued Constitutional Act 1 (see below), which laid down procedures for the trial of collaborators, the lawyers it appointed were forced to continue working with ELAS; when they found an individual had a case to answer, ELAS members often "dealt with the matter themselves": this could be execution or, increasingly, indefinite detention. Thus from November we can discern a phase of very uneasy compromise between the legal system set up by the Athens government and that set up by ELAS.[14]

On the island of Lesvos as late as February 1945, "People's Courts" were being held in all the villages. One hundred alleged collaborators were being detained by EAM in a prison in Mitilini that had been emptied of its former inmates. Lawyers appointed by Athens were kept on the sidelines, unable to investigate or even to release the inmates since there was no police force to protect them from attack. In Macedonia and Thrace, ELAS was holding an estimated 6,500–7,000 collaborators for investigation in early February. In Kavalla, "People's Courts" were reportedly trying Bulgarian war criminals. Others were in operation throughout the Peloponnese. In Thebes, the work of the Special Court was obstructed when the ELAS commander refused to hand over twelve suspected collaborators or their files.[15]

This last example is perhaps worth quoting more fully to convey the flavor and atmosphere of these uncertain months:

> Mr. C. Coutourissis, Govt Commissioner of the Special Court to investigate collaborationists, states that the National Civil Guard [EP] is carrying out arrests of royalist or conservative persons, although such persons have not committed any offence. Furthermore EP fails to report arrests to the Govt Legal Authorities. Mr. C. Coutourissis also states that ELAS and EP are a State by themselves within the Greek State. They only comply with laws of the Greek state when such laws are in conformity with their party-policy.
>
> He also stated that the 12 men arrested by EP in Thebes for collaborating with the enemy, had been sent to 2 ELAS DIV. He has already asked 2 ELAS DIV for their files, as he is unable to investigate their cases without any evidence against them. He has also asked for the whereabouts of the 12 men. No reply has so far been received from 2 ELAS DIV.

"ELAS and EP are a State by themselves within the Greek State": that is surely right, unless it perhaps exaggerates the power of the Greek state itself at a moment when it barely extended outside the center of Athens. A fortnight before the events described above, the Papandreou Government had declared all existing "People's Courts" illegal: much good that had done. On the Peloponnese, for instance, no courts were officially functioning outside Patras. Before the Dekemvriana, justice was being run very much on EAM's terms; it had the guns.[16]

Information about the workings of ELAS courts martial is hard to find. But they were not particularly secretive bodies: after Liberation, the ELAS Eleventh Division planned its sittings in the YMCA building in the center of Salonika. At Verroia in Macedonia, the ELAS Tenth Division set up a tribunal to try collaborators: its seven-man panel was composed of an ELAS major, described as a "Justice of the People"; four other junior officers; and two "comrades," one a farmer, the other a lorry driver. It was probably typical of such bodies in its members' lack of prior legal experience. Those it tried tended to be found guilty and sentenced to death, but—in some cases at least—were permitted to appeal to the ELAS Central Committee. There were some acquittals.

It is worth noting that much of the evidence suggests that by late 1944, EAM's much-vaunted "popular justice" was in fact increasingly unpopular. This was perhaps less true of the "People's Courts," which had originated in local arbitration committees and which remained popular in some areas, than it was of the ruder and more brutal justice meted out against political opposition by the EP and ELAS. But in both cases, the very novelty of EAM's procedures made local peasants suspicious. Thus on the island of Skyros the population was not happy when a certain Constantinos "Syntrofios" (i.e., "Comrade") suddenly landed with a bodyguard of seven armed *andartes*, announced that he was the "EAM organizer of the island," arrested some twenty local gendarmes, and removed them to detention in Turkey as collaborators. Although the *andartes* were not particularly disorderly, they did not succeed in winning over the islanders, a majority of whom "resent their presence and are suspicious of their intentions." When EAM held elections to set up "self-government," very few people turned up to vote. According to a British observer: "Most people are anxiously awaiting the arrival of a representative of the Papandreou Government; they cannot understand the present situation."[17]

Such doubts of course intensified during and after the Dekemvriana— the fighting in Athens between EAM/ELAS and the British in December 1944. In the aftermath of this bitter conflict both sides took hostages: the British shipped thousands of suspected leftists to camps in East Africa; EAM/ELAS herded "bourgeois" opponents and captured British soldiers on forced marches into the mountains. As news spread of the terrible brutality shown toward some of these hostages, and indeed of mass executions, popular revulsion toward EAM extremism grew. Even within ELAS and the EP, growing disquiet appears to have alarmed Communist Party officials.[18]

Yet few would have predicted, as the Varkiza Agreement was signed in February 1945 and the fighting in Athens ended, with what speed EAM/ELAS would be transformed from oppressor into victim. But this is what happened: the ending of the Dekemvriana was followed by a right-wing backlash that spiraled out of the control of either the Athens government or the British. In less than a month, the newly resurgent gendarmerie would be settling scores with its old enemies, and members of EAM/ELAS would now find that their own involvement in "People's Courts" that winter was leading them to prison or worse.[19]

The epitaph for the EAM/ELAS conception of "People's Justice" came in a series of protests that EAM addressed toward the Greek government and its British backers in early March 1945. Cataloguing the growing list of right-wing violations of Varkiza, the leaders of EAM expressed their outrage that people were being arrested for their membership in "People's Courts" and ELAS courts martial. They insisted that "the necessity of the struggle and of the maintenance of order made the existence of Courts Martial necessary; . . . consequently, persecution and arrests such as the above are absolutely illegal and astonishing." But EAM was no longer in a position to define the bounds of legality, and its astonishment was quickly to disappear.[20]

The punishment of collaborators and war criminals was a vital issue for a majority of Greeks at Liberation. That such desires were not confined to the Left is obvious from, for example, the editorial of a moderate right-wing newspaper from Patras, *Enosis*, which insisted on the need for a "purge of all traitors and the clean-up of the Gendarmerie and Security Corps." The Papandreou government, which arrived back in Greece in the middle of October, could therefore not shirk this task. But the efforts of the Greek state to restore — or establish — the judicial norms of something resembling a liberal democracy were inevitably shaped by the political forces of both Left and Right, which overshadowed and at times appeared likely to overwhelm the "political world" that returned to power in Athens after Liberation.[21]

This was evident right at the start, in Italy in September 1944, as Papandreou's Justice Minister Tsatsos prepared the Constitutional Act 1, which set up the procedures for trying collaborators in liberated Greece. Reflecting the power (and fear) of EAM/ELAS at that time, the special courts that Tsatsos announced several weeks later were themselves described officially as "People's Courts," with a mixed composition of judicial, military, and civilian personnel. The Tsatsos law provided for several degrees of collaboration, with sentences ranging from six months' imprisonment to death, but it stated that all cases must be initiated within six months of the end of the occupation.[22]

In fact, as we have already seen, the magistrates nominated by the Papandreou government in those first few months of Liberation were unable to proceed normally with their work. The civil war in December, and EAM/ELAS's subsequent loss of power, modified the original arrangements. By a further Constitutional Act, the composition of the judging panel was changed, and its "popular" character reduced. The time limit for bringing prosecutions had to be extended several times, due to the slowness of forming the special collaborators' courts. It is true that the wording of the Act was changed to make conviction of former ministers more likely. Yet the underlying reluctance to tackle the issue of collaboration was evident. Even with British pressure to accelerate the trial of prominent collaborators, no trials took place before late February. By contrast, trials of leftists for participation in the fighting in December were under way as early as the following month, and an extraordinary court martial was established to try such cases.[23]

February 1945 saw efforts against the background of the Varkiza Agreement to regularize the judicial situation created by the Dekemvriana. Martial law was lifted (except in the Athens area), and the extraordinary court martial was, in theory, wound up. An amnesty was granted for "political offences committed between 3 December 1944 and 14 February 1945"; henceforth only common-law crimes such as murder were punishable. A British legal observer wrote hopefully: "The authority of the Government will, in due course, be extended throughout the country and as a corollary, the judicial system will be reestablished and will, it is hoped, prove to be a powerful factor in restoring the confidence of the people." As will be seen below, this was to remain little more than a pious hope.[24]

In his introduction to Constitutional Act 6, which revised the composition of the collaborators' courts, Justice Minister Nikolaos Kolyvas — writing even as fighting with ELAS was continuing in the suburbs of Athens — made clear his attitude toward the quisling ministers: they had relied upon nothing and no one but the Germans, and their responsibility remained great even if it turned out that well-established political leaders had privately encouraged them to accept office. Nobody could justly be accused of collaboration if government ministers escaped censure. Nor might they plead patriotism: "The good of the Fatherland is not an objective criterion." On the contrary, the trial of quisling politicians was itself a political and moral duty: "We are bound to carry this out to set an example both to the civilised world and to future generations to show that people cannot lend their services to the enemies of the Fatherland and go unpunished."[25]

It is striking that Kolyvas justified minimizing the presence of nonlawyers on the proposed courts by explicitly denying the *political* nature of the quislings' crimes: "Their crime is not political but of ordinary penal law." Why, then, was the crime of treachery not being tried by a court martial? "Because we wish to give the accused the guarantee of impartial justice. In our country justice has functioned well. We hope that it will do its duty in this case too," the minister concluded optimistically.[26]

The showpiece trial that this legislation was designed to expedite — that of the wartime premiers and their ministers — finally got under way in late February and dragged on for several months. Indeed, a *third* piece of legislation was needed in March to speed up proceedings. During the Dekemvriana, the leading collaborators then in prison in Athens had been shipped for safety to East Africa; the necessity of this move was demonstrated by the killings of two former quisling ministers who were abducted by ELAS during the fighting. But the remainder were eventually brought back to Athens for trial.

As Kolyvas — and many others — had foreseen, the defendants based their case on two main grounds. First, they claimed, and adduced convincing evidence, that they had been encouraged to assume office under the Germans by members of the Greek "political world," including such figures as George Papandreou, prime minister at Liberation, and Nikolaos Plastiras, his successor. The enormous potential of such trials to embarrass the political elite entrusted with running the country after the war was increasingly evident. Papandreou was forced to testify; Plastiras, prime minister in the spring of 1945, was forced to resign that summer following the publication of an old letter he had written from Vichy France offering, apparently, to form a pro-German government in Athens!

Second, the defendants insisted that they had been motivated by patriotism, which, in the case of the first wartime premier, General Georgios Tsolakoglou, meant hostility to the Bulgarians, and in the case of Ioannis Rallis, premier in 1943–1944, meant hostility to the communists. Although such a defense had been ruled out *ab initio*, it was politically an appealing strategy in the months after the Dekemvriana, as the eventual verdicts showed: Tsolakoglou was condemned to death but with a recommendation to mercy (eventually heeded); the two other wartime premiers were sentenced to life imprisonment. Several ministers were sentenced to terms of imprisonment. Astonishingly, the court decided that the founding of the Security Battalions could not be regarded as a crime (though wartime broadcasts from Cairo had announced that even *membership* in them would be so regarded), since they had been formed only for the defense of public order against "criminal elements." Even the Minister of Justice could not refrain from commenting on the mildness of the sentences.[27]

But with anticommunism in the ascendant, there was little desire for further such trials within the political elite. It is indicative of official attitudes toward the trial that the only official record of its proceedings was a virtually illegible stenographic transcript that was supposed to be destroyed after six months. As a result, commentators then and now could rely only upon press reports of the sessions. The official memory of these unfortunate events was designed to be short-lived.

The power of the Right was now growing apace, and bringing with it a new immunity for former collaborators. In March, former agents of OPLA (*Organosi Perifrourisi tou Laikou Agona*, Organization for the Protection of the People's Struggle) were sentenced to death at about the same time as collaborators with the German Secret Service were given short prison terms: a senior judge ordered an enquiry into the conduct of some of the judges in the collaborationist courts, but apparently to little effect. There was further public concern when a former Battalion officer was acquitted for shooting dead a member of the EP who had tried to arrest him in central Athens the previous October. Public outrage increased in August when it was announced that a senior Battalion commander, Colonel Papadongonas, was to be posthumously promoted; a few days later the promotion was cancelled. In October, the trial of Battalion commanders and other collaborationist security officers began in almost farcical conditions, "with the President of the Court taking the side of the accused and Lambou [one of the leading defendants] himself giving orders to the police in Court."[28]

Such scenes demonstrated the power of a newly resurgent Right in the National Guard, the gendarmerie, the army, and assorted paramilitary forces over the judicial system and the established "political world." Insofar as one can tell, the public appears to have disapproved of the results: in Tripolis, a conservative town, for example, it was reported in April 1945 that "the more moderate element of the Right Wing, which forms a majority, is as impatient to see collaborationists brought to justice as it is pleased to witness the arrests of Communists and known troublemakers. It would seem as though any government which does not show at least some token action in this respect will certainly lose a great deal of popularity and support."[29]

Yet periodic commitments to purge the security services of former Battalionists and collaborators had not been carried out. In fact, the purge of the civil service envisaged by the Varkiza Agreement was now in operation, but against the Left. Individuals suspected of leftist sympathies were also excluded from the new National Guard. The Athens government had little more power in the autumn of 1945 than it had had a year earlier, only this time its authority was under challenge from the Right. Outside Athens itself, the government had lost control of policing, the prisons, the entire apparatus of "law and order."[30]

During the spring and summer of 1945, the government appointed a series of prefects and judges to take up positions in the provinces. They found terrible tensions and few signs of reconciliation: it is true that on Skiathos there were moves to bring Left and Right together, with nationalists pleading for the release of leftists from jail; and in the village of Kapandrition outside Athens, the local mayor was also emphasizing the need for political reconciliation. But these were isolated and exceptional figures.[31] Much more typical was Agrinion, where "the new force of Gendarmerie is arresting about three persons per day, mostly on charges of murder"; Levadhia, "where the soldiers and NCOs of the Gendarmerie continue to tear down pictures of Marshal Stalin"; and Tripolis, where the National Guard engaged in "beatings up, arrests without warrant for interrogation, burning of newspapers, robbery, smashing up of the Left-wing press and arming of civilians."[32]

Right-wing paramilitaries were evidently tolerated by the various police forces. In Mesolonghi, for instance, "a party of X-ites, mistaken for EPON (*Eniaia Panelladiki Organosi Neon*, United Panhellenic Organization of Youth) are reported to have been arrested by the Gendarmerie in the act of painting the walls with slogans. On revealing their identity, however, the X-ites were released and their arms handed back to them."[33] EPON, the leftists' resistance youth movement, was a target for repression; "X," an anticommunist organization that had collaborated with the Germans, was supported. The same was true for other groups, such as the collaborationist EASAD (*Ethnikos Agrotikos Syndesmos Antikemmounistikis Draseos*, National Agrarian Federation of Anticommunist Action) in Volos.

In such an atmosphere it was — to put it mildly — hard for public prosecutors to investigate collaborators. Impartial civil servants, like the prefect on Kefallonia, were often forced to resign or to tone down their activities. The public prosecutor in Agrinion had failed to bring a single collaborator to trial nine months after Liberation, even though he had 200 cases for investigation.

In fact, Agrinion, where there had been a particularly horrible massacre during the war, was in a very unhappy state. Junior gendarmerie personnel were more or less out of control: they shocked the town by desecrating the graves of former members of ELAS who had been shot by the Germans; later — and without instructions from the legal authorities — they arrested prominent members of EAM, including a former mayor of the town, on a charge of having participated in an ELAS court martial.[34]

The judiciary's inability to control the official forces of law and order was evident throughout the country. Colonel C. M. Woodhouse, formerly head of the British military mission to the Greek resistance, was sent into the Peloponnese in the summer of 1945 following rumors of an impending left-wing revolt. He found instead that the chief problem lay with the Right. The public prosecutor of Kalamata told him that the practice of arresting without warrant was "enforced solely against 'those accused of crimes during the occupation' [i.e., EAM/ELAS]." Those accused of collaboration escaped arrest because it was not thought safe to put them in the same prison as former *andartes*, and because it was believed that unlike former leftists, they would stay at home if they were not arrested! "Both arguments are nonsense," Woodhouse noted crisply.[35]

In the royalist stronghold of Gythion, most of the 290 prisoners were former ELAS *andartes*; the public prosecutor expressed pride in having three collaborators under lock and key. Often senior civil servants in these towns felt unhappy at this state of affairs, but would or could do little to alter it. The military commander of Tripolis, for instance, confessed he had not a single officer he could trust; the gendarmerie commander there emphasized that "he could not control his area as long as local officials were stupid, panic-stricken and incompetent." Such was the state of fear in Messenia, in the southern Peloponnese, that "it would take a stout-hearted man to undertake the work of a Justice of the Peace." Other senior officials made no pretense of their sympathies: the new prefect in Sparta, for example, released 300 Security Battalion personnel from jail without trial. In the meantime, leftists were arrested on the basis of hearsay, and gendarmes and former collaborators were able to work off personal and village vendettas. Tsambasis, the public prosecutor for all cases of collaboration throughout Greece, openly admitted that right-wing pressure prevented him from issuing more than a very few warrants for arrest.[36]

The situation does seem to have been slightly better in parts of northern Greece, where ELAS handed over hundreds of collaborators to the authorities in February and March 1945. Special collaborators' courts were set up in Salonika and the neighboring area (as also in Kalamata, Athens, Volos, Khalkis, and Heraklion) and began operation after many a delay in the summer. But judges' salaries were poor, and there were too few of them and too much interference from the military. In Kozani, 234 collaborators handed over to the National Guard by ELAS were immediately set free to go home to their villages. Magistrates in Salonika found the local police sabotaging their efforts to arrest well-known collaborators; when the wanted men fled to Athens, it was found that the Athens police were no more reliable.[37]

Nevertheless, perhaps the main judicial problem by mid-1945 was not the (non)-prosecution of collaborators but rather the terrible overcrowding of the country's prisons, packed full of real and suspected leftists. The earlier amnesty for political crimes committed during the Dekemvriana had simply been disregarded by the Right, as people were arrested on trumped-up charges. The official figure for the prison population in September 1945 was 17,232, including over 10,000 alleged leftists and some 1,246 alleged collaborators. The real number was certainly higher, though not necessarily as high as the 60,000 alleged by the EAM. By the end of 1945, some 48,956 EAM supporters were behind bars.[38]

In Nafplion prison, packed with 460 inmates, there were four collaborators and 407 leftists, of whom only thirty had been tried and convicted. In Mesolonghion, the conditions were described as "horrifying"; the government only fed those arrested under warrant; the rest had to be fed by their families. Inmates included children as young as nine years old. Such stories were not unusual. Despite much British pressure, there was no effective diminution in the prison population.[39]

This persecution of the Left, combined with a leniency toward former collaborators unprecedented in Europe, alarmed observers at the time. Unfortunately, the problem became worse, not better. The Royalist government, which won the first postwar election in March 1946, intensified the repression. A new historiographical consensus would now see that repression as the prime cause of the final, and bloodiest, round of the Greek civil war. Parliamentary democracy did not collapse, but the administration of justice became increasingly militarized: courts martial and special security tribunals set the framework for an ever more bloody judicial repression that formed part of Greek life for the next twenty-five years.[40]

In the months and years on either side of the Liberation, there was no single effective authority in Greece. The power of the state had collapsed in 1941 and was not fully restored until 1949. The ending of Nazi occupation brought the usual demands for revenge and punishment, but in this abnormally fluid political situation, there was no measure of agreement as to the form such justice should take. There was, in effect, a clash between competing forms of political justice. Brief, though highly effective, was the collective revenge taken against the Albanian Muslim Chams by Greek nationalists in a tiny corner of northwestern Greece between July 1944 and March 1945. Ethnic justice — or aspects of it — would assume a far greater importance with the nationalist struggle for the hearts, minds, and villages of the Slavic population of northern Greece during the final and bloodiest stage of the civil war.

At Liberation, a far more serious challenge to prewar judicial norms was that offered by EAM/ELAS, which held sway over most of the country until the spring of 1945: its "People's Courts" were popular in some areas, but increasingly resented or suspected in others. The use of

ELAS and the EP to target the "class enemy" — "reactionary" individuals or even villages — alienated many of the very country people it was supposed to attract. Hostage-taking and mass executions confirmed their worst fears.

By early 1945 the evidence suggests that many people looked forward to the Athens government reasserting its authority as a way of bringing back social peace. But although the government was under pressure to rebuild the legal system as quickly as possible, and seems to have accepted the need for collaborators to be tried as a means of assuaging popular outrage, it lacked control of the state apparatus. After the Dekemvriana, the idea of an impartial police force was pushed further away than ever. The security forces upon which Athens relied were chiefly concerned with settling old scores with the Left. Trials of collaborators continued, a trickle compared with the wave of arrests of former *andartes*. Eventually, this repression itself pushed the Left into a new armed response.

To what extent, then, can we talk of "political justice" at all in Greece at this time? Was the idea of justice anything more than a rhetorical device to justify the persecution of one's opponents? Each of the three groupings had a different conception of political criminality: for the nationalist Right, it meant ethnic affiliation; for EAM/ELAS, it meant opposition to its vision of a "People's Democracy," a form of communist justice inflected by the uncertainties, ambiguities, and moral expansiveness induced by the war; for the post-Liberation governments and their British backers, it centered on the liberal idea of individual "treachery." To ask whether any of these conceptions was necessarily superior to the others is to raise the question of the fundamental relationship between ideology and justice. It seems to me, however, that such a question is unavoidable in the context of this troubled period.

NOTES

1. Modern Greek Archive (King's College, London), info VIII, Minorities file: "Simeioma: Zitima Tsamourias," n.d.
2. WO 204/9348, "Albanian Minority in Epirus, 1940–1944," n.d.
3. FO 371/43692 R 14686/9, Leeper (Cairo)-Foreign Office, enclosing D. Wallace, "Report on a Tour of EDES 3rd Division and a Visit to the Headquarters of 1st Independent Brigade, 1–13 August 1944," 15 Aug. 1944.
4. FO 371/48094 R 8564, "Tour of South Albania April 2–6," by M. A. Hodgson, 1945; FO 371/48094 R 8331, "Report by Lt. Col. C.A.S. Palmer on Visit to Northern Greece, 9–14 April 1945," 1945. See also K. Cooper, *The Uprooted* (London, 1979), 80.

5. FO 371/48094 R 20573, Romanos-Foreign Office, 4 Dec. 1945; FO 371/48094, C. M. Woodhouse, "A Note on the Chams," 16 Oct. 1945.

6. See my *Inside Hitler's Greece: The Experience of Occupation, 1941–1944* (New Haven and London, 1993), 289

7. FO 371/43692 R 14791, Boxhall-Laskey, 12 Sept. 1944, enclosing telegrams from the field. For one blacklist, FO 371/48272, Levadhia, 18–25 May 1945. The burgeoning Aris hagiography may be sampled in the form of a recent "scholarly symposium," K. Koutsoukis, ed., *I prosopikotita tou Ari Velouchioti kai i ethniki antistasi* (Athens, 1997).

8. WO 204/8923, "Report on Work of the Legal Dept., Salonika District, ML (Greece), 16 Nov. 44 – 31 Mar. 45," 5 Apr. 1945; WO 204/9380, "Public Security: Period 16th Oct. to 9th Nov. 1944."

9. FO 371/43693 R 15765, telegrams to and from the field.

10. Ibid.

11. Ibid.

12. WO 204/9380, "Diary, 27th Oct. 1944."

13. WO 204/8835, "REPORT on a Disturbance in the Area of the Gendarmerie School at 1445 hrs., 22 Nov. 44."

14. The situation of lawyers appointed by the Athens government was especially difficult. In one case, a Salonikan lawyer appointed to the special courts for collaborationists was himself arrested by ELAS as a collaborator and brought for trial before an ELAS court martial: WO 204/8923, "Report on Work of the Legal Department," 5 Apr. 1945.

15. WO 204/8923, "Report on Work of the Legal Dept," 5 Apr. 1945; "Progress Report for Week Ending 18 Feby 45," 19 Feb. 1945; and "Re THEBES," 29 Nov. 1944; FO 371/48254 R 2815, Rapp (Salonika)-Athens, 7 Feb. 1945.

16. WO 204/8923, 18 and 25 Nov. 1944.

17. WO 204/9381, "Report on Skyros," 28 Oct. 1944.

18. FO 371/48254 R 2684, 20 Jan. 1945; FO 371/48258 R 3976, Leeper (Athens)-Foreign Office, 19 Feb. 1945, enclosing "CSDIC Interrogation Reports of British and Indian Prisoners of ELAS."

19. FO 371/48274.

20. FO 371/48262 R 443, enclosing EAM-British Ambassador, 5 Mar. 1945.

21. FO 371/48254 R 2684, 20 Jan. 1945, enclosing *Enosis* editorial.

22. WO 204/8923, 25 Nov. 1944.

23. FO 371/48253 R 2549, Leeper (Athens)-Foreign Office, 4 Feb. 1945.

24. WO 204/8923.

25. FO 371/48258 R 4024, Leeper (Athens)-Eden, 16 Feb. 1945, enclosing the text of Constitutional Act 6.

26. Ibid.

27. For a lengthy report on the trial, see FO 371/48272 R 10144, Warner (Athens)-London, 5 June 1945, enclosing "The Trial of the Quisling Ministers: Part 2."

28. FO 371/48279 R 14971, R 15076; FO 371/48284 R 18710. In November there was widespread shock at the leniency of the sentences in the Lambou trial: FO 371/48286 R 20169, Leeper (Athens)-Foreign Office, 22 Nov. 1945.

29. FO 371/48269, Tripolis, 13–19 Apr. 1945.

30. P. Papastratis, "The Purge of the Greek Civil Service on the Eve of the Civil War," in L. Baerentzen, J. Iatrides, and O. Smith, eds., *Studies in the History of the Greek Civil War, 1945–1949* (Copenhagen, 1987), 41–55; D. Close, "The Reconstruction of a Right-Wing State," in Close, ed., *The Greek Civil War, 1943–1950: Studies of Polarization* (London, 1993), 156–90.

31. FO 371/48273.

32. Ibid.

33. Ibid.

34. FO 371/48274, "Agrinion, 17–23 June 1945."

35. FO 371/48279 R 14973, Caccia (Athens)-Foreign Office, 25 Aug. 1945, enclosing C. M. Woodhouse, "Situation in the Peloponnese," 11 Aug. 1945.

36. Ibid.; FO 371/48263 R 5860, 21 Mar. 1945; WO 204/8931.

37. FO 371/48264 R 6218, Rapp (Salonika)-Athens, 5 Apr. 1945; WO 204/8931, Salonika, 10 Aug. 1945; and ibid., "Kozani: subject Collaborators."

38. FO 371/48279 R 15198, Lascalles (Athens)-Foreign Office, 7 Sept. 1945; Papastratis, "Purge," p. 46.

39. WO 204/8930, "Conditions in Greek Civilian Prisons," 26 June 1945.

40. See my "Historians at War: Greece, 1940–1950," *Historical Journal*, 38.2 (1995): 499–506.

TWO

The Punishment of Collaborators in Northern Greece, 1945–1946

Eleni Haidia

THE DEPARTURE of the occupation forces from Greek soil marked the end of a particularly harsh period for the Greek people. The Greeks were not, however, prepared to consign the events of those years to oblivion; there was a widespread determination to impose exemplary punishment on the collaborators. Resolving this thorny issue placed considerable obstacles before the smooth social transition from occupation to Liberation, and rapidly became a taboo subject, heavily charged with the emotions of the civil war that followed.

This chapter is based on the proceedings of the collaborators' trials, which were held at the Special Court in Thessaloniki between 1945 and 1949. It is confined to those that took place in 1945–1946, for both technical and historical reasons: the existing legislation was replaced in December 1946, and above all it was in 1946 that the background to the whole process changed completely with the outbreak of the civil war, which divided Greece for many years to come.[1]

At Liberation, the Papandreou government had responded to the widespread feeling that justice should be done by announcing without delay that the "National Nemesis will be implacable."[2] Undoubtedly, EAM/ELAS had had a hand in this announcement, for it was particularly sensitive to this issue; it was in the government of National Unity, its strength was unimpaired, and it was able to influence government decisions. Although the prime minister's sybilline assertion that the number of collaborators was not large certainly gave rise to some apprehension, his initial promise soon materialized in the form of Constitutional Act 1, "On the imposition of penal sanctions on those who have collaborated with the enemy," a law supplemented a few months later by the Plastiras government.[3] In January 1945, the Plastiras administration, replaced Constitutional Act 1 with Act 6, "On the Imposition of Sanctions on Those Who Have Collaborated with the Enemy."[4] As Nikolaos Kolyvas, the minister responsible, pointed out in the preamble to the new law, the aim of the Ministry of Justice was to ensure that the accused received impartial justice, not to exonerate them, as was widely rumored.

Boy selling food in the streets of Thessaloniki, winter 1946. Reproduced by kind permission of the estate of Nancy Crawshaw.

As elsewhere at this time, one basic problem was defining the term "collaboration" in the context of a judicial reckoning with the consequences of enemy occupation. What was to end up as a term of historical analysis and controversy started out as part of the legal and political process. Article 1 of the Greek Constitutional Act identified the following categories: those who had undertaken to form a government during the occupation, or had served as ministers or deputy ministers in the occupation governments, or had facilitated the task of the occupation authorities by holding public, military, administrative, or judicial posts (this applied to local government agents); those who had worked in the employ of the occupation authorities, facilitating their task or oppressing the people; those who had deliberately acted as tools of the enemy by spreading enemy propaganda, praising the achievements of the occupiers, and cultivating defeatism among the Greek people (this applied particularly to publishers and journalists); those who had denounced Greek or foreign nationals participating in the Allied struggle; those who had committed acts of violence with or without the assistance of the occupation authorities (to have received arms from the enemy was regarded as a particularly aggravating circumstance); those who had systematically informed the enemy about the movements of individuals or organizations working on behalf of the Allied struggle; those who had hindered the Allied war effort in any way; and those who, with the help of the enemy, had led movements targeting the integrity of the country. Finally, it also mentioned those who had exploited economic collaboration with the enemy, thus causing detriment to the Greek people or to Greek citizens, or who had assisted the enemy war effort or derived unusual financial benefit, and those who had profited in any way from their collaboration with the enemy to the detriment of Greek citizens or citizens of an Allied power.

Those found guilty of acts that came within the scope of article 1 received sentences that ranged, according to their status or position and the gravity or consequences of their actions, from death to life imprisonment, penal servitude, permanent exile, or, in the case of extenuating circumstances, prison terms of varying length. The death sentence was actually carried out in only eight cases;[5] thereafter, until the end of 1946, it was tacitly suspended with parliament's tolerance, initially because no temporary government was prepared to assume the responsibility with elections just around the corner, and later because the country's headlong rush toward civil war overshadowed this particular issue. We may contrast the paucity of death sentences carried out for cases of collaboration with the extensive use of capital punishment in the burgeoning civil war against the Left.

The decisions of the Special Court were final and did not carry the option of a fine. However, the condemned had the right to appeal to the Clemency Board and to ask either for a commutation of their sentence or for a reprieve. Quite a number of appeals were submitted in 1945–1946: in some cases a sentence of death was commuted to life imprisonment, and there was one case of a ten-year prison sentence being reduced to four years.[6]

It was, then, on the basis of the Constitutional Act that the Special Collaborators' Court of Thessaloniki was set up in 1945 with the same area of jurisdiction as the Thessaloniki Court of Appeal, and with the task of judging offenses committed within its district. That district originally included seven prefectures, chiefly in central Macedonia. The news that the court had been set up was particularly welcomed by the people of Thessaloniki. However, it was an indication of the difficulties that attended the court's initial operations that within a few months the Minister of Justice, Nikolaos Kolyvas, permitted smaller courts to be set up in other prefectures (Serres, Drama, Kastoria, and Florina) with a view to lightening the burden on the Thessaloniki Special Court and creating more flexible structures.[7] Time was passing and the trials had become bogged down in delays, the press was fulminating daily and the public was growing restive. Through 1945 the Special Magistrate in Thessaloniki frequently mentioned the problems confronting the judicial authorities, in an attempt to justify the delay and appease public opinion.

There were, in addition to the more general problems of administering justice in the confused and chaotic conditions of Greece in early 1945, several specific difficulties for the courts in Macedonia: in this area of delicate territorial equilibrium, collaboration was not simply a matter of working with the enemy in the hope of (chiefly financial) gain; it also threatened the country's territorial integrity. In particular, the inclusion of Slavic-speakers among the accused trained the spotlight once again on the bilingual inhabitants of Macedonia. This sensitive area of the Balkans had been put under strain by the triple occupation, particularly by the presence of the Bulgarians, whose activities were tolerated by the German authorities and sometimes assisted by the Italians.[8] The aim of Bulgarian propaganda was quite clearly to prejudice the integrity of Greece and ultimately to annex Greece's northern territories to the Bulgarian state. It was aimed at the Slavic-speaking inhabitants, especially those whose national consciousness was somewhat fluid and who were once again placed in a difficult position because of the dialect they spoke. Many had deliberately chosen to collaborate with the Bulgarians, had joined the *Okhrana* (Bulgarian propaganda) groups, and had worked against both Greek- and Slavic-speakers who did not share their own views. Others had bowed to pressure or been pushed into collaboration by poverty, attracted by the generosity of the Bulgarian Club toward its members.[9] A number of them, however, were merely scapegoats, paying for the treachery of fellow Slavic-speakers who had been prudent enough to accompany the occupying forces when they withdrew from Greece. Suspicion against them increased with the anti-communist feeling that developed after Liberation, when the Communist Party of Greece (KKE) began to promote the notion of the equality of all ethnic groups, which was perceived by nationalists as a threat to Greece's integrity.

Other minorities also formed the object of the attention of the special collaborators' courts. Wartime Italian propaganda had, for its part, talked freely of a Koutsovlach minority and the need to create an autonomous Koutsovlach state. This particular form of propaganda had been stronger in Thessaly, where the notorious Alkibiades Diamandis was active, but it also affected Macedonia after it gained supporters in the prefecture of Grevena. Diamandis, a pro-Italian lawyer from Samarina, had rallied local leaders in 1942 and, in collaboration with the Italians, established a fifth column known as the Roman Legion. His ultimate aim had been to create a so-called Principate of the Pindus.[10] On hearing Diamandis's manifesto, and indeed, motivated by the prospect of immediate material gain, a small number of the Vlach-speakers in Grevena had been moved to follow him and declare fealty to the Italian occupiers. However, the vast majority of the Vlachs had remained loyal to Greece, despite the legionaries' pressure, and this prevented the issue from assuming greater proportions in Macedonia.

Lastly, prewar Thessaloniki had possessed a large Jewish community, which found itself after 1941 in the German administration zone. From the very first weeks of the occupation, the German authorities had embarked upon a series of antisemitic measures, confiscating Jewish shops and apartments, which gradually came into the hands of those who collaborated with the Germans as rewards for services rendered. These measures culminated in the deportation of the community in 1943 and the abandonment of its property, which certainly became a major incentive for those collaborators in quest of profit. Some of the latter also found themselves under investigation, both by EAM in the winter of 1944, and by the officials of the collaborators' courts.

The problems caused by the political and legal complexity of the various cases of collaboration with the occupation authorities were compounded by difficulties of a practical nature, for the courts themselves were seriously lacking in many respects. Working conditions were wretched and staff inadequate, so that the magistrates simply did not have the time to study all the charges that were brought every day.[11] The number of prosecutions was increasing in leaps and bounds, and the deadline for lodging complaints was constantly extended. An article in the newspaper *Ellinikos Vorras* painted the gloomiest possible picture of the situation in the courts:[12]

> Only three magistrates have been summoned here, squeezed into narrow, stifling offices without seats, without writing materials, without pen-holders. The magistrates' offices are packed with detainees, advocates, and witnesses, while the magistrates themselves, crushed as they are in the narrow space, are in grave danger of suffocation. In such circumstances, there can naturally be no guarantee that justice will be done by judicial functionaries leading such a martyred existence. For how much longer are these semi-savage conditions to continue, before the authorities in Athens evince the slightest concern?[13]

At the same time, the files surrendered by ELAS[14] after it pulled out of Thessaloniki were also being examined. So long as EAM was in charge in the city (from late October 1944 until 17 January 1945), the EAM general staff continued the efforts to dispense justice that it had begun during the occupation by setting up People's Courts.[15] Its National Guard immediately started arresting suspected collaborators, one of its first achievements being the surrender of the members of the gendarmerie and the security services who were holed up in the YMCA building. The rate of arrests was such that the prisons were soon packed. The accused were brought before the People's Courts, tried, and, if found guilty, brought back to prison. In some cases, people condemned to death by summary procedures were actually executed, which provoked strong protests from the commander of British forces in Athens, General Sir Ronald Scobie, to Euripides Bakirdzis,[16] the head of the general staff of the Macedonian Divisions Group. Bakirdzis promised that a decree would be issued, but such were the shortcomings of the military commander, Christos Avramidis, and the governor general of Central Macedonia, Yeoryios Modis, that it was never properly implemented, with the result that a fresh wave of arrests took place during the December revolution. Meanwhile, quite a number of citizens, as also the British consul general, Thomas Rapp, complained that those arrested included individuals who had had nothing whatever to do with the occupying forces, but were being persecuted simply because they had opposed EAM.[17]

These problems were further compounded by the reluctance of witnesses to come forward and help the preliminary inquiries, despite constant appeals to all those possessing evidence or information. It was thus difficult to complete the investigations and set the dates of the hearings. This phenomenon was chiefly a factor in the major cases, such as those concerning Jewish property and related issues; by contrast, contractors were approaching the magistrates on a daily basis to testify against wealthy businessmen who had taken on German projects.[18] Reluctance to come forward was chiefly demonstrated by countryfolk, who often simply could not afford the expense of traveling to and staying in the city, because the state offered them very little reimbursement. Rumor was also rife that some wealthy collaborators were trying to buy off the witnesses and were sometimes even resorting to violence, and this probably frightened or discouraged some potential witnesses, who decided to get on with their lives and try to forget the past. Thus from Drama comes the following news: "The population of our prefecture has been roused to indignation by the revelation of the actions of the Armenian tobacco merchant Takvorian, who, through his employees, has been endeavouring to elicit from the tobacco growers testimonials to his patriotic activity during the Occupation." And as a trial of suspected Bulgarian agents opened in August, it was reported: "A stir ran through the court when witness Christos Vasderis revealed under questioning that, shortly before his appearance before the Court, Evangelos Gatsis had given him 10,000 drachmas in the corridor to testify in favour of his relation D. Gatsis. The bribe was confiscated by the Court."[19]

Meanwhile, all those whom the judicial authorities had decided to prosecute were remanded in custody, and the problem of space, already a headache for the authorities, soon became acute. Eptapyrgio prison had been damaged by the Germans and had not yet been repaired, and the new prison was still being built. In the face of mounting numbers of detainees, which were increasing by geometrical progression, the authorities resorted to renting warehouses and space in the Infectious Diseases Hospital.[20]

The inevitable delay in the start of the trials is apparent from the constant protests in the press, which made insinuations about the inertia of the Special Magistrate and published scathing articles denouncing the authorities' indifference to the information that many collaborators had fled to Athens and were now living there. The trials eventually began on 24 April 1945, and naturally drew large crowds, a testimony to the still lively public desire for justice.

The accused may be divided into three categories, according to whether they had collaborated with the Bulgarians, the Germans, or the Italians. Some had collaborated with all three. It should be noted that the term "collaborators" was not normally extended to include the ordinary black-marketeers, though it did cover those who had had financial dealings with the occupiers.

The first category, those who were accused of collaborating with the Bulgarians, was by far the largest group, 663 (69 percent) of the 959 people accused. Most were from central and western Macedonia, though there were also many from the prefecture of Thessaloniki, particularly in 1946,[21] when the regional courts started to operate. The number of accused in this category seems disproportionately large in relation to the number of trials, but this is due to the fact that in some cases several people (usually from the countryside) were tried en bloc. They tended to be from the same or neighboring villages, sometimes they were blood relations, and their declared occupation was either farming or some sort of manual work. So quite often more than one person stood in the dock; indeed, in trial no. 173–174/1945, the number of accused was no less than sixty-four.

One of the first trials to be held involved eight people from Rizari, in Edessa prefecture. All declared themselves to be farmers. Two were brothers and another two were blood relations, though their kinship is not specified in the records. The accusations against six members of the group were particularly serious. Witnesses for the prosecution stated that the accused had expressed pro-Bulgarian sentiments since 1941, as soon as the Bulgarian troops had arrived. They had then joined the armed *Okhrana* groups and had gone around wearing the organiza- tion's blue uniform. They had tried to intimidate their fellow villagers into joining the Bulgarian Club, denounced Greeks to the Bulgarians, ripped up Greek flags, and organized pro-Bulgarian demonstrations in Edessa. With other *Okhrana* members (there was some doubt as to whether two of the accused had participated), they had mobbed the village; in the ensuing fray, at least two men had died and one woman had been injured.

In their defense, the accused admitted that they had carried arms, but maintained that it had been out of fear of guerrilla attacks. They had not known, they said, that the *Okhrana* was a Bulgarian organization, and they denied having taken part in looting and violent assaults. The court found two of them guilty of collaborating with the enemy and oppressing the people and sentenced them to life imprisonment. The other six were sentenced to death, because, apart from the above- mentioned charges, they were held responsible for people's deaths. Two- thirds of their property was confiscated as well. These were the first collaborators to receive the death penalty, and they were executed in Eptapyrgio prison.

These people were accused of manifesting pro-Bulgarian sentiments when the Bulgarians arrived (by flying Bulgarian flags, for instance, or putting up portraits of King Boris), of joining the *Okhrana* groups, of complicity in the arrest and execution of Greek citizens, of spreading Bulgarian propaganda, and of assisting efforts toward Macedonian au- tonomy. Inhabitants of urban centers were chiefly accused of joining the Bulgarian Club (some even holding high executive positions) and of at- tending Bulgarian churches, taking part in Bulgarian celebrations, join- ing Bulgarian choirs, and so on. The list of accusations was usually very long, being relevant to many of the articles of the Constitutional Act: the charges leveled against someone accused of "national unworthi- ness" might include a whole string of offenses, such as spreading propa- ganda or belonging to the Security Battalions.

The testimonies started to grow more complicated and to reveal the true nature of the problem when the witnesses recounted the activities of an accused prisoner during the occupation who, having been a loyal friend of the Bulgarians in the early years of the occupation, would suddenly appear as a member of *Slovenomakedonski Narodno Oslobo- ditelen Front* Slav Macedonian National Liberation Front). These were the *Okhranists*, armed members of Bulgarian-sponsored units, who were quick to join the Slavic-speaking units officially under the jurisdiction of EAM in order to avoid punishment after the occupation. Some of them even chose to espouse the SNOF manifesto regarding the autonomy of Macedonia. Others seem to have moved on to SNOF after active service with EAM.[22]

Many of the accused had absconded and were tried in absentia. They tended to be either fanatical supporters of the Bulgarian cause who had accompanied the departing Bulgarian troops in October 1944, or autonomists who had managed to flee to Yugoslavia. In 1945, 51 (15 percent) out of a total of 362 accused of collaboration with the Bulgarians were absent, and in 1946, 69 (23 percent) out of a total of 301. The sentences imposed on them were particularly harsh: 253 were found innocent, but of the 410 found guilty, 78 were sentenced to death, 65 received life imprisonment, and the rest were sentenced to penal servitude or prison terms.

The second category of collaborators, those who had worked with the Germans, covered a broad spectrum of everyday life, for their activities had spread into all sectors. They included Gestapo informers, people who had worked as interpreters and secretaries in the German services, members of the Security Battalions, ordinary collaborators, and the more notorious economic collaborators. Most of them had been active in the city and environs of Thessaloniki, which had been under German administration. They included people who were known to the citizenry for their unpatriotic activities, but not the high-ranking officials, who were tried by the Special Court in Athens, or had proceedings against them dropped, as for instance in the case of Dimitrios Mandouvalos, the wartime chief of police.

The economic collaborators[23] — including civil engineers, contractors, and merchants — were a particularly interesting group, accused of entering into economic relations with the German occupiers: twenty were tried in 1945, fifty-nine in 1946. They repeatedly found themselves in the spotlight as legislative amendments, each more favorable than the last, were pushed through on the pretext of decongesting the prisons.[24] Essentially, the governments were hoping to resolve their differences with this group of collaborators by offering them the option of paying a sum of money to discharge their debt to the state; breach of the agreement for discharging the debt incurred the penalty of banishment for the defaulter's family. According to the press, the measure was implemented in the case of one G. E. Pollatos, editor of the newspaper *Nea Evropi*, which was published by the German authorities. "Maria Pollatou and her daughter are under arrest," reported the papers. "They are to be transported to Spetses because Pollatos refuses to pay his debts to the state."[25]

The huge sums they or their relatives were called upon to pay roused the ire of some of the economic collaborators from Thessaloniki, and in 1947 they sent a memorandum to the American ambassador.[26] The law by which they had been convicted was unjust and unconstitutional, they told him, and they asked him to intervene to secure their release and a reduction of the taxes imposed upon them. Their actions indicate how confident they felt of their position at a time of political polarization and growing anticommunism.

The collaborators with the Germans naturally included those who had worked as interpreters and/or secretaries in the German services.[27] Needless to say, most were quick to explain that they had been forced to provide their services because of their knowledge of the German language. Others maintained that they had assumed the post in order to collect information for resistance groups or the Allies. Since there were no British liaison officers present, nor any officials who could have confirmed their assertions (the latter appeared at a few trials), the validity of their assurances cannot (and could not) be accepted.[28]

The largest group of German collaborators—some sixteen tried in 1945, twenty-six the following year—comprised the informers, those who were accused of systematically betraying to the occupation authorities, usually in the hope of financial reward, fellow citizens who had been involved in the resistance, or had been sought because they were of Jewish origin, or were sheltering British officers. In these cases, the prosecution witnesses were usually Jews, some of whom testified that the accused had robbed them of a small fortune with promises of saving them from the German soldiers; others attested that, on their return from the concentration camps, they had found their property in the possession of the accused. This constituted incriminating evidence, because the Germans habitually rewarded their collaborators with confiscated Jewish property.[29]

The category of German collaborators also included the members of the Security Battalions. These are not to be confused with similar battalions established in the rest of Greece by Ioannis Rallis, the prime minister of the last occupation government: the Security Battalions that operated in Macedonia from early 1944[30] onward were independent of the Athens administration, owing to Bulgarian opposition and a general lack of confidence in Greek officers.[31] They were supported by the German Secret Service and the German services in general, which also equipped and armed them. They were manned by opportunists, extremists, nationalists, and victims of ELAS, and their behavior was gross and savage. A typical case was Yeoryios Poulos, a particularly cruel man who took part in many of the Germans' mopping-up operations and whose name was linked with the bloodshed in the town of Yannitsa.[32]

The Security Battalions' bloody activities roused the strong revulsion of the local people, who hoped that justice would be done after the war. But they soon realized that the political developments were on the side of the Security Battalion members. When the Germans left, the ELAS remorselessly pursued the Security Battalion members who had camped outside Thessaloniki waiting to surrender to the British and smashed their corps. Most fled to Kilkis, where some were killed during the siege of the town. Quite a number managed to flee abroad with the departing Germans, a few were brought to trial, but most took advantage of the irregular situation to blend unnoticed into postwar society, and this is reflected in the small number of trials of Security Battalion members: only twenty-seven were tried in 1945–46.[33]

The trial of the press collaborators was particularly interesting. It was held in the Thessaloniki Special Court in 1945,[34] and in the dock were journalists who had worked during the occupation for *Apoyevmatini* and *Nea Evropi*, the only newspapers that continued to be published after the German authorities closed down all the rest on 17 April 1941. These papers had essentially been organs of German propaganda and were strictly censored by the relevant bureau. Facing trial with the journalists were the two newspapers' editors-in-chief and publishers.

Many stood accused of consciously collaborating with the enemy and spreading propaganda, offenses that carried the heaviest penalties. The trial riveted the attention of the citizenry and the journalistic world, who demanded that the collaboration of people responsible for informing the public be severely punished. It brought to light some interesting facts about journalism in occupied Thessaloniki and raised many questions about the options facing the journalists. One thing is certain: the journalists who eventually decided to remain jobless had to cope not only with the problem of survival but also with constant pressure from the occupation authorities, particularly after 1942, when the Germans tried, unsuccessfully, to break up the union of editors, which had seventy members at the time.[35]

When most of the accused were convicted, one of their colleagues, Vassilis Messolongitis, who had also worked for *Apoyevmatini* during the occupation but had appeared at the trial as a witness for the prosecution, tried to justify what his seven colleagues had done by arguing that they (and he himself) had been driven to do what they did by fear, and not by any lack of patriotic feeling.[36] He concluded: "And so we became pro-German and instruments of the conqueror's propaganda since it was not easy for us to be heroes. Heroism is truly a gift from God, but He in His infinite mercy has not seen fit to bestow it upon all people, and coincidentally upon none of us eight."

Needless to say, some well-known, prominent collaborators were nowhere to be found and had to be tried in absentia. The newspapers did not hesitate to accuse the authorities of negligence, nor to reveal that these people were at liberty in Athens.[37] Specifically, 26 percent of those accused of collaborating with the Germans were missing in 1945, and 18.5 percent in 1946, a greater proportion than the absentees among those accused of collaborating with the Bulgarians. The sentences passed were no less severe than the previous ones: of 135 found guilty, 22 were sentenced to death, 16 to life imprisonment, and 97 to penal servitude.

The third category consisted of those who had collaborated with the Italians, a very small group. Their small number was probably due to the fact that most were Vlach-speakers and had been active mainly in Thessaly, setting up armed bands and propagandizing the establishment of the "Principality of the Pindus," which would unite the Vlach-speaking populations. These collaborators were committed to trial at the Special Court of Larissa, which was responsible for this specific area. Only three were tried by the Special Court of Thessaloniki.[38] One was held to have accepted Romanian propaganda, as proven by the fact that he regularly attended a Romanian church and sent his children to a Romanian school. The other two, former inhabitants of the district of Grevena, had worked with the Italians and with Diamandis in seeking the establishment of an autonomous mini-state. All three were sentenced to penal servitude.

The picture of the trials in this period is completed by the detainees of Armenian descent, who were accused of collaborating with the Bulgarian authorities.[39] A number of members of the Armenian community purportedly engaged in anti-Greek conduct during the occupation. Six trials of a total of eight Armenians were held in the two-year period that concerns us here. Four of the accused were acquitted, since there was no incriminating evidence against them and the witnesses stated that the charges had been brought for personal motives; one was sentenced to life imprisonment, and three to penal servitude.

But the rate at which the hundreds of pending cases were being heard was desperately slow. Amendments were constantly being made to the current legislation in the hope of speeding things up, but to no avail. Only 135 trials were held in 1945–1946. On 16 February 1946, Special Magistrate Spyros Alexandropoulos announced that some 1,500 cases were still pending and warned that if the regulations governing their conduct were not changed, it would take another eight years to complete the whole process.[40]

At this time, public opinion seemed to be particularly sensitive to this tremendous issue: many professional associations — drapers, journalists, lawyers — were quick to expel their unworthy members, and the Athens

Theological School called for the severe punishment of clergymen who had proved unequal to their calling, so that the Church's prestige might be restored.[41] At the same time, letters were frequently published from ever-vigilant citizens, who were quick to denounce in the press any collaborators they had seen still at large and to name others who had escaped the attention of justice. Other letters protested injustices inflicted on fellow citizens. A reading of the letters that were sent to the newspaper offices reveals both the readers' intentions and their keen concern about the course of the trials.

The climate of euphoria did not last long, however. Suspicion and concern lest any collaborators take advantage of the authorities' negligence to make good their escape restored the editors to a state of alert, and they frequently published accusations against the Special Magistrate. At the same time, the course of the trials was being closely followed in other European countries, such as France, Italy, and Belgium. Guilty verdicts abroad were published with the pointed, and somewhat unfair, comment that *serious* efforts were being made to administer justice in Europe, the implication being that the judicial authorities in Greece were not doing their job impartially.

The situation was aggravated and a climate of strong suspicion created by the government's decision temporarily to postpone executions until after elections. The public began to wonder about the government's intentions, for the number of death sentences was far from negligible (between 25 April 1945, when the trials started, and 12 December 1946, when the trials were temporarily halted by order of the Special Magistrate in view of impending changes to the existing legislation, ninety-nine people had been condemned to death; eight were shot at Eptapyrgio prison at dawn on 11 August 1945). The press bombarded the authorities with questions, to which the Ministry of Justice does not seem to have had any answers, being content merely to deny the rumor that forty-three executions were to be postponed[42] and to allay suspicions that the sentences were to be commuted to life imprisonment.

The matter of the executions returned to the headlines in 1948, when the then-Minister of Justice, Christos Ladas, decided that all the death sentences should be carried out, provoking a strong reaction by the foreign correspondents. The right-wing Tsaldaris administration was accused of being authoritarian and undemocratic, because the decision was directed mainly against the communists who had been in prison since the December revolt. The State Department sent a memorandum on the subject to all its diplomatic staff in Greece mentioning, *inter alia*, that only twenty-five collaborators and four war criminals had been executed so far in the whole country.[43] British public opinion also reacted strongly, forcing the British Embassy in Athens to contact members of the government and ask them to find a solution, since most of the condemned were communists. But in the event, the unexpected assassination of the hardline Minister of Justice, who had been the inspiration behind the decision to carry out the executions, was followed by the appointment of the moderate Georgios Melas, and the tension gradually eased.[44] It was decided that the condemned would be executed a few at a time to quiet the situation down, while waiting for the Clemency Board and the Court of Appeal to issue their decisions. The unexpected international reaction seems to have encouraged the government to question the ethics of the situation and helped it to appreciate the magnitude of the political cost.

Four years later, when steps were being taken to bring peace and reconciliation to Greece, a new law was passed commuting all death sentences imposed up to 31 October 1951 to life imprisonment, and even, in certain circumstances, permitting those sentenced for collaboration[45] to be released. The new law confirmed the suspicions of the public and the press, who had been aware of similar rumors of leniency ever since 1946. The civil war had finally managed to marginalize the issue of the collaborators, and even, a little later, when circumstances permitted, to put an end to it.

All the same, a fair amount of ink was devoted to the subject of the collaborators, at least in 1945, when the thrill of Liberation still glowed and before the menacing clouds of the civil war darkened the sky, after which interest gradually turned toward domestic political developments and the question of the collaborators began to fade from the scene. Carried away by a new acrimonious confrontation, newspaper editors took sides with the political factions whose ideology they shared and turned their backs on the major social problem of the people who had collaborated with the occupation forces. These now received very little attention, confined simply to brief accounts of the verdicts. Trials conducted in the criminal courts, however, were described in greater detail, since it was these that were now monopolizing people's interest.

The Allied countries' diplomatic delegations also followed the course of the trials in Greece. Every so often, both the American and the British consuls in Thessaloniki would send reports to their superiors, though these were usually little more than lists of statistics. Furthermore, from 1947 onward their interest, too, was focused on the criminal courts, in line with the spirit of the time. Unfortunately, the degree to which the Allied countries intervened in the task of Greek justice in 1945–1946 has not been sufficiently investigated, because the American consul arrived in Thessaloniki quite late and the French and Russian delegations never settled in the city at all.

We do know, though, that a number of special commissions had meetings with higher legal functionaries in Thessaloniki who were responsible for the trials of the collaborators, and also that they visited the correctional institutions in which prisoners on remand were being detained. On one occasion, in fact, when some British officials were visiting a rather makeshift detention center, many of the detainees began proclaiming their innocence,[46] whereupon sixty-six prisoners took advantage of the ensuing commotion and the guards' distracted attention to make good their escape. According to their members, the aim of these commissions was to form an opinion, not to pass judgment on the efforts of the Greek judicial system. Nonetheless, in July 1947, the British Embassy suggested that the government amend some of the provisions,[47] and a year later it was giving Georgios Melas advice about the executions.

All this time, it seems, the British parliament also took a particular interest in the progress of the trials, and MPs frequently submitted questions to government representatives criticizing them for supporting the Greek government in its attempts to secure light sentences for well-known collaborators. In a report to the British ambassador to Athens in late 1946, the consul general in Thessaloniki intimated that the British authorities were being strongly criticized by some of their compatriots for their attitude on the issue.[48] The report also revealed that the inhabitants of northern Greece were unanimous in their support for the exemplary punishment of the collaborators; and it made no secret of the partiality of the judicial authorities.

Any intervention by the United States was probably quite limited and certainly not apparent until after 1947, when the Truman Doctrine started to be applied in Greece. The document accompanying the aforementioned memorandum from the economic collaborators was indicative of the United States' attitude: its author, the embassy's financial adviser, explained that the matter was connected with the country's domestic affairs, but he was mentioning it because he thought it might be of interest to the American commission that was dealing with the country's economic reconstruction.

Several conclusions may be drawn from the study of postwar justice in Greece. First, postwar public opinion in Macedonia was quick to tar all Slavic-speakers with the same brush, with results that were not slow in making themselves felt. Slavic-speakers were accused of a variety of offenses, often on the basis of rumor, conjecture, exaggeration, and even sheer malice, as the witnesses' depositions reveal. Someone might be considered a "Bulgarian" because he was the butcher who provided the Bulgarians with their meat, because he happened to be related to a known collaborator with the Bulgarian authorities, or because he was having an affair with someone of Bulgarian descent. It is an indisputable fact that a number of Slavic-speakers did work with the Bulgarian leagues and actively help to spread their propaganda; but it goes without saying that not all Slavic-speakers were pro-Bulgarian, nor were matters as simple as some people tried to present them. Some statements contain indirect suggestions of the use of force or psychological pressure by armed groups, or sometimes a state of utter penury, situations that compelled some Slavic-speakers to enroll in the Bulgarian Club.

Second, suspicion still persists that judges, clerks, and even witnesses were suborned, which means that the verdicts pronounced by the Special Courts on all categories of collaborators are open to question. In some cases, too, there were charges that the accused had exerted pressure on fellow citizens to make false statements. The personal archives of two lawyers who defended a number of collaborators who had been active in Macedonia contain documents that clearly indicate the extent of the backstage activities of the parties concerned and prove the validity of the leaks and rumors that so alarmed public opinion: they contain false statements by witnesses, letters from the accused asking prominent figures to intervene on their behalf, and as reports of the recent release of proven collaborators.[49]

Third, political developments — as was no doubt inevitable — drastically affected the course of the trials. The heightening of tension between the KKE and the rest of the political world, which eventually plunged the country into civil war, influenced the witnesses' attitudes, and from 1946 on they ceased to declare proudly that they had been active members of ELAS or, more importantly, to feel certain about the impact of their depositions. Increasingly absorbed in the problem of wiping out the "Communist threat," the political world gradually backtracked on its initial post-occupation declarations trumpeting the exemplary punishment of the collaborators, effectively ignoring popular opinion. During the first two decades after the civil war, many of those convicted served part of their sentence and then took advantage of the anticommunist climate of the time to secure their release from prison; owing to the circumstances, no adverse comment was heard from any quarter. In the years that followed, British and American diplomats reported only on the criminal court decisions and the executions of communists. Whenever Greek justice was called into question, the collaborators, curiously enough, had nothing to say and were rarely mentioned. The suppression of such an important issue, however, and the tacit toleration of the guilty parties' impunity turned collaborationism into an open wound in postwar society. The authorities might have lost interest and betrayed ordinary people's hopes, but the word "collaborationism" was not forgotten; on the contrary, it was adopted by political opponents and used henceforth as a stereotypical term of abuse. Some politicians — as the Merten affair was to reveal — were forced to abandon their careers owing to their activities during the occupation; others, perhaps the majority, managed to carry on, and indeed to rise to high positions, by carefully concealing their past.

NOTES

1. Resolution 19, "On the amendment and replacement of various clauses of Emergency Law No. 533/1945 on the amendment, supplementation, and codification of Constituent Act No. 6/1945, etc.," *Government Gazette*, 17 Dec. 1946, p. 69.

2. Statement by the leader of the government, Georgios Papandreou, to the Greek people, *Government Gazette*, 18 Oct. 1944, p. 1.

3. *Government Gazette*, 6 Nov. 1944, p. 12.

4. *Government Gazette*, 20 Jan. 1945, p. 12.

5. Trial 3/45; *Fos*, no 11451 (12 Aug. 1945).

6. *Ellinikos Vorras*, no. 239 (11 Nov. 1945) and no. 451 (23 July 1946).

7. Emergency Law no. 533, "On the amendment, supplementation, and codification of Constitutional Act No. 6/45 on the imposition of sanctions, etc., as amended," *Government Gazette*, 3 Sept. 1945, p. 224; Emergency Law no. 217, "On the amendment and replacement of various clauses of Constitutional Act No. 6/45," *Government Gazette*, 24 Mar. 1945, p. 69.

8. Evangelos Kofos, *I valkaniki diastasi tou Makedonikou Zitimatos sta chronia tis Katochis kai stin Antistassi* (The Balkan dimension of the Macedonian Question during the Occupation and the Resistance) (Athens, 1989).

9. The Bulgarian Club was founded in Thessaloniki in May 1941. It tried to attract members by distributing food and other scarce goods. Only Bulgarians who were born in Macedonia, or Bulgarians of Macedonian origin, could be admitted to the club. With the intervention of the German commander of Thessaloniki and the Aegean the statute of the club changed, and only full-blooded Bulgarians could be admitted to membership. The high-ranking members of the club conducted propaganda in the prefecture of Thessaloniki and western Macedonia, which were under Italian occupation, and collaborated with the *Okhrana*. For the action of the *Okhrana*, see St. Troebst, "I drassi tis Ochrana stous nomous Kastorias, Florinas kai Pellas, 1943–1944" (Ochrana's action in Prefecture of Kastoria, Florina and Pella, 1936–1944), *Praktika tou Diethnous Istorikou Sinedriou, I Ellada 1936–1944, Diktatoria-Katochi-Antistasi* (Proceedings of Conference on Greece, 1936–1944, Dictatorship, Occupation, Resistance) (Athens, 1989). For the Bulgarian Club, see Hristos Kardaras, *I voulgariki propaganda sti germanokratoumeni Makedonia. Boulgariki Leschi Thessalonikis* (The Bulgarian propaganda in German-occupied Macedonia: Bulgarian Club of Thessaloniki) (Athens, 1997).

10. Athanassios Hryssohoou, *I Katochi en Makedonia* (Occupation in Macedonia), vol. 3 (Thessaloniki, 1951); and Ioannis. Koliopoulos, *Leilasia fronimaton. To Makedoniko Zitima stin katechomeni ditiki Makedonia, 1941–*

1944 (Plundering of Loyalties: The Macedonian Question in occupied western Macedonia), vol. 1 (Thessaloniki, 1994).

11. *Dimokratia*, no. 49 (19 Apr. 1945), and *Ellinikos Vorras*, no. 71 (22 Apr. 1945).

12. *Ellinikos Vorras*, no. 71 (22 Apr. 1945).

13. The lack of paper can be seen in the proceedings of the trials. The secretary often has to use the same paper twice, making reading it even more difficult for the researcher.

14. *Dimokratia*, no. 26 (23 Mar. 1945).

15. Ioannis Stefanidis, "I 'erithra simprotevoussa': I kiriarchia tou EAM sti Thessaloniki, Oktovrios 1944–Ianouarios 1945" (The "communist capital": The EAM rule in Thessaloniki, October 1944–January 1945), *Praktika tou sinedriou Makedonia kai Thraki, 1941–1944. Katochi—Antistasi-Apeleftherosi* (Proceedings of Conference on Macedonia and Thrace, 1941–1944: Occupation-Resistance-Liberation) (Thessaloniki, 1994, unpublished). See also Markos Vafiadis, *Apomnimonevmata* (Memories), vol. 2: *1940–1944* (Athens, 1985).

16. George Alexander, "British Perceptions of EAM/ELAS Rule in Thessaloniki, 1944–45," *Balkan Studies*, 21.2 (1980): 205–6.

17. Alexander, "British Perceptions," 209.

18. *Dimokratia*, no. 63 (5 May 1945).

19. *Makedonia*, no. 11250 (27 May 1945).

20. *Ellinikos Vorras*, no. 69 (20 Apr. 1945).

21. The Bulgarian lieutenant Anton Kaltsef, whose center of operations was Edessa, and his close associate, Italian lieutenant Giovanni Ravali, who was doing his military service in Kastoria, were both known for their action in western Macedonia. They were tried by the Special Court of Athens according to article 4 of the London Compact. This article referred to the transfer and the trial of war criminals to the places where they had committed their crimes. The two accused were sentenced to death for their action during the occupation and were executed in 1948. For this trial see I. Papakiriakopoulos, *Voulgari kai Itali eglimatiai polemou en Makedonia* (Bulgarian and Italian war criminals in Macedonia) (Athens, 1946).

22. Trials 86/1945, 106/1945, 115/1945, 132/1945, 245/1945, 28–65/1946, 173/1946, 225/1946.

23. See Eleni Haidia, "Idiko Dikastirio Thessalonikis: I periptosi ton ikonomikon dossilogon" (The Special Court in Thessaloniki: The case of the economic collaborators), *Valkanika Symmikta* (1996): 8.

24. Emergency Law no. 753, "On the decongestion of prisons," *Government Gazette*, 21 Dec. 1945, p. 311.

25. "Banishment of Collaborators," *Ellinikos Vorras*, 24 Jan. 1946.

26. U.S. National Archives, Washington, D.C. [henceforth USNA], 868.512/5-1547, from American Embassy, Athens, Greece, to the Secretary of State, "Imprisonment for Economic Collaboration in Greece."

27. In 1945, three people were tried on this charge. Of course, a large number of people were also tried whose activities put them in both categories, and sometimes also in the category of informants (see below). These people are all counted as collaborators for the purposes of this study.

28. According to one witness's statement, when the Bulgarians withdrew and the Security Battalions were hunting down those who were left, all those who had assisted the British were provided with documents to that effect.

29. Eleni Haidia, "Ellines Evrei tis Thessalonikis: Apo ta stratopeda sigentrossis stis ethousses dikastirion" (Greek Jews of Thessaloniki: From the concentration camps to the court), *Praktika tou III Simposiou Istorias "I Evrei tis Elladas stin Katochi"* (Proceedings of Third History Symposium, "Jews in Thessaloniki during the German Occupation"), Thessaloniki, 8 Nov. 1996 (unpublished).

30. L. Hondros, *Occupation and Resistance: The Greek Agony, 1941–1944* (New York, 1983), 82–83.

31. Hryssohoou, *Katochi* (Thessaloniki, 1949), 1: 144.

32. Mark Mazower, *Inside Hitler's Greece: The Experience of Occupation, 1941–1944* (New Haven and London, 1993), 336–38.

33. Yeoryios Poulos, who had evaded going abroad, eventually surrendered to the Greek authorities, was tried in Athens, sentenced to death, and was executed.

34. Trial: 215/ 216, 23 Oct.–3 Nov. 1945.

35. Vassilis Messologitis, a journalist who testified in this trial, mentioned the continuous German interference in the Editors' Union.

36. *Ellinikos Vorras*, no. 239 (11 Nov. 1945). Also Yeoryios Anastassiadis, *I Thessaloniki ton efimeridon* (Thessaloniki according to the newspapers) (Thessaloniki, 1994), 77, where not only the problem of the survival of many unemployed journalists during the occupation, but also the threats and the pressure they suffered, both from the Germans and the few Greek collaborators, are reported.

37. *Dimokratia* devoted numerous articles to this vexed question during its eight-month lifetime. With reference to Athens in particular, see *Dimokratia*, no. 104 (25 June 1945); and *Ellinikos Vorras*, no 193 (15 Sept. 1945).

38. Trials 201/1945, 30/1946, 258/1946.

39. Trials 6, 96, 256 in 1945; 19–21, 146, 264 in 1946.

40. *Fos*, no. 11605 (16 Feb. 1946).

41. *Makedonia*, no. 11378 (17 Oct. 1945).

42. *Fos*, no. 11641 (1 Apr. 1946).

43. USNA, Internal Affairs of Greece 1945–1949 (unclassified), from Department of State to American Diplomatic Officers, 6 July 1948, Memorandum on Greek Penal Measures.

44. USNA, Internal Affairs of Greece 1945–1949, 868.00/7-1448, from K. L. Rankin, Charge d'Affaires ad interim (American Embassy, Athens) to the Secretary of State, Marshall.

45. Law no. 2058, *Government Gazette*, 18 Apr. 1952, p. 1.

46. *Fos*, no. 11315 (27 Feb. 1946).

47. USNA, 868.00/ 7-1448, pp. 2–5.

48. FO 371/67075 R 488/399/19, from W.L.C. Knight to D. W. Lascelles, Thessaloniki, 11 Dec. 1946.

49. Christos Papadimitriou, "I dioxi ton dosilogon tis Katochis sti Thessaloniki (1941–1944) mesa apo ta prosopika archia ton dikigoron Ioanni

Stathaki kai Yeoryiou Mellou" (The prosecution of occupation collaborators in Thessaloniki [1941–1944] as attested in the personal archives of the lawyers Ioannis Stathakis and Georgios Mellos), *Praktika tou IE Panelliniou Istorikou Synedriou* (Proceedings of XV Panhellenic Historical Conference) (Thessaloniki, 1995), 479–83.

THREE

Purging the University after Liberation

Procopis Papastratis

THE PUNISHMENT of traitors and collaborators was an issue that preoccupied the Allied government from a fairly early stage of the war. The Inter-Allied Conference for crimes committed against civilian populations, held in London in January 1942, decided that the occupation forces and local accomplices who were guilty or responsible for these crimes would be prosecuted and stand trial, and that the court's decisions would be carried out.[1] The Lebanon Conference of May 1944, which resulted in the formation of a Greek Government of National Unity, approved unanimously a National Charter, which laid down the main issues that had to be faced during the transitional period toward Liberation. The principles on which the administration of the newly liberated country should be based were also included. The document specifically mentioned the "imposition of harsh measures against the traitors of the Country and against those who exploit our People's misery."[2] In January 1942 the adoption of such a decision in London was obviously meant to encourage the subject people of Europe and warn the occupying forces. However, on the eve of Liberation, such a decision had acquired an additional dimension whose existence, nevertheless, was officially ignored. It had become a political issue. The punishment of traitors — an expression that, following Liberation, was gradually replaced with the term "purge" — was the touchstone on which a number of issues were tested: the honesty of the political elite's intentions, the realization of wartime commitments, the integrity of postwar governments, and finally, class solidarity between prosecutors and the accused.

The Lebanon Conference met in an atmosphere of thinly disguised confrontation. The representatives of the smaller resistance organizations and the bourgeois political parties had grouped together, accepting British advice on how to face the delegates of the communist-led EAM/ELAS organizations. In such an atmosphere, the punishment of traitors was an obviously suitable issue to underline national unity, which was what this conference was ostensibly seeking to establish. Given the prevailing circumstances, it was assumed that there was a general consensus on such an issue. Until then a substantial part of the bourgeois world had adopted attitudes ranging from reluctant acceptance to open encouragement of the Security Battalions and the collaborating government of Athens. The explicit way in which the National Charter referred to the punishment of traitors provided assurance — in theory — that this attitude toward the collaborators would change. If the Greek government-in-exile had been recognized by the Allies as the legal government of Greece from the start of the Axis occupation of the country, now, on the eve of Liberation, this government, in its new guise as Government of National Unity, sought through the issue of the treatment of collaborators, to discard its image as an absentee administration, operating largely cut off from the horrors of occupied Greece.

The fundamental task it confronted was to be accepted by the people not only as a legal entity but also — more importantly and essentially — as their own legitimate government. Such an acceptance would greatly facilitate its unopposed return to a liberated Greece at a time when it was widely feared that EAM/ELAS might seek to seize power. Yet in spite of the explicit warning issued by the Government of National Unity in early September 1944 that those who still continued to serve the enemy would face "merciless punishment," an array of acts and omissions emanating from Greek or British officials created a widespread impression that the traitors would go unpunished.[3] This impression was reinforced when the quisling government of Ioannis Rallis, unperturbed by such warnings from abroad, continued to pass laws concerning the Security Battalions. These laws increased the number of regular army officers serving in the Battalions, and took care of their promotions either in these units or in those which would be created to defend law and order in the country. In addition, a special provision was inserted to allow the award of the distinguished service medal during a period when no state of war existed, as the puppet government of Athens was not at war with Germany. As a result, the award of this medal for acts performed beyond the call of duty was extended to the men serving in the collaborationist units.[4]

The promulgation of all these laws took place while the quisling government was disintegrating, with its ministers tendering their resignation. It is obvious that the message Prime Minister Rallis wanted to convey was that he was taking care until the last moment to contain the danger of subversive ideologies (i.e., communism) for Greece. In his resignation statement the day the German army withdrew from Athens, Rallis declared that he was returning to private life with a clear conscience, having performed his duty to the people faithfully, ready to account for his acts in front of competent authorities.[5]

This statement reflected a certain feeling prevailing among a considerable part of the "leading class" — to use an expression introduced a few days later by Prime Minister George Papandreou in his Declaration of

Liberation—that during the years of occupation they had functioned inside Greece as a beleaguered outpost of the national conscience. This feeling was vividly described by the vice-rector of the University of Athens, who, when referring to the day the Germans left Athens—a day of immense jubilation—pointed out that "no one can accuse the University, because, at least, it did not raise the EAM flag."[7]

An official commitment to the punishment of traitors was recorded in no uncertain terms in the Declaration of Liberation. Simultaneously, however, the Declaration included the first attempt to exorcise the problem, as the same document asserted that the number of guilty persons who had become "unfaithful to the Nation" was not substantial. In fact, the Government of National Unity had already started the procedure for the punishment of traitors before its return to liberated Athens. The Constitutional Act referring to this issue was approved and published while the Greek government waited impatiently in Cava dei Tirreni—a small village near Salerno—for the British to transfer it to Athens. It was published in the *Government Gazette* twice more, in Athens this time, but with certain amendments. The main amendment, which undoubtedly indicates a change in attitude, is shown in the title of this law. The initial title, "On Imposing Punishment on Traitors," was changed to "On the Imposition of Sanctions on Those Who Have Collaborated with the Enemy."[7] It is obvious that the aim of this amendment was to lessen the significance of the collaborators' crimes.

The Dekemvriana temporarily suspended all developments on the question of collaboration. Thereafter, radical changes in the political scene directly affected the issue of collaborators. The purge was now enlarged to include those who had participated in or contributed to the outbreak of the "mutiny of December 3"—in other words, encompassing Left as well as Right. It was also expanded to include those who had demonstrated weakness of character and dishonorable or "antinational" behavior since the establishment of the Metaxas dictatorship in August 1936.[8]

These modifications enhanced the democratic image of the governments formed after the December events, and seemed also to provide them with a formulation allowing an even-handed if not objective assessment of the political surgery required. At the same time, they underlined the distance separating the parliamentary regime emerging after the Liberation from the dictatorial and collaborationist regimes that had just collapsed. Additionally, this purge aimed at lessening British pressure on the Greek government to improve its record on this issue. Britain, for its own long-term reasons, wanted to see normal political conditions quickly restored in Greece. And London considered a satisfactory conclusion of the purges to be an important prerequisite to this.

This double purge—on the one side against those involved in the communist-inspired "mutiny of December 3," and on the other side against the collaborators and those exposed for unbecoming behavior during the Metaxas dictatorship—also had another dimension. It demonstrated the failure of these two extremes of the political spectrum and thus strengthened the credibility of the political formation occupying the middle ground.

It is within this context that all appointed governments up to the 1946 elections insisted on purging the universities. Their insistence, however, was characterized by hesitations and retrogression: although four Constitutional Acts on this issue were promulgated over a period extending little more than six months, there was a marked reluctance to proceed with the publication of this legislation. The government had made its intentions clear on the subject in October 1944, but the relevant laws only started appearing in the second half of 1945.[9]

Prime Minister Papandreou had used harsh words to describe the situation in his Declaration of Liberation on 18 October 1944, the day the government entered Athens. He had stated then that during the Metaxas dictatorship, the university, as well as all other institutions that in a republic constitute the leading class, had become morally bankrupt, with a few notable exceptions. In the middle of November, Papandreou returned to the issue and, adding salt to the wound, told a committee of professors from the Faculty of Law of the University of Athens that all professors appointed since the establishment of the dictatorship in August 1936 would be fired. The professors in question were well aware that the government was moving toward this decision. There was consequently considerable commotion during the meeting of the Senate of the University of Athens at the end of November 1944. The prevailing feeling among the members of the Senate was that the university was under siege.[10]

The question of whether to insist on the professors' resignations acquired a new dimension with the far-reaching purge so boldly proclaimed by the prime minister. The insult was further driven home by a request for the Ministry of Education to examine the Proceedings of the University in order "to use them against the University," as a member of the Senate put it. This attitude of the government was leaving the university "exposed against the Nation," remarked another member. "Most of us are under purge," protested yet another Senate member, "either because we were appointed during the dictatorship or due to the age limit."[11] At the time, the government had introduced the revolutionary idea of lowering the age limit for professors. Consequently a great many were up in arms and wanted to repel this double assault on their chairs. It was agreed at the end of 1944 that the Senate should insist on resigning—

the Faculties of Law and Medicine were already following this course of action—and only Papandreou's own resignation from the premiership released the Senate from this inconvenient pledge. At the same time, with barely concealed indignation, if not contempt, the largely conservative professoriate witnessed an eruption of revolutionary zeal among the student body that they were hardly able to contain. This politically charged atmosphere threatened to abolish the last vestiges of the university as "the sacred and spiritual cathedral of the Hellenic Nation," of which they considered themselves to be custodians, as a professor of medicine argued.[12]

It is obvious that the developments in the University of Athens were mirroring the political situation prevailing in Greece at the time, with the majority of the students involved in activities greatly at variance with what the Senate deemed as correct behavior. A characteristic example of the existing relationship between the two sides on the eve of Liberation was the students' decision to rename the university a "Foundation of Freedom and Reconstruction," provoking strong disapproval within the Senate.[13]

But the purge in the universities was also becoming tangled up with those personal animosities which so often develop in the world of academia, with serious differences based on scientific disagreements, and with institutional rivalries.[14] The purging procedure introduced in early April 1945 for the Faculties of Divinity and Medicine of the University of Thessaloniki was undoubtedly inspired by a combination of all these factors. All professors appointed during the occupation were dismissed. For the necessary reconstitution of these two faculties, the government turned for assistance to the University of Athens. As a result, the professors of the Faculties of Divinity and Medicine in Athens were asked to decide who should replace their purged colleagues in Thessaloniki.[15]

It can easily be argued that this particular purge should have proceeded in the opposite direction, that is, toward those same faculties of the University of Athens. Indeed, the government very well knew that the purging professors of Athens were themselves under threat of purge. Yet it showed great hesitation in implementing this threat, for the first Constitutional Act introducing purges to all universities was delayed for another three months. In the interim, the Ministry of Education collected information regarding the occupants of those chairs which had been established during the occupation. The authorities at the University of Athens, clearly obstructive in producing this information, were on the other hand taking all measures to expel those who had participated in the National Liberation Front during the occupation. It must be noted that the Ministry of Education handled the dismissal of the professors appointed during the dictatorship and the occupation with particular attention. Until it was decided to expand the purge across the universities, these professors enjoyed the privilege of being excluded from the purge of the civil service that the government had initiated. When they were finally dismissed, the term "purge" was not mentioned in the title of the relevant law. In an effort not to affront the universities, a less-offensive title was chosen. Appearances were thus kept up with anodyne references to the restoration of university autonomy.[16]

Attitudes among the faculty, ranging from self-imposed inaction to ideological identification with the victors of the Dekemvriana, were evident at the general meeting of the Athens professoriate. This impressively titled group, far from being a collective body in the modern sense, met irregularly whenever either congratulations or condemnation were deemed necessary. After Liberation, this body had convened in order to visit and congratulate the commander of British forces in Athens, General Sir Ronald Scobie, for his role in the December confrontation. In January 1945 it met for a second time to condemn the "professors of the *resistance*" in no uncertain terms. One hundred and one professors appended their signature to the damning document produced by this gathering. Very few dissenting voices were openly heard in the university against this measure. In the Senate, only one member — an opponent of the purge in the universities — expressed his strong criticism of this practice of "forced signatures," as he called it. In the Faculty of Law, only three professors refused to sign this document.[17]

As has been already mentioned, the university moved quickly against those involved in the December insurrection. The Senate itself — where conservatives were clearly in the ascendant — asked the Ministry of Education to take the necessary measures against these professors with the aim of restoring order and tranquility in the university.[18] By the middle of February 1945, most of the professors had submitted reports on the conduct of the staff under their supervision, either academic or administrative, since the occupation. All incriminating evidence was sent to the Ministry of Education for it to take the appropriate action. For reasons, no doubt, of political expediency, any action against those accused of leftist sympathies or activity was postponed until after the Varkiza Agreement, signed on 12 February 1945. But in the new atmosphere that was gradually prevailing in the university, members of the Senate did not have to register their indignation any more when their students shouted at them, as had happened shortly after Liberation in the Theological Seminar, "You are (morally) bankrupt, purge, purge."[19]

In March, the Senate decided to visit the prime minister and the Minister of Education demanding as minimum punishment the suspension of EAM professors. It addressed a circular letter to the faculty — excluding those under investigation — requesting any evidence against colleagues, and used this evidence to put pressure on the government, especially with regard to those professors who had left Athens during 1944 to join PEEA (*Politiki Epitropi Ethnikis Apeleftherosis*, Political Committee for National Liberation) in the mountains.[20] It is worth noting that two of these had become ministers in the wartime Government of National Unity; they were highly respected academics, and most were socialists. Only months earlier, the goverment had officially restored the EAM professors to their chairs in appreciation of their participation in the resistance.[21]

While the Senate and the general meeting of the professors concentrated their wrath on the EAM professors, they were exceedingly reluctant to assist the Ministry of Education in its attempt to purge the faculty of academic staff appointed during the occupation. It was only after the Minister of Education (until recently the vice-rector of the University of Athens) personally interfered that the Senate formed a committee to look into the matter. At the end of June 1945, the Senate postponed any decision on this issue, as none of the university faculties had answered the documents the Ministry of Education had sent them. This sequence of events showed that the delay in complying with the minister's instructions—far from being another example of bureaucratic inertia—was based on deliberate calculations of institutional and individual self-interest. A few days later a law abolishing all posts established in the public sector during the occupation took care to exclude the university professors, along with other selectively chosen functionaries, from its implementation.[22]

The case of the sacked EAM professors demonstrates a more general phenomenon, which large sections of the Greek society experienced within a very short time—namely, an abrupt and total reversal of the political situation. Its long-term repercussions were not discernible at the time. The harshness of the occupation and the several forms of resistance against it were combined in the collective memory of the Greek public with an optimism that, having survived this ordeal, better days undoubtedly lay ahead. At the same time, however, it was becoming increasingly evident that the government, apart from its inability to face the desperate economic situation, was unable to carry out its promise regarding an issue that directly affected the self-respect and dignity of a people who had suffered greatly. As has already been mentioned, the purge of the universities was attempted with the help of three Constitutional Acts that were published in the *Government Gazette* in a period of little more than six months. This impressive array of laws proved unable to survive the spirited resistance of the universities themselves. A fourth and more determined attempt by the government was cut short by the regent, Archbishop Damaskinos.

The fifty-year rule that Greece applies to its archives and the subsequent lack of evidence, the silence of those involved, as well as a certain reluctance to approach the subject due to the embarrassing character of the issue of collaboration, has resulted in a considerable delay in research into this question. Contrasting the text of these laws and the reaction they produced, however, yields certain interesting results. The purge that was introduced with the first Constitutional Act at the end of June 1945 covered the period from 1932—when Law 5343, "On the Organization of the University," was published—to the end of the Axis occupation. It was the basic law on this issue for the period under examination. It referred to chairs that were arbitrarily founded and modified as to their subject, as well as to the incumbent professors whose chairs were abolished. Nevertheless, the severity of this law was short-lived. Less than one month later, a new Constitutional Act introduced milder measures against a number of professors appointed during the Metaxas dictatorship.

A further shift in the attitude of the Ministry of Education was recorded a few months later. In early October 1945, a third Constitutional Act revealed the government's displeasure at the delay with which the universities were proceeding with the implementation of the purge. It also underlined its decision to enforce a faster and stricter framework to promote this effort. As a result, disciplinary boards were established with the authority to call the rector of the university before them if he did not adequately supervise the implementation of this particular law. Yet the continuing inactivity of the university authorities forced the Ministry of Education in January 1946 to introduce a new draft law, its fourth attempt. This action produced an eruption of protests among the professoriate. This reaction was caused neither because the term "moral unworthiness" was now introduced in order to define when a professor had conducted himself in a manner unbecoming to his position, nor because a shorter procedure was introduced to reach a conclusion on this matter; the real bone of contention was who controlled this process. Unlike previous Constitutional Acts, the innovation of this draft law was that the university risked losing control of the purging procedure.[23]

Simultaneously, another sensitive issue was introduced, the perennial question of the retirement age for professors. It is on this last issue that the professors conveniently centered all debate, while the purge was not considered a matter of first priority. The Senate of the University of Athens and the general meeting of the professors, which was reactivated for the occasion, denounced the new measures as directly jeopardizing the autonomy of the university, precipitating a lively press debate between faculty and ministry.

The student body, in a newly conservative guise, was also involved in this issue. According to one press report, Athens students went on strike in support of the professors, shouting, "Hands off our academic institutions"; other reports, however, suggest that some students remained critical of the politically compromised faculty. The rector addressed the striking students, told them not to meddle in the professors' affairs, and advised them to return to their lectures. In the end, the rector of the University of Athens proved to be right. The threatened professors had no need for the support offered by students ideologically akin to them. This issue was more quietly and effectively solved by approaching the regent himself directly, circumventing both the Minister of Education and the Cabinet, which, by that time, had approved the law in question. At the end of May 1946, the rector informed the Senate that, accompanied by the vice-rector and the Dean of the Faculty of Law, he had been received in audience by the regent. The regent asked whether he should sign the Constitutional Act referring to the purge in the universities, adding that he would base his decision on their opinion. The three professors unanimously stated that the publication of such a law just a few days before the general elections would be unsuitable, and for this reason they were against it. The regent, whose signature would ratify this Constitutional Act, followed their advice, and at this point the attempt to purge the universities ended: the first elected government in postwar Greece — further to the Right than any of its predecessors — was not inclined to pursue the matter. A highly conservative elite weathered the threat of reform and held at bay all efforts to come to terms with a decade of compliance with undemocratic regimes.[24]

NOTES

1. I. Venezis, *Emmanuel Tsouderos* (Athens, 1966), 266–67
2. G. Papandreou, *The Liberation of Greece* (Athens, 1945), 77–78. The Greek prime minister, G. Papandreou, based his hardly concealed eagerness that his government should extend its function in the post-Liberation period on the implementation of this commitment.
3. Papandreou, *Liberation*, 144. On the readiness to accept the services of the Security Battalions that was permeating considerable sections of the Government of National Unity, see the diary of the poet G. Seferis, a career diplomat who followed his government in exile and observed with anger and sarcastic indignation its inability to rise to the occasion. G. Seferis, *Political Diary A, 1935–1944* (Athens, 1979), 251, 254, 255, passim. On the British and Greek governments' attitudes toward the Security Battalions, see M. Mazower, *Inside Hitler's Greece* (New Haven and London, 1993), 328–64; and P. Papastratis, *British Policy towards Greece during the Second World War, 1941–1944* (Cambridge, 1984), 209–11.

4. *Government Gazette*, no. 232, 6 Oct. 1944, Laws 1924 and 1937; no. 237, 9 Oct. 1944, Law 1941; no. 240, 10 Oct. 1944, Law 1967.

5. *Government Gazette*, no. 242, 12 Oct. 1944.

6. Proceedings of the Senate of the University of Athens, 6th session, 17 Oct. 1944.

7. *Government Gazette*, no. 36, Cairo, 14 Oct. 1944, Constitutional Act, "On Imposing Punishment on Traitors," approved by the Greek Cabinet on 1 Oct. 1944; no. 12, Athens, 6 Nov. 1944, Constitutional Act 1; no. 12, Athens, 20 Jan. 1945, Constitutional Act 6.

8. *Government Gazette*, no. 67, 22 May 1945, Constitutional Act 25.

9. *Government Gazette*, no. 167, 30 June 1945, Constitutional Act 60, "On Restoring the Autonomy of the Universities." This law was subsequently modified by Constitutional Acts 67 and 72 of 19 July and 6 October 1945, respectively. The last modification, introduced by the Ministry of Education in late January 1946, failed to materialize, for reasons examined in this chapter.

10. *Proceedings*, 11th session, 28 Nov. 1944.

11. Ibid.

12. The Papandreou government obliged the University Senate on this issue by resigning when the conflict of December ended. The Senate was thus able to decide that, the reasons for its resignation having ceased to exist, it could continue with its duties. *Proceedings*, 12th session 16 Jan. 1945.

13. *Proceedings*, 6th session, 17 Oct. 1944. On the reaction of the university authorities to the problem emanating from the political activity of the student organizations, see *Proceedings*, 8th and 9th sessions, 7 and 14 Nov. 1944.

14. On the ideological conflicts that led to the establishment of the University of Thessaloniki, see Rena Stavridou-Patrikiou, "Inter-University Equilibria and Their Overthrow (1910–1926)," in *Proceedings of the International Symposium: University Ideology and Education*, vol. A (Athens, 1989), 215–22.

15. *Government Gazette*, no. 85, 4 Apr. 1945, Constitutional Act 34. The Faculties of Divinity and Medicine, although part of the initial group of faculties when the University of Thessaloniki was established in 1925, were reestablished in 1942 during the Axis occupation. There was a long history of intervention by the government in university affairs. In 1938 the Metaxas dictatorship was considering transferring the Faculty of Philosophy from the University of Thessaloniki to the University of Athens. B. Kyriazopoulos, *Fifty Years of the University of Thessaloniki, 1926–1976* (Thessaloniki, 1976), 238–39.

16. The Cabinet started discussing the question of purging the universities toward the end of March 1945. The relevant law was eventually published three months later: *Kathimerini*, 21 Mar. 1945; *Government Gazette*, no. 167, 30 June 1945. On the purge of the civil service see P. Papastratis, "The Purge of the Greek Civil Service on the Eve of the Civil War," in L. Baerentzen, J. Iatrides, and O. Smith, eds., *Studies in the History of the Greek Civil War, 1945–1949* (Copenhagen, 1987), 41–55.

17. *Proceedings*, 19th session, 6 Mar. 1945; National and Capodistrian University of Athens, *One Hundred and Fifty Years 1837–1987: Catalogue of the Exhibition* (Athens, 1987), 86.

18. The general meeting of the professors condemned their EAM colleagues

in a strongly worded petition issued in the middle of January 1945. A few days later the Ministry of Education instructed the university to examine whether its academic and administrative staff was involved in the December insurrection: *Proceedings*, 13th session, 23 Jan. 1945. The Varkiza Agreement of February 1945 followed the civil confrontation of the previous December and introduced a number of measures to restore normal political conditions in postwar Greece.

19. *Proceedings*, 11th session, 28 Nov. 1944.

20. *Proceedings*, 21st session, 13 March 1945. The newspaper *Rizospastis*, the official organ of the Communist Party of Greece, was rather restrained when blaming the university authorities and the government for the persecution of the EAM professors: *Rizospastis*, 4 Mar., 15 and 17 May 1945. The Senate proceeded with its action against the EAM professors in its 30th session (27 Apr. 1945). PEEA was the Government of Free Greece, as it was commonly known, which EAM had established in central Greece in the spring of 1944.

21. The EAM professors were reinstated in their academic positions in November 1944. *Proceedings*, 18th session, 27 Feb. 1945; *Rizospastis*, 4 Mar. 1945; *Proceedings*, 21st session, 13 Mar. 1945. In addition to the five professors suspended in Athens, a number of professors from the University of Thessaloniki suffered the same fate. Approximately seventeen members of the academic staff of the Greek universities were finally suspended.

22. *Proceedings*, 35th and 37th sessions, 5 and 19 June 1945; Constitutional Act 59, 27 June 1945.

23. A lively debate between the protesting professors and the Minister of Education developed through the press. The former, arguing that half of them would be dismissed, threatened to resign en bloc, while the latter reassured the journalists that none would eventually resign. It would be a blessing if they did, he added, as the university would thus be self-purged. *Kathimerini*, 25, 26, 27, 29 Jan. 1946; *To Vema*, 1, 23, 25, 29 Jan. and 2 Feb. 1946. For the official correspondence they exchanged, see *Proceedings*, 21st session, 5 Feb. 1946.

24. *Kathimerini*, 30, 31 Jan. and 5 Feb. 1945; but also *Rizospastis*, 30 Jan. and 1 Feb. 1946; *To Vema*, 27 Jan. 1946; *Proceedings*, 22nd and 29th sessions, 12 Feb. and 26 Mar. 1946.

FOUR

Between Negation and Self-Negation: Political Prisoners in Greece, 1945–1950

Polymeris Voglis

KOULA ELEFTHERIADOU was accused of being a person better known as "Maria" who had recruited guerillas.[1] The only prosecution witness was a gendarme who was alleged to have collaborated with the German occupation forces. Eleftheriadou was sentenced to death on 1 May 1947, and five days later was executed at the age of twenty-four. One night before her execution she wrote to her family:

> My beloved. The way that I'm dying may seem to you a hard shock. But if you think about it twice you'll see that it is better to die for my ideals, honestly, which are the ideals of all the workers, than to live dishonestly, betraying my party, which stands for the avant-garde and leads our people in its struggle for national independence and people's freedom. I am proud because I die like a people's fighter and within the ranks of the heroic Greek Communist Party.[2]

Koula Eleftheriadou's letter is built upon three strong oppositions — death and life, fighter and traitor, honesty and dishonesty — all coupled with a locative correlation, "within the ranks." Her death was justified, as opposed to those who chose to live dishonestly and "outside the ranks."

In this chapter, these two "sides" — those awaiting death and those political prisoners who signed declarations of repentance — will be brought together. I argue that whereas the regime, in an escalating crisis that ended in the outbreak of the civil war (1946–1949), adopted a strategy of negating its leftist political opponents, for the political prisoners themselves this strategy was experienced as self-negation. The different forms of self-negation, like self-betrayal or sacrifice, illuminate the complexity of the power mechanisms in action and the way in which political prisoners tried to make sense of their own deeds.

THE STRATEGY OF NEGATION

Thousands of people were prosecuted, arrested, imprisoned, and exiled during the years that followed the Liberation of Greece in October

A member of the Democratic Army of Greece, western Macedonia, 1946–47. Reproduced by king permission of the estate of Nancy Crawshaw.

1944. The starting point was the battle of Athens in December 1944, in which EAM/ELAS units fought against the government and British troops, and were defeated. The Varkiza Agreement, signed in February 1945 between EAM/ELAS and the government, signaled the defeat of the former. According to that agreement, first, the guerilla units had to be disbanded and surrender their arms, and second, all the offenses committed during the December events, or Dekemvriana, were pardoned, except "common-law crimes against life and property which were not absolutely necessary to the achievement of the political crime concerned." This last clause turned out to facilitate the mass prosecution of EAM/ELAS members. In 1945, according to the British Legal Mission to Greece, 50,000 people had been arrested; in October of the same year, 16,700 were held in jail. Moreover, the demobilization of ELAS gave ultra-right and royalist bands the opportunity to terrorize the countryside: within one year after the Varkiza Agreement, through February 1946, 1,192 people had been murdered, 159 women raped, and 6,413 wounded by the ultra-rightists.[3]

The abstention of the Communist Party and smaller socialist and centrist parties from the elections of March 1946, and the reemergence of leftist guerilla activities (more organized from 1947 onward), provided an opportunity for the government of the Populist party — and later a coalition of the Populist and Liberal parties — to take harsher repressive measures against leftist political opponents. The hard line adopted by the government, backed by Great Britain and the United States, was mirrored in the introduction of special legislation and of extraordinary courts-martial, the establishment of massive detention camps on barren islands (like Makronisos, Yiaros, Trikeri), and the mass persecution of the Left. In September 1947, according to a report of the Communist Party, 19,620 political prisoners were in jail and 36,948 in exile. By the end of the civil war, in September 1949, the total number of prisoners and exiles was nearly 50,000; almost one year later, in August 1950, and after the closing down of the Makronisos camps, 23,457 were still in prison and 3,407 in exile. Within this context of mass persecution, declarations of repentance, in which the detainees recanted their political beliefs and the Communist Party, constituted a particular and important feature of the whole process.[4]

Declarations of repentance did not appear for the first time in the postwar era but had already been a feature of the Metaxas dictatorship (1936–40); it is estimated that 45,000 declarations were signed, and many of them publicized, during the four years of the dictatorship.[5] For the regime, the significance of the declarations had been highlighted by the Minister of Public Order, Konstantinos Maniadakis, who wrote in a confidential order issued on 19 June 1939, "The acceptance of such declarations aims not so much at the prosecution of the organized Communists, as it does at the smashing of the party's internal cohesion. The declarations of repentance have spread so much confusion among the party members that suspicion and mutual distrust prevail."[6]

In the postwar era, the goals of the authorities did not change, and nor did the importance of declarations. In the following paragraphs, the case of those who signed declarations of repentance (*dilosies*) will be discussed both as an attempt to deconstruct the individual and liquidate the prisoners' sense of collectivity, and as an example of disciplining and stigmatizing difference, of drawing the dividing lines that construct a political identity.

A recent study of the Corfu prison gives a detailed account of the formal procedure surrounding the declarations of repentance.[7] Once a prisoner had signed a declaration of repentance, the governor of the prison communicated it to the public prosecutor of appeal. The public prosecutor sent the declaration to the Ministry of Justice, and to the church and the municipal authorities of the prisoner's residence for public knowledge. Sometimes the declaration was sent to the local military authorities and the press. The declaration of repentance was accompanied by a lengthy memorandum, in which the prisoner renounced his or her ideas. The diversity of legal, political, and social institutions interested in the declarations indicates the importance attached to them, their various uses, and the close cooperation of the state apparatuses on this issue during the civil war.

Declarations of repentance constituted a crucial phase in the process of interrogation and imprisonment. Political detainees knew that such a declaration might stop the torture or open the way for their release. Statutory articles anticipated that exiles and prisoners could be released, and even death sentences could be commuted to life imprisonment, if the detainees renounced their ideas.[8] Nonetheless, detainees were seldom willing to sign such declarations. Interrogations that could last for days or weeks, solitary confinement, torments, humiliation, rumors that caused anxiety and fear, and anything that could inflict pain in the detainee's body and psyche was used to disintegrate the detainee's world. The authorities' aim was to bring detainees into such physical and psychological exhaustion that they would sign a declaration of repentance like the following:

> I, the undersigned R. Elias, . . . state that I renounce the Communist Party for the completely anti-Greek methods that it employs and that I am ashamed for having been its follower. I assure you that in the future I shall lead my life as a true-born Greek, faithful to the patrimonial national heritage, which a few evil so-called Greeks tried to ruin. I call on all the misguided young to follow my example.[9]

Within the process of interrogation the declaration of repentance marks the disintegration of the detainee's world and his or her self-negation. As Elaine Scarry argues, "World, self, and voice are lost, or nearly lost, through the intense pain of torture and not through the confession, as is wrongly suggested by its connotations of betrayal. The prisoner's confession merely objectifies the fact of their being almost lost."[10] Notwithstanding the world-destructive enterprises of interrogation and torture, declarations of repentance are important because they specify and formulate self-negation. The declaration is the moment when the whole procedure comes to be literally transcribed into the language of power, when it is the detainee who is written rather than the detainee who writes.[11]

In the above-mentioned declaration of repentance, R. Elias had to denounce not only the Communist Party, but also his past as a follower of it. The past was a mistake, a fallacy; he had been misguided, deceived, led astray; but now that the truth prevailed, now that he knew the truth about its anti-Greek role, he was denouncing and renouncing it; his present and future are inscribed into the domain of truth. From this point of view, the penitentiary and internment processes are transformed into mechanisms for the production of truth and error, to use Foucault's terms. The error is the past, the truth is the present. But, inasmuch as the past experience is constituent of an individual's identity, the renunciation of the past distorts one's self-identity. One became ashamed of the past because in 1947 a member of EAM/ELAS would be labeled as "traitor" and "Bulgarian." The past, as societal ties, as individual and collective values, habitus, and vision of the world, is discredited, and this, for the individual who signed a declaration, was perceived as a self-betrayal, a self-negation.

Moreover, a declaration of repentance was just the beginning in a process of humiliation and degradation; those who signed had to prove that they had truly repented by informing against friends and comrades, and by sending public letters repudiating communism. In the camps on Makronisos, where soldiers, and later civilians, suspected of leftist beliefs were concentrated under a state of violence and terror, this process seemed endless. The repentees had to give talks to their colleagues, as for instance Yiorgos S., a "well-formed cadre" and student at the law school, who finally, after three months of interrogation and torments, gave talks on "the collaboration of Bulgarian and separatist organizations with ELAS" and similar issues.[12] Others had to write letters to newspapers, send letters to their hometowns praising Makronisos penitentiary and denouncing the Communist Party, or deliver speeches to their fellow citizens, like Lambros K., who gave a talk in Igoumenitsa under the title "How I Fared on Makronisos," in which he argued that he "found the way of God and Motherland at this great National University called Makronisos."[13] At the end of this process in the Makronisos camps, the repentants had to turn themselves literally against their unrepentant colleagues. They had to become tormentors, to beat, harass, and insult the unrepentants, or, to use the camp director's words, "to assist the few officers so as to point out to their colleagues with incontestable arguments and facts beyond doubt, their gross mistake and the consequences resulting thereof."[14]

In the last case, the boundary between repentants and unrepentants is replaced by the dividing line between detainees and authorities. Under the extreme conditions in the Makronisos camps, "repentance" had to be demonstrated every day, and self-negation was intended to end up in the production of a new subject, that of the "reformed" soldier who would insult and beat the "unrepentant" colleagues, carry ministers in his arms, cheer for the king, and sing, "Even if criminals betrayed us / and contaminated our souls / now once more / our life belongs to Mother Greece."[15] Because the boundary between repentants and unrepentants in many cases, as I shall argue, became less and less discernible, the authorities' aim was to secure and demonstrate that there is no middle ground between the authorities and the unrepentants. The achievement of this goal was to a large extent due to the fact that the party mechanism, too, had adopted this separation. I suggest that the subjectivity of the repentant is conditioned by a double negation. The first negation, on the part of the authorities, rejects the past of the repentant as a resistant and a member of leftist organizations. The second, on the part of the party mechanism, rejects the present situation of the repentant and excludes him or her from the prisoners' collectivity.

THE STIGMA OF THE REPENTANT

On 27 July 1947, in a front-page article, the editor of the communist daily *Rizospastis*, Kostas Karayiorgis, wrote,

> And the "declarations" [of repentance] are *ten times more* sinful than then [i.e., during the Metaxas dictatorship]. Now it is an all-or-nothing struggle! We are living in a tragic and epic period, when modern Greece's drama is reaching a climax and is heading quickly toward its katharsis. The faint-hearted do not have a place near us and will never find a place among us. . . . There will be no *unworthy* who will not be able to hold their views like a *fortress*.[16]

The view of the Communist Party could not have been more adamant. The epic topos that the author employs in order to stress the importance of the times and the eschatological connotations that words like "sin" or "katharsis" carry (it is not a coincidence that "sin" and "repentance" derive from the same rhetorical paradigm) depoliticize the civil war. The categories are not political but ethical. Declarations, for instance, are not a political mistake but a sin, while *dilosies* are not less politically conscious but faint-hearted. Everything is turned into an is-

sue of moral superiority. Political arguments that might exclude prisoners who were not members of the party are not stated; instead, more
inclusive moral considerations are put forward. It is not the communists
who exclude the repentants; it is the fearless and dignified who exclude
the faint-hearted and the unworthy.

A few years later, the secretary-general of the KKE, Nikos Zachariadis, would delineate not only the ethical but also the political and social profile of the repentant.

> The issue related to the declarations and the *dilosies* . . . is this: the petit-
> bourgeois has defeated the fighter. He didn't endure the difficulties, gave in to
> the hardship, cracked, capitulated, was brought to his knees, and many times
> committed acts of betrayal. . . . For the member of the KKE there is no capit-
> ulation, retreat, or compromise on the total dedication to the struggle even if
> it is to sacrifice one's life.[17]

The stigmatization of the repentant as a petit-bourgeois, a coward, a
compromised individual, or a traitor forged the identity of the political
prisoner against the repentant, who was becoming the Other among the
political prisoners. Declarations of repentance were considered as a
breach of the party discipline and an undermining of the prisoners' collective spirit. The fear that the morale of those who did not repent
would be undermined, that the coherence of the prisoners' collectivity
would be threatened and party discipline loosened, led to their exclusion. *Dilosies* had no place among political prisoners; they served as the
negative defining example. From this viewpoint, the political prisoners'
collectivity was itself a power mechanism with its own strategies of exclusion and punishment.

There were three forms of punishment: exclusion, stigmatization, and
segregation. First, repentees were excluded from the party. The Seventh
Congress of the KKE in 1945 was quite clear on this point: considering
the declarations as "apostasy and treason," it was decided that "the
dilosies would not be admitted again to the KKE."[18] Second, the stigma
of the declaration was indelible, even when the individual was readmit-
ted to the party (this was the case of *dilosies* in Metaxas's dictatorship
who had joined the resistance organizations during the occupation).
The declaration remained a stain upon the individual in the party files,
as a suspicion and an explanation for possible actions against the party.
Aris Velouchiotis, the most notorious of the three leaders of ELAS during the resistance, disagreed with the Varkiza Agreement and didn't surrender his arms. The party had not forgotten that Aris Velouchiotis had
signed a declaration of repentance during Metaxas's dictatorship and
denounced him as a double traitor: he had betrayed the party as a repentant and as a dissident.[19] The third, and perhaps the harshest, form

of punishment inside prisons was segregation. Even when repentants were not transferred by the authorities to a separate ring or cell or camp location, they were isolated by their fellow inmates; the contacts between them and the unrepentants were limited, and they were excluded from prisoners' collective activities. Once again, but from the other side, there was to be no topos between the authorities and the unrepentants.

Nevertheless, many *dilosies* still felt attached to the party and their comrades. Driven by pain, fatigue, fear, or despair, they signed declarations, and that decision was as painful as the torture.[20] Later, however, many *dilosies* proved that they had not "repented" at all. Petros Stratigareas was one of them. Like thousands of soldiers suspected for leftist political beliefs, he was sent to the Makronisos camps in 1949. He underwent the process of "rehabilitation," finally signed a declaration of repentance, and sent letters denouncing communism to the parish of Chaidari, his neighborhood in Athens. A few years later, however, when Stalin died, Stratigareas decided to send a letter to a right-wing newspaper to express his and his fellow Chaidari inhabitants' sorrow for Stalin's death; on top of that, he sent a letter to the same newspaper to express his sympathy for the communist political prisoner Manolis Glezos. After all this, he was not surprised when he was arrested, and on 10 July 1953, he was banished for being "dangerous for public order and security."[21]

After 1949, when the executions stopped, many of the *dilosies* withdrew their declarations. This was the case, for instance, in Akronafplia prison, where 373 were classified as "repentants" and were separated from the 330 "unrepentants." On 16 June 1950, twenty-four repentants pushed the guard "away from the open door of the Communist dormitory and entered. The Director has stated that there are thirty-six more repentants who wish to be transferred to Left Wing dormitories and who wish to withdraw their declaration of loyalty."[22] Classified and categorized by the authorities or by the "bureau" of the party mechanism, but not by themselves, political prisoners transgressed the boundaries and showed the fragility of the dividing lines that categorized them. The categories of repentants and unrepentants were questioned by (re-)establishing the main feature of the subjectivity that they had in common, that they were political prisoners.

There is no point in discussing the sincerity of the declarations of repentance. During and after the civil war, all kinds of declarations and statements found their way into newspapers. A father publicly renounced his whole family (his wife, his two sons, and his daughter) because "the family lost its way and turned against the interests of my country"; numerous letters from individuals stated, "I have never been a communist and member of similar organizations like EAM, EPON, etc., which collaborate with Bulgarians and Slavs and whose aim is to subjugate my country."[23] The fundamental point is that no one has to declare that he is not a communist, unless he is "asked" to do so. Such statements were products of a polarized society under the reign of terror and violence, not of free will. Moreover, in the case of declarations of repentance, the authorities' aim was to construct a passive consensus for the regime through their publicity, and to dissolve, at least inside prisons, the prisoners' collectivity by dividing political detainees into repentants and unrepentants.

For the political prisoners themselves, given the views of the Communist Party on this issue, declarations of repentance represented a violent deconstruction of their identity, a self-betrayal; to use their own words, "The real objective with the publication of declarations . . . is our humiliation, discredit and our moral suicide," so that "the Left should be wounded, exhausted, decease morally."[24] And many political prisoners, instead of the "moral decease," chose actual death.

EXECUTIONS

On 16 July 1946, two political prisoners, a certain Sapranidis, twenty-five years old, and Kalemis, thirty years old, both villagers from the Kilkis district in Macedonia, were executed in Salonika. The two men were first accused under article 1 of Resolution C of trying to detach a part of the Greek territory from Greece. When this charge failed, they were charged under article 2 of the same law with "organizing armed bands."[25] They were the first political prisoners executed since the Liberation of Greece in October 1944. But they were not the last.

The executions of political prisoners that commenced in July 1946 stopped shortly after the end of the civil war, in September 1949. It is difficult to estimate the number of executions, since there are no official documents from the government side. Several scholars assume that out of 7,500 death sentences, between 3,000 and 5,000 political prisoners were actually executed.[26] In any case, the lowest estimation is given by British sources, according to which from 1946 to 1949, 3,033 persons were executed as sentenced by extraordinary courts-martial, and 378 as sentenced by civil courts.[27]

Executions and the legislative framework that made them possible were inextricably related to the events of the civil war. Two and a half months after the elections of March 1946, the first sporadic attacks of armed units against gendarmerie stations occurred. The government of the Populist party, with the support of a parliament where the parties of the Left were not represented, passed Resolution C, 18 June 1946, "on extraordinary measures concerning public order and security." Its first article introduced the death penalty for those who intended "to detach a part from the whole of the country." The offenders of Resolution C were tried by extraordinary courts-martial that had been set up in eleven cities of Thrace, Macedonia, Epirus, and Thessaly (gradually, extraordinary courts-martial would be set up throughout the whole country). In December 1947 the formation of the Provisional Democratic Government, the guerillas' government, provided the government the opportunity to pass Compulsory Law 509, 27 December 1947, "on security measures of the State, the regime, and the social order, and the protection of citizens' liberties," which outlawed all leftist parties and organizations and imposed the death penalty on those who were "seeking to apply ideas, which overtly aim to overthrow the regime or the established social system by violent means, or aim to detach a part from the whole of the country."[28]

Some evidence of the severity of extraordinary courts-martial is provided by my research in the archives of the Ministry of Justice. In these archives there is a large number of reports on decrees (total 11,545) of extraordinary courts-martial from 1946 to 1949. Out of the 7,771 convicted, 1,185 (15 percent) were sentenced to up to one year's imprisonment, 1,956 (25 percent) were sentenced to from one to ten years, 1,290 (17 percent) from ten to twenty years, 1,309 (17 percent) to life sentence, and 2,031 (26 percent) were sentenced to death—one out of four convicted individuals.[29]

From 1945, the leftist political opponents were first rendered powerless, then excluded, and finally negated in the growing polarization of the conflict during the civil war. At the first level, negation meant that political opponents were categorized and stigmatized in such a way that some qualities were silenced while others, newly invented, that contradicted the previous ones, came to the foreground. The resistants became bandits, common law offenders, and, in the end, traitors to their country. They were attributed the stigma of the "Other." They had committed a "crime," that of treason, which had alienated them from the rest of the community, namely the nation. The Minister of Press, Michael Ailianos, expressed this form of negation very well when he stated that "the Greek Government denies, once again, that there have been any executions for political crimes. It also emphatically denies that there are any individuals of the above category detained in prisons."[30] The transformation of political prisoners into criminals facilitated and justified their negation at a second level, their literal negation in their execution. Executions as a form of punishment were the demonstration and affirmation of the absolute power of the state over its political opponents.

The impact of the executions upon political prisoners was profound. Anyone who did not show signs of "repentance" could be sentenced to death, and many of those sentenced to death knew that they could be executed within a few days. There was no appeal against decisions of extraordinary courts-martial, and actually, a great number of those convicted were executed within three days of the sentence so that they would have not enough time to submit petitions for reprieve to the Council of Pardon.[31]

Hundreds of those sentenced to death became moribunds and found themselves in a state of almost total heteronomy: their lives, literally speaking, were dependent on the state rather than on themselves. They were incorporated into the strategy of a regime waging a civil war. The days that followed the assassination of the Minister of Justice, Christos Ladas, on 1 May 1948 left no doubt about this. On 6 May, twenty-four political prisoners were executed in Athens; these were followed two days later by thirteen executions in Athens, eighteen on Aegina, eleven in Salonika, and ten in Lamia; on 7 May, seventeen more were executed on Aegina, and on 10 May, another fifteen political prisoners were executed in Volos.[32] The 109 political prisoners executed within five days served as an example for the regime to demonstrate outside and inside prisons its determination to reestablish its power, even through sheer violence. For this reason I suggest that executions of political prisoners, as the literal negation of political opponents, not only are closely interrelated with the culminating crisis of the civil war, but also became an essential part of the regime's strategy.

SACRIFICE AS A MEANINGFUL DEATH

Executions became the constant anguish of the political detainees sentenced to death. The overall situation inside prisons changed, especially in those that were transformed into places of concentration for prisoners to be executed. This is the case, for instance, for the Averoff men's prison, where in two years, 1948–49, 296 political prisoners were executed—202 within a week of their transportation to that prison.[33] Corfu, Kefallonia, Aegina, Akronafplia, Eptapyrgio, Lamia, Xanthi, and Itzedin (Crete) were among the other prisons to which prisoners might be taken for execution. Hunger strikes, appeals to Greek and international authorities and organizations, and appeals to the public were the only means that the prisoners had at their disposal to stop the executions, yet these demonstrations could not alleviate their fear that perhaps the next time would be their turn, their names would be called by the guards. They were living with death.

The moribunds who were chosen for execution were transported during the night; when the guards entered the chambers of those sentenced to death (though they were not always separated from the other prisoners), the steps of the guards and the sounds of keys and doors put them on the alert. The only thing to discover was whose turn it was that night. The political detainee who was taken for execution always cried out a few words to his fellow inmates, like "Farewell brothers, it's my turn now. I promise to do my duty, dying with my head high. I hope that I'll be the last one. Long live the Greek people. Long live our Party."[34] These words were not just a farewell, but proof that they were not afraid of death and a gesture of encouragement to their fellow inmates.

Then, the moribunds were transferred to solitary confinement cells that the detainees called *Golgothas* (Calvary). This is the topos of pain and martyrdom, where the innocent one suffers alone before his or her death—the connotations of the metaphor carry the burden of the eschatological traditions (to be found in religion and political ideologies) and of the popular habits that tend to dramatize events according to great narrative patterns. In this cell a detainee would spend the few hours till dawn (when executions took place) alone or, more often, with some fellow inmates: they would eat, drink, sing, sometimes even dance, and write their last letters to their families and partners.

Within this context, the last letters of the moribunds may give us an insight into the way in which they were making sense of their deaths, the meaning they were attaching to their executions. Yiorgos Katsimichas, a driver from Livadeia, was executed on 10 May 1948, at the age of twenty-seven. In his last letter from Corfu prison, he writes to his family:

> At the moment that I'm writing to you they are taking me and other comrades for execution. Father and Mother, I promise you that I will walk to the firing squad with my head high and a song on my lips. You should know that I shall honor our family, our Immortal National Resistance, Greece, our People. My wish is the following: I don't want you to wear mourning clothes nor to cry nor sing dirges, upon hearing the bad news. What I'm asking you is to hold your heads high and give yourselves wholeheartedly to the struggle of our people, the struggle for Freedom—Democracy—Independence. Let the cry be a song and the dirge be a dance.[35]

Yiorgos Karayiannis, in a letter sent from the Averoff prison on 27 March 1949, writes to his relatives:

> Neither you nor my little girls should feel pain for my loss. You have to encourage them because they are so small. I write about my kids with great sorrow; I loved them so much that I have been seeing them in my dreams every night. I'm leaving them with great anguish. I hope they remember me in good and bad times and say "Wish our father was alive." When you meet my

Beloved Theologia kiss her for me. I loved her so much at the time the enemies separated us. I don't want her to carry her head down but high for I've
never done anything wrong to anybody. . . . I kiss you for the last time.[36]

Orestis Makridis, on 25 June 1948, wrote a letter from the Averoff
prison to his imprisoned wife, a few hours before his execution:

My dear wife, I am sending you my last greetings from the moribunds' cell.
Despina, our separation is cruel but I don't believe that you will be grieved
because you know the reason I'm dying. And you should know that I die
happy and proud. . . . My dear Despina, my last wish is, as soon as you 'll be
free, to find a nice man, one of ours, and to get married. I'm giving you my
last kiss.[37]

The pain of loss is dominant. And beyond or after grief and pain, what?
"Be proud," "Do not mourn," and "Remember." The executed should
be honored and remembered because they died for high ideals such as
democracy and freedom. Notions of pride and honor are crucial in
these letters. On the one hand, the execution is unjust, politically motivated ("never done anything wrong to anybody"), and in this way the
stigma of the executed criminal is removed; on the other hand, those
about to be executed are proud ("die with the head high") because they
are doing their duty. Their deaths in the present will contribute to the
future realization of the ideal. The future trajectory is their main concern, the life that they will not live and that they try to anticipate (to be
remembered and honored) and settle (for instance, permission to the
beloved one to get married).

There is a concept of sacrifice underlying this meaningful death, this
notion of "dying for something." To die for the people, the freedom, the
party, is an attempt, as Zygmunt Bauman points out, "to render meaningful (indeed noble and desirable) what unless culturally processed
would appear an unalloyed absurdity."[38] The way these prisoners were
dying was closely related to the way they had lived, and this close relation was bringing together a meaningful life and a meaningful death.[39]
Nikos Zachariadis wrote in 1946 that one of the qualities of the Party
member was "the invincible superiority of the communist to be dedicated, to be devoted and to sacrifice himself, if necessary, for the highest
and greatest ideal."[40] The communist should be ready to die, to sacrifice
himself for the cause, in the war or in the prisons. Such an attitude
toward death presupposes not only a subject who is not highly individualized, but also, somehow, one who has a certain familiarity with death.
Greek society throughout the 1940s did not enjoy a period of tranquility — the Greek-Italian war, the occupation and resistance, the civil
war, all together constituted almost ten years of violence and death.

Many political detainees had lost relatives or friends in battle or in executions. Dionysis Goumas, for example, knew, long before his arrest in 1949 and his death sentence, what death meant: three out of five members of his resistance unit were found dead in the streets of Athens, and his three brothers had been executed by the Germans during the occupation.[41]

Affiliated with the experience of death, sacrifice was opening the way to the pantheon of people's heroes and was transforming death, which thousands of people were facing every day inside and outside of prisons, into a comprehensible and justified contingency. "Brothers / the victory is all ours / as we defeat terror / any kind of death," wrote the moribund Kostas Yiannopoulos.[42] Transforming death through sacrifice, they were situating themselves beyond the realm of death, negating it. To give one's life for an ideal was a form of self-negation that presupposed an entity or a symbolic universe worth demanding, intermingled with a world-building enterprise that was giving a sense of identity, purpose, and place to the persons.[43] First, sacrifice as meaningful death confirmed an identity, that of the communist as a people's fighter, as a hero, who was dying according to the paradigm set up by the resistance: not dying for oneself, but for high ideals, as heroes do. In this way they were also reestablishing their identities by removing the stigma of the criminal or the traitor that the regime had attributed to them. Second, sacrifice demonstrated a purpose, that of doing their duty: to die like they had lived, faithful both to their own ethics and principles and those of the party. Third, sacrifice gave them a place in the imaginary past and future. Their death was opening the way to the collectivized immortality of people's heroes (the past) and was contributing to the fulfillment of the cause, the victory of the Left (the future).

The dead body of the executed and the living "truth" of the repentant were interlaced within the framework of a complex negation involving different attached meanings. Negation was the key strategy of the regime as well as of the party to expand their domain under control by canonizing the diversity and disciplining the difference in the polarized context of the civil war. Moreover, the strategy of the negation was positive, in the sense that the negative example served to construct the ideal individual, the loyal national-minded (*ethnikofron*), from the perspective of the regime, and the image of a fighter worthy of the people, from the perspective of the party.

The political prisoners who signed declarations of repentance found themselves in a precarious situation. Forced by physical and psychological violence, they renounced their pasts and their identities. Self-betrayal, as a form of self-negation, was reinforced by the fact that they were segregated from and excluded by the rest of the political prisoners. Moribunds, again, facing absolute negation on the part of the state, they had to make sense of their own deaths. Sacrifice, offering oneself for something, a form of self-negation as well, was affirming political prisoners' identities; it was establishing a continuity with the past of the resistance and providing a paradigm that sustained the coherence of the prisoners' sense of solidarity.

Thus, as negation and self-negation were interrelated to the past (the identity of the resistant), the present (the status among the political prisoners), and the future (the imaginary and actual life or death) of the political prisoner, they were creating different topoi. The topos of death for the moribund was that of the imaginary collectivity, whereas the topos of life for the repentant was nonexistent in the symbolic universe of political prisoners.

NOTES

1. This chapter is part of my research project on political prisoners in Greece from 1945 to 1950. An earlier and very different version was presented in the framework of Professor Luisa Passerini's seminars at the European University Institute in May 1997. I would like to thank Philippos Iliou, Antonis Liakos, Mark Mazower, and Luisa Passerini for their helpful comments, and Kathrin Zippel for her help in editing the chapter.

2. Archeia Synkronis Koinonikis Istoria [Archive of Contemporary Social History, hereafter ASKI], EDA (*Eniť Dimokratiki Aristera*) Archives-National Resistance Archives, Letter of Koula Eleftheriadou from Eptapyrgio prison, Salonika, 5 May 1947; FO 371/67019 R 7957, Report of Mr. Francis Noel-Baker MP, 6 June 1947; FO 371/67076 R 9371, Executions carried out on previous sentences, 1 to 31 May, Salonika to Foreign Office, 30 June 1947.

3. Report of the British Legal Mission to Greece, London, His Majesty's Stationery Office, 17 Jan. 1946, p. 15; *Rizospastis*, 12 Feb. 1946. For the Varkiza Agreement text translated in English, see Heinz Richter, *British Intervention in Greece: From Varkiza to Civil War* (London, 1985), 561–64.

4. ASKI 425 F 25/5/105; FO 371/87668 RG 10113/28, Athens to Foreign Office, Figures of political prisoners in Greece, 1 Sept. 1950; David H. Close, "The Reconstruction of a Right-Wing State," in Close, ed., *The Greek Civil War, 1943–50: Studies of Polarization* (London, 1993), 156–90.

5. George Kousoulas, *Revolution and Defeat: The Story of the Greek Communist Party* (London, 1965), 130; Angelos Elefantis, *I epangelia tis adynatis epanastasis: KKE kai astismos ston mesopolemo* (The promise of the impossible revolution: KKE and bourgeoisism in the interwar) (Athens, 1979), 256.

6. Maniadakis's archives, cited in Kousoulas, *Revolution and Defeat*, 132.

7. Dionysis Moschopoulos, "Politikoi kratoumenoi stis fylakes tis Kerkyras, 1947–1949" (Political detainees in the Corfu prison, 1947–1949), in *Geia sas adelfia . . . Fylakes Kerkyras, 1947–1949 — Martyries* (Farewell brothers . . . Corfu prison, 1947–1949 — Testimonies) (Athens, 1996), 19–66.

8. Nikos Alivizatos, "The 'Emergency Regime' and Civil Liberties, 1946–1949," in John O. Iatrides, ed., *Greece in the 1940s: A Nation in Crisis* (Hanover and London, 1981), 220–28.

9. *Acropolis*, 8 May 1947.

10. Elaine Scarry, *The Body in Pain: The Making and Unmaking of the World* (Oxford and New York, 1985), 35.

11. Paul Gready, "Autobiography and the 'Power of Writing': Political Prison Writing in the Apartheid Era," *Journal of Southern African Studies*, 19.3 (1993): 489–523.

12. ASKI 421 F 25/3/132, Letter of K. Zacharoudis.

13. *Skapaneus*, vol. 11, 28 Nov. 1948, p. 20, republication of the speech, which originally appeared in the newspaper *Foni tis Thesprotias* (Voice of Thesprotia) on 12 Sept. 1948.

14. FO 371/87647 RG 10106/18, General Director G. Bairaktaris's report on Makronisos's reformative organization, 24 Jan. 1950; Louis de Villefosse, "Makronisos, laboratoire politique," *Les temps modernes* 51 (Jan. 1950): 1287–99.

15. See *Acropolis*, 1 Oct. 1947; *Scapaneus*, vol. 1, 28 Oct. 1947, pp. 14–15.

16. *Rizospastis*, 27 July 1947, emphasis in the original.

17. Nikos Zachariadis, *Provlimata kathodigisis sto KKE* (Problems of leadership in KKE), Edition of the Central Committee of KKE (1952), 231–33.

18. Seventh Congress of KKE, Resolution on the declarations, 6 Oct. 1945, in KKE, *Episima Keimena* (Official documents), Athens, Synchroni Epochi (1987), vol. 6, p. 127.

19. Resolution of Polit Bureau of the Central Committee of KKE, 15 June 1945, in KKE, *Episima Keimena*, p. 21. The denunciation of Aris Velouchiotis had been decided at the Eleventh Plenum of the Central Committee, in April 1945, but remained secret. See Ioanna Papathanasiou, "I logiki ton sygkrouseon stin igesia tou KKE, 1945–1948" (The reasons for conflict in the leadership of KKE, 1945–1948), *Istorika* 23 (1995): 407–20

20. Nikos Margaris, detained at that time on Makronisos, gives a vivid description of that decision:

> I touched his forehead with my palm. It was obvious that he was burning with a temperature. . . . He gripped me and the trembling resumed. "I am so much afraid. The declaration turns over constantly in my mind, doesn't let me calm down, it follows night and day close behind me." He coughed huskily and resumed: "I will sign, I am worn out, I am thirsty, I am burning," he said slowly, shakily. . . . He was silent for a while.
> "I love life," he resumed. "I want to live, no matter how they will let me live," and a shiver shook him. "I'm exhausted," he stammered out. "I will sign," and sobbed his heart out.

N. Margaris, *Istoria tis Makronisou* (History of Makronisos) (Athens, 1986), 2: 334.

21. Modern Greek Archives/League for Democracy Archives, Info IV, First Degree Public Security Committee of Attica, Banishment decree 61/10 July 1953.

22. FO 371/87772 R 1642, British Police Mission Headquarters, Monthly report—June 1950, 19 July 1950.

23. *Macedonia*, 22 July 1951; *Acropolis*, 20 July 1947. For a discussion on

the broader topic of practices of denunciation, see Robert Gellately, *The Ge-stapo and German Society: Enforcing Racial Policy, 1933–1945* (Oxford, 1990), esp. 129–58; Sheila Fitzpatrick, "Supplicants and Citizens: Public Letter-Writing in Soviet Russia in the 1930s," *Slavic Review,* 55.1 (1996), 78–105; Eric A. Johnson, "German Women and Nazi Justice: Their Role in the Process from Denunciation to Death," *Historical Social Research,* 20.1 (1995): 33–69; and the special issue on "Practices of Denunciation in Modern European History," *Journal of Modern History,* 68.4 (1996).

24. Memorandum of political exiles on Ai-Stratis, 17 September 1950, in *Ta thymata tou monarchofasismou katigoroun* (The victims of monarchofascism accuse) (Nea Ellada, 1951), 64; Margaris, *Istoria tis Makronisou,* 1: 327.

25. *Greek News Agency,* 17 July 1946; *Acropolis,* 19 July 1946. It may be considered as public execution since it was reported that "the people of Eptapyrgio neighborhood saw the executions from a distance"; see *Eleftheri Ellada,* 17 July 1946.

26. Lawrence Wittner, *American Intervention in Greece, 1943–1949* (New York, 1982), 143–48; Amikam Nachmani, *International Intervention in the Greek Civil War: The United Nations Special Committee on the Balkans, 1947–1952* (New York, 1990), 95–98; Giorgos Katiforis, *I nomothesia ton varvaron* (The barbarians' legislation) (Athens, 1975), 63; Nikos Alivizatos, *Oi politikoi thesmoi se krisi, 1922–1974* (Political insitutions in crisis, 1922–1974) (Athens, 1995), 520; Roussos Koundouros, *I asfaleia tou kathestotos: Politikoi Kratoumenoi, ektopiseis kai taxeis stin Ellada, 1924–74* (The security of the regime) (Athens, 1978), 133–34.

27. FO 371/87668 RG 10113/11, Athens to Foreign Office, 6 Apr. 1950.

28. Alivizatos, *Oi politikoi thesmoi,* 495–523.

29. Archives of the Ministry of Justice, *Anafores apofaseon ektakton stratodikeion* (Register of decrees of extraordinary courts-martial). These reports were sent from the "local" extraordinary courts-martial (there is a small number from "divisional" courts martial as well, which are not included in my sample) to the Ministry of Justice/Department of Criminal Affairs. These reports from extraordinary courts-martial cover mainly northern and central Greece (and occasionally Chania, Mytilene, and Thebes), but do not constitute a series. The assumed leniency of the extraordinary courts-martial toward women seems to be questioned, since 19 percent of the convicted women were sentenced to death, whereas 27 percent of the convicted men were sentenced to death. Nonetheless, it is difficult to generalize a conclusion because in this sample the vast majority of the decrees concern men (87 percent).

30. FO 371/72354 R 6123, Statement of the Minister of Press and Information Mr. Michael Ailianos to foreign press correspondents, 14 May 1948.

31. Executions were more likely for persons who had been sentenced to death unanimously or by a majority of four to one, since the government had issued instructions to prosecuting officers of extraordinary courts-martial to suspend execution of persons sentenced to death by a majority of three to two. See FO 371/67079 R 15861, Salonika to Athens, 1 Dec. 1947.

32. FO 371/72353 R 5593, Athens to Foreign Office, 6 May 1948; FO 371/72353 R 5666, Athens to Foreign Office, 8 May 1948; FO 371/72353 R

5667, Athens to Foreign Office, 8 May 1948; FO 371/72353 R 5780, Athens to Foreign Office, 11 May 1948. Also see *Acropolis* 5, 6, 7, 8, and 11 May 1948. According to other sources, the number of executed was 154; see Memorandum of the moribunds' relatives, in *Matomeni Vivlos* (Blooded book) (Nea Ellada, 1949), 113–23; Tasos Vournas, *Istoria tis synchronis Elladas: O Emfylios* (History of contemporary Greece: The Civil War) (Athens, 1981), 204.

33. Averoff prison archives, *Evretirio katadikon fylakon Averof* (Index of convicts of Averoff prison). In 1947, 8 political prisoners were executed; in 1948, 185; and in 1949, 111.

34. Mitsos Roupas' testimony, in Vardis Vardinoyiannis and Panayiotis Aronis, eds., *Oi misoi sta sidera* (Half of them in irons) (Athens, 1996), 283. Several testimonies from political prisoners on executions are published in this volume, see pp. 263–436.

35. ASKI, EDA Archives-National Resistance Archives, Letter of Yiorgos Katsimichas from Corfu prison (no date).

36. ASKI 422 F25/4/1, Letter of Yiorgos Karayiannis from Averoff prison, 27 Mar. 1949.

37. ASKI, EDA Archives-National Resistance Archives, Letter of Orestis Makridis from Averoff prison, 26 June 1948.

38. Zygmunt Bauman, *Mortality, Immortality and Other Life Strategies* (Cambridge, Mass., 1992), 27. The case of the Irish hunger strikers is a similar example for the concept of self-sacrifice among political prisoners; see Daniel J. O'Neil, "The Cult of Self-Sacrifice: The Irish Experience," *EIRE-Ireland*, 24.4 (1989): 89–105; George Sweeney, "Irish Hunger Strikes and the Cult of Self-Sacrifice, *Journal of Contemporary History*, 28.3 (1993): 421–37.

39. Norbert Elias, *The Loneliness of the Dying* (Oxford, 1985), 58–66.

40. Nikos Zachariadis, *O kommounistis laikos agonistis melos tou KKE* (The Communist people's fighter member of KKE) (Athens, July 1946), 9.

41. Modern Greek Archives/League for Democracy in Greece Archives, Info XI, Individual dossiers.

42. ASKI, EDA Archives-National Resistance Archives, "Our Last Hour," poem of the moribund Kostas Yiannopoulos, Aegina prison, 1948. Kostas Yiannopoulos was executed on 7 May 1948; see Aegina prison archives, *Evretirio katadikon fylakon Aiginis, 1948* (Index of convicts of Aegina prison, 1948).

43. Peter Berger and Thomas Luckmann, *The Social Construction of Reality: A Treatise in the Sociology of Knowledge* (London, 1971), 110–12; Philip A. Mellor, "Death in High Modernity: The Contemporary Presence and Absence of Death," in David Clark, ed., *The Sociology of Death* (Oxford, 1993), 3–30.

FIVE

Children in Turmoil during the Civil War:
Today's Adults

Mando Dalianis and Mark Mazower

"AT FIVE P.M. on Wednesday, April 13, 1949, the heavy iron door of Averoff prison was opened to admit me, and my name was added to the register of prisoners awaiting trial." Mando Dalianis, the daughter of Asia Minor refugees, had graduated not long before from the Athens medical school when she was accused of illegal political activities and arrested. She was held in the Averoff women's prison in Athens for twenty-one months before being tried, acquitted of the charges against her, and released. In that time, she forged close links with other women inmates and with the young children they were permitted to keep with them.[1]

Conditions in the prison were harsh. It had been built in 1889 as an annex to the larger central men's prison in order to house the country's female prison population, normally 100–120 in number. Expanded during the German occupation, it had been badly damaged in the Dekemvriana fighting, and the prisoners had to be temporarily rehoused. In January 1947 the prison reopened, and its population—like that of all prisons in Greece—increased rapidly. By the time of Dalianis's arrest, it housed more than ten times more women than had been originally anticipated. The inmates all had left-wing backgrounds and faced long terms of imprisonment, or execution.

Despite the harsh and overcrowded conditions—the entirely inadequate furnishings, diet, and sanitary facilities—by 1950 some 119 children had spent time in the prison with their mothers. Waking up on her first morning in prison, Dalianis met "Alexis, who was then eight months old. He was sitting on his mother's bed and she was standing beside him." The children were not registered as prisoners, nor were they included in the prison rations; they were shut, like the adults, for sixteen hours a day inside the wards. "The only objects visible to the children were the campbeds, the walls, the chapel and the palm-tree." In 1950, the prison administration ordered the children's removal in order to punish the women for protesting against the execution of political prisoners. Fifty-four of the children went to foster parents, because

A nun, the prison governor and a group of older children, Averoff Women's Prison, Spring 1949. From the collection of the late Mando Dalianis

their mothers were afraid that they would otherwise be indoctrinated against them, but some thirty-seven were placed in official institutions, where they remained until the early 1960s.

These children and their mothers became the subject of Dalianis's research. She had looked after them in prison, and kept in touch with many until 1956, when she left the country. In 1980 she carried out a follow-up study, reestablishing contact both with the mothers, some of whom had not been released until 1960, and with the children themselves, now adults with, in many cases, families of their own. In all between 1980 and 1986, she visited, questioned, and interviewed 993 individuals over three generations. In particular, she tried to compare the experiences and life paths of children who had been in prison with those of children who had remained outside, separated from their mothers. She also compared the physical and mental health of these two groups with that of the Greek population as a whole. The result was a unique long-term study of the impact of war and civil war upon the Greek family, with many implications for the broader debate about how wars and other traumatic events affect individuals in later life. In this chapter, based entirely upon Dalianis's materials, we shall try to bring out the rich variety of paths followed by Greek families in the aftermath of the civil war before concluding with some more general reflections.

Most of the mothers incarcerated in the Averoff prison were born between 1915 and 1930, and their experiences reflected the diversity of Greece's national history in those years. Some were from Athens, but most were born either in country villages or in the diaspora. About one-quarter (a figure in line with the proportion of refugees in the Greek population as a whole) came from refugee families. Iris, for instance, had been born into a well-off shopkeeper's family in Izmir in 1920, but grew up in the refugee quarter of Kaisariani on the outskirts of Athens, where her mother worked as a domestic servant in order to raise the money for her children's education. Popi, another refugee child, had been born in a village near Constantinople before the Balkan Wars: her father died during the flight to Greece in 1922. Dora, born in 1910, was an only child whose father had emigrated to the United States when she was one and had brought up another family there. Many of Dalianis's cellmates were already used to the exile, familial separation, impoverishment, and emotional strains that the 1940s would force into their lives.

A large number of these women were from farming backgrounds, and nearly half were completely illiterate; the rest had primary, or at the most a few years of secondary, education. Ariadne, who had attended university in Athens before the war, was, like Mando Dalianis herself, unusually well-educated by these standards: in the prison she worked as a volunteer teacher, helping the other women to learn reading and writing. Yet on the whole, these women were not especially poor in terms of Greek society: nearly two-thirds had their own homes.

A few of the more educated prisoners had a history of trade-union or Communist Party activism dating back to before the war. But in general it was the experience of Nazi occupation that had politicized them, usually through their involvement in the resistance. For most women, this was the point at which their horizons expanded beyond their domestic worlds. Most of their husbands served as soldiers during the war, and the vast majority had either been active themselves in EAM/ELAS, or had been related to members. This involvement continued through the civil war.[2]

Through the stories these women told Dalianis, we can see the pressures that led to such involvement. Some kept out of politics but were married to men who did not. Others faced arrest after 1945 because of their husbands' partisan activities and fled to the mountains, in at least one case while pregnant. Families, and especially newlyweds, tried to stay together at all costs, even if this meant a flight into illegality.

As a result, many of their children entered life under the harshest and most extreme conditions. Some were born on the mountains, while many of those born at home lived in an atmosphere of fear, anticipated arrest, and forced separation. The case of Heleni is indicative: she and her husband Kostas farmed land near Mt. Taygetos and had three very young children when Liberation came. Kostas had been arrested by the Germans for partisan involvement and was repeatedly attacked by local right-wing gangs in 1946–1947; this continued even after the family moved to the town of Gytheion and opened a shop. Kostas's brother was killed, and Heleni and Kostas were eventually forced to close their shop. In 1947, Kostas decided to join the Democratic Army for self-protection, and his wife and children joined him early in 1948. They lived together in the wild for about a year. When the Democratic Army began its retreat, women and children were not allowed to join the partisans lest their crying give away their positions. Heleni and the children hid in a cave while the fighting raged around them. When found by army soldiers, the children were emaciated, covered with urine and feces, and ridden with lice, and they could neither see nor walk.

These women, still breast-feeding their babies and looking after older children, faced some terrifying dilemmas. One was whether to stay with their husbands even when this might mean abandoning their children. Aspasia, for instance, who followed her husband into the hills with their newborn baby, came to the point where her wounded husband needed her to stay in the cave with him, while their starving child required her to leave if she was to survive. "I went mad and started to roar," she told Dalianis. "My roar reverberated through the forest. I did not care. Let them find me. Let them kill me." In this case, Aspasia took her child and managed to surrender, thus saving its life. Her husband, she learned later, was shot in the cave where he lay wounded. It seems certain that other women made the opposite decision, and abandoned their babies or children, but this was perhaps the darkest secret of all, and it is not surprising that even thirty years on, none of the women interviewed by Dalianis admitted to having done this. In at least one case, where Dalianis suspected that the mother had actually killed her child on the mountain, the woman's husband did not allow her to get near the subject during the interview.

The transition back from illegality to legal existence — through surrender or arrest — was often equally or even more traumatic, and was filled with uncertainty and hazard. Army soldiers and paramilitaries were trigger-happy, especially near the battlefield, and they executed people out of hand. It was thought safer to surrender in daylight than at night, and preferably in the view of a large number of people. Women who surrendered were called all sorts of names and often beaten up. Many suffered torture, especially at the hands of the secret police, and some were raped. On the other hand, conscript soldiers in particular often behaved kindly toward their children. The children — and this was to be critical in affecting the later development of family relationships — were also crucial to the fate of their mothers, since pregnancy or motherhood was often enough to save a woman from execution. Twenty-two-year-old Artemis, for instance, was pregnant when she was captured with two wounded partisans on Olympos in April 1947: the soldiers shot her two comrades but spared her life. In another case, two-year-old Dimos was *sent* to the prison in order to save his mother Chloe from execution. At least one mother whose baby was *not* in prison was executed.

For those women who were sent to be tried in the special military courts that had been set up during the civil war, judgment lay in the hands of an unpredictable group of men with mostly right-wing sympathies. Little research has yet been carried out into the Greek judiciary, either regular or military. Dalianis, however, had her own personal experiences on which to rely, and she describes many of these men as "fanatics." Stassinopoulos, the chief prosecutor in her own case, was, in her words, "a real sadist." To his question: "Is this a civil war or a war between Greeks and Bulgarians?," Dalianis answered: "I don't know. History and further research will give us the answer." "You intellectuals are the catastrophe of the poor Greek people," retorted the judge. On the other hand, personal contacts, as so often in Greece, sometimes softened such harshness—the president of the court in Dalianis's trial, for instance, was a good friend of her cousin—as did the gifts—gold sovereigns, electric heaters, and flowers were common presents—that defendants often presented to the prosecutorial team. But the costs of the law strained the family finances of many poor women. "We sold the sheep—fifty drachmas per sheep—to pay the lawyer," recalled one, decades later.

The women were often, as in Dalianis's own case, detained in prison or detention camps for many months before they came to trial. They were separated from their husbands and did not immediately discover their spouses' fate. It happened more than once that men were executed without their wives being told: Filio and Vivi, for example, were being held in Athens when their husbands were executed in Lamia in November 1948. Their relatives said nothing, and the women only guessed the truth after the relatives came for a visit dressed in black. Family news spread fastest through such visits, since letters were censored by outgoing and incoming prison administrations and could not be more than twenty lines long.

Conditions varied greatly from the temporary detention camps on the islet of Trikeri (near Volos) to the jails of the secret police, in the army camps, provincial prisons, and the Averoff prison itself, their final destination.[3] The first director of the Averoff was an educated woman called Petrantis, a solicitor, who showed kindness to the children and was suspected by her superiors of being too close to the prisoners and swayed by ideas of prison reform. Consequently, she was replaced by a harder and more conservative character, the former chief warder, who had trained as a midwife but had no qualifications in prison administration. The warders themselves were nuns, mostly from poor refugee and village backgrounds, who also tended to be highly conservative. They tried to encourage the women to sign repentance declarations, promising extra milk for their children as an inducement.

The whole system of public recantation, which was such an important part of the state's assault on the Left, left its mark on all involved—women, their children, and their families. It was not just the warders who urged prisoners to repent: their children and relatives often did so, too. Nor was the choice between Party and family—for this was often what it amounted to—an easy one. Mika's mother visited her in prison and urged her to renounce her beliefs for her children's sake. Mika's refusal meant that she did not see her children until after her release. Rea's stepmother told Rea's son that his parents ought to "renounce their ideals and get out." The boy could not understand why his parents did not do so, and worried that they did not love him. Nor, of course, did making a statement of repentance guarantee domestic harmony: one woman did this for her children's sake, only to find that they felt hostile toward her and preferred the company of their grandmother.

Women who succumbed were shunned or harassed by their cellmates before their release. But one can sympathize with the poor illiterate mother from Lefkada who had married in 1946, lost one child on the mountains, and had another baby in prison, or with Iris, who recanted while on death row, fearing to leave her daughter parentless (since the father was also in prison). In 1951 Jeny, her daughter, was brought into court at the age of six to plead with the judge — successfully, as it turned out — for Iris's release. Thirty years later, Jeny still remembered the scene vividly, and felt mixed feelings toward her parents' political passions: "I respect my parents for their commitment to the struggle for a good cause," she told Dalianis, "but feel bitter because they combined having a child with their fight for social justice. They had no right to do that. I told them, I would not participate in any struggle, if I had a child."

For those inside, the prison became their social world, a place for working, child-rearing, and acquiring an education. Many worked in the thriving prison economy, earning money through piecework for Athenian businesses. One inmate, Jiana, was the "prisoners' employer," acting with her sister as a contact between the other prisoners and the business world outside. Jiana was only there for having sheltered her brother's son. She had been badly tortured on her arrest and suffered occasional relapses in which she howled uncontrollably.

For the children, prison life tempered deprivation and lack of liberty with a strong sense of community. The women prisoners evolved a system in which each child was given one or more godparents from among their number, and Dalianis was to attach considerable importance to the feeling of affection and security this engendered when she came to explain the psychological resilience of the children in later life. Mika, whose own children had remained with her parents in the village, felt that the prison children "had not only their mother to protect them like an eagle, but also those in the prison who provided them with love, affection, care and support." The children themselves seem to have adapted fairly quickly to this strange life, which was often after all more orderly and predictable than what they had experienced in the months immediately preceding it. Theodora, who had been born under a chestnut tree in the mountains at the height of the fighting, nearly dying of starvation at the age of seven months, was just over one year old when she entered the Averoff with her mother. At first she was frightened by the large number of women, and scratched anyone who came near her "like a wild cat." Within a few months, however, she played happily with other children and women. She was christened in the prison chapel, named after her father (who had died in the civil war), and acquired twenty godmothers from among the inmates. Two-year-old Mimi, who had endured the harsh winter of 1948–1949 on the mountains and survived flooded rivers, heavy snows, and the last battles in the Peloponnese, fell ill on admittance to the Averoff and was briefly separated from her mother. On being reunited, she first refused to go near her, but then adapted quickly to prison life.

The children whose lives Dalianis studied were invariably reared in an atmosphere of enforced separation. Their fathers were often dead, in prison, or in exile behind the Iron Curtain, where many raised new families in places like Prague and Tashkent. The children themselves were either in prison with their mothers, cut off from contact with the wider family, or being raised by grandparents, aunts, or cousins, cut off from their imprisoned mothers. Almost half the prison children had brief periods of separation from their mothers because of hospitalization or holiday visits with relatives.

In August 1950, the prison authorities ordered all children above two years of age to leave the prison: nearly half went into the care of foster parents; almost a third went into official institutions. Leaving prison was, for many, like leaving home, and many, when asked in the following months where they were from, replied: "From the Averoff prison." The state was minimally involved in the fostering process, which operated chiefly through parental initiative. The mothers tried hard to arrange for fostering because they feared that their children would be indoctrinated against them in the official institutions, and relied heavily on grandparents and other relatives.

For those children without a foster home, the first port of call was usually the Children's Shelter in Kifissia. This once-luxurious villa with hot water had been stripped of most of its furniture by the authorities and quickly ran out of funds, becoming overcrowded and dirty. Eventually conditions became intolerable, and the prison governess and the Red Cross persuaded Queen Frederika to admit the children into a home at Kalamaki. From there they were either collected by relatives or transferred to one or more of the Children's Villages that had been built by the Welfare Organization of Northern Greece in the late 1940s to house displaced children and others uprooted by the war and civil war. There were, by the end of the decade, more than fifty such Children's Villages, mostly on the outskirts of large towns; even today, eleven remain in operation.

Conditions inside these Villages in many ways resembled prison life, and there was the same rigid sense of a division between "inside" and "outside" worlds, separated usually by walls or guarded barbed-wire fences. They were run on quasi-military lines, often by former officers, who employed corporal punishment and made the children wear uniforms. Letters were censored, just like in prison, and the atmosphere was generally unfriendly. As in prison, there were no clocks or calendars, and the day was regulated by the ringing of a bell. The children were marched everywhere, even on occasional visits to the world outside, to the cinema or a local park.

Most teachers were indifferent or cruel to their charges, though there were some exceptions, and the atmosphere varied from place to place. Verria was "like a concentration camp," according to one former pupil, while Rhodes was far better, with greater and more positive contact between the school and local people. Athina, during her years in the Village in Kavalla, was allowed to attend a local secondary school and made friends with the other pupils there. In Larissa, the Apostle Paul's Children's Village had a well-designed and well-equipped primary school on the premises, as well as an unusually sympathetic principal. Here — in one or more of these Villages — the children received the bulk of their formal education, often even after their mothers were released from jail.

The return of children to their mothers was not automatic but depended upon the verdict of a supervisory committee. Thus, for example, on 27 August 1953, Mrs. Antonopoulou, a member of this committee, reported that Pepi E's mother had been released and was now working as a room cleaner in a hotel in Amaroussi while her husband was unemployed. Because their house had been destroyed, they did not want to return to their village, and they had received official permission for residence in Amaroussi. They asked for six months before taking their daughter back. "It would be better for the little E," advised Mrs. Antonopoulou, "to stay for this period to avoid distress and deprivation." Her advice was followed in this case, though not in that of little Georgios P., whose mother — now released — "is able to care for her son in her village (in Thrace) but leads an immoral life." Georgios was sent home, against the advice of Mrs. Antonopoulou, with a new set of clothes. Indeed, in most cases, the authorities seem to have been keen on reuniting children and mothers as quickly as possible.

The mothers' fears that their children would be indoctrinated while in official care were certainly not groundless. In most places they were subjected to twice-weekly "political education" and sang songs praising "our mother, sweet Queen Frederika, who saved us from the terrorists." The children were, on the one hand, told that their parents were criminals and traitors, and on the other, reassured that they were now under the beneficent protection of the royal family itself. "Our parents and their comrades, the former partisans, were portrayed as bandits, gangsters, traitors, killers," recalled Aris. "The queen and king were our caring parents. Both, especially the queen, visited the Village on many occasions with their children. I started almost to believe it and felt flattered by the idea that the king and queen were my parents." A child who was educated in the Larissa Village recollected how "the staff had stressed that all the pupils ought to be deeply grateful to the queen (Frederika) for her loving care and financial support for their upbringing and education." In Rhodes, where the children lodged in a former Italian army barracks, the inmates wore black on the death of King Paul.

This ideology of royal paternalism was not very successful in the long run, however. It was undermined by the many inadequacies of the environment of the Villages themselves, whose staffs were mostly untrained and unskilled in the arts of persuasion. It was not easy to feel loyalty to institutions that offered such limited educational opportunities and such hostility from those in positions of authority. Many children were, of course, influenced by what they were told. But more listened to older children and what *they* told them, and even those who did swallow the official line appear to have realized its biases soon after rejoining their families.

As soon as the mothers were released, they tried to rebuild their families, rejoining their husbands where that was possible and collecting their children either from the Villages or from foster parents. Most of the children were reunited with their mothers immediately upon the latters' release, having been separated for as much as ten years. The children's average age at this time was about ten. For only one-third of the prison children was their father at home at this time; for the rest, he was dead, missing, in prison, or in exile.

In every respect, reunion was an arduous and painful matter. Parents were strangers to each other, and often remained such. At first, many women could not help their thoughts returning to the prison, especially to their friends who were facing execution. The children often found it hard to regard these women as their mothers, and one mother sadly noted, "The word 'mother' did not exist for my children." Elli could not say "mother." Rea was initially called "communist" and "antipatriot" by her son, while Popi called her mother "granny." Thus while some remembered the moment of meeting as a joyful one, for others it was very painful. Many mothers felt grateful to their children for effectively saving their lives, but such feelings were not reciprocated. Many children had distanced themselves from the prison, and found that seeing their mother awakened disturbing memories. They were often reluctant to leave their foster parents, and even the institutions, where they had friends.

These strains were compounded by the difficulties that immediately faced the ex-prisoners as they tried to rebuild a normal life. Emerging from prison into poverty, they were kept under strict surveillance and reported regularly to the local police. They returned to burned homes and wasted fields, and the village in particular was generally a hostile environment where they could not escape the eye of the local gendarme or his associates. Neighbors and relatives had often plundered property and laid claim to land, necessitating costly lawsuits from the outset. As mostly husbandless leftists, these women were in a most vulnerable social position, dependent upon whoever would give them help and employment.

"I didn't even have a spoon to eat with. Nobody knocked at my door. I slaved night and day," was how one woman remembered the six to seven years she spent in the ruins of her burned-out house, before sending her daughters out of the village "to work like slaves in strangers' houses" as servants. Many of these women eked out a living in the fields, or collecting wood from the forests. Some could not leave their villages without permission. Others overcame the rural mistrust of city life and migrated to the towns — where a little more anonymity was possible. "Moving to Athens, where they were strangers amongst strangers in a strange place, helped them start a fresh life, free from social stigmatisation," Dalianis writes of one family. Job openings — as seamstresses, factory workers, hairdressers — were more plentiful in the city than in the countryside, but the women still experienced the harassment that was a constant factor in their lives. They were, in their words, "hunted" by the police and shadowed by their agents, as were their families. Emigration was one way to escape this surveillance, but it meant obtaining a passport, which was often refused them. A very few emigrated illegally.

Finding employment in the state sector was ruled out in these circumstances, as it was for almost all their children (and even grandchildren) right through the 1970s. Yet the great sacrifices that many of these mothers made for their children appear on the whole to have been rewarded. The latter, despite the obstacles placed in their path by the state, appear to have made highly successful careers in the private sector, often starting up small family businesses. As electricians, builders and engineers, businessmen and artists, they, too, profited from the booming postwar Greek economy, and made the transition to a largely urban lifestyle.

To Dalianis, one of the most important questions to be tackled concerned the psychological adaptation of the prison children in later life — their ability to form stable relationships and families. Expecting to research a history of trauma and phobia, she found instead a pattern of personal and psychic development that did not differ substantially from the Greek norm. In general, the children had turned into adults in good physical and mental health. To be sure, there were instances of phobia and trauma among both children and mothers. Some mothers suffered from persecution complexes, in one case to the extent of believing her son and fellow prisoners were traitors and police agents. One child, who had witnessed his mother being tortured by gendarmes, still lived in fear of policemen. Others feared dogs, the dark, and confined spaces. But these phenomena were not common, and although there were suicides and breakdowns, again the incidence of these was not higher than the national average.

The children were often late developers sexually, which was scarcely surprising given the attitudes toward sex on the part of the authorities in the Children's Villages, where girls suspected of sexual relations with boys were beaten and often expelled. Yet Greek society generally in the postwar years was still highly conservative in matters regarding sex education, and once again Dalianis's findings were that in later life, the prison children did not seem very different from the national norm in their behavior as marriage partners and parents.

Seeking to explain the absence of trauma, Dalianis focused upon what she saw as "protective factors." These included the affection lavished on the children when they were young by extended family — notably grandparents, whose role was vital — by godparents, and in the prison itself by the community of fellow prisoners. Many of the children also took pride in the cause for which their parents had suffered and in some cases died. They quickly abandoned, where they had accepted, what they had been told at school and identified themselves with their parents' struggle. Often this identification took a powerfully symbolic form through naming: the dead father, in particular, was idealized and immortalized by having his children named after him (often at his express wish). But even where this did not happen, many children idealized their fathers' memories and interpreted their deaths as sacrifice. Zoe, tyrannized by a right-wing teacher, was "proud of my [dead] father," who belonged to "the flower of youth."

This pride, however, coexisted with more complex and troubling feelings, especially toward the mother. Many children felt their lives had been blighted by their parents' political obsessions and resented this. Rita, who had as a child been separated from her mother for the best part of ten years, and who had moved seven times from one home to another, felt strongly on this score. She appreciated the great efforts her mother had made on her behalf, trying to keep the family together. Nevertheless, she told Dalianis: "I admired her ideology but hated the people in her party. They destroyed our family. I am convinced: I would never abandon my child for my ideals. I am absolutely certain: I would renounce my ideals for the sake of my child." Naturally, this kind of anger was felt especially keenly in the few cases where a child's choice of partner was vetoed by parents on political grounds. It was also hard to come to terms with loss where a parent's fate was uncertain, or where the father had emigrated and perhaps started a new family elsewhere. As a child, Hector had imagined his father as "a very strong, ideal man, a hero fighting for a better world"; later, as an adult, in contact with the father who lived in exile in Romania, his attitude became much more critical.

The mothers, for their part, were inclined to try and make up for the suffering they had brought on their children by lavishing love and material comfort on them. Yet it is difficult to see such behavior as unique to this group. The reaction against ideological commitment — not incompatible with pride in the part played by one's family during the 1940s — as well as the effort to make up for the deprivation of the war years with an abundance of love and material goods, were both important features of postwar social development in Greece, as in much of Europe.

Dalianis concludes by suggesting that a continuing mother-child relationship may be less vital than had previously been believed to a child's subsequent psychological health, especially if a strong bond is formed in the very first stages of the child's life, and if they are able to grow up later in a warm and loving community, such as had been provided by the fellow prisoners in the Averoff. But her research also points to the importance of belief, of how suffering at one stage of one's life is subsequently interpreted: by identifying themselves with their parents' struggle and idealizing their suffering, the children turned their past into a source of pride and affirmation. The contrast with the equivalent generation of Holocaust survivors and their children, for whom the idealization of suffering in this way is not possible, is striking. But Dalianis cautions that while her study illustrates the "human individual's enormous capacity to adapt," it should not lead us to ignore the "tremendous human price" the children paid. They felt "robbed of childhood and youth," and more than one felt simply that they had had "no childhood" and that "we didn't have a normal life." Leonidas felt bitter that "I was always restricted, never free to do or become what I wanted." On the other hand, it was difficult to say what was normal in this context, as many children retained positive and happy memories from their time in the Villages and even from the Averoff prison itself. It was, after all, outside of these institutions that their social marginalization had begun.

Solidarity with what we might call the community of the Left and its ideals bolstered many of these families through the postwar decades of exclusion, marginalization, and repression that were a lasting consequence of civil war. The socialist government's policy of national reconciliation in the early 1980s spoke directly to their concerns with success. But even before politics caught up, the extended family had proved itself indispensable in assisting recovery—at the individual, social, and economic level—from the traumas of the 1940s. Dramatic economic growth and urbanization also played their part. If most of Dalianis's mothers had been poorly educated village women, their grandchildren lived in cities and planned to go to secondary school, if not university, with the backing of their families. The result was that in less than four decades, the animosities of the civil war had receded much further from the forefront of people's minds and lives than anyone might have predicted at the time.

NOTES

1. This chapter was written by Mark Mazower, based entirely on the published and unpublished work of the late Mando Dalianis, and its unusual parentage warrants explanation. In 1994 Dalianis published a monograph entitled *Children in Turmoil during the Greek Civil War, 1946–49: Today's Adults* (Stockholm: Karolinska Institutet) that comprised a longitudinal psychiatric analysis of her research findings and a collection of family case histories. By the time of her death, two years later, she had also prepared several articles for publication (which have since appeared in *Thetis* and *Acta psychiatrica*). In July 1996, already gravely ill, she delivered the paper at Sussex University that forms the basis for this article. The following month, I spent a week at her home in Stockholm to discuss how we might collaborate. We agreed that I should present her findings and material in such a way as to bring them to the attention of historians, social scientists, and others who might not normally be expected to have access to her monograph. This chapter is the result, and readers interested in a more detailed account of her work can turn to her monograph. All quotations here are taken either from the monograph or from documents in Dalianis's possession. I would like to express my gratitude to Mando's husband Dimitri Dalianis, to their children, to Professor Per-Anders Rydelius of the Karolinska Institute, and to Professor Dimitri Ploumbidis of Athens University for their support.

2. T. Vervenioti, *I gynaika tis Antistasis. Ieisodos ton gynaikon stin Politiki* (Athens, 1994), gives the fullest account of how women's lives were changed by the war.

3. For life on Trikeri and in other womens' camps, there is a remarkable collection of photographs, V. Theodorou, ed., *Gynaikes exoristes sta stratopeda tou emfyliou: Chios, Trikeri, Makronisos, Aï-Stratis, 1948–1954* (Athens, 1996).

SIX

Left-Wing Women between Politics and Family

Tassoula Vervenioti

IT WAS DURING the German occupation that Greek women entered the public sphere en masse for the first time. Strange, perhaps, that war and a triple occupation could be associated with happiness and fulfillment, yet even today women members of EAM or the KKE feel that they acted as historical subjects and gained self-confidence, equality, and esteem through their resistance activity. Such feelings outweighed the everyday difficulties of those years. For teenage girls in particular, who had not yet completely accepted traditional gender roles, the radical spirit of the resistance and the difficulties of the struggle provided opportunities for initiatives and activities that had been unavailable in peacetime: women formed the majority of *Ethniki Allilengyi*, (EA: National Solidarity) and were crucial in the auxiliary services of ELAS. Young girls formed some 45 percent of EPON's strength in Thessaly, for instance, in the summer of 1944.

Just as periods of social upheaval and crisis often act as vehicles for the expansion of women's roles, so their ending forces women back into their "traditional" duties.[1] This process of forced domestication was especially painful in postwar Greece, for several reasons. First, the break with the past was particularly great because of the extent of female involvement with the resistance. Second, wartime resistance itself had been explicitly linked to demands for social reform, and the creation of a new society — People's Rule (*laokratia*) — in which there would be gender equality. Finally, the civil war sharpened a woman's basic dilemma, since in the late 1940s choosing between traditional gender roles or continuing the struggle for social liberation was often a life-or-death matter.

This study of the feelings, experiences, and decisions of women in the left-wing resistance is based upon a research project that has lasted for more than ten years. Over this time I have conducted more than 100 interviews with such women, who ranged from former senior Party figures to members of the rank and file. Despite their varied backgrounds and wartime experiences, all were persecuted after the war; seventeen were imprisoned, sixteen exiled, and four had experience of both. Nineteen fought in the civil war in the Democratic Army, while twenty stopped their political or resistance activity at some point during the civil war.

Many women with backgrounds on the Left were reluctant to be interviewed, claiming their activity was not important, or that other women had more meaningful testimony. Women who had held senior positions and had managed — usually with the help of relatives from the "other" side — not to be arrested did not like to talk about their experiences. One woman who had passed through the ELAS officers' training flatly refused to grant me an interview; it is likely that the reason was that subsequently she had married a man "of the Right." Marriage was, after all, often one way to avoid arrest. The more privileged might also escape through their studies or professional occupations. All these women had lived for years with the fear of having their resistance activity detected, and had tried to wipe out its traces. They were forced, many times in their lives, to repudiate their past. For them, the firing squad had aimed straight at their memories.

Women who continued as activists talked more easily. All speak very emotionally about their experience of collective action, for many the most memorable event of their lives. They talk about the festivals they organized, the plays they performed, how they taught the illiterate to read or prepared young girls for their university exams. All this they want to become known. On the other hand, they avoid — consciously or subconsciously — referring to the problems that emerged among them in prison or exile, regarding these as "private" matters. This is their way to protect the "honor" of "their own" people from the "others," the "outsiders." This concern with honor no doubt stems from the value system of the rural society that exerted such a decisive influence upon both EAM and Greece as a whole. During the war, the resistance and its leading party (KKE) had gained "honor" that they had to preserve carefully, not least by hiding internal differences or tensions from outside eyes. Refusing to defend himself against false charges emanating from the Party for which he had worked for so long, Nikos Ploumbidis insisted that "the honor of the Party is above my personal honor."[2]

After their defeat, EAM/KKE activists lived for decades in an utterly hostile environment. They could not criticize their own leadership, nor even mention a comrade's petty failings, since this might be considered as harming the movement — in the words of the time, "putting water into the mill of reaction." Hence these fighters tried to preserve a perfectly unified image of themselves, an increasingly idealized memory constructed largely inside prisons or in exile, which became *the* memory of their youth and bravery. This even today constitutes the "official" memory of the Left.[3]

As time passed, especially after 1989, and following a series of public ruptures within the Greek Left, some dared to confess—even to the tape recorder—that not all of them were heroes. They mention the painful breaks in exile, the quarrels in prison, the strain of living up to the exalted ideals of heroism they themselves shared. But their words falter: "I don't know. I don't remember. I was young and didn't understand." Probably they do not want to recall that people were executed without having the chance to make their farewells, simply because the Party had decreed it. They prefer to remember the heroic Stathoula, who danced around the palm tree before her execution.

To some extent these problems can be overcome if one knows the right way to raise such difficult matters. At the time, people did not talk freely, after all, about sensitive subjects like love affairs or Party business; they relied upon a kind of jargon in which love is "a feeling," a noncommunist is termed "uncoloured," the Party's decision is simply "the line," while someone who had fallen into official disfavor had been "hit."

But as oral historians have come to expect, what is often most striking are the gaps and lacunae in even the most detailed memory accounts. For members of the Democratic Army, for instance, the civil war years often overshadowed memories of the wartime resistance. Sometimes this reflects tragic incidents they lived and want to forget, whether a rape or a violation of their principles. Above all, combatants tried to see themselves as victims or heroes, not as human beings who enjoy their lives, fail, hesitate, or even on occasion feel fear. One woman confessed to me that when she was transferred from a camp to Athens for her court martial, she managed in the ten-hour journey to delete from her memory every recollection of the years 1946–1948 in order that others should not be imprisoned because of her. She succeeded so well that even today she can hardly remember faces or events of that period. Another woman told me the Party's "line" was that "when they arrest you, you should not even exist. Best not even to say your name. Because if you start talking you will say everything. Get 'amnesia.' It's the best defense." This defense lasted approximately thirty years.[4]

Women of the Left belonged not only to the Party, but also to their family. Before the war, nobody disputed that a woman's place was in the home, and that her destiny was to marry and to bring up children. The male family members' chief duty was to arrange for the marriage of a daughter or sister. The prerequisite for a good marriage was a hard-working, healthy, modest, and above all "moral and honorable" girl. Her morality and honor depended upon her virginity and the absence of any kind of relations with men outside the family. The latter were off limits to married women, too, who otherwise might be considered "dis-

Women members of the Democratic Army of Greece, western Macedonia, 1948.
Reproduced by kind permission of the estate of Nancy Crawshaw.

honored," "immoral," and "a disgrace to the honour of their family."
Father, brother, and husband had to "protect" a woman's "honor" — by
controlling her time and space — since her purity affected their own
honor and that of the family.[5]

The economic and social changes that had begun between the wars
and accelerated after 1941 breached this ideology of the patriarchal family. The loss of property either in the city — because of famine or the black
market — or in the countryside — because of antiguerrilla reprisals —
together with a more general uncertainty about the future, all weakened
the role of the family. Dowries were lost, and with them the prospect of
a traditional marriage settlement. The inability of males to protect their
womenfolk also weakened their control over them. This was one of the

factors that allowed women to be "organized" in the resistance and to enter the public sphere.

Meanwhile, the resistance itself—for reasons of its own organizational growth and ideology—came to encompass some of the functions formerly attributed to the family. The honor of EAM or the KKE depended on the moral behavior of its members. For the *andartes* of ELAS, who were the basic defenders of the nation's honor, any love affair was forbidden, even glancing at, still more walking with, a woman. Inside the political organization, things were less strict, though relationships there, too, were under the control of the leadership. It is true that in the resistance there was considerably more gender equality than in the traditional family. Even today, women generally believe that in EAM or the KKE there was no discrimination between men and women. Partly because they believed this, they felt an especially deep loyalty to "the organization."

Everything functioned smoothly so long as Party and family kept pace with each other. But when forced to choose between the two, KKE cadres faced a terrible and confusing dilemma. On 29 January 1948, a sixteen-year-old girl from Crete was arrested and exiled with her mother to the islands of Ikaria, Trikeri, and Makronisos. Grandmothers and a younger sibling were left at home. Early in 1950, she met her father on Makronisos: "And my father came and said to me: 'My child, listen to me. We have struggled. We gave whatever we had and it was worth giving. We are defeated for the moment. We are not the leaders and we can't stay here. We must go back. You are a small kid. Your mother and I can't go home and leave you here. Please help me.'" After being tortured, she eventually signed a *dilosi* (declaration of repentance). "That was one of the most tragic moments of my life. . . . For one month I didn't get out of bed at Makronisos. My nightgown was pink and it turned black. I did not even want to wash myself or change my clothes. I suffered a mental breakdown." Even today she feels she betrayed herself and her beliefs: "When I came back I joined the underground organization and married a man from Makronisos. . . . Another victim, this one. He had gone insane. When he left he was a sick man."[6]

Those who did not sign a *dilosi* are tortured by feelings of guilt for the suffering they caused their families: "I'll never get rid of the feeling of guilt toward my father. My brother was in England. His two girls were in prison. He would read the newspapers and say: 'Now they will kill them.' He felt he had been weak. . . . Things like that. And he went crazy."[7]

The KKE considered the signing of the *dilosi*—even when it was the result of intolerable tortures—not only as a violation of its principles but as a source of great shame. The fact that Aris Velouchiotis, like many other wartime activists, had "repented" during the Metaxas years was used against him when he deviated from the Party line in the summer of 1945. That earlier generation of repentees was the subject of intense discussion within the Party during 1945, and that autumn a new Party constitution prohibited them from membership. Thereafter, a party cadre who signed automatically put himself out of the Party; where married to another Party member, the spouse was expected to denounce and divorce the expelled member, or be expelled as well. Party loyalty, in other words, was supposed to override any intimacy between a man and a woman. There are several known instances where an imprisoned wife of a Party member signed a *dilosi* because she feared otherwise losing contact with her children; she thereby kept the children but was "isolated" by the Party and often repudiated by her spouse.[8]

The repentee was a traitor, not only for members or followers of the KKE, but for political opponents as well. Changing sides did not save someone from social stigma; after all, no one trusted someone who had betrayed his or her own people. Hence, repentees feel ashamed of admitting what they did, even today. A woman who signed in order to keep her job confessed to me after we turned off the tape recorder: "I felt so humiliated. Tired."[9]

Reflecting the powerful role the family played in society, and in people's minds, one of the major characteristics of the government's "emergency measures" was the reassertion of the family's collective responsibility in law. This applied to the entire postwar legal system from the reactivated 1871 brigandage law to the 1948 loyalty oath (AN 516/8.1.48). Familial collective responsibility stretched to the "certificates of social morality," used since the Metaxas dictatorship, which one had to present for the issuing of a passport, a driving license, or entry into the university.[10]

The doctrine of collective family responsibility led to "preventive" arrests of relatives of *andartes*. This was such a common practice that the writ that was issued summoning Democratic Army members to court martial stated: "And at home were no other relatives by blood or marriage to the third degree, older than sixteen years, neither children nor parents, nor brothers." Sometimes, when only an old and illiterate woman was to be found at home, the priest or village council president received the writ. In the village of Kokkinoplos near Elassona, no relatives at all could be found for fourteen defendants. The ones who were finally arrested were mainly women. They refused to sign a *dilosi* as requested, not because they were Party members (not all were) but because signing implied a betrayal of their own people and submission to the "others." "It was like giving them bullets to kill our own people," I was told by a woman from a village outside Lamia. An Athenian woman of intellectual background put it very similarly: "Your submission symbolized the submission of the group you belonged to. It was a matter of dignity for us. A matter of honor."[11]

For the Left, the collective responsibility of the family had a different meaning, and opened up a new route to political engagement for some women. The woman as mother was a highly respected figure in society, and in the resistance itself mothers had enjoyed the right to speak at EPON conferences, sharing and participating in their children's struggle. If her children were male, a woman's position was unimpeachable. In the late 1940s, mothers, sisters, and wives of imprisoned men played an important role in protesting state repression of the Left, in publicizing what was happening on Makronisos, and eventually in getting it closed down and executions stopped.

Their first effective intervention took place in June 1949 at the trial of sixteen EPON members. When news came via the prison information network in Athens that three of the defendants faced imminent execution, one of the mothers threw herself in front of the military commander's car and the execution was postponed. Later, a group of mothers used the Soviet news agency and Soviet diplomats to publicize their plight in the United Nations and mobilize international support. They dressed in black and attended the mass trials, keeping vigil outside Parliament and, on one occasion, storming the prime minister's office to beg for clemency.

In October 1950 a group of women formalized such involvement by founding PEOPEF (Panhellenic Union of Families of Political Exiles and Prisoners), which agitated effectively despite police harassment on behalf of leftists in prison. The extent to which PEOPEF was itself a KKE initiative as opposed to a grass-roots movement is not yet clear, though the Party was evidently used to mobilizing such movements, as indeed it had done during the war itself. Yet what made it possible for the women of PEOPEF to act was the fact that they were defending their own families — and by extension *the* Greek family — something that constrained their opponents and to some extent ensured their respect. In the words of a 1952 PEOPEF brochure: "Into that atmosphere of terror, defying the dangers and threats, the Mother raised her voice." Thus the president of the court martial that tried the PEOPEF leadership itself in May 1951 termed their organization's work as "sacred, national, patriotic, and Christian" before acquitting the defendants. These women were on the streets, in the public sphere, because they were fulfilling their duty toward their families.[12]

Beyond the honor of the family and the Party was the honor of the nation. In the civil war, love of homeland and the desire to preserve its honor was professed by both sides. Signing a *dilosi* was, in the eyes of the state, the guarantee of a suspect's *ethnikofrosini*, or "national-mindedness." EAM activists found it hard to accept the reversal demanded of them. I wondered why. "We had done our duty and gone unselfishly into the mountains to fight the occupiers,'" wrote the chief medical officer of the ELAS Tenth Division, later chief medical officer in the Democratic Army.[13]

Yet their opponents accused them, as communists, of having no homeland, of not believing in God, and of wanting to dissolve the family. Such accusations were not new, but they were sharpened by the civil war. Right-wing bands taunted leftists after the Varkiza Agreement with the slogan "Moscow-Sofia is your dream": Communists were neither Greeks nor patriots. When the minister of justice introduced the law outlawing the KKE, he contrasted the "Hellenes' fighting for the salvation of their *patrida*" with their opponents, "deniers of *patrida*, family and religion."[14]

A twenty-two-year old girl from a village near Volos, an *andartissa* in the DSE (Democratic Army) since 1947, was arrested in May 1948 and detained in a camp near Larissa. Her older brother was also in the DSE; her younger brother was back in the village with her mother. In her confession to the court martial in 1949, she called her own brother a "bandit" (*symmoriti*) and agreed that she had been unwillingly recruited and had voluntarily surrendered to the army. In 1951, from jail, she renounced the "bandits" and claimed that they had threatened her with "physical and psychological violence" and that her only aim was "to surrender to the National forces and to return to my Homeland and my family. . . . I'm Greek and will remain Greek." She was then released.[15]

The concept of *ethnikofrosini* meant not only defense of the country but defense of traditional Greek values as well. For women it meant a return to domesticity and submission to the rules of the patriarchal family. While men of the Left were identified with Greece's northern neighbors and called *eamovoulgari* (EAMoBulgarians), women were called not only "Bulgarians" but "whores," too. The woman who cared about things outside her home was considered "a woman of the street," a "public" woman, or in plain Greek, a "prostitute." Military judges referred to them in such terms. The title *synagonistria* (fellow-combatant) — an honorary term of address throughout the resistance — became a synonym for a woman of "loose morals." A right-wing song claimed that *andartisses* had sexual relationships with many men and did not know who fathered their children. Unmarried women in the ranks of the DSE who were captured had to undergo a gynecological exam to prove their virginity. More generally, the presence of women on the political scene threatened the whole concept of *ethnikofrosini*: such women were not merely traitors; they were also a "shame" for the nation and their families.[16]

The effort to bring resistance women back to their traditional duties involved not only propaganda but also raw violence. Men tortured women and realized their sexual fantasies on women's powerless bodies. Right-wing bands and men in the gendarmerie and the army raped left-wing women because they regarded them as already "dishonored" and beneath contempt. The teacher Pepi K. said she was raped while unconscious: "Then the sergeant who was watching [the rape] brought me to the cell and threw me in a corner. I asked him for a blanket. He said he didn't have one. I was begging for water but what he brought me was salty." One should also note that the ideological attitude of the Left itself was not very different: when referring to rapes, as in the 1947 DSE memorandum to United Nations investigators, the authors often used the term "dishonored" as a synonym for rape.[17]

As in Liberation France, women were also punished and made the subject of public ridicule by having their hair cut. Normally village women did not cut their hair but plaited it. Wearing short hair was a city fashion and was connected with emancipation and uncertain morality. During the war, ELAS punished women accused of sexual relationships with the occupiers in the same way. Antonios, the Metropolitan of Ilia, stated that ELAS, which, "as an austere guardian of our national honour, imposed moral order on society," used this method and regarded it as "a great achievement of our *andartes*." One leading Party cadre listed among the five achievements of the armed struggle that the "haircut" stopped "the tide of Greek prostitution with the occupiers."[18]

After the war ended, opinions as to which women were prostitutes changed. The "haircut" entered song, and opponents of left-wing women chanted at any who dared to walk the streets: "Old-time comrade, you who know so much, I'll come in the night to cut your hair." In the cities they used razors, in the countryside, scissors or knives. "I was beaten and had my hair cut. . . . Three girls from my village: me, another *andartissa*, and another who was not an *andartissa*, but a member of EPON. They had two scissors and cut the hair of one with a knife. She was badly hurt.[19]

Whether to continue or to end their involvement in politics after the war was over was for most women of the Left not an easy or deliberate decision. Only a few of the more educated ones, with clearly formed views, usually political activists, made the decision to go on. Yet most women did not want to go home because they had developed a taste for social participation and had come to visualize the outlines of a "new society." In the first period of civil war, they tried to combine participation in the struggle for social liberation with their personal and domestic interests. But events complicated matters.

During the occupation, the KKE demanded that its members sacrifice their immediate personal interests for the sake of the collective whole. The young, who made up the majority of the movement, had disciplined themselves and their personal emotions. The slogan of the time was: "It is not the time for all this. When the war is over. . . ." They hoped to be able to act on these accumulated and suppressed desires at Liberation. But when the moment finally arrived, "there was an anxiety. . . . You could understand that something was wrong. . . . We had expected a day of celebration that would change everything, that would give power to the People to that they would be able to shape their lives in their own way. . . . And out of all these high expectations, the only thing that actually happened was agony and participation in endless demonstrations until December came." The Varkiza Agreement did not alter this disappointment.[20]

Marriage was complicated because of high unemployment and economic difficulties. Because affairs outside marriage were socially reprehensible, the Party pressed for their legalization via a swift engagement. Some couples did get married, but found the acute housing shortage did not allow them to have their own house; they stayed with their parents and remained active in the Party.

After Varkiza, two main movements of population took place. One was from the countryside to the cities, where the greater anonymity and the illusion of legality attracted people. This was an option open to men and young unmarried women; married women in rural areas had to stay at home and care for children, parents, and their fields. The other movement was toward the mountains. Increasingly, as right-wing repression increased, men who had been involved with the resistance could not sleep at home. Eventually entire families went "to the Mountain" with as many of their belongings as they could carry. These constant population shifts eroded family relations and introduced uncertainty, instability, and separation. Together with economic distress, these shifts made a return to normal social life all but impossible, especially after the March 1946 elections legitimized the rule of the Right and the civil conflict escalated. Women faced the old dilemma more starkly than ever: Should they continue the struggle for social change — a vision slowly fading — or pursue happiness in their personal lives? Should they continue to act in the public sphere or stay at home like "good women"?[21]

Many were soon living in a state of semi-legality, especially with the outlawing of the Communist Party in December 1947. At any moment, a woman might be arrested, be court-martialed, or face exile, execution, or flight to the mountains. The first woman to be executed in the history of modern Greece was a teacher named Mirka Ginova, otherwise known as Irini Gini, a Slavomacedonian and thus, according to the patriotic logic of the time, a likely "unpatriotic element." She was one of twelve executed in July 1946.[22]

The number of women in prison or in island camps grew rapidly between 1946 and 1949, as the state haphazardly presided over a nationwide system of incarceration. All inmates faced pressure to sign repentances not only from the state but also from their own relatives. Husbands threatened to divorce their wives if they did not sign, and some divorces actually happened. Relatives emphasized the difficulty of looking after a woman's children, while unmarried girls were told not to spoil their youth or were urged to think about their parents. Women in the island camps faced additional strain since the administrative decision on their detention was reviewed every year. If in some ways these women had a freedom of movement denied to prison inmates, they were still allowed less freedom than their male counterparts, and had also to endure Party-imposed restrictions upon their movements and behavior. Male comrades inside as well as outside remained guardians of "their" womens' morality.

In April 1949, 1,200 women exiles were transferred from Ikaria and Chios to a monastery on the deserted island of Trikeri, already in use as a detention center for women held under preventive custody. Ships brought more women from western Macedonia and Epiros as well as young DSE *andartisses*. By the autumn there were some 4,700 people on the island, including children. Under the overall administration of Makronisos, the women's camp was renamed the Special School for the Reeducation of Women (ESAG), and some 1,300 women and children were sent to Makronisos itself.[23]

As stories about the reality of the Makronisos reeducation camp filtered out into the Greek and international press, shocking public opinion and creating embarrassment for the government, the inmates started gradually to be sent home under "temporary release papers." George Papandreou, the deputy prime minister, announced that women would no longer be held on Makronisos, and in July 1950, 500 women—each having refused to sign a *dilosi*—were shipped back to Trikeri, where some spent several more years.[24]

As bad as exile and prison were, worst of all was living in clandestinity. Those living underground in cities saw flight "to the Mountain" as salvation, but this salvation was closed to many women, not only because passage out of urban areas was difficult, but also because in order to leave they needed the Party's permission, which was relatively rarely granted to women. In 1948, however, the DSE started to recruit women as well, mostly from villages or towns in areas it controlled. Women in these areas had three choices: they could join the DSE, flee home at the first opportunity, or surrender to the government forces.

Because choices were generally made under pressure, the difference between a willing and an unwilling volunteer was often obscure. Maria Ferla, a wartime *andartissa* captain, married KKE cadre Georgoulas Beikos in 1945 and decided against further involvement in "the movement." But when her husband and her brother got arrested, she arranged to escape to the mountains. In 1947 she joined the DSE, despite having originally wished to be a housewife. In fact, there were many married women in the DSE: a woman joined either with her husband or after his enrollment, murder, or arrest. Some women brought their children with them; others left them with relatives. Many women partisans who gave birth during the civil war left their children and returned to the ranks.[25]

The partisans of the DSE in some ways saw themselves as the successors to ELAS. They believed that following the Germans, they were fighting against "new occupiers," the English and the Americans, who were propping up the "monarcho-fascist government." There were no separate women's combat units, as there had been in ELAS. On the other hand, the DSE partisans began a women's newspaper — *Machitria* — in August 1948, and organized a separate women's union that remained in existence even after the defeat of the Democratic Army. In theory, each unit had a woman officer entitled "assistant to the political commissars," and there were meetings of women cadres.

Living conditions for the women partisans were extremely harsh, especially after the spring of 1949. They walked continuously through the night across the mountain paths and in this way helped demolish the myth of female weakness, not least in their own minds. Fueled by a combination of pride ("A woman is capable of everything. I couldn't believe how capable I was!") and fear of how they might be treated by their opponents, they fought on, dreaming of home: "Once we were sitting and talking about what we would like to have," recalled Maria Venetsanopoulou. "One was saying: Ah, if only I had a good pie. Another wanted a roast lamb. I said I wanted a door handle. To open the door and go inside. They burst out laughing. Maria has gone crazy, they said. I missed home badly."[26]

The ending of the civil war brought that dream of domesticity closer to most women, but the reality turned out to be a domesticity beset with enormous political and economic hardships, especially for women of the Left. The younger ones tried to continue their studies, but encountered new obstacles: "I went to take the exams in 1945. I was good in maths but failed composition. The topic was 'What are the ideals of the new generation?' I wrote about EPON and was failed. . . . In 1946–47 I went back to high school. . . . In the end I never managed to take my certificate. I was exiled and when I returned I needed thirty drachmas for the stamp, which I didn't have. I didn't take it and I didn't need it. Everything was barred to us. All doors were barred."[27]

Doors were often barred to relatives, too. Anyone hiring someone from a left-wing family was pressured by the authorities to dismiss them. Katina, a midwife and nurse, made endless efforts to find a job: "We were like lepers. Nobody spoke to me. I did not have a job. I did not even have money to buy coffee for my mother. I starved! Do you understand? And then I felt the greatest misery in my life. Because outside [in exile] we may have suffered, we were beaten but we talked to each other and it was fun. There I was by myself. . . . It was an internal exile." She never returned to the Party, nor did she find a husband.

Sasa and Kyriakos married in July 1944. They lived in semi-legality until 1947, when Kyriakos went to the mountains. Sasa was in prison from 1948 to 1960. Kyriakos was arrested after returning from the hills and also imprisoned until 1960. They then faced the problem of children. "I told him times had changed. How could we have a child? He agreed with me. I did not dare to have a baby." In 1967 Kyriakos was again arrested. When the couple was reunited in 1972, it was too late for children.

Many women who suffered imprisonment or exile complain that they spent the best years of their life without enjoying life's pleasures, and above all that they have never enjoyed love. "I left jail when I was thirty years old, and my entire love life consisted of one kiss that one of my comrades once gave me." The heroine of *The Wedding Gift* by Victoria Theodorou says: "I longed to have four walls of my own, the body of another and love, whose lack tortured me for years and threw me into painful fantasies." When she decides to get married, she goes to her teacher, who has just been released from jail, and asks her advice. "You have to understand that they had arranged everything to bring you to this point. To break you down and make you crave a bedroom and kitchen, a red flannel gown and a pair of mules. . . . Deceitful men, how well they have arranged everything. . . . Resist one more time." But the heroine does not resist. She gives up her studies, marries, has two children, and goes into debt to build a house, where "I spent a second exile."[28]

It was tragic to realize that "when the Movement was defeated, the comrades became masters again. Yesterday's brothers-in-arms became simply men." Women have many such complaints about their Party comrades: "He had a different mentality, he was one of those primitive communists, who regarded happiness as a sin. . . . He didn't dare to say the word 'love,' the words 'I love you.' One time he said 'My Maria'; when he said the word 'my,' I asked him what he meant and he told me he hadn't meant anything."[29]

Mothers found they were criticized for the harmful impact of their political activities on their families. Their children, who had been sent to orphanages under the aegis of the queen during the civil war, returned home, and many found it hard not to judge their own parents: "My older daughter, most of all, puts the blame on me and says: 'What were you? I would never leave my kid for any Party. Do you understand?'"[30]

Meanwhile, the political struggle for women's rights inevitably took another path. In the light of the outcome of the civil war, it would not be the Left that would take the crucial steps toward granting those rights and liberties necessary for gender equality. In the late 1940s, the prospects for gaining such rights did not, in any event, seem good. Upholding an ideology of traditional patriarchal values, the victorious postwar state — despite its democratic pretensions — was very slow to grant women the vote and refused to modify the family law code introduced under Metaxas. Nor did it face much pressure from below: prewar womens' organizations had never enjoyed large memberships. On the Left, relations between feminists and the KKE had been competitive and antagonistic. Their mutual mistrust had been only partly overcome in the 1930s, when the rise of fascism and the Comintern's new Popular Front strategy allowed female communists to cooperate with "bourgeois" feminists of the League for the Rights of Women.

Female activism on the Left shrank in scope and numbers as certain limitations and contradictions in the Communist Party's approach to womens' issues became clearer. After Varkiza, the KKE tried to attract women in two ways. First, it tried to get more to enter the Party, and second, it wanted to infiltrate ostensibly neutral or nonpolitical organizations. In October 1945, Party secretary Nikos Zahariadis stated, "We still need more women in the Party to tidy us up." The Party agreed to appoint women cadres and to aim for a major increase in the number of women members. When the target was not achieved, Chrysa Chadzivasileiou, a member of the Politburo, remarked revealingly that this was due not to "eternal" objective circumstances but to the fact that even the (male) communists were "slaves of medieval perceptions about women."[31]

As part of its strategy outside the Party, womens' unions started mushrooming all over Greece, drawing membership especially from women who had participated in EAM and adopting as their key demand the right to vote. But this kind of mobilization, which culminated in the formation of a Panhellenic Union of Women in 1946, was cut short by the burgeoning civil war, which allowed the state to use anti-communism as a reason for dissolving womens' groups. Right-wing women, most notably Lina Tsaldaris, the widow of former conservative prime minister Panagis Tsaldaris, became increasingly prominent and influential in the suffrage debate.[32]

Right-wing governments did not seem enthusiastic about granting women the vote. In 1949 women won the right to vote in municipal or local elections, but only if they were above the age of twenty-five, perhaps to exclude precisely that politicized generation which had played such an important part in the resistance. In fact, Parliament required two years to ratify even this limited concession. But then, once the local elections of March 1951 dissolved fears of the radicalism of a female electorate, progress was surprisingly swift, and the 1952 constitution granted women the right to vote in national elections: in early 1953, a by-election in Thessaloniki led to Greece's first female deputy, Eleni Skoura, taking her seat. Three years later, as women voted in national elections for the first time, Lina Tsaldaris headed the conservative list in Athens and became the first-ever woman minister, in charge of the Ministry of Social Welfare. Was this not perhaps the final irony, that women of the Left, forced back into an unwelcome domesticity, increasingly disenchanted by the Party for which they had sacrificed so much, were now forced to watch as women of the Right made their own entry onto the national political stage?

NOTES

1. L. Rupp, *Mobilising Women for War: German and American Propaganda, 1939–1945* (Princeton, 1978), 3–7; M. R. Higonnet and P. Higonnet, "The Double Helix," in M. R. Higonnet, ed., *Behind the Lines: Gender and the Two World Wars* (New Haven, 1987), 31–47

2. See Adamantia Pollis, "Political Implications of the Modern Greek Concept of Self," in *British Journal of Sociology*, 16 (March 1965): 32–33; J. K. Campbell, "Traditional Values and Continuities in Greek Society," in R. Clogg, ed., *Greece in the 1980s* (London, 1983), 186; J. du Boulay, "Lies, Mockery and Family Integrity," in I. G. Peristiany, ed., *Mediterranean Family Structures* (Cambridge, 1976), 397, 405. On Ploumbidis, see D. Papachristou, *Nikos Ploumbidis: Engrafa* (Athens, 1997), 97.

3. J. Hart (*New Voices in the Nation: Women and the Greek Resistance, 1941–1964* [Ithaca, N.Y., 1996]), by interviewing mostly well-known activists, basically reproduces the "official" memory of the Left, but makes a number of basic errors of fact, asserting, for instance (pp. 95, 135–37, 212) that the structure of EAM included women's organizations (on which see more below).

4. For an extensive analysis of the problems of memory for this generation,

see the concluding chapters of Riki van Boeschoten, *Anapoda chronia: Syllogiki mnimi kai istoria sto Ziaka Grevenon (1900–1950)* (Athens, 1997). Interviews with Ioanna Sotirakou, 7 June 1996; Katina Karra-Eleftheriou, 28 Aug. 1989.

5. E. Friedl, *Vasilika, a Village in Modern Greece* (New York, 1962), 56; N. Skouteri-Didasakalou, *Anthropologika kai to gynaikeio zitima* (Athens, 1984), 202; I. Georgakas, "Messiniaka ethima: Erevna," in *Archive of Private Law*, vol. H' (1941): 181.

6. Interview with S.R., 5 June 1997.

7. Interview with M.K., 30 May 1995.

8. The whole subject of the *dilosi* remains to be explored; see also Chapter Four above. For the debate within the KKE in 1945, see P. Roussos, "Koinoniki synthesi kai diafotisi ton melon," *Kommounistiki Epitheorisi* [KOM.EP] (Aug. 1945): 8–11; idem, "To katastatiko tou KKE," *KOM.EP* (Sept. 1945): 14–18; also Zisi Zografos, "To KKE kai oi diloseis. Xekatharizomeno to Komma dynamonei," *KOM.Ep* (Sept. 1945): 19–22.

9. Interview with K.X., 20 July 1994.

10. N. Alivizatos, *Oi politikoi thesmoi se krisi, 1922–1974* (Athens, 1983), esp. 487–497.

11. Larissa Criminal Court brief 14/1952, unclassified.

12. See Maria Karra, *Emeis oi apexo. PEOPEF 1948–1954. Mia mikri epopoiia* (Athens, 1994), 49–50; O. Papadouka, *Kentrikai gynaikeiai fylakai Averof* (Athens, 1981), 90–92; D. Kousidou and S. Stavropoulos, *Aristeri neolaia Hellados, 1950–1953* (Athens, 1993), 550–83; interview with Maria Karra, 9 Sept. 1988. The archive of PEOPEF is held as part of the EDA archive at ASKI (Archive of Contemporary Social History) in Athens.

13. E. Sakellariou, *Diathesame ti zoi mas* (Thessaloniki, 1991).

14. Alivizatos, *Oi politikoi thesmoi*, 181–90, 511–23.

15. Larissa Criminal Court brief 16/1952, unclassified.

16. *Tragoudia tis Antistasi kai tou emfyliou* (Athens, 1975; reprint), 93–94.

17. *Rizospastis*, 28 Dec. 1946; see P. Rodakis and B. Grammenos, eds., *Etsi archise o emfylios. I tromokratia meta ti Varkiza, 1945–1947. To ypomnima tou DSE ston OHE ton Martio tou 1947* (Athens, 1987).

18. See T. Vervenioti, *I gynaika tis Antistasi. I eisodos ton gynaikon stin Politiki* (Athens, 1994), 144–52.

19. Interviews with Allegra Felous-Skifti, 21 June 1995; Maria Venetsanopoulou, 16 Feb. 1993.

20. Interview with P.H., 1 Mar. 1995.

21. See A. Laiou, "Population Movements in the Greek Countryside during the Civil War," in L. Baerentzen, J. Iatrides, and O. Smith, eds., *Studies in the History of the Greek Civil War, 1945–1949,* (Copenhagen, 1987).

22. Alivizatos, *Oi politikoi thesmoi*, 389, 496–511. According to one source, courts martial sentenced 7,800 people to death, of whom 5,000 were executed; see G. Katiforis, *I nomothesia ton varvaron* (Athens, 1975), 31–64. KKE General Secretary Zahariadis made a speech in Thessaloniki (12 April 1946) in which he accused the government of planning a massive wave of repression against the Slavo-Macedonians: "I katastasi sti notioanatoliki evropi kai i thesi tis Elladas," *KOM.EP* (May 1946): 207–11

23. R. Koundouros, *I asfaleia tou kathestotos: Politikoi kratoumenoi, ektopiseis kai taxeis stin Ellada, 1924–1974* (Athens, 1978); V. Theodorou, ed., *Stratopeda gynaikon* (Athens, 1976); M. Mastroleon-Zerva, *Exoristes* (Athens, 1985).

24. K. Hariati-Sismani, *Chios-Trikeri-Makronisos-Trikeri, 1948–1952* (Athens, 1977); Theorodou, ed., *Gynaikes exoristes sta stratopeda tou emfyliou: Chios, Trikeri, Makronisos, Aï Stratis, 1948–1954* (Athens, 1996).

25. Interviews with Maria Beikou, 13 Mar. 1990, 28 June 1995, 3 July 1995, 26 Oct. 1995; Vasso Skopidou, 2 June 1995.

26. Interview with Katina Latifi, 25 Sept. 1995; Roula Koukoulou, 20 Sept. 1995; Vera Foteva, 18 Apr. 1996; Theodora Zikou, 8 Apr. 1992; Maria Venetsanopoulou, 16 Feb. 1993.

27. Interview with Elissavet Theodoridou-Sozopoulou, 2–3 May 1990; Chrysa Krania, 22 June 1995.

28. Interviews with Anthoula Stavropoulou-Christakea, 26 Dec. 1995, 14 May 1996, 16 May 1996; V. Theodorou, *Gamilio Doro* (Athens, 1995), 20–21.

29. Interview with Eleni Kamoulakou, 18 June 1987, with K.M., 9 Sept. 1988.

30. Interview with T.L., 9 Sept. 1988.

31. KKE, *To 7o Synedrio tou KKE* (Athens, 1945); C. Chadzivasileiou, "I panelladaki kommatiki syskepsi gynaikon," *KOM.EP* (Mar. 1946): 117.

32. L. Tsaldari, *Ethnikai, Koinonikai, Politikai Prospatheiai* 2 vols. (Athens, 1967).

SEVEN

The Impossible Return: Coping with Separation and the Reconstruction of Memory in the Wake of the Civil War

Riki van Boeschoten

"WE LEFT for three days and returned after thirty years". This catch-phrase summarizes much of the postwar experience of the inhabitants of Ziakas, a village in the mountains of northern Greece — husbands and wives living apart for decades, children growing up without their parents, feelings of estrangement poisoning the happy reunion of beloved ones, the difficult survival of those who stayed behind amidst the scattered ruins of the material and social body of their village. These are the realities that they have in mind when they speak about their past and that have shaped their vision of it. For them, as for many other mountain villagers of northern Greece, the war in a sense never ended. The "unruly years" of the 1940s are with them forever.

Ziakas was one of the many so-called little Moscows of wartime Greece — villages that linked their fate to the Left through their participation in the resistance and their support of the Democratic Army in the civil war. Before the war, Ziakas was a community of poor but self-sufficient smallholders and transhumant shepherds, marked by its egalitarian social structure and a great degree of cohesion. The village was located in the foothills of the northern Pindus range, in the valley of the Venetikos River, west of the market town of Grevena. Amidst open fields, scrub hills, and oak trees, its one- or two-story stone houses looked toward the valley with the rocky formations of Mount Orliakas in the background. A mule track coming from the city of Grevena crossed the village and then continued toward the Vlach villages higher up in the mountains, or toward Epirus (Metsovo, Zagoria, Ioannina). The journey to Grevena used to take about five hours on foot. The community of Ziakas also included the tiny village of Perivolaki, with 100 inhabitants, which was hidden in the forest, at a distance of about one hour on foot. This village could be reached only by a steep mountain track. In all, the community had about 1,100 inhabitants in 1940.

In 1948 depopulation on an unprecedented scale occurred when about 90 percent of the villagers left the country and were settled in

Musicians, western Macedonia, Spring 1947. Reproduced by kind permission of the estate of Nancy Crawshaw.

eastern Europe. The majority of these political refugees returned to Greece only in the 1980s, but most then settled in the towns, where their children found jobs. Many visit the village now only during summer holidays. The few inhabitants that stayed behind after 1948 lived through the postwar period as the remnants of a mutilated social body, isolated from their kin behind the "Iron Curtain."

Under these circumstances it is problematic to speak of the reestablishment of family and communal life, for the community was never reconstituted as it was before the war. After Liberation in 1944, the ensuing civil war deregulated the norms of family and communal life and disrupted even the physical sense of community, with the village destroyed and its inhabitants dispersed all over the globe. And yet fifty years later, both the community and the family have clearly survived the disruptive forces of this postwar odyssey, both as social institutions and as loci of social memory. As I hope to show in this chapter, this is the result not only of specific actions or events, but also of ongoing mental processes, conscious or not: the elaboration of coping mechanisms and survival strategies, the symbolic reconstruction of points of reference, and the structuring of past experience into a collective memory, continually updated in terms of the present.

The most tangible signs of these processes are recorded oral testimonies. Important though they are, they represent only the tip of the iceberg, the top layer of subsequent reworked versions of the past inscribed on the palimpsest of memory. Can we ever hope to unearth lower levels, at present hidden from sight, and reconstruct the whole process of memory structuring? Here we stumble right away on two of the major methodological problems confronting any scholar who ventures into less conventional ways of "doing history": the tricky nature of memory and the slippery, though challenging, field of subjectivity. And yet, if we want to get at these deeper social and mental processes, the tools of traditional historiography are insufficient. The use of oral testimonies and an anthropological reading of data offer an enormous potential for a changed perspective. They are in fact a necessary counterpart to research based on documentary evidence. How can we, as historians, reconstruct past "realities," without taking into account the hopes and fears of historical agents, their interpretations, which served as guidelines for their actions, or their views of the past in the present?

I shall come back to these methodological issues in due course. Here I just want to stress that a sensitive and careful analysis of this kind of material can open up new historical insights. The advantage of a micro-historical perspective is that it offers the possibility for a Geertzian "thick description" of complex sociocultural processes that interact with the historical environment and help to determine the course of events, while remaining out of focus in most traditional historical work.

I started my work in the village of Ziakas in 1987, just after I had completed earlier research, which dealt with the ideology of partisan songs. For the next nine years I visited the village for a few months every year and collected interviews (eighty in all) with all age groups, male and female, both in the village and in neighboring villages. This effort was supplemented by documentary research and anthropological fieldwork. The time covered in the interviews spans from 1900 until today and, in terms of people, three generations. As work progressed and I began to formulate my first hypotheses, I received a considerable amount of feedback from interviewees, some of whom actively cooperated in the production of a book with oral testimonies.[1] The long duration of the research proved to have unexpected advantages. It was precisely during the research period that the different branches of the collective memory came together and engaged in a new memory-structuring process. As a result, I did not have to make any particular effort to learn about the community's past, which was a topic of daily conversation. Moreover, I was able to follow day by day and year by year the whole process of memory structuring, including the gradual integration of the refugees in mainstream Greece and the effect of major events, such as the breakdown of "real socialism," which until then, in spite of it all, had served as a point of reference.

If we want to understand how the people of Ziakas tried to cope with the fragmentation of their families, we should first uncover some of the basic aspects of their domestic environment. What were the nature and social role of the family before the war? How were normal family relations affected by the abnormal circumstances of the war? How have the people of Ziakas reacted to outward impulses in the past, and how did they interact inside the community? What were the social and cultural attitudes informing their actions?

As elsewhere in southern Europe, family relations played an important role: emotionally, socially and at the level of production. As a highly endogamous village, most families were in some way related to each other, providing each family with a network of relatives on whom they could rely. In view of the absence of dependent labor relations, all labor was shared by the members of one household, whereas in peak periods people resorted to the exchange of labor, preferably among relatives. The system of kinship was that prevailing in continental Greece: bilateral with agnatic bias, virilocal residence, and partible inheritance.[2] In the 1930s the most common form of household was the cohabitation of two or more married brothers with their offspring. Under this system, women and children had very little to say. Women were extremely vulnerable, as they had no property of their own. Therefore a widow usually remarried soon after her husband's death. More important than the system itself, however, is the way it was lived and interpreted in daily interactions. If we compare, for example, the social practices of Ziakas with those of the Sarakatsani, a pastoral community on the same mountain range with a structurally similar kinship system and economy, it appears that both communities had a different habitus, which had developed as a response to outside pressures and inspired the beliefs and actions of their inhabitants. Rigidity of social norms protected the nomad Sarakatsani from a hostile environment and confined relations of trust and friendship within the inner core of its social structure, the family, linking kinsmen by bonds of categorical obligations. This closed and corporate society forms a striking contrast with the flexibility of social norms in Ziakas and the group cohesiveness of its inhabitants, where loyalty, trust, and cooperation were not restricted to kinsmen alone, but extended also to unrelated families. In Ziakas, social relations were ruled by pragmatism, the principle of reciprocity (exchange of favors), and the avoidance of conflict. Violations of the socially accepted rules of behavior (e.g., premarital sex) were tolerated to some extent and did not call for exclusion or severe punishment. This particular habitus based on cooperation, flexibility, cohesion, and pragmatism developed partly as a response to the strains of the 1930s, when the village was drawn into a market economy. It facilitated the acceptance of new ideas and practices, and it mitigated some of the worst effects of the civil war.

The massive participation of the villagers in the resistance organizations of EAM/ELAS and in the institutions of local self-government brought about major changes in the family itself and in its relation to the community. Adolescents and women acquired voices of their own and relative autonomy of action. Both groups greeted this change with great enthusiasm.

> We liked those meetings, they attracted us. That's why we used to go there. We wanted to stop being ordered about by men, "Get up, sit down!." Because men were then like a kind of dictatorship![3]

> At first some parents did not want us to have mixed meetings of EPON, they feared the girls would be "led astray." People then had rather puritan views. But there was nothing to fear: each boy had his own sisters in the organization. And so the parents got used to the idea. And we worked together, boys and girls. Every Sunday there was a meeting of EPON, followed by a feast. That's why I remember that period as the best time of my life.[4]

The second important change was the broadening of the public sphere, not only because women and adolescents participated in public activities, but also because the collectivity was endowed with competence over issues formerly settled in private. In the public hearings of the "People's Court," matters such as adultery, parental authority, inheritance, and even wife-battering were openly debated and decided upon. Thus the social control of moral issues shifted from the family to the village square. The emancipation of women and adolescents was a radical break with the past, and as such it is remembered, whereas the expansion of the public sphere built upon and was facilitated by the close ties that had always existed between the family and the community. The structure of the collective memory, in which these changes occupy a significant place, points to a major and lasting shift in the social frame of reference.[5]

This period of expansion and social stimulation was followed, in the civil war, by a period of contraction and enclosure. The village was gradually cut off from contacts with the town and with neighboring villages, which were evacuated by the National Army in 1947, and its fate was increasingly linked to that of the Democratic Army. Adult men went into hiding to escape the violence of right-wing bands. From 1947 onward, the village remained practically without men: most had joined the guerrillas or had been drafted into the National Army. Many were killed or captured and sent to jail. Women and children had to bear alone, amidst heavy fighting and bombardments, the double burden of ensuring the survival of their own families and providing material support to the guerrillas.

The last phase of the civil war was what led to the final disintegration of the village and its physical destruction. In the spring of 1948 most of the children, about 300 of them, were evacuated to eastern Europe by the partisans. The transhumant shepherds, who had spent the winter on the Thessalian plains, were not allowed to return to the village and remained in Thessaly until 1951. In the summer the rest of the villagers followed the partisans to Mount Grammos and into Albania. On their way, many women were forcibly recruited into the Democratic Army. In the autumn of 1949 the remaining refugees were sent into eastern Europe. Only about 10 percent of the villagers stayed behind: these were the shepherds who had found themselves in Thessaly, those who were in jail or serving in the National Army, and some individuals who fled to the town or got lost on their way to the border. As a result, nearly all the families were divided, not only by the Iron Curtain, but also inside eastern Europe itself. Refugees were spread around eastern Europe according to the availability of housing and the labor needs of the host country. Reuniting families was only a secondary consideration, taken into account only after hard pressure from the refugees. All the decisions on this matter were made by the Greek Communist Party (KKE), in cooperation with the Communist Party of the host country. With increasing bitterness, the people of Ziakas realized that the Party they had fought and died for had turned into a bureaucratic mechanism that had divided their community and families. In the powerful words of one woman, a party activist during the civil war, the Party cadres "carried along their briefcases and did not care for people." In the first years of exile, correspondence with Greece was strictly forbidden. In defiance of this rule, some established contact through relatives in America, the only way to find out the fates of their loved ones. The reunion of married couples inside eastern Europe was achieved within a few years, but those divided by the Iron Curtain lived apart for decades, or were separated forever.

Most children were sent to Czechoslovakia, where they were settled in luxury buildings, former residences of the local aristocracy turned into boarding schools. But these homes were often far from their parents' residences. Many children were settled in a different country from their parents. Mothers who had arrived with their children were strongly "advised" to put them into the homes. The reasons given for these measures were that the children would be able to complete their educations while women would be free to take part in the production process.

COPING MECHANISMS

The tragic consequences of this separation for people's personal lives are more than evident from individual biographies. Here are a few examples. "Spiros" had been engaged for nine years when he left for Tashkend with the other partisans. His fiancée stayed behind. When he heard she had married, he decided to marry another woman. Many years later, when he learned his fiancée had not married after all, but had been waiting for him, he became ill with cancer and died shortly afterwards.

"Kostas" had been captured and jailed, while his wife had joined the Democratic Army and ended up in Poland. They corresponded with each other until 1977, when his wife finally managed to return to Greece. When she died only five years later, his grief was so unbearable that he wanted to commit suicide. He found the courage to live on only by writing a poem to her memory.

"Maria" faced a crucial dilemma when she found herself in Albania in 1949: either to accompany her child to Czechoslovakia or to follow her husband to Tashkent. She decided to do the latter. When she was at last reunited with her child, the child did not recognize her as a mother: she had become a stranger.

"Eleni" left with her two children, leaving her husband and her elder son behind. Although she received many proposals, she refused to live with another man, out of respect for her husband, who had never treated her badly. When she finally returned to Greece, her husband had just passed away.

How can people resume their daily lives, when the recent past has thoroughly shaken or destroyed the very foundations of their identities? How can they preserve those identities against the odds of separation? How can they reconstruct their families, when the traditional role of the family has been completely deregulated? In his seminal work on the influence of calamities upon human society, the Russian sociologist Pitirim Sorokin compared the social texture of communities affected by a major calamity to a "tattered spider's web," in which "old loyalties and social ties are either weakened or destroyed, and new ones not yet established." Under these circumstances, human behavior becomes "form-

less, chaotic, uncontrolled by any clear-cut norms, increasingly dependent upon casual external circumstances." Few societies, however, are
completely destroyed. In fact, calamities can also form a favorable
ground for the emergence of new social forms. Society then becomes
like "half-melted wax, out of which anything can be moulded." In
which direction this reconstruction will go depends to a large extent
on the preexisting culture of the society in question. Referring more in
particular to the effects of war, Sorokin pointed to the existence of two
opposed coping mechanisms: either an egoistic stimulus of self-preserva-
tion gains the upper hand, or a social stimulus directed toward the preservation of or loyalty to the community does. Drawing on a vast literature concerning human history since ancient times, he suggested that the
second response is more likely to occur when the society in question has
a well-integrated system of values that are neither limited to material
aspects nor rooted only in ideology, but also are based on conduct. This
definition corresponds more or less to the concept of habitus, as out-
lined by Pierre Bourdieu.[6]

When the people of Ziakas tried to cope with the disastrous effects of
the civil war, the second, community-directed, response prevailed. The
specific habitus that they had elaborated during the interwar era and
that had ruled their social relations was an important factor in molding
their individual and collective reactions. In the aftermath of the civil
war, when they found themselves shattered and dispersed, they set
about reconstructing their families and community, their personal and
collective identities. In doing so, they resorted to the tools that were
available to them: the same habitus, but enriched and diversified by the
experience of the civil war, as well as new coping mechanisms that they
invented in order to integrate entirely new experiences into their lives.
In fact, the setting was no longer a self-sufficient face-to-face community. Both in Greece and in eastern Europe, a third factor interposed
itself between the community and individual families. In Greece it was
the postwar, anticommunist state and its institutions, in eastern Europe
the Stalinist regime with the Greek Communist Party as its intermediary.

One of the consequences of long-term separation was the appearance
of extramarital alliances. Under certain conditions this form of cohabitation was no longer viewed as adultery, but as a kind of "provisional
marriage," justified by the conditions of exile. This flexibility with respect to prewar moral standards was rooted both in the community's
habitus and in the legacy of the civil war. The tolerance of extramarital
alliances was favored first of all by traditional pragmatism, according to
which the natural condition for a man or woman is to live with an
individual of the opposite sex. A second factor was the practice of informal marriages among partisans, which had developed with the massive

recruitment of women partisans in the last phase of the civil war: "If a partisan fell in love with a girl, he would take her as his wife. You would send in a written application to the brigade, to Bartziotas, to those big ones. And they would give you this piece of paper and that was it."[7] Finally, the dispersion of local communities and their integration into a new social structure had slackened the social control of sexual relations. However, social control was not abolished altogether; rather, it took a different form. A new moral code was established, centered on the provisional yet semi-permanent nature of the refugees' settlement in the host country. These new moral standards defined as illicit both unstable, occasional relations and permanent relations that were contracted without the knowledge of the legal partners in Greece. The implicit condition was that if and when return to Greece became possible, each of the provisional marriage partners would return to his or her legal partner. To avoid complications, contraception was used to prevent the birth of any children. However, this rule was not always observed, with all the tragic consequences this implied. Sometimes a pregnancy was deliberately provoked by one of the partners to avoid separation. Needless to say, many of these "illegal" partners spent more time with each other than with their legal partners, and the second separation was often more painful than the first one.

Another form of social control was the Party meeting, in which personal relations were often a matter of public debate. During meetings of the local Party organization, people could be called to account for their personal behavior, or even face public outcry. To some extent, the moral standards of the Party coincided with the moral code elaborated by the refugees themselves, but those standards were less easily accepted, because they were imposed from above. On the other hand, the fear of public contempt operated as an inhibiting factor preventing the involvement in "illicit relations" (e.g., sexual partnership with a married man or woman, or with more than one partner at a time). An extremely painful episode for these veteran resistance fighters in their relation to the Party was the process of "reassessment of Party membership," known as *anakatagrafi*, which took place in the early 1950s. Each Party member had to stand up in the Party meeting and declare in public who his parents were, his social background, to whom he had been engaged, and who his present partner was, and consequently the local Party branch would decide if he was worthy to continue being a member of the Party or if instead he should be expelled.

For many refugees, if not for most, however, the reestablishment of family life did not imply the establishment of new relations, but took rather the form of a symbolic reconstruction. Their choice to lead a single life was part of a survival strategy that they had adopted already during the civil war. They tried to cope with the deregulation of the social texture by insisting on the cohesion of the family and, implicitly, of the community. They tried to reunite family members scattered around eastern Europe. They tried to stick together and continue their traditional activities and practices (for example, they preferred to work in agriculture instead of in industry, despite lower wages; they continued traditional matchmaking and marriage strategies and observed local customs and holidays). And finally, they insisted in elaborating their own version of their history, their collective memory, in which the concept of cohesion forms the leading thread.

In many cases these efforts implied conflicts with the Party leadership, and often a final break with the Party. For rank-and-file Party members, family matters played an important role in these conflicts. They were embittered, for example, by the long delays often involved in bringing back children to their parents' country of residence, or by a refusal to allow travel to other eastern countries to join family members, visit sick relatives, or attend a parent's funeral.

Back home, for the fifty-odd people who were left in Ziakas, out of a thousand before the war, the symbolic reconstruction of the family went hand-in-hand with that of the community. This is best exemplified by a moving ritual these who remained continued for many years whenever a letter arrived from abroad. The whole village gathered at the belfry, and the letter was read out in turns by members of the audience, amidst sobbing, laughter, exclamations of surprise.

> We took the letter and started to read. Resurrection, they are alive! And it took six months for the letter to arrive. We couldn't read the letter, we were weeping, as we were standing there at the belfry. When we received a letter then, we used to read it aloud for the whole village to hear. We continued that practice for many years, we had great joy, it was an event. So we started to read, I couldn't, I was weeping, then another one tried, he was weeping too, then it was Vangelis's turn, he was illiterate, and there we were four men weeping. It was a real resurrection.[8]

How did the children cope with separation? They were less distressed by it than might have been expected. The fate of the child refugees has been a highly sensitive issue, both sides accusing each other of snatching away children against their parents' will.[9] The story of these children, in their own voices, looks very different from the public discourse of either side. Their memories present a "private image," leaving room for doubts and fears, and are less influenced by the social precepts they would have acquired later on in life. According to this story, the children were not objects, but subjects with their own will. Most children wanted to leave for abroad and some even left in secret, against the will of their parents.

> We left with the children and, as for me, I had decided to leave in secret, I wanted to leave by my own will. I was about fourteen by then. I heard the children would go there to be educated, and I did not want to stay behind. I had loved learning since I was a little boy and for so many years we couldn't go to school. And I organized quite a lot of children, whose parents wouldn't let them go, so they could leave in secret. My father didn't want to let me go, because he wanted me here to look after the flock, but I had decided to leave.[10]

Among the reasons that induced the children to leave were of course hunger and fear of the war, but also the desire not to be separated from the other children, to escape a shepherd's life and to be educated. These attitudes were rooted in the experiences of the war period: the emergence of the young as a peer group, their increased autonomy and responsibilities in the support of the guerrillas and the survival of their families. The children's response also reflected the community's culture: they displayed the same sense of cohesion as the adults, but focused on their own age group.

A surprising fact that came out of the interviews was that most children did not refer spontaneously to feelings of grief over the separation from their parents, and when questioned they said that this was not their main concern. This image forms a striking contrast with most Cold War literature, the best-known example being *Eleni* by Nicholas Gage. In the words of one boy: "We got used to living without our parents and my mother was like a stranger to me. She used to weep and beg, but it took a long time before I was able to come back to her. Something had happened in my inner self in those years." Among the more apparent reasons for this behavior, one might mention their continued involvement with their peer group, the excitement of new experiences, and the improvement of their standard of living compared to what it was in the village (many used the word "paradise" to describe it).

On the other hand, the more sensitive children especially were profoundly disoriented by the terror of the civil war and the uprooting of their traditional way of life. The absence of norms in their formative years have marked them forever. This is expressed in the interviews by repeated remarks such as, "I did not know what was right and what was wrong," or, "I was only a little child." In such moments, the absence of their parents was extremely painful. Yet most missed their parents only later in life, usually at crucial moments of their career.

The separation of the child refugees from their families had one more important consequence: they were cut off from the ongoing process of memory-structuring — an issue to which I shall return. Many took part in the structuring of the collective memory only after they had returned to Greece as adults. In the process, many myths they had lived by were destroyed, while new ones emerged.

Methodological Issues

In the discussion of the evidence so far, there is a clear subtext that refers to the more general methodological issues raised by the kind of approach I have adopted in this inquiry. It seems appropriate to reflect further on some of these issues and to draw some general conclusions. A major point I want to make is the importance of culture. I have stressed the multiple ways in which sociocultural attitudes and practices of the past, as well as the experiences of the war period, shaped the inhabitants' reactions to their new situation. The concept of habitus, launched by Pierre Bourdieu, is extremely useful in research that explores the intersection of objectivity and subjectivity As a set of predispositions shaping attitudes, evaluations, and actions, as a kind of hidden second nature or "forgotten history," the concept of habitus can fill the gap between the conscious experiences expressed in the praxis — which is a fairly accessible area of investigation — and the more volatile underlying structures of subjectivity. Used in this way, it can help to avoid the pitfalls of arbitrary interpretations of the subjective level. Another implication of my analysis is that the habitus is not static, but is itself subject to change. This is not always evident from Bourdieu's work, which focuses on the present. I have tried to show how the survival strategies of the villagers were rooted both in their prewar habitus and in the experiences of the civil war, which modified and updated that habitus in the light of new conditions. Finally, both the old and the new habitus shaped the space in which new responses could be invented.[11]

Husbands and wives separated by the Iron Curtain resorted to two different tactics to cope with separation. One option was the material reconstruction of family life by engagement in provisional yet semipermanent extramarital alliances. The second option was a symbolic reconstruction by insistence on the cohesion of an individual's family and community. There was a symbolic dimension in the first option, too. To avoid complete deregulation of the social texture, it kept intact the original family in a symbolic way by inventing a new moral code centered on the provisional nature of the new partnership. The children who were separated from their parents by their early evacuation to eastern Europe and their subsequent settlement in children's homes adopted yet another survival strategy. They replaced the cohesion of their original family with the cohesion of their peer group, and they tried to take advantage of the new opportunities offered by the educational system of the host country, without, however, severing their ties with their family and community. All three groups continued the symbolic reconstruction of their family and community throughout the years of exile in two additional ways: by resisting those aspects of the Stalinist regime that kept them divided, and by elaborating their own collective memory.

Though the importance of cultural patterns and practical attitudes might be easily acknowledged, it leaves unanswered the question of how to discover such attitudes in the past. One of the answers I have given is to resort to the tools of anthropology. But is retrospective anthropology really possible in historical research? Luisa Passerini, the leading Italian oral historian who introduced the issue of subjectivity as a potential for oral history in her classic study of the Turin working class under fascism, doubted whether this was possible at all and suggested that oral historians should complement their interviews with written primary sources. She did so herself with great success, using, among others sources, police reports. Her doubt stems from the historian's inability to make use of the classic tool of anthropology, participant observation, in order to distinguish between personal opinions and social values on the one hand, and actual behavior on the other.[12]

Yet the preconditions for retrospective anthropology vary according to the target group, and, as I discovered during the research in Ziakas, its potential is enhanced in a micro-historical project. First of all, in a small community, it is possible to investigate, through participant observation, those aspects of the sociocultural environment that have survived the erosive forces of time and social change. Second, by cross-checking information from different informants, it is possible to distinguish between practices and attitudes that belong to a shared culture and those that are related to individual experiences. This does not mean, however, that this "shared culture" has always been there. This is a major problem that presents itself in a different form in relation to the "archaeology of memory" that I discuss later on. I solved this problem in part by paying particular attention to "unintentional messages." When people tell a story, they usually want to make a particular point, and their narration is tailored to that effect. But in the flow of narration, casual remarks are often made that have never been part of the narrator's effort to make sense of his world, because they belong to the doxa (another term borrowed from Bourdieu), the obvious implications of his daily life that need no further comment. These casual remarks can thus reveal past behavior in a rather "innocent" way, because they are not influenced by later interpretations. They may also point to preexisting underlying mental structures, which can be considered as "markers" of the community's culture. The habitus of the people of Ziakas was revealed to me mainly by such remarks, which were often made in private and unrecorded conversation. For example, much of the evidence about prewar flexible attitudes, the exchange of favors, reconciliation practices during the civil war, and extramarital alliances was presented as self-evident facts of life to a knowledgeable audience (the researcher or co-villagers), but was not necessarily mentioned in the recorded interviews. Needless to say, such qualitative information can hardly be found in documentary evidence. And yet it is from such material that a "thick description" of the community can be constructed in a much similar (though less immediate) way, as in research done by anthropologists in a contemporary setting.

Another important tool was the comparison of oral witnesses with official discourse. In this I was led by another important insight I gained from Jan Vansina, namely the distinction between a public and private image: "People in many cultures tend to create two portraits of themselves. One is a mask or a public image built up in terms of roles and statuses, values and principles—the noble mask of themselves. The other portrait is much less often limned and reveals traces of doubt and fear as quite contradictory experiences are remembered." Vansina stressed the reliability of such data, especially when they run counter to fashion and do not conform to ideal types. In my research this was the case in particular with the private memories of women and children. Women presented themselves neither as heroes nor as victims, as they appear in the coeval literature of left-wing organizations, but more as "heroes in spite of themselves." Though they obviously enjoyed some of the new rights they acquired during the resistance and adopted patterns of behavior previously considered as male, they also stressed the overwhelming feelings of fear and disorientation and the multiple ways in which they tried to cope. The private image of children, stressing their relative autonomy and the concept of peer group, forms a striking contrast both with the Cold War literature and with the official discourse of the communist leadership.[13]

THE ARCHAEOLOGY OF MEMORY

The elaboration of collective memory is a long-term, never-ending process, which starts with the initial (conscious or subconscious) encoding of experiences, as they happen. These initial messages are then modified, updated, or erased from memory, as people try to integrate new experiences and to make sense, privately or in conversation, of their past in terms of the present. One might argue that it is impossible to determine in any way what people thought and felt fifty years ago, because their original memory is modified by later experiences. My research showed, however, some ways of getting around this difficult problem. In the first place, people sometimes refer explicitly to the "hindsight effect," by making a clear distinction between what they believed then and now. It is also very useful to look at age cohorts and at social frames of reference, instead of analyzing the oral witnesses as an undifferentiated whole. This approach gives a better insight into the different layers of social memory, but also into the processes of lasting social change. For example, in the general economy of the interviews, the memory of the resistance has been occluded by that of the civil war. However, people who were then in their teens or early twenties retained an extremely vivid memory of the resistance period, which seems to reflect the initial layer of memory. I explained this by pointing out that their participation in the resistance coincided with their emancipation from parental authority, which has marked their personal lives thereafter. If this is true, then the important place these experiences occupy in their memory indicates a turning point in the social frame of reference at the very moment when these experiences were inscribed in the memory. As a result, these particular memories were "frozen" more or less in their original forms.[14] The same is true, to some extent, for women. Their emancipation from male authority during the resistance marked a break with the past and changed their social frame of reference. Their memories of this period were reinforced by later experiences both during the civil war and during the years of exile.

Obviously, things are more difficult when later events contradict earlier experiences and have modified or "silenced" related memories in a more permanent way. This is the case, for example, with the negative experiences the villagers had with the communist leadership in eastern Europe. In many instances, these experiences "covered up" the initial enthusiasm, which had resulted in the massive recruitment of villagers to the Communist Party. In such cases, the analysis of other primary sources is extremely useful, and a necessary counterpart to an interpretation based only on present oral witnesses. But "covered-up" memories can leave their traces in present discourse and pop up unexpectedly—either because the cognitive patterns on which they were based have survived in latent memory and, when they come to the surface through the act of narration, contradict the narrator's present views; or because former views have led to actions, which can be recalled more easily. Finally, these latent memories can be reactivated when the factors that led to their suppression cease to exist.

A sensitive analysis of the available material can exploit all these possibilities to improve insight into the archaeology of memory. On the other hand, the liabilities of memory can be turned into a virtue, by concentrating on present memories and trying to understand how people cope with the crumbling of their hopes and expectations and what role this particular past plays in their present lives.

COLLECTIVE MEMORY IN THE PRESENT

For some of the returned refugees, young and old, past experiences and the demystification that accompanied their return resulted in unbearable psychological stress, unstable personal relations, and even suicide. Yet since the 1980s, a new, more balanced view of the recent past is emerging, a precondition for the villagers' integration into modern Greece. The collective memory is playing a crucial role in this process of reconstruction by blending its three branches into a unifying, yet not uniform, whole: the memory of adult refugees, the memory of the children, and the memory of those who stayed behind.

Although they are based on a common layer of experiences and initial interpretations, postwar experiences have affected the transformation of memories in different ways. If we want to understand the present process of reconstruction, it is necessary to take a quick look at what these postwar experiences were and how they affected the articulation of the collective memory in its three components. There is one point, however, that the reader should keep in mind: for all three branches of the collective memory, the civil war operated as an "interpretative turning point." According to Gabriele Rosenthal's definition, these are "biographical turning points which lead to a reinterpretation of the past, the present and the future." This happens when certain events in a person's life acquire a new and fuller significance and are consequently reinterpreted in the light of later developments. In other words, people could not remember the resistance period as if the civil war had never happened. The last interpretative turning point in an individual's or a community's life has immediate bearings on its present worldviews and should therefore be considered as a "threshold to the present." For most inhabitants of Ziakas, the civil war is such a threshold to the present. It is exactly for this reason that they refer to it as if it happened yesterday.[15]

The memory of the people that stayed behind has been deeply marked by the persecution they experienced as former resistance fighters in the postwar period. When the traditional structure of the village economy broke down, many settled in urban centers, especially in the area of their winter pastures (Tirnavo, Larissa). As it was extremely difficult to find a permanent job without a "loyalty certificate" (*pistopiitiko kinonikon fronimaton*), some emigrated to Sweden, Germany, or the United States. These postwar hardships were experienced as a continuation of the right-wing violence that started after the Varkiza Agreement in early

1945. The resistance and the vision of social change it embodied remained a positive pole of reference, but its memory remained for many years in a more or less "frozen" state, as it was too dangerous to speak about it in public. Yet to repudiate that past would imply the denial of personal involvement in the resistance, and disavow relatives killed in the civil war or living abroad. Moreover, those who stayed had no direct experience of the Stalinist practices experienced by their relatives in eastern Europe, and whenever they were told of specific incidents, they found them difficult to believe. Thus, until the 1980s, the abstract idea of socialism also remained a positive pole of reference.

The adult refugees, on the other hand, experienced a second "interpretative turning point": they reinterpreted the civil war in the light of "real socialism." Their life in the "fatherland of socialism" had both positive and negative aspects. On the one hand, they found unprecedented levels of material prosperity, with respect to both their lives in the village before the war and the living conditions of their relatives in Greece. On the other hand, the daily conflicts with the leadership of the Greek Communist Party prevented them from identifying the positive aspects of "real socialism" with the Communist Party. As they did not have a global vision of the phenomenon of Stalinism, the vision of socialism remained in suspension, defined by both its negative and its positive poles, until the breakdown of the Berlin Wall. For both groups, the memory of the resistance period, with its emphasis on self-rule, local autonomy, and direct democracy, remained a valid alternative model for society, different both from the postwar regime in Greece and from the Stalinist model in eastern Europe.

The third branch of the collective memory is fragmentary. The child refugees, growing up without their parents, were cut off from family and community memories. Their own private memories only gave a partial account of events. For many years they had but sporadic opportunities to speak with their relatives about what had happened in the village, while being constantly exposed to the public version of history, as it was transmitted by their teachers. This latter version was centered on the legacy of Greece, especially of ancient Greece, and the struggle for democracy. As a consequence, these children grew up with many unanswered questions about their recent past. Moreover, the idealization of Greece did not prepare them for the difficult process of adaptation after their repatriation to a fatherland they did not recognize. Most of these children connected to the collective memory of their parents, when they were already in their forties and had established their own families. At that point of their life cycle, the reconnection with the past was no longer a top priority.

After the repatriation of the political refugees in the 1980s, these three branches of the collective memory started to interact and to blend. The most important effect of this process was the integration of the experiences of the refugees into the memories of those who had stayed behind. As a result, this latter group experienced in its turn a belated "second interpretative point," through which its members came to see the civil war in the light not only of their own postwar experiences, but also of the experiences of their co-villagers under "real socialism." To put it more bluntly, the stories they were told about arbitrary decisions by Party cadres, about the problems encountered in the reunification of families, and about the repression of dissidents could no longer be waved away as "anticommunist propaganda." The recognition of this fact facilitated the reconnection of these later experiences with earlier examples of Stalinist practices they had lived with in the civil war, or even during the resistance. As a result, their memories of the civil war, previously dominated by their treatment as second-rate citizens by the postwar regime, became more balanced. This process smoothed the way to their integration as full citizens into the modern Greek nation-state.

There were other factors that contributed to the same effect. These factors were of both an internal and an external nature. In fact, the present recomposition of the collective memory is taking place in a new setting. The scale of interaction is no longer the small face-to-face community in which communication is dominated by oral discourse. Under their new living conditions, the people of Ziakas are directly exposed to the influence of national and international events and to "public history." Their children live in urban centers as modern citizens, every home is directly connected to the outside world through television, and for the first time in the community's history, patron-client relations have begun to play a role in people's lives. Among the global events that are affecting the collective memory, one should mention in particular the official recognition of the resistance by the PASOK government (1982), the breakdown of the former socialist bloc (1989), and the emergence of nationalism around the Macedonian issue (1991–1992). The available space prevents a full discussion of these factors, so I shall concentrate on the first, which is also the most important. The official recognition of the resistance implied a positive reevaluation of left-wing resistance fighters who fought in the ranks of EAM/ELAS. It also involved moral as well as material rewards (the granting of resistance "certificates," state pensions, and the recognition of pension rights for former refugees). These measures took away much of the bitterness these resistance fighters had felt ever since 1945 over the fact that they had been chased down as common criminals soley for resisting the national enemy. This development enhanced the process of integration of this group into Greek society, which had started immediately after the fall of the junta. It also facilitated the process of reconciliation between the two camps, which had been divided since the Cold War era. However, the kind of consensual public history that has emerged from this process presents the war period as a "national liberation struggle," glossing over social and ethnic cleavages, the social message of EAM, and the entire civil war. The "national reconciliation" that is emerging from this form of "useful history" can only be a very superficial one.

In the case of Ziakas, this sanitized version of recent history has only a marginal hold over the collective memory. The social message of EAM, and in particular its model of social change, continues to operate as a central point of reference, not only with respect to the past, but also for the present. The experiences of the inhabitants in the modern state — the alienation of citizens from the process of decision-making, growing inequalities, the overwhelming power of Athens-based central authorities — reinforce the memory of an alternative model of social organization, which they had tested in practice and found satisfactory.[16] Their memory of the resistance recognizes the existence of social conflicts, some of which were at the root of the civil war. They cannot "forget" the civil war, precisely because it still operates as a "threshold to the present." Their memory of this period has become less "black and white," and especially less black, than it used to be. On the contrary, the people of Ziakas are trying to draw some positive lessons that can allow them to come to terms with their past and to pick up the threads that were broken in 1948. The preservation of the community's cohesion and the local practices of cooperation among political opponents under the strained circumstances of civil strife have reinforced feelings of collective identity and local belonging and have paved the way for a more substantial reconciliation with their former enemies. It is mainly for this reason that the memory of the civil war has not been covered up, blocked out, or replaced by a more innocent "screen memory." The collective memory of the civil war is extremely painful, but not unbearable, because there has been no total breakdown of traditional practices and values. The recognition of this fact and the creative way in which the people of Ziakas are trying to come to terms with their past are essential preconditions for a real reconciliation. In this respect, the case of Ziakas might set an example for Greek society at large, in which the public history of the war period hampers rather than enhances the prospects for such reconciliation.

NOTES

1. See R. van Boeschoten, *Anapoda chronia: Syllogiki mnimi kai istoria sto Ziaka Grevenon (1900–1950)* (Athens, 1997).

2. This refers to a kinship system in which the individual gives priority to relatives on his father's side of the family, where newly-wed couples take up residence at the husband's home, and the family property is equally divided among the sons at the father's death. For a description of this system, see J. Campbell, *Honour, Family and Patronage* (Oxford, 1964).

3. Interview with Soultana Boubari, b. 1920, member of the women's organization of EAM in Ziakas, 1 Sept. 1988.

4. Interview with Nikos Papanikolaou, b. 1925, secretary of the youth organization EPON in Ziakas, 16 July 1988.

5. Unfortunately, documentary evidence on the real-life practices of village courts is extremely scarce. For some exceptions, see Mazower, *Inside Hitler's Greece* (New Haven and London, 1993), 273; Th. Tsouparopoulos, *Oi laikoi thesmoi tis ethnikis antistasis* (Athens, 1989), 235–61. The operation of People's Justice in Ziakas is described in some detail in van Boeschoten, *Anapoda chronia*, ch. 4.

6. P. Sorokin, *Man and Society in Calamity: The Effects of War, Revolution, Famine and Pestilence upon Human Mind, Behaviour, Social Organisation and Cultural Life* (New York, 1942), 120, 180; for a dramatic exception—the case of the Ik, a nomadic mountain people in Uganda, who were affected by famine to such an extent that society was completely disrupted and the family simply ceased to exist—see C. Turnbull, *Mountain People* (New York, 1972). On habitus, see P. Bourdieu, *Outline of a Theory of Practice* (Cambridge, 1977).

7. Interview with "Katerina" (pseudonym), b. 1928 in Ziakas, served as a partisan in the Democratic Army, 17 Aug. 1988.

8. Interview with Nikos Papanikolaou, b. 1925, 28 Aug. 1988.

9. For a balanced account, see L. Baerentzen, J. Iatrides, and O. Smith, eds., *Studies in the History of the Greek Civil War* (Copenhagen, 1987).

10. Interview with Apostolis Vergos, b. 1932, in Perivolaki, 2 Aug. 1988.

11. L. Niethammer, "Fragen-Antworten-Fragen," in L. Niethammer and A. von Plato, eds., *"Wir kriegen jetzt andere Zeiten": Lebensgeschichte und Sozialkultur im Ruhrgebiet, 1930 bis 1960*, vol. 3 (Bonn, 1985), 429; P. Bourdieu, *Esquisse d'une theorie de la Pratique* (Paris, 1972), 178.

12. L. Passerini, *Fascism in Popular Memory: The Cultural Experience of the Turin Working Class* (Cambridge, 1987), 2; Passerini, *Storia e soggetivita* (Florence, 1988), 18.

13. J. Vansina, *Oral Tradition as History* (Madison, Wis., 1985), 8.

14. H. Schuman and C. Rieger, "Collective Memory and Collective Memories," and J. M. Fitzgerald, "Autobiographical Memory and Conceptualizations of the Self," in M. A. Conway et al., eds., *Theoretical Perspectives on Autobiographical Memory* (Dordrecht and Boston, 1992).

15. G. Rosenthal, *Erlebte und erzählte Lebensgeschichte* (Frankfurt, 1995).

16. This is one of the reasons why Ziakas is still a left-wing village. In recent elections the right-wing New Democracy obtained less than 10 percent of the votes, the rest being shared between the PASOK and the Left (KKE and Synaspismos).

EIGHT

Red Terror: Leftist Violence during the Occupation

Stathis N. Kalyvas

THIS CHAPTER AIMS to question, and help revise, one of the central, indeed hegemonic, assumptions in the study of the Greek civil war: that the Left (the National Liberation Front—EAM—and the Communist Party of Greece—KKE) has been the main (or even the only) victim of violence.

The emergence and domination of such a view should come as no surprise. On the one hand, defeat in a civil war tends to be total; hence supporters of the defeated side suffer disproportionately. Indeed, most descriptions of the violence suffered by the supporters of the Left usually focus either on the period immediately following the end of the occupation—often described as the period of the "white terror" (1945–1947), or on the final phase of the civil war (1947–1949) and its aftermath. On the other hand, references to left-wing terror, as plentiful as they were vague, became a key weapon in the ideological arsenal of the Greek Right. The collapse, in 1974, of the ideological hegemony of the Right erased all references to leftist terror. Indeed, recent scholarly historical research has tended to overlook,[1] minimize,[2] or whitewash[3] leftist terror.[4] Even serious scholarship has tended to minimize leftist terror in a variety of subtle and implicit ways—including the choice of a skewed vocabulary. For example, Riki van Boeschoten dubs the violence of EAM "revolutionary violence" and the violence of the Right "terrorism."[5] Moreover, the rare references to leftist terror are typically followed by explications that hasten to posit its limited, insignificant, or exceptional character. In short, the claim is that leftist violence was an "aberration."[6] Although this claim is based on partial and mostly biased accounts, it remains unchallenged to this day primarily because of the absence of systematic empirical research on violence during the Greek civil war. The only sources are anecdotal: either the openly biased memoirs of right-wing and left-wing veterans of the conflict, or the contemporary accounts of British Liaison Officers (BLOs), which also need to be used with care because of their anti-Left bias.[7] Recently, a few single-village studies have provided useful insights, but remain of limited value as they cannot be generalized beyond the confines of the villages they focus on.[8]

In contrast, my account of leftist ("red") terror is based on the first (and to this date only) systematic and large-scale empirical investigation of violence during the Greek civil war. Based on extensive research carried out primarily in the region of the Argolid (but also in the adjoining areas of Korinthia and Arkadia), in the northeastern Peloponnese, this (ongoing) research is based on (1) close to 200 interviews with participants and ordinary people covering the counties of Argos and Nafplia in the prefecture (*nomos*) of the Argolid; (2) extensive archival evidence from the Court of Appeals of Nafplion, as well as British, German, and American archives; and (3) published and unpublished memoirs, autobiographies, and local histories.[9] Thus, the empirical basis of this chapter is both comprehensive (since it includes an area populated by about 40,000 people living in close to sixty villages) and reliable (since it combines oral and written, contemporary and retrospective, right-wing and left-wing sources, and accounts of both active participants in the conflict and ordinary people). Based on this research I was able to compile, among others, the full list of civilian casualties in two out of three counties of the Argolid. Although violence can take many forms, violent murder is unquestionably one of its most extreme expressions.

My goal is not to contribute to a meaningless partisan debate on comparative cruelty: it is clear that all sides resorted to terror. Instead, the focus on the red terror is necessary for two reasons: first, to set the record straight, and second, because a full exploration of the nature of violence during the Greek civil war requires a comparative analysis of the uses of terror by all political actors. While our understanding of right-wing violence, especially during the occupation, has been furthered by recent research,[10] the same cannot be said about left-wing violence.

First I show that in the Argolid, the red terror was a centrally planned process, key to EAM's and the KKE's strategic goals; I also discuss how my findings apply to the rest of the country. I then show how the red terror is intimately connected to the violence initiated first by the Germans and their local allies during the occupation period, and second by right-wing bands following the liberation of the country. I argue that a full understanding of the dynamics of violence during the civil war can only come from a comprehensive analysis that links the uses of terror by various political actors; the integration of single isolated events into the entire sequence to which they belong; and the combination of many different bodies of evidence. I illustrate these points by showing how seemingly straightforward instances of German terror and rightist "white" terror can prove misleading when not connected to the red

terror and placed into the full sequence of events to which they belong—something that can only result from the creative combination of
many different bodies of evidence.

RED TERROR: STRUCTURE AND GOALS

The Argolid: Social, Economic, and Political Background

The Argolid is located in the northeast part of the Peloponnese.[11] Its two
main towns are Nafplion, the administrative capital (and the first capital of Greece), and Argos, the market town. The Argolid lacks religious
and ethnic cleavages, even though it is not culturally homogeneous;
about half its population is of Albanian descent, known as Arvanites:
Christian Orthodox people, bilingual in Greek and *Arvanitika*, conscious of their distinct cultural identity, but with a strong sense of Greek
national identity. Indeed, this potential ethnic cleavage was not politicized during the civil war. Arvanite and non-Arvanite villages were
equally likely to side with the Left or the Right and equally disposed in
their propensity to exhibit violence.

Like most of rural Greece, the Argolid is overwhelmingly dominated
by family farming. Big landed property disappeared through successive
reforms in the course of the late nineteenth century. As a result, almost
every peasant family owned the land it tilled. In the plain of the Argolid
(where data for the 1940s are available), there were 5,090 farms for
5,360 families. During the late 1930s the last sizable land tracts, belonging to a few monasteries, were distributed to the peasants of the
surrounding villages. The number of families with no land property did
not exceed 5 percent. The great majority of the families owned farm
property equal to what they could till without hiring extra labor; very
few families owned more land than they could farm on their own. The
situation was similar in the hills and the mountains. Hence, the class
cleavage was not salient. Although the villages displayed a measure of
internal social stratification reflecting differences in the sizes of family
farms, this "class" structure was trumped by a high level of social mobility and the presence of fluid and changing vertical village factions
that included members from all "strata" of the village—often, but not
always, on the basis of lineage and kin.

Monarchist parties were dominant, as was generally the case in the
Peloponnese; the Communist Party was very weak. This political profile
was even more pronounced in the counties of Argos and Nafplia, where
the combined score of three Monarchist parties in the 1936 elections
(the last free elections before the advent of the Metaxas dictatorship)
reached 71.3 percent; Venizelist parties won 27.1 percent and the Com-

munists less than 1 percent (0.75 percent).[12] These scores were distributed quite evenly across the region, suggesting the absence of internal regional cleavages. The Argolid lacked a tradition of rebellion or mass violence. Since the Greek War of Independence in the 1820s, the main points of high conflict had been a successful military rebellion against King Othon in 1862 and the so-called national schism (1916), both of which produced no significant violence.[13] Indeed, Panayiotis Lilis, a KKE district leader from the village of Gerbesi, begins his (unpublished) memoirs by underlining the absence of a tradition of social and political struggle in the Argolid.

The Emergence of EAM

The Argolid was occupied by Italian forces from 1941 to September 1943, and by German forces after the Italian capitulation until September 1944.[14] In spite of their weakness, the few Communists of the Argolid benefited from the province's proximity to Athens and were able to quickly begin working toward the development of a mass-based movement, EAM. In contrast to the situation in the mountain regions of central Greece, EAM was organized as an effective political organization before the emergence of its army, ELAS (the National People's Liberation Army). Eventually, in the Argolid, EAM became far stronger than ELAS, which recruited relatively few men.[15] The leading personalities of the resistance movement were political cadres rather than guerrilla chieftains.

The first meeting of EAM in the Argolid took place in December 1942, after the Communist Party sent a cadre in the region to coordinate EAM and KKE activities.[16] In a January 1943 meeting, the decision was made to expand the still-clandestine EAM organization throughout the Argolid. Guerrilla activity in the northern Peloponnese took a serious turn in the summer of 1943, after a group of sixty ELAS guerrillas were dispatched by Aris Velouchiotis to the Peloponnese to spur the growth of ELAS. Their first action was to disband a number of small nationalist bands mainly composed of Greek Army officers and, thus, establish a monopoly over the resistance movement. The Italian capitulation in early September 1943 greatly boosted ELAS: it provided weapons and supplies, while creating a power vacuum in the area. ELAS took advantage of the situation and began attacking (the few) mountain outposts of the gendarmerie. By October 1943, most gendarmes had fled to Argos and Nafplion, where the Germans were garrisoned. With the exception of a few small village outposts in the coast and the plain, the Argolid came under full EAM control.

In short, the formerly conservative and monarchist Argolid had suddenly, but clearly, turned into EAM country. All my informants, regardless of their present political affiliation, pointed out to me that during this period support for EAM was close to unanimous.[17] That an area with no tradition of social struggles and with almost no communist presence could be swayed in such a quick and overwhelming fashion points to the importance of occupation (and its effective collapse) as a central and independent factor in shaping political developments.

By November 1943, EAM openly governed the Argolid villages through local and regional organizations.[18] By January 1944, Communist Party cells were in place in almost every village, and the Party was growing rapidly. EAM collected taxes, provided logistical support for the fighting units of ELAS located in the mountains, issued permits for village-to-village travels, mobilized the population into a variety of ancillary organizations, policed the area, and administered justice though a network of "People's Courts." In other words, EAM had evolved into a state structure. Many authors have quoted Woodhouse's statement about the benefits that the rise of EAM brought to mountain Greece: "The benefits of civilisation and culture trickled into the mountains for the first time. Schools, local government, law-courts and public utilities, which the war had ended, worked again. Theatres, factories, parliamentary assemblies began for the first time. . . . EAM/ELAS set the pace in the creation of something that Governments of Greece had neglected: an organised state in the Greek mountains."[19] However, these authors fail to note that state-building does not only bring benefits; it also brings state-like levels of repression.

In my estimation, close to 90 percent of all violent civilian deaths in the Argolid that occurred in the context of civil strife, from the beginning of the occupation (1941) to the end of the civil war (1949), occurred between September 1943 and September 1944.[20] Four distinct periods of violent conflict in the Argolid can be distinguished during this time: winter 1943–1944; spring 1944; June–July 1944; and August 1944.

WINTER 1943–1944

Up to the winter of 1943 there was a lack of open polarization or widespread violence in the Argolid. Few people lost their lives, mostly cattle thieves executed either by the occupation authorities or by the first ELAS bands. (One of the most important consequences of occupation and the decline of state authority had been the increase in criminal activity in the countryside.) In addition, EAM killed some of the most hated collaborators of the Italians. These collaborators, mostly criminal types, were universally despised because they systematically blackmailed and robbed peasants: their motivation was clearly material rather than ideological. The liquidation of collaborators and cattle thieves, as well as the establishment of effective policing, met with almost universal approval and led to a substantial increase in safety — and this was the case across Greece.[21] An EAM cadre in Epiros captures this feeling: "Even if ELAS had had no other objective, its effective policing [which] led to the emergence of full-fledged order and security in the areas under its control [was sufficient as an achievement]."[22]

This is not to say, however, that the seeds of polarization had not already been sown. Below the appearance of universal support for EAM, many local conflicts were played out, especially concerning the staffing of the EAM village committees. As Lilis points out in his memoirs, the initial recruitment efforts in his village were marred by assertions such as: "I am not joining the organization, because so-and-so is already a member." Moreover, some people were punished by EAM for minor offenses, real or not; punishments included fines and beatings but no killings. These developments generated resentment, especially when the victims were influential men in the village and the victimizers young village toughs of lower status.

The first systematic campaign of civilian assassinations in the Argolid began in November 1943 and was organized by EAM — *not the occupation authorities*. The first wholesale destruction of a village in the Argolid by the German occupation troops also took place in the first days of November 1943, following the (accidental) killing of three German soldiers by ELAS *andartes* (as the guerrillas were known). As a reprisal, the village of Berbati was burned down, and four villagers were killed while trying to flee. However, no mass reprisals took place.

The EAM terror campaign of winter 1943–1944 was hardly peculiar to the Argolid. A similar wave of killings swept the entire Peloponnese during the same time,[23] and most probably the whole country as well.[24] This campaign of assassinations was carried out by EAM's newly formed OPLA squads — a combination of secret police and death squads. (OPLA is the Greek acronym for Organization for the Protection of the People's Struggle; the acronym also means "weapons.") These groups established very rapidly a reputation for ruthless violence that is still alive in the memories of many among my informants. In an interview he gave me, a former OPLA member described his job starkly: "I was not a regular guerrilla; I was a devil's guerrilla."

Charles Tilly has pointed out that "violence is rarely a solo performance; it usually grows out of an interaction of opponents."[25] It would be unsatisfactory to just say that EAM initiated this wave of violence without accounting for its origins. This wave of violence can be understood as the local reflection of two significant national developments: first, the decision in the summer of 1943 by the Athens collaborationist government to raise Greek auxiliary units, generically known the Security Battalions (SB) — a decision that resulted from the realization that most of the countryside had come under EAM control and that German forces could no longer police the Greek territory effectively; second, the subsequent decision by the KKE leadership to preempt this development, which they viewed as a major threat.

In the Argolid, the Security Battalions did not appear until May 1944 — although they came to neighboring Korinthos in January 1944. However, EAM's winter 1943–1944 assassination campaign produced twenty-nine victims. In addition, a significant number was abducted from the two towns and killed in the surrounding mountains. At the same time, two isolated monasteries (near the villages of Borsa and Heli) were transformed into concentration camps to handle the prisoners and their interrogation, torture, and eventual execution. Likewise, the isolated hill village of Limnes was used as a detention and execution ground. The geographical distribution of these camps was strategic: they spanned the Argolid from west (Borsa) to East (Heli); Limnes was located at the center, forming an arc that surrounded the plain.

Although some of the victims, particularly in the towns, had been working for the German occupation authorities, the great majority had not. Indeed, they were described by EAM cadres as "reactionaries" rather than "traitors." They were typically notables: mayors, doctors, merchants, petty officers, that is, individuals who were seen as both potentially disloyal to the EAM cause and able to influence many villagers. Their potential disloyalty was connected to what were rather trivial issues: traveling to a (German-occupied) town too often, hiding or refusing to hand in a gun, refusing to pay a tax or perform some duty requested by EAM, criticizing EAM or even poking fun at a local EAM member in the coffee shop, and so on.

These were trivial issues insofar as criticizing EAM did not spring, in the great majority of cases I examined, from narrowly political considerations, such as a preference for monarchy. Almost every villager at this point shared EAM's proclaimed goal of national liberation, while at the same time not suspecting the KKE's behind-the-scenes powerful role. Still, many villagers resented the daily demands for food and labor that the building of an army entails; many fragile local balances were upset by the composition of local EAM committees; and many newly empowered local EAM village leaders (known as *ipefthinoi*, "the responsible ones") began to use their positions to settle scores and humiliate personal enemies. After the killings, any villager hostile to the local EAM leadership realized that the stakes were high and shut his mouth.

In this sense, EAM's terror campaign was successful: it generated widespread fear, mutual suspicion, and the collapse of trust within communities. In doing so, it cut short any challenge to EAM's monopoly, and deterred people from engaging in actions against EAM. The purposeful creation of fear is a feature that consistently came up in interviews with both right-wing *and* left-wing villagers.[26] "You wouldn't talk here," a (left-wing) woman told me, "because you didn't know what could happen to you. There was fear. Fear and terror." A leftist man from the mountain village of Frousiouna expressed this point:

> We, the village boys, we hadn't really understood what was going on here. We hadn't understood what "revolution" really meant. And Doctor Michalopoulos [a moderate local EAM leading figure], who was my uncle, gave me the following advice. He told me: "Listen, with this established situation, you won't say no. You will execute [whatever] orders [you receive] without objecting. They want the mule, you'll give them the mule. This is a revolution," he told me. "They can kill both you and the mule, and they will be accountable to no one. You won't talk. You'll listen."

Two elements struck the villagers as particularly shocking. First was the arbitrary character of the terror, conveyed in the recollection above — strongly resembling both Jacobin and Soviet terror.[27] Often there was no apparent reason for an arrest. "We never learned why so-and-so was killed" is a statement that comes up again and again in my interviews. In many instances, my informants could not even speculate on why a certain individual had been killed. The second shocking element was its novel character. Nothing like this had ever befallen these people — or their parents. Never had the Greek state authorities resorted to such a practice. Neither personal disputes nor political conflicts had ever given rise to such violence. As the American ambassador to Greece wrote in one of his dispatches: "People familiar with the relatively bloodless 'Greek revolutions' of the past may well have been astonished as well as horrified by what has occurred in this one."[28] This point was also emphasized by a British journalist:

> Here in Greece there used to be furious feeling between Venizelists and Monarchists and coup upon coup d'état, but never any corpses piled up. . . . Greeks never before shed Greek blood as they have done this autumn [1944] in the Peloponnese and Macedonia. The factious spirit is that of the old Venizelist-Monarchist squabbles, but its expression has a new ferocity, so that Athenians, horrified at the tales that come in, plead with the stranger to believe that such things — the mutilation and murder of prisoners, the taking of hostages, the massacres in EES villages [i.e., villages that collaborated with the Germans in Macedonia] — are the doing not of Greeks but of Bulgars and Germans infiltrated into the ELAS ranks.[29]

What is more, while the violence exercised by the occupying authorities could be comprehended as part of foreign occupation, the violence exercised by EAM, involving neighbors and meted out by Greeks in the name of the liberation of the country, must have initially appeared incomprehensible. I stress this point, because I think it is fundamental in understanding the intensity of the reaction against EAM that was to follow.

Successful terror is intended to achieve a maximum amount of compliance with a minimum amount of violence. Yet, terror also produces resentment. As a British Liaison Officer active in Korinthia and Achaia put it: "Above all [the villager] hates having his only mule 'borrowed' by people for whom he has no respect. He has talked it all out in some dark corner with his brother villagers, he has plotted against and schemed to rid himself of at least the EAM in his village, but he has no gun; so he sits there quietly biting his first finger in that significant way which means 'All right, you are on top for now, but you wait.'"[30] As long as the balance of power remained unchanged and control was in EAM's hands, this kind of resentment was contained and violence remained limited and circumscribed. However, when and where the balance of power was upset, things went awry. This is precisely what happened in the Argolid in the spring and summer of 1944.

SPRING 1944

The situation began to change in late April 1944, as a result of the escalation of the conflict in neighboring Arkadia and Korinthia. This escalation was triggered by the arrival of Security Battalion troops in Korinthos in January 1944, and in Tripolis in March 1944. The core of these Battalions, made of mostly marginal elements recruited in Athens, was under the command of junior officers from the region who had fled to Athens after the winter wave of assassinations. Upon their arrival in the two provincial capitals, the Security Battalions proceeded to recruit locally, mostly among three categories: thuggish elements from the towns; demoralized gendarmes who had been idle in the towns after being chased from the countryside (and being consistently the target of assassination by OPLA teams); and the kin of those previously killed by EAM, together with young villagers who had been harassed by village EAM committees, often on the basis of personal grudges—both groups having fled their villages for the towns. The arrival of the Security Battalions set off a process of escalation of violence, aptly described by a British Liaison Officer: "ELAS' attitude to them was one of extreme hostility; and many of the worst ELAS atrocities were carried out against SB prisoners and against their families, who were normally removed to concentration camps. ELAS' fury against the Security Battalions grew with what it fed on, and the Battalions themselves proved no less masters of the arts of intimidation and terrorisation."[31]

At the same time, the German occupation authorities escalated their reprisals in the region. On 22 April, as a reprisal for an ELAS action, they shot eleven hostages from Nafplion.[32] In May, a small SB detachment (about twenty men) finally arrived in Argos and quickly dispatched a unit in Nafplion. This detachment was led by three captains of the Greek Army (Dimitrios Moustakopoulos, Spiros Robotis, and Panayotis Christopoulos). Eventually the Argolid unit reached a size of about 150–250 and was able to seal off effectively both Argos and Nafplion from EAM, stop most of the kidnappings and assassinations, and destroy the underground EAM organizations. Some EAM members were shot, and most fled. Likewise, most EAM organizations in the villages located near the two towns were forced to go underground, and their most visible cadres had to flee. Overall, the Security Battalions dealt a devastating blow to EAM in the towns and the villages of the plain. "Some people there," recalls Lilis, "came to believe that if the *andartes* came down to the plain they would kill them, and this is why they saw their salvation in the continuation of the German occupation. The blow we suffered within a few months because of the terrorism and the propaganda [of the Security Battalions] was devastating. They were able to shift the people's spirits; whereas a sizable part was at least neutral toward us, they now turned against EAM's struggle."

The role of the kin of EAM's victims is central in understanding the wave of terror launched by the Security Battalions. As soon as they realized that the Security Battalions were willing to help them overthrow EAM in their villages, the victims' kin lobbied the SB to organize raids and supplied the Battalions with crucial information about the EAM organization of their villages. More than sixty years later, many among these people have no qualms about their actions, which they view as either just retribution for the distress suffered under EAM rule or as the inevitable result of the only defense that was available to them. For instance, a man whose parents had both been killed by EAM before he joined the Security Battalions, told me: "I went to the Germans. What should I have done since there was no one else to turn to?"

Raids began to be carried out against villages of the plain in May 1944. They took the following form: a combined force of Germans and Battalionists surrounded the village and forced all village men to gather in the central square. There, one or two villagers following the raiding party would single out key EAM cadres. These would then be sent to the German concentration camp of Korinthos, to be either shot in some reprisal measure or placed in the grisly cages that had been attached to the trains' front ends in order to deter sabotage; if they were lucky or wealthy enough to bribe their way out of the camp (but not so wealthy as to buy their freedom), they would be shipped to Germany to be used as slave labor. To an outside observer, these raids would appear as instances of indiscriminate violence exercised by the occupiers against innocent civilians. It is clear, however, that they were *also* selective acts of retaliation in the context of an escalating local conflict. Close to forty people, in my estimation, were killed in these raids during May 1944.

In response to this attack, EAM stepped up its campaign of terror in the areas under its control. The launching of the first major mopping-up operation by German and Security Battalion troops deep into EAM territory during late May, June, and July 1944 proved to be another critical step in the process of escalation.

JUNE–JULY 1944

Mopping-up operations, the goal of which was to annihilate the *andartes* by cordoning off an entire area and then proceeding to thoroughly "comb" through it, produced a high level of primarily indiscriminate violence and triggered a new sequence of violence and counterviolence. The first raid began on 17–18 May and lasted until 1 June; it involved about five thousand men and targeted the eastern Argolid. The aim was not to occupy territory on a permanent basis but to encircle and destroy the *andartes*. A large number of civilians, 134 in my estimation, mostly elderly people, women, and children, were shot and killed in the fields while attempting to flee from their villages. Most had few active ties to EAM.[33] The main cause of the indiscriminate character of this violence was the absence of local informers (such as existed in the plain villages), primarily because there had been little or no EAM violence in these villages during the previous months.

An important development that took place in the course of this operation was the collective defection of a number of villages to the German side. After the Germans and the Security Battalions moved into a village that was strategically located (close to a railroad line or to an important mountain passage), they would gather all the villagers in the central square and would offer them a choice: take up arms and join them in the fight against the *andartes* or suffer collective punishment. The village mayor, in consultation with the most prominent villagers, would typically accept the deal. Interestingly, many among the people active in such deals had been among the most prominent EAM supporters in their villages. To induce commitment, the Germans would then request that the villagers deliver some EAM sympathizers to them. Usually these hapless sympathizers would be shot on the spot. The decision of villages to enter into these deals hinged greatly on expectations. This was the first time villagers were witnessing such extensive military operations, and they believed that the *andartes* (who had fled) had been totally defeated. This was a crucial factor (together with the threat of collective punishment) that led them to defect. A typical sentence from my interviews goes like this: "The [villagers] thought that because such a big operation was going on, because the mountains were laden with Germans, that the guerrillas had been destroyed. 'Well,' they said, 'then let's join the Germans.'"[34]

The rampage going on in the eastern Argolid was carefully observed by villagers and EAM cadres in the western Argolid. Both groups were frightened by the unprecedented amount of violence used by the occupation troops. Some villagers, including EAM sympathizers, began fleeing to the towns so as to avoid being killed in what they anticipated would be the next target of German raids. At the same time, EAM leaders were worried by the collective defections in the eastern Argolid, and their worries increased when villagers began to flee to the towns. To stop this trend, a new wave of terror was launched, as a result of which many people were arrested and interrogated. Fifty-six (including women) were shipped to a concentration camp in the St. George Monastery in Korinthia and were executed by having their throats slit. These killings produced a commotion in Argos, home to many of their relatives, and led to new retaliations. Andreas Christopoulos, a writer and resident of Argos who recorded his impressions from the occupation in a book published in 1946, recalls the situation in June 1944: "One person goes to the Gestapo offices to tell them that the *andartes* arrested his family tonight, another person tells them that they burnt down his house, and yet another one that they exterminated his family because he was a reactionary."[35]

After having "pacified" the eastern Argolid, the occupation troops turned their attention to the west. On 17 July, they launched a big operation to destroy ELAS bases in the mountains further west. The villagers fled upward and were generally lucky; they were able to escape and suffered relatively few casualties. However, a few days before this second mopping-up operation, an additional fifty villagers had been arrested and put to death by EAM in a series of preemptive actions intended to both punish suspected "reactionaries" and thwart additional ones by spreading terror. The arrests this time were even more arbitrary. For example, some people were killed just for spreading rumors, as indicated by the following excerpt from an interview:

Diamandis Kostakis was tilling his field of maize. The adjacent field was tilled by a man named Vourdoulas. They were watering the fields when he told Vourdoulas, "You know, Vazeos [the ELAS commander] defected to the Security Battalions." This was German propaganda. Vourdoulas reported this [exchange] to Barba-Sotiros Sotiropoulos. Barba-Sotiros told it to Yannis Papadopoulos, who reported it to the teacher Liberopoulos, the village *ipefthinos*. The teacher, fearing [the consequences of not reporting this], told it to Stef-

anakis, another teacher who was a member of the regional committee. Stefanakis came in and interrogated Papadopoulos: "Who told you?" [Papa-
dopoulos] replied: "Sotiros [told me]." "Come here Barba-Sotiros," [the
teacher said], "who told you?" "Vourdoulas," [Barba-Sotiros replied]. "Vourdoulas, who told you?" "Kostakis," [Vourdoulas responded]. Kostakis was
brought in: "Did you say this thing?" "Yes," he replied. Stefanakis hit him
very hard, he beat the hell out of him, then they took him and killed him.

No collective defections took place in the mountain villages since
there was no one to defect: everyone had fled. However, the inhabitants
of the villages located in the hills of the Argolid had been encircled and
were forced to return to their villages: it was impossible to hide in caves
for more than a few days. Upon their return to their homes, those who
had fled were contacted by Security Battalionists and relatives from
Argos, who urged them to join them. Having undergone the terror of
EAM during June and July, a terror amplified by rumors that new
blacklists with up to fifty names per village had been drawn by EAM
members, these villagers were willing to defect. They rounded up a few
EAM cadres and sympathizers unlucky enough to have remained behind and delivered them to the Germans. Often they took the initiative:
having rounded up the few members of EAM they could find, they
marched them to Argos in order to exchange them with German weapons.[36] The prisoners were a proof of commitment and an indicator that
the villagers could be trusted by the Germans — who, however, failed to
arm these villagers (they, probably, did not consider their villages to be
of strategic interest). What is particularly ironic about these developments is that when the word "revolution" came up during my interviews, it was mostly used by the people from these villages describing
their uprising against EAM: "Our villages revolted," they told me; or,
"This was the time of the revolution."

AUGUST 1944

The balance of power shifted once more in late July and August.
Once the German army decided to leave Greece, the "pacified" hills
were evacuated and, by mid-August, the *andartes* began returning —
literally, with a vengeance. They took a tremendous toll in the "trai-
torous" villages of the eastern Argolid, killing 119 people. Like the Germans, they burned some villages down to the ground. In one village
(Heli), they took between sixty and eighty hostages, mostly elderly people (including women), slaughtered them, and threw their bodies into a
well, in what was probably one of the most grisly acts of mass violence
in the area.[37] In other villages, entire families were rounded up, taken to
the mountains, and slaughtered. For example, in one massacre that took

place on 15 August 1944 in the village of Gerbesi, the *andartes* arrested twenty-three people, most of them members of five families — including five children, aged sixteen, fifteen, fourteen, five, three, and a baby of just eighteen months.[38] The tragic feature of these massacres was that some of the victims had already lost close family members during the German operations of June. The selection of the victims was heavily informed by personal grudges and exacerbated by the violence of the past months.

Fortunately, this rampage was not repeated in the western Argolid, where most people fled to Argos and Nafplion before the arrival of the *andartes*. These villages were deserted, and the *andartes* burned them down. As the Germans were leaving the Peloponnese, the *andartes* gradually reasserted their control over the entire Argolid. The Germans evacuated Argos on 19 September, and the Security Battalions surrendered their weapons in Nafplion on 5 October, and left for the island of Spetses under British supervision. Contrary to what one might have expected, little violence took place during this period. (The only exception was a massacre in the village of Achladokambos following a deadly battle between the victorious *andartes* and the resisting village Battalionists, on 18 September 1944.) While the spirit of revenge ran high, EAM managed to police the villages with great effectiveness and prevent acts of retaliation. Many arrests took place,[39] and EAM promised that those responsible for crimes committed during the occupation would stand trial after the country's liberation. Most of these people were freed after the Varkiza Agreement.

All in all, I estimate the number of *civilians* killed between September 1943 and September 1944 in the area I investigated to be around 670 — close to 2 percent of this area's total population. EAM was responsible for roughly 55 percent of these killings, and the Germans and their collaborators were responsible for about 45 percent.

The Structure of Red Terror

When not overlooked or dismissed as right-wing propaganda, EAM terror is typically presented as the result of isolated actions of a few uncontrolled guerrilla chieftains or fanatic communist cadres.[40] However, there is substantial evidence strongly suggesting that terror was a centrally planned (though regionally implemented) policy pursued consistently by the KKE and EAM throughout Greece. In fact, we can safely talk of a *system of terror*. Its goal was to ensure civilian compliance and maximize control over the population.

This does not imply that terror was the only instrument used by EAM to generate compliance. In fact, terror can (and did) coexist with ideological appeals and the provision of material benefits. Nor does this imply that every member of EAM or ELAS was involved in terroristic activities. As it turns out, the system of terror was mostly administered by specialized quasi-professional teams rather than ELAS—although it required the active collaboration of hundreds of village EAM committees. Furthermore, a distinction should be made between terror and violence. Terror is a *method* of rule, whereas violence is an *outcome* of terror. The use of terror does not necessarily imply mass violence. In fact, successful terror produces low levels of violence, because its objective is intimidation, not extermination: "Kill one and scare one thousand," goes a Chinese saying. In a different formulation, high levels of violence are indicative of a breakdown of terror. For example, although EAM killed less than thirty people in the villages of the Argolid during the winter of 1943, it was able to deter all opposition. This point is important because it allows us to explain both interregional and intra-regional variations of violence. Within the Argolid, the further a village was located from German control, the less severe was the violence used by EAM. In the mountains of the Argolid, for example, only a few beatings took place during the same period. This appears to have been true for the mountain villages of central and northern Greece, which were not threatened by German incursions. When, however, the mountain villages of the Argolid came under German attack, EAM resorted to higher levels of violence to deter civilians from defecting to the Security Battalions. Likewise, the mountain villages of central Greece, which suffered little EAM violence during the occupation, underwent left-wing violence during the last phase of the civil war, when they came under attack by the Greek National Army: the experience, in 1947–1949, of the mountain villages of Evrytania or Thessalia, which had been relatively free of violence in 1944, resembles strikingly that of the mountain villages of the Argolid in 1944.

How was the system of terror implemented? Although the first Security Battalions were only formed in Athens in 1943 (and did not begin operating in the countryside until January 1944), the leadership of the Communist Party decided to take preemptive action against them. OPLA was formed in the summer of 1943.[41] Immediately after (25 August 1943), the leadership of ELAS in the Peloponnese requested that regional EAM branches form "a special organ" in order to "isolate at the right moment" the "leaders of the reaction."[42] The central committee of ELAS issued an announcement on 7 December, warning anyone planning to join the Battalions that they would be punished with death, that their families would be arrested, and that their property in "Free Greece" would be confiscated.[43] This announcement was echoed by a similar one issued by the Political Bureau of KKE on 21 December.[44]

These decisions were quickly transmitted to the communist leadership in the Peloponnese, operating under the acronym KEPP (Central Committee for the Peloponnese Region). The program of "elimination of the reactionaries" was further communicated to the Peloponnesian district KKE representatives at a meeting in the Arcadian village of Strezova held on 26 November 1943.[45] The EAM newspaper of Achaia captured the spirit of this meeting, attended by about 250 representatives from the entire Peloponnese: "Gestapo Men and Traitors, the People Will Hang You in the Central Square."[46] The British Liaison Officer George Tavernarakis referred to this meeting in his report: "At the last general conference of ELAS Peloponnesian representatives, principles of dealing with 'reactionaries' were laid down. Reaction was distinguished as either Active or Passive. Those who indulged in the former were to be shot, while Passive reactionaries (defined as persons known to disagree with it without taking any definite action) must be sent to concentration camps, of which a good many now exist."[47]

In December 1943, the EAM and KKE press in the Peloponnese was reproducing warnings and threats against potential Security Battalions recruits — worded in a surprisingly similar fashion. For example, the KKE newspaper of Achaia ran a central article entitled "The Greeks with Greece, the Traitors with the Gestapo," which contained the following telling passage: "This is why we warn them for the last time to leave [the SB]. Otherwise we will exterminate them, we will burn their houses and we will destroy all their kin."[48] These were not empty threats. They were acted upon across the entire Peloponnese: violence was carried out against the relatives of men who joined the Battalions, fled to the towns, or were just suspected of being disloyal to the EAM cause. At the same time, EAM began to systematically threaten the Greek army officers to join it so as to undermine their availability for the Security Battalions.[49]

The KKE's ability to implement a system of terror was made possible by its centralized structure and its domination over EAM. Two features are worth underlining. First, the smallest village was connected to the KKE's regional committee through ascending organizational links, thus making possible the local implementation of national directives. Second, the KKE was organized at a higher level than EAM: whereas there was a KKE regional committee (*periferiaki epitropi*) covering the entire Argolid & Korinthia prefecture, the highest EAM authority in the region was the provincial committee (*eparchiaki epitropi*), covering only the Argolid (a second EAM provincial committee covered Korinthia). In addition, the regional secretaries were directly appointed by the KKE's Peloponnesian bureau (to which they were accountable) and often carried the title "representatives of the Peloponnesian bureau."[50] Finally, whereas the KKE committee was composed of seasoned communist cadres, the EAM committee was composed of mainly urban, middle-class, middle-aged, higher-profile but powerless noncommunists — though headed by a dedicated communist from the town of Nemea (Andreas Froussios, alias Gravias). The terror system was implemented and monitored directly by the KKE organization. There was nothing flashy about the KKE cadres: even their aliases were bland and distinctly unheroic (in contrast to the ELAS chieftains' flamboyant heroic aliases): Stathis, Gavos, Gravias, etc.

How were regional directives conveyed at the village level? My interviews with a number of surviving EAM *ipefthinoi* (village leaders), members of EAM village committees, and KKE cadres (most of them still supporters of leftist parties), as well as the analysis of court documents, make it possible to reconstruct accurately the organizational ties that connected the villages with the regional leadership.

In the fall of 1944, a series of meetings took place at the village level. These meetings brought the local EAM committee (typically composed of six to eight members) together with district or regional cadres. In the villages of Argos county, the second secretary of the regional KKE committee, Dimitris A. Andreadakis (alias Mitsos Gavos) attended these meetings. Gavos asked the local committee to identify the village "reactionaries" and consent to their elimination. As one participant told me: "In September or October 1943, the [village] committee held a meeting with [the regional committee representative] in order to arrest three men, to clean up the reactionary elements." A number of names would come up and be discussed; sometimes the discussion would include anonymous denunciations of specific individuals. Often a vote would take place, but sometimes the decision was reached through deliberation of the KKE members in a closed meeting.[51] Gavos would then ask the committee members to sign a document pertaining to the decision. The local committee might also gather signatures from the villagers regarding a specific case.

A few nights later, an OPLA squad composed of men unknown to the villagers descended on the village, met a local guide (who was, in some cases, hooded), knocked on the victims' doors, arrested them, and delivered them to the KKE authorities located in the mountain villages. These arrests went smoothly; the victims were told not to worry, because they would be taken just for a "little interrogation" (the standard expression used comes up in many interviews and written sources: *mia anakrisoula*) and would quickly return to their village. Typically, the victims did not worry too much because nobody had been killed up to that moment. Upon arrival in some EAM facility in the mountains, these persons were interrogated and often tortured (typical tortures included beating, *falanga*, and flogging). A few were let go (largely depending on whether they knew some high-level cadre who could intervene on their behalf), but most were executed a few days later, usually by having their throat slit. Their bodies were dumped and often remained unburied for a long time. Relatives were often reassured by the village committee members that the victims were alive and well taken care of. In some cases, relatives were asked to provide food and clothes for them (which were then appropriated by EAM cadres). Many relatives of victims told me that even more than the deaths of their loved ones, it was the uncertainty and lies that followed that really distressed them.

The collaboration between the EAM village committee members and the regional KKE leadership affected not just *how* the victims were selected but also *who* was selected. On the one hand, the KKE cadres sought to eliminate influential people who could turn a village (or a substantial portion thereof) against EAM: village mayors, village doctors, petty officers, etc. On the other hand, many committee members used their power to settle personal accounts. For example, a village mayor who was abducted and killed in the fashion described above was both suspected of harboring anti-EAM feelings and happened to be involved in a bitter personal dispute with a committee member for having reneged on his promise to marry the committee member's sister. This process echoes Jan Gross's remark about Soviet terror in West Poland as being "characterized by *privatization* of the instruments of coercion."[52] It is important to emphasize here that no one was killed in the winter of 1943–1944 unless consent from the village organization was secured in the way I described above.[53]

During the spring, regional party meetings were held to discuss these issues anew and set general guidelines. A key meeting in this respect was the Peloponnesian meeting of the KKE, which took place in a mall hamlet near the Arkadian village of Strezova, on 19 April 1944. Initially set for 26 March, this meeting had to be postponed because of a combination of bad weather and German operations. Panayotis Lilis, a district secretary from the village of Gerbesi in the Argolid, attended this meeting together with seven other representatives from the Argolid and Korinthia and describes it in detail in his memoirs.[54] The meeting was addressed by the secretary of the KKE's Peloponnesian bureau, Achilleas Blanas, who analyzed in detail the decisions of the Tenth Plenum of the KKE's Central Committee (held in January 1944).[55] Party leaders pointed out that in the period between the Tenth Plenum and the Peloponnesian meeting, "the measures concerning the attack against the reaction had been relaxed" and more decisive measures were needed, such as "disappearances of traitors and reactionaries" that would be carefully planned and carried out—as opposed to the prevalent practice of careless assassinations following which corpses were left unburied and were used as reactionary propaganda against the party.[56] KKE representatives were briefed about the role of OPLA, whose squads were to be composed of two to three members directly accountable to each regional committee secretary.[57] OPLA men were supposed to shoot to kill in only two cases: when operating in German-occupied territory (as assassination squads), or when the suspect resisted arrest. Otherwise, their main function was to carry out arrests. At this point during the meeting, Lilis recalls, a man got up in the room and asked the speaker: "Hence OPLA will be the future *Gepeou?*"[58] Blanas replied that "such things are told by those who are opposed to EAM's struggle, those who confuse EAM's liberation struggle with the party's goals and struggles."[59] The man who had raised the point about OPLA was then asked to leave the room. The meeting closed with the appointments of the regional secretaries. Theodoros Zengos (alias Stathis or Triandafyllos) was appointed first secretary for the Argolid and Korinthia regional committee.

Once more, the decisions taken in this meeting reached the local level with remarkable speed. KEPP issued a set of directives regarding the creation and staffing of interrogation units and the guidelines for discreet arrests, interrogations, and "disappearances" of traitors and reactionaries; these directives advised the regional committees to "exterminate the reaction."[60] In May 1944, the EAM newspaper *Lefteros Morias* published an inflammatory central article with the telling title "Knifeblade for the Reaction" (*Lepidi-Lepidi stin Antidrasi*). A KKE cadre from Korinthia recalls: "This is how the party line reached [us]: 'We must eliminate the reaction. No one who can sway the people must survive. We must even do away with reactionaries who can influence five people and push them against us.'"[61] By May 1944, new concentration camps housed in isolated mountain monasteries were created to handle the fledging numbers of prisoners, while the campaign of terror was stepped up decisively.[62]

An additional indication of the impressive ability of the Party and EAM to coordinate activities throughout the Peloponnese peninsula is provided by the staging of "spontaneous" demonstrations in villages of the EAM-controlled areas.[63] These demonstrations unfolded following a similar script: the inhabitants of many villages would converge in a bigger village, where they would listen to speeches by regional EAM leaders and would then approve a petition demanding relief from the Red Cross, weapons from the British mission, and the punishment of the "traitors"; these petitions were worded in remarkably similar terms across the peninsula. In one case (Ano Belesi, in the Argolid), such a demonstration also included the execution of a "traitor." EAM's ability to mobilize thousands of villagers in a time of war both across and within regions points to its remarkable organizational strength. An additional testimony of EAM's impressive ability to control violence at the local level is its prevention of violence following the defeat of the Security Battalions in September and October 1944.[64]

Two elements strike me as central to the red terror. The first is the convergence of the local logic of village organizations and the supra-local strategic concerns of the regional (and national) organizations. This point is missed by both "top-down" historians, who lack information about local developments and tend to interpret terror as an indiscriminate process implemented from above against unsuspecting civilians, and anthropologists, who view terror as a process primarily informed by "local vendettas" — in the words of Stanley Aschenbrenner, "a sequence of action and reaction that needed no outside energy to continue, though it was of course exploited by outside agents."[65] The second element is the highly bureaucratic character of the red terror — an element that sets it apart from the intensely localist violence meted out by right-wing bands during 1945–1947.[66] This bureaucratic character is manifest in the way the system of terror was implemented: countless reports on specific individuals and their activities were drafted, discussed by committees, submitted to hierarchically superior committees, appealed, or acted upon. Countless meetings were held, thousands of signatures were collected, and hundreds of petitions circulated. Violence was professional and impersonal, characterized by a startling division of labor: an execution would be decided by one group, confirmed by another group, and implemented by yet another group, or set of groups.

Let me provide just two illustrations — both from left-wing sources. Stratis Papastratis, an EAM activist, recounts the story of Yannis Satiris, the mayor of the village of Avlonari in South Evia. Upon learning that he had been included in an EAM blacklist, Satiris traveled to (German-occupied) Halkida, the capital of Evia, to plead his case with higher EAM authorities; when this proved insufficient, he even went to Athens to see leading EAM cadres![67] Ilias Yannakos, a mid-level EAM cadre in Epiros (and a faithful communist until his death), describes in his memoirs how he himself became the target of an EAM assassination attempt.[68] Apparently because he had voiced a critique of an EAM action, he was blacklisted by the EAM organization in Konitsa and slated for execution. Unsuspecting about this fate, he was taken by a local guide to the village of Vassiliko, where the local *ipefthinos* had been told to arrange his execution (this was before the formation of the OPLA squads). The guide handed him to the *ipefthinos*, asking him, as Yannakos recalls, for "a delivery receipt, as if I were some piece of merchandise!" The *ipefthinos* took extreme precautions in feeding and caring for him, fearing to be later denounced as having being too friendly with a blacklisted man. Eventually the *ipefthinos* called the execution off, but what is interesting is the bureaucratic nature of his justification for doing so: he claimed that his village, Vassiliko, was under the jurisdiction of the Pogoni EAM organization rather than the Konitsa organization, which had requested the execution![69]

The bureaucratic character of the red terror becomes even more striking (I would even say eerie) when one takes into account the social and historical environment in which it unfolded: poor, mostly illiterate villages, in a time of occupation and war.[70] It is particularly ironic, of course, that all this violence was part and parcel of a struggle for the "national and social liberation" of Greece.

The Causes of Red Terror

EAM violence was not restricted to the Argolid; the entire Peloponnese was affected as well.[71] Although we lack systematic evidence, it seems that many other regions were also particularly affected, especially central and western Macedonia.[72] Conversely, some regions seem to have avoided the worst excesses of EAM violence. Understanding the causes of the red terror requires an explanation of this variation. Although this task cannot possibly be undertaken in the absence of systematic data on violence from all over Greece, it is possible at this point to disqualify some established arguments.

Most EAM apologists, be they veterans of the resistance and the civil war or historians, tend to account for EAM violence (implicitly rather than explicitly) by pointing to the personal characteristics of regional KKE and EAM leaders: intolerant and paranoid because of the persecution they had suffered before the occupation, they easily resorted to ruthless violence. Such an interpretation seems to fit the case of the Argolid. Both Theodoros Zengos (the first secretary of the KKE regional Argolid & Korinthia committee) and Dimitris A. Andreadakis (the second secretary) proved overly zealous in implementing the Party directives on spreading terror. Indeed, the Communist Party condemned Zengos's actions and dismissed him from the Party after the liberation of the Peloponnese in October 1944. The regional KKE newspaper *Lefteros Morias* published, in its issue of 14 October 1944, the dismissal decision: "KOPP is dismissing from the party Triandafyllos or Stathis because [he was found guilty of] criminal distortion of the party line in the organization he led. . . . He used against citizens methods which have no relation to the party morale and behavior and damaged the party's authority."[73]

Very little is known about Zengos.[74] A native of the Volos area and a prewar communist, Zengos is described as a wiry and intense man. An employee of the state telecommunication service (TTT), he was working in the Peloponnese when the war began. He is described as extremely fanatical by Communist Party cadres who knew him, able to terrorize into silence his subordinates.[75] When the commander of the ELAS Sixth Regiment, Major Vazeos, criticized him for having ordered some executions, he was told by Zengos to "watch out."[76] It even appears that Zengos demanded that a fixed quota of "reactionaries" be liquidated in every village under his jurisdiction.[77] In short, there is no doubt that the presence of Zengos at the head of the Communist Party in the Argolid and Korinthia explains part of the violence exercised by EAM during 1944.

However, an interpretation that lays all (or even most) of the blame on particular persons would be both unsatisfactory and misleading. First, personalistic accounts fit with the view of the red terror as an aberration. Yet there is something preposterous about branding as "deviant" a behavior that appears to have been a widespread pattern as opposed to an exceptional occurrence. Blaming Zengos (and a few other cadres) tells more about how the Communist Party tried, at a crucial juncture, to evade its responsibility for the atrocities than it does about what caused these atrocities in the first place. Second, such an account fails to explain why there was such a concentration of extremist communists in certain areas, such as the Peloponnese.[78] Third, it also fails to explain the variations of violence within regions: why did some villages in the Argolid suffer disproportionately from the red terror? Fourth, while Zengos was overzealous, he still followed the party directives for the elimination of the "reaction" — as I showed above. Moreover, Zengos was never really punished. The actual accusations that led to his dismissal from the Party were trivial compared to his actions.[79] What is more, Zengos was quickly rehabilitated. He was given a new position in central Greece, on Aris Velouchiotis's recommendation, before being transferred to the infamous KKE Bulkes camp; he ended up in Poland, where he died a natural death years later.[80]

A better way to explore the causes of the red terror is the following hypothesis: the use of terror by EAM was a function of the severity of the challenge faced by EAM.[81] Moreover, the likelihood of widespread violence depended on this challenge being (repeatedly) acted upon. According to this hypothesis, local factors, such as social conflicts and the personalities of local cadres, should only account for residual differences. In other words, the best predictor of the number of EAM victims should be the strength and activity of organizations, such as the Security Battalions, that challenged EAM's authority; such organizations were stronger in the Peloponnese and western Macedonia, precisely the areas where EAM resorted to widespread violence.[82] In turn, the growth of the Security Battalions can be accounted for by a combination of factors: the prewar politics of the region, the military importance of the area for the Germans, and the available resources.[83]

As I pointed out above, mountain villages far removed from the threats posed by the Security Battalions were less likely to be targeted by EAM, as opposed to hill villages, where the probability of a villager coming into contact with the Security Battalions was higher. For example, the mountain village of Frousiouna in the Argolid, which suffered little EAM violence, had never been visited by the occupation troops until it was attacked by them in July 1944. In a letter they sent to the Red Cross authorities, the inhabitants of the village pointed out that "never had the occupation army and the SB come to our area and never did the population imagine that such a raid would take place given that our region is mountainous and deprived of any roads. As a result of this psychological state, the people failed to take any preventive measures."[84] The confirmation of this hypothesis demands sustained empirical investigation.

VIOLENCE: INTRODUCING SEQUENCE

Malandreni and German Terror

The village of Malandreni, located in the western part of the Argolid, affords an edifying example of the problems of an exclusive reliance on archival material when studying violence, namely the tendency to generalize from only one aspect of a complex set of events.[85] This relatively prosperous hill village (population in 1940: 883) appears in the German archives under the name of Melandrina; a report mentions that the village suffered indiscriminate looting by a group of sixteen German soldiers, who also beat up a woman who protested. The German territorial commander in nearby Korinthos was so appalled by what he saw as "gangster methods" comparable to behavior in the "Wild West" and indicating a wholesale deterioration in military discipline that he wrote a scathing report to his superiors. Mark Mazower uses this case as one example of the German army's brutal behavior and of its imposition upon the Greek population of a "daily threat of an apparently random and undiscriminating violence [that] became central to their experience of the occupation."[86] This is a valid point and, indeed, the brutality of the German army in occupied Greece (and elsewhere) has been amply documented. However, the image of the Greek experience of the occupation conveyed by this example is incomplete. Placing German terror in the context of a sequence of local developments reveals a complex and nuanced picture of this experience.

EAM came to Malandreni in August 1943, when a communist from the nearby town of Nemea secretly visited the village and founded a local committee of EAM composed of two teachers, a doctor, a student, and a farmer, none of whom was a communist. However, all were equally excited about the prospect of contributing to the resistance movement, the echoes of which could be heard from central Greece. The main activity of EAM in Malandreni became the collection of food for the supply of an ELAS unit stationed in the nearby mountains. EAM also focused on fighting petty crime. For example, the mayor of the nearby village of Sterna who had received Italian monies for his village's contribution to the construction of a road but refused to pay the village workers was threatened by a group of EAM members and forced to pay the villagers. When three boys stole money from a shepherd, EAM played an active role in retrieving it. As Yannis Nassis, a leading member of the Malandreni EAM explains in his memoirs, "It would have been a success for the organization if we could find the thieves."[87] Indeed, he succeeded in finding the culprits and had them return the money. However, this case provides an early example of how things began to unravel with potentially catastrophic consequences. When an ELAS unit visited Malandreni for the first time, its commander asked the villagers if they had "traitors or thieves" among them. Without a second thought, the shepherd's wife named the three boys. The ELAS commander demanded that the boys be delivered to him for punishment, but Nassis managed to save them and the matter stopped there. In many instances, the first people to have later joined the Security Battalions were precisely young men who had been publicly humiliated by EAM.

The EAM organization suffered a relative decline during the last months of 1943 as the two teachers left for other villages. A reorganization took place in January 1944; at the same time, a secret five-member KKE cell was formed. The key KKE and EAM members overlapped. The village notables refused to participate in the EAM committee for fear of possible reprisals by the Germans who were in nearby Argos and paid frequent visits to Malandreni. Nassis points out that he warned them: "The organization will have to be formed, willingly or not. If you participate you will guarantee your own security. If you don't, you will be the first to be in danger."[88] Though these men did not join, they supported EAM like everyone else in the village. Participation was then universal, Nassis recalls: "The village was like a bee-hive. Everyone was a member of the organization, some in Popular Justice, some in security (observation posts, outposts, transportation, supply)."[89] However, the seeds of discord were being sown. Small disputes connected to compulsory labor and requisitions would be blown out of proportion in a matter of few months.

The rise of EAM provided incentives for many people to settle past grudges. Personal disputes began to blend with politics from the very beginning. For example, one of the first men to be arrested by EAM had been accused of having denounced to the Italians a number of his co-villagers who were hiding weapons; as it turned out, however, this man had been falsely accused by his sharecropping associate, who wanted to keep the farm's crops to himself.[90] A few people who had been beaten up by the Italians because they had refused to surrender their weapons began to agitate against the village mayor, whom they accused of being an associate of the Italians — and whom they also disliked for a variety of personal reasons. The village *ipefthinos* consulted with the ELAS commander about his case and was told that only traitors were to be liquidated, not mayors. However, the mayor's enemies kept conspiring against him and, during April 1944, bypassed the local EAM committee and sent an anonymous denunciation to the regional committee. They fingered a number of people, including the mayor, whom they accused of collaboration with the Germans. The regional committee carried out interrogations that showed that the accusations were really, as Nassis points out, about "oil, lambs, etc., the usual stupid stuff."[91] Nobody was arrested.

The relative proximity of the Germans and the threat of reprisals proved an important inhibiting factor for the inhabitants of Malandreni, who had to tread very carefully. In October 1943, the British Liaison Officers active in the area (Major James and Captain Fraser) decided to sabotage the Argos airport, built and used by the Germans. Their attempt failed, partly because, as the BLO Captain Fraser pointed out, "the inhabitants of Malandreni did not wish to be involved with the Germans, who, in Argos, were only 20 minutes away."[92] In mid-April 1944, a Greek-speaking member of the German occupation forces, who went by the Greek name of Anestis, began to pay regular visits to Malandreni as part of an effort to lure the village to his side. The EAM village committee handled these contacts very carefully, to avoid exposing the village. During one such visit, EAM members from a neighboring village asked the Malandreni EAM members to ambush the Germans. The latter refused to do so, fearing German reprisals. As a result, the Malandreni EAM members were reprehended by these (safely) radical EAM members. In the meantime, "Anestis" announced that he would pay a visit to Malandreni during the local festival of St. Athanassios, on 2 May. Again, radical EAM members from neighboring villages began lobbying in favor of attacking the Germans. Nassis went to see Zengos (alias Stathis), the regional committee secretary, in order to lobby against the ambush. Zengos's reception was very cold: "Who do you think you are, comrade?" he asked Nassis, "A representative of the Germans?" Nassis replied: "No, comrade, I just came to compare the benefit [of ambushing the Germans] with its cost, this is why I came." "The Germans burned many other villages," Zengos replied, "but these villages joined the *andartes*."[93] Following this exchange, Nassis met with other cadres ("the big guys") and eventually got the second secretary of the regional committee to vouch that no ambush would take place: "The village knew about these developments and when it learned how the matter was decided there was great joy," Nassis recalls.[94]

However, on the day of the festival, armed *andartes* came to Malandreni. They told the local EAM members that Zengos had overruled the second secretary and green-lighted the ambush. Using the extensive telephone network set up by EAM, the Malandreni EAM members called Zengos, who confirmed this decision. The Malandreni committee relented: "Since Stathis gave orders," Nassis points out, "who were we to refuse?"[95] The villagers heard of these developments and immediately deserted the festival in anticipation of the German reprisals; they quickly gathered as many of their possessions they could carry with them and fled the village. "Anestis," who in the meantime had arrived with a couple of soldiers, saw the villagers fleeing, got suspicious, and left quickly; the ambush failed. After two weeks (21 May 1944), the Germans returned to Malandreni. Their intentions were now different. They killed a man in a neighboring village and arrested a teacher who, under pressure, informed them about EAM (around this time two young men from Malandreni also joined the Security Battalions in Argos). They looted a few houses, but did not destroy Malandreni. This is the event that appears in the German archives, an altogether rather minor event in the tragedy of Malandreni.

At around the same time, the German troops and the Security Battalions launched their deadly mopping-up operation against the villages of the eastern Argolid. Both individual villagers and EAM cadres in the western Argolid, including Malandreni, became frightened by the unprecedented amount of violence. As I pointed out in the first section, the mopping-up operations in the eastern Argolid led many villages to defect to the Germans. Entire villages accepted weapons from the Germans and joined them in the fight against ELAS. EAM leaders became extremely worried about this development. Their worries increased when scores of villagers, including EAM sympathizers, began to flee to Argos in order to avoid being killed in an area that they anticipated would be the next German target. Among them was Nassis's brother

Spiros, a student, who was so thoroughly scared that he decided to flee to Argos in spite of his brother's warnings. He knew a doctor who admitted him in a clinic — a safe place to hide. The party leaders decided that this had to be stopped. On 6 or 7 June, the EAM provincial committee met and asked the Malandreni organization to force all the villagers who had fled to Argos to return to the village, and threatened sanctions. Back in Malandreni, this decision gave rise to rumors that those who had fled would be executed. Instead of causing those who had fled to return, these rumors caused a new wave of fleeing. Fearing for their lives, close relatives of those who had previously fled left for Argos. As soon as they arrived there, they cautioned their relatives against returning to Malandreni.

On the afternoon of 9 June, a group of German soldiers and Security Battalionists raided Malandreni.[96] Some of them, dressed as a peasants and guided by one of the men who had fled during the previous days, entered the village and caught everyone by surprise. Nassis was shot in the leg but managed to escape. Others fled to the nearby village of Douka, where the KKE regional organization was holding a meeting. According to Nassis:

> Stathis told them to go back to the village. Then, Christos [Dassaklis] without thinking about the consequences told him: "Where will we go comrade? They almost killed one of us. Don't you see, we have traitors." Christos said this and then he couldn't stop and he began to name names, any name that came to his mouth. "Let's go," Stathis told him, and ordered [an OPLA] group to go to the village and arrest the traitors.[97]

Thirteen people, mostly relatives of those who had fled to Argos, were arrested in the night of 13–14 June 1944. Their houses were burned down and thoroughly looted. The prisoners had their hands tied with barbed wire and were taken to Douka, and from there to the concentration camp located in the St. George Monastery in the Feneos Mountain, where six were released and the remaining seven were killed by having their throats slit.[98] The most tragic individual story is probably that of Yannis Nassis's brother, Spiros, and his fiancée, Kiki Kalantzi.[99] Her mother and brothers had been arrested by the Italians because they had sheltered British soldiers, left behind in the British retreat from Greece. After being freed, her two brothers joined ELAS as guerrillas. Her sister, Mina, who worked for the BLO team, had just been executed by EAM in its campaign against villagers who were seen as too close to the British — and after being denounced by her fiancé, who had heard that she was carrying an affair with a British Liaison Officer. Kiki was arrested to exert pressure on Spiros Nassis to return from Argos, where he had fled. A few days after the killings took place

(Kiki was among the victims), relatives of the victims who found Nassis's whereabouts in Argos denounced him to the Germans in an act of revenge. He was arrested, sent to a concentration camp, and shot in August, in a reprisal execution. An observer unaware of these complex dynamics could interpret these two killings as that of a "left-wing resistant" killed by the Germans[100] and of a "collaborator" killed by EAM. It is obvious how erroneous such an interpretation would be.

Nassis claims that he attempted to intervene and save his co-villagers—and I found his claim plausible. His efforts were hampered by his wounded leg. In spite of this wound, he went to the mountain village of Douka to argue his case. He saw Zengos, Gravias, and Gavos. He attempted to get the local KKE organization to act: "Whatever these people have done," he told them, "they are not traitors."[101] A report was drafted and sent to the regional committee—but to no avail. Unfortunately, Nassis had been badly discredited by the previous developments and had lost his control over the younger members of EAM in Malandreni.

One day after the arrests, a team of Germans led by the Malandreni men who had fled to Argos came to the village in the hope of saving their kin. Most villagers had fled, so the main thing they could do was loot a few houses belonging to EAM men and burn them down—in the process killing a thirteen-year-old girl who was hiding in one of this houses. They caught a villager whose brother was an EAM cadre; they took him to the church and beat him to death. They finally found four young men from the nearby village of Borsa who were guarding an outpost and killed them.

Unfortunately, this story does not end here. During June and July many more arrests took place. Seventeen more villagers were executed in the killing grounds of the Feneos Mountain by having their throats slit.[102] They were mostly men, including brothers, and fathers and sons. Most were closely related to EAM men—many were first cousins. Many more houses were burnt down and looted by the EAM members.[103] The choice of the victims was haphazard, as every member of the local organization was trying to save his skin by fingering as traitors an increasing number of their co-villagers. Likewise, some villagers were saved for purely coincidental reasons. For example, shortly after Vangelis Kyriakopoulos fled to Argos, his two daughters were arrested by EAM. Kyriakopoulos decided to hand himself over in order to save his daughters. He had been taken to the St. George Monastery, where he was slated for execution, when he met one of the executioners, named Kostas Serbetis, whom he had sheltered in his house for some time. Serbetis managed to free him, and this is how he escaped death. Indicative of the absurd arbitrariness of the whole process is the case of a young man named Liakos Dassaklis. His father Christos, a drunk, had accused him in April 1944 of being a German collaborator. Nassis had Liakos brought to him and interrogated him about the accusation. Liakos was stunned and denied any collaboration: "Me, Barba-Yanni?" he told Nassis, "Me, with the Germans?" Nassis called his father in:

> "Sit down, I told him. Barba-Christo, what is your problem with Liakos?" "What is my problem? He doesn't listen to me, he doesn't respect me." "But you don't say that in your accusation, you say that he is collaborating with the Germans." He began to lose it and [to say] that they must take him "up" [in the EAM-held mountains], they must teach him how to behave. "You should be ashamed Barba-Christo. Get out of here!" I turned to Liakos: "Listen to me: you listen to your father, otherwise I will keep the denunciation, I will send it up and they will teach you a lesson." He left. It must have been March or April. In July they took Liakos up and he never returned.[104]

After the second wave of executions in July, the Malandreni villagers who were in Argos lobbied the Germans to go to Malandreni and evacuate the villagers—which they did. They also burned fourteen more houses belonging to EAM families. To many villagers, the Germans were the liberators who freed them from the regime of terror under which they had been forced to live![105] Altogether, twenty-four villagers had been victims of the red terror. Following the collapse of EAM in February 1944, the victims' relatives began to retaliate. Surprisingly, only one killing took place in the village—but it was a grueling one. The widows of EAM victims attacked the mother of an ELAS guerrilla; they beat her to death and mutilated her. As a right-wing villager told me:

> The mother of an *andartis* had gone to Nemea, and the widows learned about it and ambushed her outside our village; and they attacked her, they did many bad things to her, and they killed her there. The widows, whose husbands had been killed [by EAM]. Yes. Revenge. But what had this woman done to them? For example, my son is twenty-five or thirty years old, he might have been a guerrilla, and they come and kill his mother? Why? Was this woman guilty? She wasn't. But such things happened then.

Many EAM members were arrested. Eight were tried and condemned to death, but no one was executed: they served from eight to nineteen years in prison. As a right-wing villager told me in an interview: "They went to prison and returned to the village. But what about those who were killed? Did they come back?" Some EAM members went into hiding and took part in the last phase of the civil war in 1947–1949. Finally, some others managed to switch allegiances. Nassis bitterly notes that the some of the same people who under EAM were denouncing their co-villagers to EAM as collaborators of the Germans, were now denouncing them to the right-wingers as communists.[106]

Many EAM members justified the crimes committed in the context of the red terror by putting forth a political argument. The appeal of Kostantinos G. Katsaros from Korinthos, accused of crimes committed by EAM during the occupation, is representative of this mode of thinking:

> If patriotic organizations committed harmful patriotic acts, these acts can be considered only patriotic wrongful acts, fully necessary for, and inevitable in the successful completion of, the patriotic struggle, which was successful, justified, and nationally recognized; it is impossible to separate and prosecute them as self-contained wrongful acts since they are linked to the patriotic struggle; they cannot be considered punishable.[107]

Nassis shuns this kind of whitewashing. He concludes his remarkable account by connecting the local developments to the decisions taken by the KKE leadership:

> Beginning of May, end of April, a KKE meeting took place in Arkadia. All the secretaries of the regional committees took part [he refers to the meeting near Strezova recounted above]. I know this from second-hand accounts. All the cadres of the movement said that an organized reaction existed. This remark was generally correct. The decision was taken to strike at the reaction. This is easier said than done because, to a large extent, action and reaction mingle together and you can't separate them even when you want to, even if you are experienced. You'll either take innocent lives or you'll leave out guilty lives. . . . So what was Stathis [Zengos] supposed to do? It is obvious. He had been told what to do in the Arkadia meeting. He had to act, but he picked the wrong target. The target was in Argos and Nafplio, not in Malandreni. Instead of striking at the head, he struck at the feet. . . . This was wrong. The decision was to strike at the reaction, not to strike at everyone. It wasn't right because when we clear the field from weeds we will take out wheat as well. But humans are neither wheat nor weeds.[108]

Douka and White Terror

On the evening of 22 May 1946, four men broke into a house in Nafplion, where they machine-gunned and killed Giorgos Kostakis, his three-year-old daughter, and a sixteen-year-old boy named Stavros Papadimitriou; Kostakis's one-year-old daughter escaped miraculously. The victims were killed while sleeping on the floor of the basement room they rented.

This grisly crime carried a clear political connotation. Both the perpetrators, led by Vassilis F. Doris and his brother-in-law Ilias K. Rotzokos, and the victims came from the same village: Douka, a mountain village of the western Argolid (population in 1940: 182). On the one hand, the adult victim, Giorgos Kostakis, had been an EAM sympathizer, while Stavros Papadimitriou's family were the main supporters of EAM in Douka (moreover, the two families were related). On the other hand, the perpetrators had formed a right-wing terrorist band. This was an instance of the "white terror," the violence unleashed by the right-wingers against the leftists after EAM's defeat. To an outside observer, this was clearly an instance of right-wing violence against left-wingers. However, a careful examination of this case unearths a far more complex reality.[109]

The judges who were assigned this case in 1946 noted that the Doris and Papadimitriou families were locked in an "enraged criminal struggle whose planned and implemented goal is the annihilation of the biggest number of each family's members."[110] The story goes back to 1942 (and maybe even deeper in the past). Vassilis Doris, a young shepherd, had a crush on a village girl, Vassiliki Papadimitriou. Vassiliki rejected Vassilis's advances in favor of his brother Sotiris. In normal times the story would have probably ended here, but this was the time of the Italian occupation. When Italian troops came to Douka to collect the villagers' hunting weapons, Vassilis Doris told the Italians that Vassiliki was hiding weapons. As a result, the Italians beat her up badly. In 1943, EAM came to Douka, and the members of the Papadimitriou family became the main EAM supporters; one brother even joined the ELAS guerrillas. They immediately began drafting reports demanding Doris's arrest for collaboration. However, their reports[111] went unheard: Doris might have been a scoundrel, but he was no traitor, and EAM saw no reason to believe the allegations against him. However, things changed in the course of the summer of 1944. The third report was sent directly to the provincial EAM committee in the beginning of July. This time around it was also signed by the *ipefthinos* of the neighboring hamlet Tsiristra as well as many Douka villagers. Most importantly, this was also when the KKE regional committee had reached the decision to weed out the "reactionaries" in the area; as a result, this report was welcomed and acted upon immediately.

On 8 July 1944, at around 10 a.m., Sotiris F. Doris and his brother-in-law Giorgos K. Diamandis were arrested in their village. The arrests were carried out by two OPLA men unknown to the victims. The next morning, at around 8.00 a.m., OPLA men arrested Sotiris's brother, Vassilis F. Doris. They told him that they were taking him to an interrogation at the provincial committee, in the mountain village of Tatsi, where the headquarters of the Argolid EAM and KKE regional committees were located. On 10 July , they were taken together with eight more prisoners to the monastery of St. George in Feneos. Doris's deposition to the court of Nafplion provides a rare glimpse into the bureaucratic process through which EAM ran its terror system.[112]

The concentration camp at the St. George Monastery was full of prisoners, including close to fifty villagers from Valtetsi, mostly old people, women, and children in rags.[113] Doris was asked to hand over his personal belongings and was told that they would be returned to him upon release. He was then taken for an interrogation, which he describes as painless, smooth, and quick.[114] No torture or beating took place. Most prisoners were poorly dressed farmers, but some were well dressed and seemed "educated." Among them was the lawyer Vassilis Tsorvas, a regional EAM cadre who told him that he had been arrested because of something improper he had said during a speech he had given in a village.[115] No one in the monastery knew the fate of the people who were taken from there.

In the early hours of 18 July (around 3.00 a.m.), a guerrilla came in the cells and called up twenty names: nineteen men and one woman. The prisoners were told that they would be taken to the headquarters of the ELAS brigade; they were immediately taken to the courtyard and tied with ropes in sets of two. They were marched up in the mountain by six men for some time, until the sun had come out. After four short resting stops, they stopped. Unknown to them, they were only 200 meters away from the site of their execution, where a deep cave was being used as a convenient burial ground. The procedure followed was impersonal and routinized: the prisoners were not insulted, abused, or mistreated during the march. They were told to sit down and wait. At this point, Doris's bland description turns dramatic: "At this moment, crows were flying above us cawing ghastly, while at the same time, yellow corpse flies struck our faces, forcing us to shake up our heads like horses, since our hands were tied." Two men, the executioners as it turned out, left for the execution site while the prisoners were guarded by the remaining four. After a few minutes, two of the four remaining men began to shuttle to the execution site, take two prisoners at a time. The execution consisted of slitting the victims' throats and push their bodies down the cave. It took about twenty minutes to expedite each set of two. During this time the remaining prisoners began to worry about their fate. Sotiris Doris told the guerrilla guarding him: "Comrade (sinagonisti), our faces have lost their color; is a knife awaiting us?" — at which, the guerrilla replied with sympathy: "Who told you this? Don't be scared, the brigade is down there, it is a big camp, a whole army is there, but there are operations going on in the village of Kionia and this is why we brought you here." After about ten people had been killed, the Doris brothers' turn came. As soon as they arrived to the execution site, they saw the two executioners smiling at them, each smoking a cigarette and holding a knife.[116] In the meantime, Doris had managed to untie his hands; he hit the man who guarded him, ran away, and escaped in spite of the shots fired at him. After a few days he made it to Argos, were he was hiding until the Germans evacuated the area. A day after his escape, in an act of retribution for his escape, EAM arrested and executed his other brother, Nikos F. Doris.

Doris managed to hide until February 1945. In March he joined the newly formed National Guard in Athens, but he immediately deserted with his weapon and returned to the Argolid to exact revenge. He formed a band composed of friends and relatives "whose objective," according to the judge's report, "was the criminal annihilation of the Papadimitriou family." Indeed, this was the *main* objective of Doris's band, as it did not seem to have participated in many other attacks. In this, this band did not differ much from most right-wing bands that only operated within a village or cluster of villages.

Doris soon caught Vassiliki Papadimitriou, beat her up, shaved her head, and probably raped her — although, interestingly, he refrained from killing her. On 12 April 1945, he killed Panayotis Kostakis, a relative of the Papadimitriou family, whom he accused of having being involved in the denunciation of his family. The next round came when two Papadimitriou brothers, Nikos and Ilias, attacked Dimitrios Koukoulis, a brother-in-law of Doris, and killed him, together with Anastasios A. Kostakis, in June 1945. On 13 February 1946, Doris and his band attacked the Papadimitriou house in Douka and killed Vassiliki Papadimitriou's mother and her young son Yorgos. Only her younger son, a fifteen-year-old named Stavros, was able to escape from the slaughter by hiding inside the house. Doris's band then proceeded to loot the house. Following this attack, Vassiliki Papadimitriou fled to Nafplion, together with her brother Stavros, her brother-in-law Giorgos Kostakis, and his two children, age one and three. In Nafplion they rented a basement, where they lived under constant fear. Kostakis went to see the president of the Court of Appeals, I. Galanos, and begged him for an escort of gendarmes so that he could go to Douka and harvest his wheat.

Unfortunately, Doris learned about their whereabouts and attacked them on 22 May 1946. Vassiliki Papadimitriou had left the basement to visit a neighbor, but her brother, Kostakis, and Kostakis's children were sleeping on the floor. After breaking in, Doris and his men systematically machine-gunned them, killing Stavros Papadimitriou, Giorgos Kostakis, and his three-year old-daughter Panayota. The gendarmerie counted twenty-one bullets. Fortunately, one-year-old Efstathia was saved, as she had slipped during her sleep toward her father's legs.

In his 1945 deposition to the court of Nafplion, Doris painted himself as an anticommunist who was singled out by EAM because of his ideas. Justifying a criminal act with a reference to political conflict was a certain way to avoid punishment. In this way, his thinking mirrored the argument of many leftists (although the outcome of the trials differed widely). Indeed, Doris and his associates were tried in July 1947, but the jury of the Korinthos court acquitted them. They also evaded additional charges by taking advantage of the Sophoulis amnesty law. After a few years, Doris emigrated to the United States, where he died many years later. Nikos and Ilias Papadimitriou served prison sentences and went to live in Athens. One-year-old Efstathia Kostaki was adopted by a family in Australia. Vassiliki Papadimitriou was rumored to have joined the Communist Democratic Army in the central Peloponnese. She survived, but the people I interviewed in Douka did not know of her whereabouts. As a Douka villager told me, "Vassilis [Doris] and Vasso [Papadimitriou] began the whole affair; they survived, but everyone else around them was killed."

CONCLUSION: THE NATURE OF CIVIL WAR VIOLENCE

What are we to make of the events in Malandreni and Douka, and the hundreds of similar events that took place in the context of the Greek civil war? A straightforward point is that the red terror is intimately connected to the violence initiated first by the Germans and their local allies during the occupation period (the "black terror"), and second by right-wing bands following the liberation of the country (the "white terror").

Disaggregating the nature of the violence during the civil war is a trickier issue. Consider the example of Douka. Were these events an instance of political violence or a case of a private vendetta? For the judges of the Nafplion court as well as for the villagers of Douka (then and now), these events constituted a clear instance of a private feud. "As is well known to everyone," a 1945 affidavit points out, "the Doris family was engaged in a conflict with the Papadimitriou family for years. . . . And it is well known that the former resorted to the Italians and the latter to the *andartes* in order to exact revenge, but the hatred grew on probably because they were not satisfied [with the intensity of the revenge]." This statement is revealing and points to what I deem to be the core of civil war violence: neither just private feud nor just political violence, but both simultaneously.

This case was not just a private feud. To begin with, unlike other areas in the Peloponnese, such as the Mani, the Argolid lacked a tradition of blood feuds. Moreover, unlike blood feuds, the competing factions of Douka began fighting against each other only when outside actors made it possible for them to do so, either by soliciting their denunciation (the Italians and EAM) or by providing impunity for their actions (the postwar Greek state). While blood feuds are a carefully scripted and regulated localized mechanism of social control (typically excluding women, children, and the elderly from the roster of possible targets), the violence of Douka degenerated into a process akin to social anomie, where no holds were barred. In accounting for the violence that struck his village, a Douka villager resorted to the same metaphor used by the German commander about Malandreni—that of the Wild West: "During these years," he told me, "our village was like Texas." This violence was clearly not just another iteration of a process taking place from time immemorial, as is the case with blood feuds; it was totally new and bewildering. Nothing like that had befallen Douka before. The political aspect of the violence is also indicated by the fact that people identified themselves with opposite political parties, and that killings typically affected only individuals whose political identities differed from that of the local "ruling party" (in other words, retaliation was impossible when the opposite side was in control).

Nor was this case just one of political terrorism. Individual motivations were mostly nonideological: no one got killed because of their political preferences in favor, for example, of a communist regime or the king—at least *not just* for them. The main individual actors were local people involved in personal and local conflicts. In most of my interviews, in most of the trial cases I have read, in most of the participants' memoirs, references to personal and local conflicts come up again and again. In fact, it is difficult to find cases in which personal or local conflicts were *not* an issue! This, it should be pointed out, is hardly an idiosyncratic characteristic of the Greek civil war. It is a staple of civil wars, both ethnic and nonethnic. Consider the following statement by Jan Gross about the violence in western Poland during the Soviet occupation: "Yet, much as the violence represented an explosion of combined ethnic, religious, and nationalist conflict, I am nevertheless struck by its intimacy. More often than not, victims and executioners knew each other personally. Even after several years, survivors could still name names. Definitively, people took this opportunity to get even for *personal* injuries of the past" (emphasis mine).[117] Gross quotes from survivor accounts that could have been taken directly from the Greek case: "Soviet authorities conducted searches and arrests . . . directly in response to denunciations by neighbors who had personal accounts to square"; "Accusations, denunciations, and personal animosities could lead to arrest at any moment. People were officially encouraged to bring accusations and denunciations"; "Whoever had a grudge against somebody else, an old feud, who had another as a grain of salt in the eye—

he had a stage to show his skills, there was a cocked ear, willing to listen."[118]

Hence the key issue: while the script of civil war violence is often that of a blood feud with its escalating rounds of individualized retaliation and counterretaliation, it is also a violence that would never have taken place without the constant prodding, encouragement, assistance, and support of political organizations.[119] The case of Douka was neither a case of a personal vendetta nor an instance of political terrorism; it was *both*. The Italians who were searching for hidden weapons and sheltered British soldiers, the Germans who were looking for ELAS guerrillas, the communists who were looking for reactionaries, and the postwar Greek Right, which was looking for communists, all *had* to rely on local people to carry out their plans. At the same time, local people were not just innocent bystanders being tramped upon by elephants. They were willing to manipulate these political organizations in order to settle their own accounts with a ferocity that was as novel (and probably as bewildering) to them as the situation in which they found themseleves, where the wish to see a neighbor beaten up or humiliated triggered processes of (initially) unanticipated mayhem. How could young Vassilis Doris, who used the Italians to take revenge on the woman who had shunned him, possibly have imagined in 1942 that, largely as a result of his action, both his own family and the woman's would be utterly destroyed six years later?

It is this *convergence* between local concerns and supra-local imperatives, nonideological motivations and strategic goals, that lies at the heart of civil war violence and endows it with its intrinsically distinct character. The mix of identity and strategy, the personal and the political — in other words, the destruction of the boundaries between the two — emerges with clarity in Dimitrios Pirgakis's apology in the court of Korinthos. Pirgakis, a KKE member from the village of Ellinohori of Korinthia, was tried for the murder of twelve villagers by EAM in July 1944:

> I believe that personal hatred probably played the leading role in the decision to kill them, because the village *ipefthinos* D. Trimis disliked the Tsoungos family with whom he was competing in the olive-press market. The village party leaders argued that these people had to be slaughtered because they were the "black reaction," which if not attacked, would attack them.[120]

The recognition of the distinct character of civil war violence is just the beginning of serious research on the issue. Any attempt to understand violence in civil war will require both innovative theoretical analysis, and systematic and creative empirical research.

NOTES

1. C. Tsoukalas, *The Greek Tragedy* (Harmondsworth, 1969); N. Svoronos, *Episkopisi tis neoellinikis istorias* (Athens, 1982); A. Collard "Investigating Social Memory in a Greek Context," in E. Tonkin et al., eds., *History and Ethnicity* (London, 1989), 89–103; J. Hondros, *Occupation and Resistance: The Greek Agony, 1941–1944* (New York, 1983); J. Hart, *New Voices in the Nation* (Ithaca, N.Y., 1996).

2. E.g., O. Smith, "The Memoirs and Reports of the British Liaison Officers in Greece, 1932–1944: Problems of Source Value," *Journal of the Hellenic Diaspora* 11.3 (Fall, 1984): 9–32; H. Fleischer, "The National Liberation Front (EAM), 1941–1947: A Reassessment," in J. Iatrides and L. Wrigley, eds., *Greece at the Crossroads: The Civil War and Its Legacy* (Pennsylvania State University Press, 1995), 49–89.

3. E.g., A. Elefantis, "Mas piran tin Athina . . . Apo tin ideologia tou konservokoutiou stin ideologia tou prodomenou ellinismou," *Dokimes* 6 (1997): 19–50; K. Broussalis, *I Peloponnisos sto proto andartiko, 1941–1945: Apeleftherotikos agonas kai emfilia diamachi* (Athens, 1997).

4. The few (partial) exceptions include M. Mazower, *Inside Hitler's Greece: The Experience of Occupation, 1941–1944* (New Haven and London, 1993); and D. Close, *The Origions of the Greek Civil War* (London, 1995).

5. R. van Boeschoten, *Anapoda chronia: Syllogiki mnimi kai istoria sto Ziaka Grevenon (1900–1950)* (Athens, 1997).

6. Fleischer, "The National Liberation Front," 58.

7. Smith, "Memoirs and Reports." British Liaison Officers were generally hostile to EAM.

8. S. Aschenbrenner, "The Civil War from the Point of View of a Messenian Village," in L. Baerentzen et al., eds., *Studies in the History of the Greek Civil War* (Copenhagen, 1987), 105–25; van Boeschoten, *Anapoda chronia*.

9. The results presented here are preliminary as I am still processing this material.

10. Mazower, *Inside Hitler's Greece.*

11. The discussion is based mostly on E. Karouzou, "Cultures Maraicheres dans la Mediterranee: Les Transformations de la Plaine et al Societe Argolique, 1860–1910," Ph.D. thesis, European University Institute, Florence, 1995; and N. N. Anagnostopoulos and G. Gagalis, *I Argoliki Pedias* (Athens, 1938).

12. The national score was as follows. Monarchist parties, 47.59%; Venizelist, 44.17%; Communist Party: 5.76%

13. I. Zenginis, *To Argos yia mesou ton aionon* (Athens, 1996), 399–404.

14. I use the term "German" generically. In the Argolid there were many Poles and French soldiers serving in German units.

15. There are no data on the composition of ELAS's Sixth Regiment, which operated mostly in Korinthia and the Argolid. However, the military commander of the Sixth Regiment, Major Emmanouil Vazeos, provides in his memoirs a full list of the regiment's 147 men killed in action. Of these, only 14.9% were from the Argolid. E. Vazeos, "Ta agnosta paraskinia tis Ethnikis Antistaseos eis tin Peloponnison," unpublished ms., 1961.

16. This section is based mostly on the unpublished memoirs of Panayotis Lilis and the account of the local historian Kostas Danousis, "Anagennisi," *Opuscula Argiva XIII* (1994), 321: 4–13.

17. This is also supported by British Liaison Officers reports. See, for instance, Public Records Office, London (PRO), HS 5/699, "Report by Lt. Col. R. P. McMullen on Present Conditions in the Peloponnese."

18. EAM government is often described as "self-government." However autonomous it might appear on the surface, the local goverment was created and remained closely controlled by EAM and the KKE; regional government was openly in the hands of these two organizations.

19. C. Woodhouse, *Apple of Discord: A Survey of Recent Greek Politics in their International Setting* (London, 1948), 147.

20. Numerical estimates refer to homicides — both an unambiguous and an extreme form of violence.

21. Close, *Origins*; G. Margaritis, *Apo tin itta stin exegersi* (Athens, 1993).

22. I. Yannakos, *Selides mias mikris istorias yia ena megalo skopo* (Athens, 1986), 156.

23. PRO HS 5/698 "Report by Capt. P. M. Fraser on Some Aspects of the Peloponnese, July 1943–April 1944."

24. National Archives and Record Service (NARS), Record Group (RG) 59/868.00, Dispatch by Lincoln MacVeagh, 16 March 1945.

25. C. Tilly, "Revolutions and Collective Violence," in F. I. Greenstein and N. W. Polsby, eds., *Handbook or Political Science: Macropolitical Theory* (New York, 1975), 512.

26. The creation of an atmosphere is confirmed by accounts from other regions, such as Ilia in the Peloponnese: see P. D. Skaltsas, *Stis ochthes tou Kladeou* (Athens, 1994), 131–32.

27. C. Lucas, "Themes in Southern Violence after 9 Thermidor," in G. Lewis and C. Lucas, eds., *Beyond the Terror: Essays in French Regional and Social History, 1749–1815* (Cambridge, 1983), 152–94; J. Gross, *Revolution from Abroad: The Soviet Conquest of Poland's Western Ukraine and Western Belorussia* (Princeton, 1988).

28. NARS RG 59/868.00, 16 March 1945.

29. R. Capell, *Simiomata, A Greek Notebook, 1944–1945* (London, 1946), 127.

30. PRO HS 5/699, "Report by Lt. Col. R. P. McMullen on Present Conditions in the Peloponnese."

31. PRO HS 5/698 "General Report by Major Andrewes, Area Commander."

32. Municipal Archives, Nafplion (MAN), E 32/1945.

33. As a right-wing villager told me: "Most of the people who were killed then were right-wing people, good people."

34. The same logic about defection comes up in accounts of similar developments in other areas, such as Evia: see K. Skarlis, *Me to 7o Syntagma tou ELAS sta Vouna tis Evias* (Athens, 1986). For a description of similar developments in western Macedonia (though complicated by ethnic politics), see PRO HS 5/234, "Report by a Supporter of EAM on the Development of the Situation in Western Macedonia."

35. A. Christopoulos, *Oi Italogermanoi stin Argolida* (Nafplion, 1946), 116.

36. The Macedonian villages that accepted German weapons to fight against EAM often acted on their own initiative as well. See Margaritis, *Apo tin itta stin exegersi*, 509.

37. G. Papalilis, *I Ethniki Antistasi stin Argolida* (Argos, 1980), 31, provides the only written account of this massacre that I know of — and a highly biased one.

38. This massacre, like most, remains unrecorded. I traced it through interviews. This information was then corroborated by detailed references in the court archives.

39. Arrests took place all over EAM-controlled territory during this time, especially the formerly occupied towns. For example, when ELAS left Korinthos in the wake of its defeat in Athens (11 January 1945), it took with it 115 hostages: Historical Archive of Argos (HAA), Archives of the Nafplion Court of Appeal, ABE 175/207.

40. Van Boeschoten, *Anapoda chronia*, 129.

41. NARS, RG 59/868.00.

42. Contemporary Social History Archives (ASKI): (KKE archives), 418/F30/4/142.

43. *Kimena tis Ethnikis Antistasis*, vol. 1, (Athens, 1981), 283.

44. *Deka Hronia Agones, 1935–1945* (Athens, 1977), 180–83.

45. ASKI 418/F24/2/114.

46. *Leftheria*, 15 Dec. 1943.

47. PRO HS 5/232 "Tavernarakis Report" (which confuses EAM with ELAS).

48. *Odigitis*, 8 Feb. 1944.

49. PRO HS 5/232, "Tavernarakis Report."

50. ASKI 418/F24/2/102.

51. This was the case, for instance, in the village of Ellinochori in Korinthia (HAA ABE 176/228).

52. Gross, *Revolution from Abroad*, 117.

53. At later stages, the regional committee ordered many executions that bypassed the majority of reluctant local committees. In one exceptional instance, the EAM leader of a Korinthia village was executed for resisting executions and claiming there were no reactionaries in his village (ASKI 418/F24/2/114, as well as my interviews). In many cases, EAM members were arrested and threatened with execution for intervening in favor of "reactionaries."

54. The detailed description of the meeting matches the references about this conference that I found in the KKE archives and confirms the reliability of Lilis' memoirs.

55. Blanas was a longtime party cadre from Messenia, closely attached to Siantos: K. Karalis, *I istoria ton dramatikon gegonoton Peloponnisou, 1943–1949*, 2 vols. (Athens, 1958), 1: 80. He was later criticized in an internal KKE report drafted by Polyvios Issariotis as sectarian and short-sighted (ASKI 418/F24/2/90).

56. ASKI 418/F24/2/102.

57. More specifically, the OPLA teams were supervised by so-called second bureaux, which were under the direct control of the first secretary of each regional KKE committee: Karalis, *Istoria*, 1:215; I. Nassis, unpublished memoir, Malandreni, Argolis, 1995.

58. GPU referred to the Bolshevik secret police.

59. Lilis adds that this man was not a party representative. He was in the village to carry out another EAM-related mission and somehow infiltrated the meeting.

60. ASKI 418/F24/2/102.

61. V. Kladouchos, *Apomnimonevmata, 1920–: I psichri kai dikaia katagrafi Mias Zois* (Argos, 1995), 69.

62. Karalis, *Istoria*, 1:216.

63. In an interview he gave me, the EAM leader of the village of Kaparelli in the Argolid described in detail how he was requested by the regional leadership to bring his fellow villagers to the demonstration.

64. See Edict 546/15 (8 Sept. 1944) of the Secretary of the Interior of PEEA, signed by Georgos Siantos, which laid down a code of conduct for the newly formed EAM police (Politofylaki): MAN E 27/1944. Even though many villages were full of people willing to take revenge and settle accounts with their neighbors who had collaborated with the Germans, EAM was able to impose the law and prevent violence from erupting. This also bears out the allegation that the many mass massacres of Security Battalionists in September 1944 (e.g., at Meligalas in Messenia, where between 800 and 1,000 were executed) were planned, not spontaneous.

65. Aschenbrenner, "Civil War from the Point of View of a Messenian Village," 116. This otherwise excellent account contains no information about the regional and local institutions that made possible the escalation of the violence the author describes in the village of Karpofora.

66. Whereas the Left combined a local selection of targets with a supra-local implementation of the violence, right-wing bands typically fused selection and implementation at the local level.

67. S. Papastratis, *Sta chronia tis fotias* (Athens, 1992), 36–39. Papastratis adds that the appeals did not succeed. Although Sotiris received guarantees for his life, when he returned to his village in October 1943, he was arrested and executed.

68. Yannakos, *Selides*, 167–68, 203.

69. Yannakos was doubly lucky because he escaped from death immediately after, when the killer (apparently an amateur) hesitated to kill him in the ambush he had prepared.

70. Mazower (*Inside Hitler's Greece*, 265–66) notes that EAM was hardly a monolithic organization and that it operated within a world of "rumours, confusion, fear and ignorance, in which the state and society had disintegrated at the national level and opinions and stories circulated locally." This assessment is correct at the national level; at the regional level, however, especially in the mountain areas it tightly controlled, EAM was, if not monolithic, certainly bureaucratic.

71. An internal KKE report (ASKI 418/F24/2/90) sketches a pattern of atrocities that took place across Peloponnese, and provides a scathing indictment of Achilleas Blanas, the head of the central committee of the region.

72. Evidence is provided in Kalyvas, "Uses and Forms of Terror in the Greek Civil War: Argolis and Beyond," paper presented at the conference on "Domestic and International Aspects of the Greek Civil War," King's College, London, 18–20 April 1999.

73. KOPP is the acronym for Communist Organization of Peloponnese Area.

74. The main sources are Vazeos, *Agnosta paraskinia*, 78–88; Karalis, *Istoria*, 1:234–35; Kladouchos, *Apomnimonevmata*, 68–70; Lilis, n.d.

75. Lilis, n.d.; Kladouchos, *Apomnimonevmata*.

76. Vazeos, *Agnosta paraskinia*, 79.

77. According to Vazeos (ibid., 79), the quota was 5% to 10%; 12% according to Kladouchos (*Apomnimonevmata*, 70); 15% from every village plus 3% for EAM members, according to a deposition by an EAM member in Korinthia (HAA ABE 176/228).

78. See the extensive comments in PRO HS 5/699: "Second Report of Col. J. M. Stevens on Present Conditions in the Peloponnese, 22 June 1944." Stevens was in the north in a period of little violence, and in the south in a period of great violence.

79. Zengos was directly accused only of the execution of about ten villagers in a village lying outside his area of jurisdiction (Strezova in Arkadia), and of not following the standard procedure for death sentences. He was not accused of the mass slaughters of the Argolid and Arkadia: ASKI 418/F24/2/102).

80. Kladouchos, *Apomnimonevmata*, 69–71; Karalis, *Istoria*, 235.

81. Mazower, (*Inside Hitler's Greece*, 291) points out this logic as well.

82. According to a Special Operations Executive (SOE) report (PRO HS 5/232, "March 31st, 1944 — Greece: Political. Internal Situation. Situation of the Greek People in March 1944"): "During January and February 1944 the most frightful reports have been received from Macedonia and Peloponnesus."

83. The Peloponnese had a strongly monarchist tradition, but it was also was seen by the Germans as a front-line area vulnerable to Allied operations. Its network of communications was relatively extensive, making guerrilla activity easier to combat: C. M. Woodhouse, *The Struggle for Greece, 1941–1949* (London, 1976).

84. Quoted in K. Papakongos, *Archeio Persson: Katochika Documenta tou DES Peloponnisou* (Athens, 1977), 241.

85. The main source for events in Malandreni in 1943–1944 is the memoir of Yannis Nassis, a local EAM leader and KKE cadre. His memoir gains credibility from the fact that the author, who spent years in prison because of his active participation in EAM, and who remains a faithful communist, displays an unusually open and broad mind, shown in his willingness to criticize the actions of his own camp. I also conducted interviews with villagers from Malandreni and surrounding settlements, and extensively with Nassis himself. I also used the materials from the trial that took place after the war over the crimes committed in Malandreni.

86. Mazower, *Inside Hitler's Greece*, 217–218.

87. Y. Nassis, unpublished memoir (Malandreni, 1995), p. 4.

88. Ibid., 7.

89. Ibid., 8.

90. Ibid., 4.

91. Ibid., 15.

92. PRO HS 5/698 "Narrative of Capt. P. M. Fraser;" I. Kordomenos, *Protoporos kai nikitria I Argolida stin Ethniki Antistasi, 1941–1944* (Argos, 1994). In fact, Malandreni was more distant from Argos than Fraser acknowledged.

93. Nassis, memoir, 11.

94. Ibid., 13.

95. Ibid.

96. I failed to find the rationale behind this raid.

97. Nassis, memoir, 23.

98. HAA ABE 176/238.

99. I have changed her name, as this remains a sensitive story in the village.

100. Spiros Nassis's name is included in the memorial of resistance victims in Korinth.

101. Nassis, memoir, 25.

102. HAA ABE 176/238.

103. Nassis, memoir, 31.

104. Ibid., 16.

105. Similar reactions are reported in T. Valtinos, *Orthokosta* (Athens, 1994); and Ch. Zalokostas, *To Chroniko tis Sklavias* (Athens, 1997).

106. Nassis, memoir, 15.

107. HAA ABE 175/207.

108. Nassis, memoir, 42–44.

109. This account is based on interviews and archival records of the Nafplion court of appeals: HAA ABE 175/207.

110. HAA ABE 175/207.

111. The second report was drafted in mid-March 1944.

112. I cross-checked Doris's description with KKE cadres and an OPLA man from the Argolid whom I interviewed: they confirmed its reliability.

113. Valtetsi, a village in Arkadia, had joined the Security Battalions. ELAS troops attacked it in the summer of 1944 and killed many of its inhabitants.

114. The interrogator asked him: "What are you accused of, my son?" Following his denial, the interrogator told him: "Well, my son, go out. Bring in the next one."

115. Tsorvas was eventually freed and testified in the trial. He was drafted in the Greek National Army and killed in the last phase of the civil war.

116. Doris claims that he saw two severed heads as well, but this sounds like an exaggeration.

117. Gross, *Revolution from Abroad*, 42.

118. Ibid., 119–20.

119. S. Wilson, *Feuding, Conflict and Banditry in Nineteenth-Century Corsica* (Cambridge, 1988).

120. HAA ABE 176/228.

NINE

The Civil War in Evrytania

John Sakkas

> During the occupation I experienced fear and terror, but also
> loyalty, patriotism and true heroism. We were deprived of
> almost everything we take today for granted. Yet I feel we
> were rich, because we learned the value of human
> relationships, compassion and responsibility for each other.
> Though I would not choose to live it over again, I do look
> back at that time with a certain sense of loss. We had
> something worth living for, fighting for; some even died for it.
> It was a lesson for life.
>
> — Village man

THE MUNICIPALITY of Ktimenion is situated in the center of mainland
Greece, in the mountainous province of Evrytania. It shelters in the
foothills of the rugged and extensively wooded Mount Velouhi and is
twenty to thirty miles northeast of Karpenisi, the capital of the province, or about 180 miles northwest of Athens. The two asphalt roads
that lead to Karpenisi from the cities of Agrinio and Lamia join the
asphalt road that circles the villages of the municipality—Agios Haralambos, Agia Triada, Domiani, Petralona, Hohlia, Vraha, Kleitsos,
and Fourna—but is not yet quite finished, the section between Hohlia
and Vraha still a rough dirt and rock track. All eight villages, with the
exception of Domiani, are located on this main road. In the early 1940s
they had a combined population of about 6,400 inhabitants, and
Fourna was their administrative center.[1]

The municipality of Ktimenion played a predominant role in the resistance movement and during the civil war (1942–1949). This chapter,
based primarily on field research carried out between 1993 and 1997,
assesses that role by examining the process of consciousness transformation and the motives and norms of behavior of a number of peasant
men and women who were involved in the national events of the "troubled decade"—actively or passively. It begins by focusing on the
pre-1940 social and political climate prevailing in the municipality of
Ktimenion; it moves on to discuss the emergence of the resistance and

Wartime muletrain in the mountains of Evrytania, 1943–44.

its ability to gain the support of a large section of the local population; then it explores the origins of the "white terror" and the motives of its agents, finally measuring the impact of the civil war on the people in the area under consideration.

PREWAR LIVING CONDITIONS, SOCIAL NORMS, AND LOCAL POLITICS

Before the outbreak of the Second World War, the standard of living in Evrytania was desperately low. The mountains supported a population of more than 50,000, more than twice as many as in 1991, the vast majority of whom lived in villages and hamlets. Practically the whole of a family's budget went toward food, and it is noticeable how little, or how badly, the villagers ate. As the cultivable land was particularly meager and not especially productive, most villagers occupied themselves with cattle-raising, which provided milk, cheese, yogurt, wool for homespun clothes and blankets, and very occasionally meat, at important religious and family celebrations. Given the shortage of grain, the bread or *bobota* was made from maize, often of low quality, and was usually accompanied by cheap products such as beans, onions, lard, and potatoes. Other vegetables, and even most fruits, were a luxury. Some peasants were employed in the forests, where fir, oak, walnut, and chestnut trees predominated; others, especially in the winter, when agricultural work was scarce, eked out a scanty living by migrating to the nearest cities. They built their own houses of gray, uncut stones, on one floor or, at best, on two: humans above, animals below. The homes were poorly furnished: a few stools, a table, and a chest to hold the best clothes and any other treasured possessions. Beds were uncommon; most peasants simply slept on earthen floors covered with straw.

Successive governments had done almost nothing to develop the province by establishing the necessary groundwork, such as telecommunications, roads, medical and hospital care, or sizable factory units, to exploit the existing natural resources. Another obstacle to development was the archaic educational system and the high percentage of illiteracy. Primary education was compulsory, at least on paper, but nobody tried to enforce attendance. The local councils showed little interest, the teachers were low-paid and demoralized, the parents were uncooperative. Furthermore, teaching was excessively formal, the keystones always being, both for teachers and for pupils, discipline and unquestioning obedience to state norms. Classical and religious studies, remote in content from contemporary society and quite irrelevant to children's real needs, formed a large component of the curriculum. The medium of instruction, *Katharevousa*, was the language of the state, closer than the vernacular to classical Greek, and unintelligible to most children. Only a few of them continued their studies at the Gymnasium in Karpenisi; the remainder abandoned school by the age of twelve.

The microcosm of the peasants in Evrytania, as in the rest of prewar Greece, was centered on two social institutions that equally decisively determined social norms and patterns of behavior: the family and the Church. The family's structure was multiple and vertical, in the sense of having more than one married couple and more than two generations living under the same roof, as well as patriarchal and authoritarian. The eldest male of the family enjoyed more power and greater rights, privileges, and prestige than any other of its members. The position of the women was subordinate, and, in spite of their hard and exhaustive work in the fields, their influence was restricted to the domain of the household. They took care of the children and the very old and fulfilled numerous and time-consuming household tasks. But they had no political rights, and duties involving public contact were kept to a minimum. The children, meanwhile, were obliged to respect and obey their parents, at least up to early adulthood.

It might be expected, given the families' hierarchical and binding internal structures, that the degree of contact and cooperation between them would be very limited. In other words, here one might expect to find confirmation for Marx's famous remarks on the peasantry being a sack of potatoes, isomorphous entities without contact between them.

This was not the case. In prewar Evrytania, people were not yet deeply divided, as elsewhere in Greece, along political, social, and cultural lines.[2] On the contrary, they formed a rather homogenous society distinguished for its strong sense of communal solidarity that was favored by the almost similar economic conditions, the absence of social mobility, and the close links of kinship.[3]

The Orthodox Church was the second institution with a predominating influence, not just in Evrytania, but in most parts of rural Greece. For the great majority of poor and illiterate villagers, it constituted their only consolation and spiritual hope. But it also played an important part in their daily lives. It powerfully shaped their gender roles and social values, and with its musical and dancing ceremonies, such as the *panigyria* (festivals to celebrate the patron saint of a local church), it interrupted the monotony and boredom of rural life, provided chances for frequent social contact and entertainment. With regard to the latter, it is noteworthy that the only nonreligious recreation available was the *kafenia* that stood close to the central square of the village — in some places there were two *kafenia* — and generally served as both cafe and general store. It was in these *kafenia* that people mixed rather freely, cards and games were played, local stories were listened to and told, newspapers were read and politics were discussed.

Politically, Evrytania was a conservative province partly because of its geographical isolation, political neglect, and economic backwardness. The clientelist framework within which the bourgeois parties traditionally operated contributed to its conservatism as well. These parties were seen by the majority of ordinary people not only as embodiments of the proper set of beliefs (patriarchal family, Orthodox Christianity, national culture, private property, public order and stability — socialism was almost unknown in the province and was simply taken to mean the deprivation of individuality and the abolition of religion), but also as highly centralized patronage-based machines distributing benefits to members and voters. In an area where families were large, misery was endemic, and the staffing of the local bureaucracy was carried out almost entirely on a patronage basis rather than through competitive examinations, the possibility of even one member of a family gaining access to the lower rungs of the clientelistic ladder was compelling. A public position in Karpenisi, or a job with a local company in the nearby towns of Lamia and Agrinio, was an inestimable prize, for it meant a stable income and pension. In return, the favored was expected to express his or her preference for the traditional parties at election time. Clientelism was widespread particularly in those communities where local affairs were controlled by politically powerful lineages and socially prominent personalities. Two such lineages existed, for example, in Fourna, both held republican views and belonged to the conservative wing of Venizelism. In Agia Triada, authority was vested in the royalist lineage of Karapiperis. Most presidents of the village council elected in the interwar years belonged to that lineage and had close ties to Thomas Karapiperis and his political friends in Karpenisi, who in turn had well-developed national party connections. By contrast, Kleitsos and the village of Karoplessi, some miles away, had no such lineages, and their political life was largely influenced by educated persons with liberal and left-wing views. Such persons in prewar Evrytania, however, were the exception, not the rule. It is characteristic that in the whole of the province there were no more than twenty or thirty communists. Yet in less than two years after the beginning of the triple Axis occupation in May 1941, the situation had changed profoundly. Evrytania was suddenly transformed from a backward and conservative province to the main stronghold of the Left resistance organization, the National Liberation Front (EAM), and its powerful military wing, ELAS (National People's Liberation Army).

THE MOMENT OF THE GREAT RUPTURE

In Evrytania the first signs of a radical political awareness appeared in the mid-1930s, among ex-emigrants and seasonal laborers (road workers), among students of the Gymnasium in Karpenisi, and among teachers and journalists.[4] Political events at the regional (for example, the foundation of a communist branch in Karpenisi) and national levels, and international developments such as the world economic crisis, the coming to power of Hitler, and above all the civil war in Spain, exercised a strong influence upon their political consciousness, pushing them to the Left, and even to the Communist Party (KKE). Teachers and local journalists became particularly active mediating between the village and the outside world and broadening the views of their co-villagers. On 23 July 1933, two communist teachers, George Kospedaris and Stefos Thanos, along with a few other villagers, founded the "Union of the Friends of Progress" in Karoplessi, a year later, they also established the so-called Conciliation Committee, aiming at developing the local economy and providing local justice. The nearby villages copied Karoplessi's example and, with the encouragement and moral support of Panos Vasileiou, a journalist and historian from Agia Triada who was later exiled for his participation in the resistance, began to set up local committees to tackle some of their pressing problems. On 26 July 1935, representatives from these committees gathered in Agia Triada and petitioned the government, demanding, *inter alia*, the foundation of a medical center, the fixing of a low price for maize, the building of bridges, and the appointment of an agronomist. Similar initiatives were also undertaken by progressive societies in more distant villages, such as Laspi, Micro Xorio, and Megalo Xorio, and in August 1935 a "Pan-Evrytanian Conference" was planned to take place in Karpenisi that would debate the social and economic difficulties facing Evrytania.[5] A year later, however, under the dictatorship of Ioannis Metaxas, the conference was not allowed to convene.

A new and more radical phase of popular mobilization emerged during the early years of the occupation, and culminated in 1944, the year in which EAM established its "government of the mountains" and put into full practice its administrative and social policies. The positive consequences of EAM's administration on the rural population have been acknowledged even by C. M. Woodhouse, head of the British Military Mission to the Greek resistance, in his well-known and much-quoted book *The Apple of Discord*:

> Having acquired control of almost the whole country, except the principal communications used by the Germans, they had given it things it had never known before. . . . The benefits of civilization and culture trickled into the mountains for the first time. Schools, local government, law-courts and public utilities, which the war had ended, worked again. Theatres, factories, parliamentary assemblies began for the first time. . . . EAM/ELAS set the pace in the creation of something that Governments of Greece had neglected: an organised state in the Greek mountains.[6]

Yet, for all their importance, the experiments in local self-government in the 1930s and the experience of "Free Greece" during the occupation are not in themselves sufficient to explain the rapid growth of the resistance in mountainous Greece. Unlike the resistance in the towns and the plains, the resistance in Evrytania was not caused by the sudden foreign occupation or by the sudden collapse of the old order and its replacement by the EAM administration.

Partly because of its inaccessibility, Evrytania was never actually occupied by the Germans. In June 1941, an Italian garrison was stationed in Karpenisi. In general it appears to have maintained good relations with the local people. Later, it would be entrusted with keeping away guerrillas from the villages and guarding the vulnerable mountain passes that military detachments, flocks of livestock, and caravans had to cross. The only immediately tangible effects of Italian rule were a few reprisals, the occasional drafting of men for construction projects, and some drain on food resources due to requisition or theft.[7]

Nevertheless, thousands of ordinary Evrytanians, among them moderate conservatives and royalists, who had never seen a German or an

Italian, took the decision to align themselves with EAM/ELAS as soon as the first guerrilla bands appeared in their periphery. Their response was spontaneous, but their motives were many and complex. Patriotism must be considered of prime importance. EAM clearly placed patriotic duties ahead of political or ideological considerations, and the acronym ELAS was pronounced in the same way as Ellas — that is, Greece — which made it particularly effective in focusing on the national aspect of the war. Eighteen-year-old N. Diamantis from Kleitsos, who had just received the valuable, at that time, certificate of graduation from the Gymnasium in Karpenisi, met an ELAS unit in his way to Fourna and happily followed it because "it was his duty to fight the Germans." S. Galimanis, from the village of Dafni, thirty-two miles from Karpenisi, became a follower of ELAS mainly because he thirsted for revenge after his brother's death in the fortifications of the Beles mountain range in Macedonia in April 1941. It is not by chance that the first armed bands in central Greece appeared in Domnista (7 June 1942), southeast of Karpenisi, a village that had mourned the loss of ten men during the Italo-Greek war (1940–1941) and in which the hatred toward the Axis ran deep. It should be noted, however, that some middle-class patriots were not so willing to fight the enemy. N. Kyros, for example, a conservative merchant from Fourna living in Karpenisi, believed that the German army was invincible:

> I loved my country but I was really impressed by Nazi Germany's military successes. What could we do against them? I dare to say today that I and some other citizens in Karpenisi thought at that time that the outcome of this war would be determined exclusively by our Allies, England, America and Russia. . . . Surely, there was a sense of defeatism and vanity among some of us.

Linked to the villagers' patriotism was the acute sense of *filotimo*, a notion embodying honor and shame. The inhabitants of Evrytania had the traditional reputation as being always free, wild, and ungovernable. They had kept their autonomy throughout the difficult era of Ottoman rule (1393–1821) and had taken an active part in the 1821 War of Independence. Now they felt a moral obligation to defend their glorious past and protect their pride and dignity against the threats and insults of the new enemies. In Karpenisi some people joined ELAS because they could not bear to hear the Italians — whom they had defeated and even humiliated at the front — singing "the children of the Duce went to the villages of the *tsoliades* [collaborationist units]." An event that accidentally took place prompted another inhabitant of Karpenisi, Th. Tsiamtsiouris, to join ELAS, even though he was an *ethnikofron* (nationally minded) and firm supporter of the monarchy:

I was walking in the town when I suddenly came face to face with an Italian. I looked at him. He thought I was laughing at him and he slapped me. I felt angry and humiliated. I left immediately and joined the first ELAS band I encountered. And I stayed with them until 1944. Why should I leave? They were fighting the enemy. That's what I also wanted.

Tsiamtsiouris's spontaneous change of political camps is not surprising. In the villages of Evrytania the boundaries between Right nationalism and Left patriotism were sometimes blurred. A typical example is the similar political course of two prominent activists, Georgoulas Beikos and Dimitris Bakolas. The son of a farmer from Kleitsos, Beikos joined the Communist Party, as he himself states in his two books on wartime Greece, at the age of seventeen, but soon afterward he became involved in the activities of Metaxas's youth organization, EON (*Ethniki Organosis Neon*, National Organization of Youth), in Larissa.[8] When the Greek-Italian war broke, out he joined the National Army, fought at the front, and, upon returning to his village, began to organize the first communist cells in Evrytania. In the 1950s he was exiled to various islands of the Aegean, and after the colonels' coup d'état in 1967, he worked as a foreign correspondent of the outlawed leftist newspaper *Avgi* in Moscow until his death in 1975. His friend and comrade Bakolas, a thin, gentle-looking lawyer of transparent honesty and integrity from the village of Mavromata, was also a Metaxas sympathizer before the war. The German invasion of Greece and the sudden collapse of the old order, however, exerted a strong influence on his political thought, and in mid-1941 he came in contact with the KKE Central Committee in Athens. He was then authorized to set up a party organization in Evrytania and, at the same time, took over the editorship of the *Foni tis Evrytanias*, a former pro-Metaxas local paper that appeared once a week.[9] Thanks to his efficiency and fierce determination, the KKE and EAM organizations in Karpenisi increased their memberships considerably. But after Liberation, the KKE Central Committee, instead of rewarding Bakolas for his valuable wartime services to the cause, and at the instigation of ELAS leader Aris Velouchiotis, sent him off to Party branches first in the town of Nafpactos and then in the province of Evvia, instructing them to isolate him. In mid-1945 he was arrested on a trumped-up charge and assassinated in a police station. His father, uncle, and cousin were executed during the civil war, and all the households of the Bakola lineage in Mavromata were burned down.

Behind EAM's membership expansion in Evrytania lay another factor of equal, if not greater, significance: the rapid deterioration of living conditions, particularly during the first half of the occupation period.

Many villagers, goaded beyond restraint by the *pina* (hunger, starvation), the spread of infectious diseases (polio, malaria, typhus, tuberculosis), and the hardships of daily life, joined EAM in their desperate effort to get the elementary means for their survival.[10] EAM placed particular emphasis on relief measures calculated to meet the villagers' immediate needs and in time restore the standard of living to its prewar levels. It concentrated its efforts on supervising local production, organizing soup kitchens within the villages, and monitoring the movement of goods in and out of them. In Agia Triada, almost all of the seventeen EAM members, ten of whom also belonged to the Communist Party, were young and lived in extreme poverty. For them, the fight against the Nazis and the struggle for a new dignity as human beings went hand in hand. Galimanis recalls:

> I was so poor that I could not provide for my family even a piece of bread or a pair of shoes. Hunger was then my permanent friend; he never left me for a moment and partook of all I had. I decided to join the resistance after my brother's death and when I was told that EAM was the only solution to our miserable economic situation.

EAM/ELAS prestige was further enhanced by its wholehearted support for the traditional and much-respected institutions of the Church and family. Even the communists within EAM were reluctant to go along with their clear-cut Marxist slogans and risk leaving the peasantry in isolation and their alliance strategy in tatters. Some *kapetans* (guerrilla leaders) agreed that Orthodoxy and communism had many points in common, and Aris Velouchiotis himself often stressed the importance of the Church and extolled the virtues of the Greek family, based on monogamy, strict morality, and sacrifice for the collective good. Many priests took part in the resistance, and two Church dignitaries backed EAM, the Metropolitans Ioacheim of Kozani and Antonios of Ilia. The contradiction between the KKE's silence on religion and defense of the family and the *Communist Manifesto*'s advocacy of their eventual abolition was not taken seriously or reflected upon. It was not until 1977 that the communists organized a conference on religion, family, and society, and even then there seemed little recognition by the leadership of how important the issues were.[11] "What many of us in the resistance wanted," remarks Dimitris Karathanos, a lawyer now living in Athens and one of the few communists in Agia Triada before the war, "was not the abolition of Orthodoxy or the dissolution of the traditional family, but *laokratia* [People's Rule] founded on the values of egalitarianism and solidarity and the principles of direct popular participation and social justice."

Yet the Communist Party had no clear idea how to exploit the very new conditions created by the war and establish *laokratia*, a term that, for all its vagueness, exercised considerable intellectual and political fascination. At a practical level, the KKE's deep uncertainty, if not outright confusion, about both its long-term strategy and its day-to-day tactics became visible when the dilemma of patriotism (national unity) versus ideology (people's self-government) came to the forefront. In mid-1942 five young communists, among them Beikos and Thanos, founded a committee in the village of Kleitsos that structurally and functionally belonged to the KKE organization in Karpenisi and was responsible for the neighboring municipalities of Ktimenion and Dolopes. In December 1942 this committee, without any previous consultation with the KKE or EAM headquarters in Karpenisi, decided to fill the political vacuum in their area of responsibility by drawing up a code — popularly known as the Poseidon Code — for village self-government and people's justice. Article 1 provided for the formation of local five-member committees in each community, if the people desired to do so. According to Beikos, "The Code laid the basis for a soviet model of administration." His superiors in Karpenisi, who were not prepared to sacrifice national unity on the altar of their "revolutionary" convictions, curtly dismissed the committee's ambitious scheme as being antiparty. In fact, what they particularly feared was the reaction of the small noncommunist component of EAM, the Union of People's Democracy (ELD). "Do not forget," they replied to a stunned Beikos, "that we have EAM, a program of EAM, a position of EAM for the solution of the internal problem after liberation. The main issue is that of national liberation. All other problems are subjected to it." Although they officially refused to collaborate with the committee, in practice this stance was less rigidly maintained. However, Beikos and his close comrades were left with little doubt that the party's desire was to check the autonomous tendencies in the mountains of Evrytania and gradually replace the Kleitsos model of self-government with an "officialized" and "bureaucratized" system of administration.[12]

The centralization of EAM/ELAS's rule in Evrytania and elsewhere remains unexplored or inadequately analyzed. But it was not the only grim side of the resistance. Another one was the increasingly coercive aspects of ELAS policies. This is a subject that deserves a separate study. Here I will only point out that Aris Velouchiotis — "the fighting genius of ELAS," as he was described by Woodhouse[13] — and other ideologically fanatical *kapetans* were not only self-disciplined and capable of great feats of physical strength and endurance but also capable of a brutality that was by no means confined to action against collaborators and informers; it also included Italian and German captives and prisoners as well as resistance rivals and innocent civilians.[14] To explain this behavior, it is not enough to argue that this was a "natural" response to the problems of the guerrilla war.[15] ELAS controlled almost the whole of Evrytania, while the Italians in Karpenisi displayed a tolerant attitude toward the local population. Yet ELAS's repression was so intense that many villagers were forced to join the resistance or get involved in the institutions of self-government simply to avoid charges of treason and threats to their lives.

Some guerrillas resorted to violence because they had been hardened by having been deprived of their youth, their families, and a normal existence during the Metaxas dictatorship. Aris was one of those who had developed a fiery temperament after suffering many years' cruelty as a party activist at the hands of the police before the war. During the resistance, he punished severely his "fellow-combatants" for such minor offenses as stealing chickens; but at the same time, he himself often behaved improperly toward the local population. In mid-October 1942, for example, he ordered the arrest of four respected family men from Kleitsos, among them a teacher and a doctor, charging them with stealing some wheat from the village storeroom. For almost a week he tortured them mercilessly and unceasingly. When Beikos informed Bakolas about Aris's behavior in Kleitsos, the latter simply commented: "Lucky for you, he didn't kill all of you." Many years later one of the store guards confessed to the village priest that the four men were innocent because he had committed the offense.[16]

There were also a few guerrillas who simply continued the long tradition of brigandage.[17] Like the freedom fighters that manned the Greek War of Independence, known as *klephts* and *armatoli*, they had to prove their "worth" to their leaders and, especially, the peasantry; through violence and terror they made themselves feared, achieved recognition, and secured a position of power and influence. Sotiris Drakos, Aris's close friend and comrade, was one of those *kapetans* who were able to attract the support and admiration of the common folk out of fear of reprisals rather than out of sympathy. On 8 October 1942, Drakos and his men murdered two little girls in the village of Hohlia, five miles from Agia Triada, because their father had deserted the resistance a few days earlier and gone to Italian-occupied Karpenisi. When Beikos asked Aris to bring the "butchers" before a People's Court in Hohlia and sentence them to death, the ELAS leader replied with astonishing coolness: "What's done cannot be undone."

Relations between ELAS fighters and their political advisers, usually members of the KKE, were not always harmonious. Some *kapetans* treated party functionaries with the utmost suspicion and contempt, particularly those who were not under their control or influence or who refused to tolerate their excesses. Powerful *kapetans* usually disregarded any political authorities who ventured into the territories they controlled, and ruled as petty despots. "Aris," wrote Bakolas to the KKE Central Committee in the winter of 1942, "knows not what rule and proper behavior mean"; he implored the committee to intercede with Aris, so that he and his followers might show more respect for his authority. The Party allowed Aris to continue his activities, but in early 1943 sent Andreas Tsimas, one of its most educated and able cadres, to keep an eye on him.[18]

The indisputable existence of black stains on the history of the EAM/ELAS resistance little affected the popular enthusiasm for the new style of political and social practice in Free Greece, which, generally speaking, remained high throughout the occupation. What had marked the wide appeal of EAM/ELAS were not only, and even not primarily, its ideological aims and political projects, but also its practices and everyday activities. For the first time in modern Greek history, people who had been almost continually ignored by governments in Athens from the establishment of the modern state were mobilized in the political and social sphere and were called upon to be directly involved in the construction of a new institutional order; and for the first time in modern Greek history, long-established concepts of legitimacy came under attack, and traditional power structures, either bureaucratic or based on a personalistic network, were shaken or discredited in the previously neglected mountainous regions, where inhabitants had traditionally been regarded as apathetic and conservative. In the words of Beikos, the resistance represented "the moment of the great rupture with the past, a break which opened the way to a more direct and socially just form of democracy and state."[19] However, the great hopes of so many people were not to be realized. For although the immediate objective of the KKE and EAM was not a socialist revolution, as has often been argued,[20] but the expulsion of the foreign invaders and the continuation of national unity after Liberation, the British government under Churchill, who lacked the slightest sympathy for communism, was determined to maintain its traditional hegemony in Greece at all costs, and thereby to safeguard what was still considered to be a major strategic line to the oil fields of the Middle East and to India. In December 1944, the British prime minister decided to intervene militarily, and an expeditionary force was dispatched to Athens to crush the ELAS forces. After five weeks of fierce fighting, EAM was forced to sign an agreement at Varkiza, outside the capital.

ORGANIZED VIOLENCE AND MANUFACTURED CONSENSUS

The Varkiza agreement, however, did not bear the fruits for which most people had hoped. For although EAM conformed to its terms, the government carried out none of its obligations.[21] As a result, within a few months the entire leftist coalition of the occupation years came under severe persecution by para-state forces aided by agents of the official state. The judges of the People's Courts were accused of murder, the tax collectors for PEEA (Political Committee for National Liberation, the provisional government of Free Greece) of theft, and the *kapetans* of "moral responsibility" for crimes. In May 1945 EAM was forced to publish a White Book, detailing murders, arbitrary arrests, and attacks on left-wing offices and newspapers; in September, the Greek government admitted to some 16,225 prisoners held on political charges.[22]

By that time, rightist terrorism in Evrytania had assumed enormous proportions.[23] Its agents in Karpenisi and the nearby villages were the state representatives, the National Guard, and, after late summer 1945, the gendarmerie and the so-called Society of the *Ethnikofrones*. Government appointees, such as the prefect (nomarch), G. Stamatis, a member of Papandreou's Socialist Democratic Party, the mayor, N. Karras, who was replaced in late 1945 by D. Kotsibos, a well-meaning and simpleminded conservative, and the city council, felt it was their task to keep in with the local elites who sympathized with monarchism. They therefore were more preoccupied with breaking EAM's authority and reducing its influence in the province than with tackling the daunting tasks of reconstruction and rehabilitation. Among the first measures they adopted immediately after their installment were the diversion of supplies of the United Nations Relief and Rehabilitation Agency into royalist and black market hands, the purge of democratic elements from the public services and municipal councils, and the prohibition of pro-EAM meetings and festivals. The responsibility for the implementation of these measures lay with the National Guard, a militia commanded by Greek army officers. It consisted largely of volunteers raised to fight ELAS in December 1944 and former members of the German-armed and -trained Security Battalions. The prefect, the mayor, and the National Guard maintained friendly relations and a personal network with the Society of the *Ethnikofrones*, which had been formed in June 1945 in order to coordinate the fight against EAM in Evrytania by some respectable *ethnikofron* citizens, among whom were P. Papaspyrou, a doctor; N. Papageorgiou, a lawyer; and the director of the Gymnasium in Karpenisi, I. Siakavelas.

In the distant villages of the Ktimenion municipality, where the state's authority was even more precarious, the leading part in hunting and persecuting leftists was taken by the notorious Grigoris Sourlas from Thessaly and Vourlakis from Fthiotida, and by local young right-wing extremists such as Lambros Voutselis, Giannis Lozos, Giannis Karabas, Kostas Tziavos, and Kostas Samaras. By the winter of 1945 there were more than 600 right-wing paramilitaries in Evrytania.[24] Sourlas had a long penal record for brigandage and acted under the protection of Zervas's EDES, the wartime anticommunist resistance organization. His base was in Farsala, and his 250 permanent armed men were organized by the ex-collaborator Major Toliopoulos in bands from ten to thirty strong, but often grouped in larger units. Vourlakis was an aggressive and extremely dangerous bandit who acted in central Roumeli. His band persecuted and killed tens of innocent people, even from his own village. Both these terrorists enjoyed a semiofficial status, having established close links with government authorities in Athens.[25] The local bands, consisting mostly of illiterate villagers, were usually small in number, poorly disciplined, and ill equipped, and often acted in cooperation with National Guard, the extremist political organization "X," the village EOBs (*Ethniki Organosis Vasilikofronon*, National Organization of Royalists) and the Society of the *Ethnikofrones*. The latter was responsible for financing Voutselis and Lozos, two former shoemakers, and Karabas, a convicted murderer with a history of psychiatric problems, whose band included the cynical chief shepherd and big landowner K. Malamoulis. The Society gave them every practical assistance they needed to "restore" law and order in the area. This the three bandits were only too glad to do. In the absence of any determining ideology, the continual discovery of "enemies" was essential, as their sole legitimate raison d'être. They broke into homes searching for guns; intimidated, threatened, and kidnapped innocent girls and women; and tortured and killed unsuspecting villagers, often for no other reason than because those villagers had expressed misgivings about what they were doing, or because some member of their band had a personal grudge against them. As Voutselis and Karabas had no legal status and were bound by no regulations or code of conduct, their "police" actions were arbitrary and erratic, and frequently outraged the sensibilities of those conservative sections of society whose approval and support the authorities were anxious to retain. As early as mid-1945, Voutselis had become so repulsive to the Society of the *Ethnikofrones* that it demanded and achieved the dissolution of his band.

Yet rightist terrorism was not just thuggery. Some *ethnikofrones* joined the existent bands or formed their own because they saw little difference between the equally antimonarchist liberals and communists, and no possibility of compromise with either. During the civil war most were absorbed into the infamous MAY (*Monades Asfalias Ypaithrou*,

Rural Security Units), which enjoyed army help. Samaras, an EOB member in Kleitsos, and Tziavos, a field guard from Petralona and one of Zervas's most loyal and trusted followers, were not only admirers of King George, but also blindly fanatical anticommunists. Dimitris Kavadias from Agia Triada, who knew personally both Samaras and Tziavos, explains the reasons why he joined a rightist band:

> I feared the communists . . . they wanted disorder and dishonor for our country. They were godless . . . a terrible thing. We, the patriots, loved and prayed to God. We loved our parents as much as our country and our country as much as our parents. We loved the king who personified our free and glorious country. We felt love and graditude for all those who had gived their blood for Greece. . . . Why did I personally join the band? For three reasons: because I wanted to be free, not a slave in a communist country; because I wanted to rescue our Macedonia from the Slavs; and, more importantly, because I wanted simply to survive by killing the *EAMovoulgarous* [EAM-Bulgarians] before they killed me.

At no time between the Varkiza Agreement and the first postwar elections, in March 1946, were opponents of the white terror capable of making a decisive or sustained initiative against its onslaught. Communists and noncommunists were never able to find sufficient common ground for alliance, nor were they organized for physical violence, unlike their adversaries.[26] The KKE organization in Karpenisi had been thrown into disarray, as many leftists, among them Bakolas and Beikos, had been murdered or had gone underground to avoid arrest. Moreover, many moderates who had experienced the rigid activism of ELAS during the occupation feared the "red menace" and the possible overthrow of the state by the Left far more than they feared the white terror, for all its thuggery. This resulted from the fact that the white terror advanced not only by means of intimidation and murder, but also by virtue of its ever-intensifying organization of consensus through psychological pressure and propaganda. It was to the manufacture of this consensus that the governments of 1945–1946 attempted to harness every means of communication available to them, ranging from institutions such as education at all levels to the auditory and written word. Thus, after Varkiza, a former resistance member could easily be stigmatized as "communist" and "unpatriotic," the latter being a reference to the KKE's alleged support for Slav Macedonian secessionism, and forced to repudiate his principles and enroll in the villages' royalist societies. On the other hand, most of the national and local newspapers, the radio, members of the economic and social elites, politicians, and state officials in Karpenisi tended to present a very one-sided view of the situation in the province, to the detriment of the Left, and to the credit of the bandits, the "defenders of law and order." As a result, a substantial section of the formerly radicalized public opinion, especially in Karpenisi, gradually underwent a conversion to tolerance or even support for the agents of the white terror.

In the municipality of Ktimenion a number of villagers remained discontented with rightist acts of violence but, in the absence of any noncommunist alternative to that imposed by the Right, found it expedient, indeed realistic, to adapt themselves to the changed circumstances of national life. They simply reverted to their habitual way of life behind closed doors or among their friends, compromising themselves minimally with the regime in carrying out the task required of them in their jobs and professions. There were also other more abrasive forms of this essentially passive opposition, found particularly among former resistance fighters. They were often manifested as an unwillingness to demonstrate even token public identification with the regime, such as refusing to collaborate with the authorities, take part in official celebrations, act as informers, or obtain the "certificate of national probity," even though this stubbornness frequently led to harassment in their daily lives.

It was the institutionalization of the white terror with the adoption of emergency legislation, which amounted to martial law, by the newly elected government of Constantinos Tsaldaris during the critical months of the summer of 1946, and the restoration of the monarchy after the dubious referendum in September, that caused the first serious cracks in the heterogeneous structure of the manufactured consensus. In the face of the virulent anticommunism that permeated the entire state apparatus, and as rightist terrorism intensified day by day, an increasing number of people in the communist and noncommunist Left found that they had no other choice than to take refuge in the mountains and meet violence with violence. The civil war was only a matter of time.[27]

THE CIVIL WAR: HUMAN SUFFERING, MORAL DISINTEGRATION AND SOCIAL EXCLUSION

A few months before fighting broke out between the KKE's embryonic Democratic Army and the National Army toward the end of 1946, leftist villagers in Evrytania, on their own initiative, had begun to form self-defense units (*Aftoamyna*) and collaborate with the few bands of former ELAS *kapetans* (Pelopidas, Lefteris, Korozis, Nikitaras) that continued to exist, despite the Varkiza terms, in the mountains, especially between Kleitsos and Karoplessi. These bands operated independently and without coordination and, for the most part, confined their activities to threats, both to obtain food and to maintain their domination in the area. Their tactics changed in August 1946, when a small gendarme contingent was unexpectedly attacked on Mount Trifyla, near Kleitsos, in the course of which a MAY terrorist and two civilians were killed. From then on, guerrilla retaliatory attacks on rightist bands and gendarmes increased, and in December a guerrilla unit led by Ermis (Vasilis Priovolos), a former member of ELAS and admirer of Aris Velouchiotis, entered Fourna, shut down the local gendarmerie station, and made the nearby village, Vraha, the temporary seat of the guerrilla headquarters for the municipalities of Ktimenion, Dolopon, and Agrafon, consisting of twenty-five communities.[28] In Agia Triada, twenty-eight villagers, six of whom were young women, joined the Democratic Army, either because they and their relatives felt unprotected and at risk of being abused or because some of them had been badly treated by bandits. At the same time, men of the Right in that and other villages, especially those who had been prominent in or were leaders of this side and had in some way been involved in terrorist acts, began to depart from their areas and concentrate at Karpenisi, where, they thought, it would be possible, with government reinforcements, to hold out against and finally defeat the guerrillas. Their departure for the town indicates how fragile their post-Liberation dominance over the Left seemed in their own eyes.[29]

Indeed, their anxiety was justified. By mid-1947 there were more than 1,500 Democratic Army fighters in Evrytania, 10 percent of whom were ELAS veterans. They controlled nine-tenths of the province. Only Karpenisi and its surroundings remained in government hands. In late January 1949, the Democratic Army decided to launch its last major offensive in central Greece. Two divisions numbering about 3,000 men led by the *kapetans* Giotis (Harilaos Florakis) and Diamantis (Giannis Alexandrou) attacked Karpenisi and successfully overpowered the garrison. The town was held for about three weeks, and during the last three days, when the guerrillas had decided to withdraw, several executions were carried out, shops and public buildings were ransacked, and hundreds of rightists were taken hostage or forcibly recruited into the Democratic Army ranks.[30]

Only an approximate estimate of the losses of the civil war in the villages of the Ktimenion municipality can be made, since civilians were killed as readily as people in uniform, and much of the worst killing took place in areas where, or at times when, nobody was in a position to or cared to count. The casualties show deep political divisions within some villages: Agia Triada lost 50 villagers, 18 from the Right (10 were killed in action, 7 were captured and executed after the guerrilla occupation of Karpenisi, 1 was victim of revenge) and 32 from the Left (15 in action; 17 civilians were victims of revenge, of whom 2 were burned

Political commissar, Western Macedonia, 1947. Reproduced by kind permission of the estate of Nancy Crawshaw.

alive at the beginning of August 1947 and 10 were literally slaughtered near the village of Domiani on 8 July 1948). Petralona lost 26 villagers, 9 from the Right (1 in the battle of Karpenisi; 6 civilians were executed, a girl was shot in the village, 1 died from the cold near Karpenisi) and 17 from the Left (5 in action; 9 civilians were executed by Tziavos in May 1947, a girl named Kiki Vasileiou was executed in Lamia *after* the end of the civil war, 2 captive guerrillas were burned alive). Hohlia lost 8 villagers, of whom 4 were executed by the guerrillas in revenge for their terrorist activities, 1 leftist was executed by the village's MAY band, and 3 guerrillas were killed in action. In Agios Haralambos, with the exception of a priest and a young girl who were killed by accident after a bomb explosion, six guerrillas and soldiers killed in action, and the execution of a rightist murderer, there were no other casualties during the civil war. The reason for this is that at the end of 1946 the leftists agreed with the local authorities to avoid fratricidal fighting and protect their village. By contrast, Domiani mourned more than 50 guerrillas, soldiers, and civilians. The exact number of casualties from each side is difficult to estimate. What is known for certain is that on 8 July 1948, 18 Domiani civilians, men, women, and small children, were arrested, brutally tortured, and finally executed, along with others, by fanatical rightists. Vraha lost more than 25 villagers; at least 17 died in action, while several civilians were executed by guerrillas, 5 of whom because they allegedly owned a wireless set, and a girl, forcibly recruited to the "movement," because she had deserted the Democratic Army ranks. More than 40 villagers from Kleitsos perished in action or were executed, while about 45 guerrillas from the capital of the municipality, Fourna, were lost in various battles, one of which took place inside the village in April 1948.[31]

The heavy human death toll was only one of the disastrous consequences of the civil war in the municipality of Ktimenion. Within a few years the area was profoundly transformed at almost every level—physically, demographically, economically, politically, and socially. Private houses and public buildings were destroyed, and hundreds of people were left homeless and unemployed. Before the Second World War, Evrytania had had a population whose rate of increase (births minus deaths) was quite high, even by Greek standards: about seven per thousand from 1920 to 1940. During the 1940s the population declined dramatically—the result of the casualties, enforced evacuation, and migration for direct political reasons—as Table 9.1 shows.

The transformation of the municipality's economic landscape was also dramatic. Transport and communication networks were severely damaged, trade came to a standstill, the production of most goods was abandoned, and livestock nearly disappeared. By September 1949, the cost of living was 254 times that of before the war, and for most people starvation was close at hand.[32] According to a woman from Vraha living in Athens, who asked to remain anonymous, at the end of the civil war several men in her village "looked skinny and weak. Even at ten in the morning they looked as though they just didn't have any energy left. There were also some children whose heights and weights met the medical definition of chronically malnourished."

Beyond the human suffering and physical losses, the civil war affected fundamentally general models of social relations and expected patterns of behavior. It created situations in which the villagers could not trust anything or anyone, thereby eating into the social fabric at numerous points, and poisoning or breaking down traditional relationships of sol-

TABLE 9.1
Population Trends in the Municipality of Ktimenion

Communities	1920	1940	1951
Agia Triada	576	773	535
Petralona	217	297	193
Hohlia	301	357	231
Agios Haralambos	226	295	206
Domiani	671	698	557
Vraha	825	857	629
Kleitsos	—	1,489	1,080
Fourna	1,457	1,591	1,110
Total	4,273	6,357	4,534

idarity. Apostolis Skartsiounis from Agia Triada corroborates this from his own personal experience:

> My village was split into two. The civil war divided people, it ruined families, kinships, friendships. On one side there were the real patriots, "the saviors of the nation," and on the other there were the "Commies," the traitors. At the local we were always on our guard, we always looked round before we said anything; after all, it only took one word out of place and you were in trouble.

With the onset of the civil war, the prewar sense of collectivity disintegrated and the "passions of instinct" came to prevail.[33] Villagers who previously were kind, generous, and politically indifferent or neutral were fanaticized and began to persecute relatives and friends with unprecedented ferocity. Whole families were split or uprooted, or perished altogether. In Agia Triada only one girl survived from the Skodrianos family. Her parents were burned alive, her two brothers and one sister were killed in action, and another sister was arrested, tried, and executed on the charge that she came from a guerrilla family. In Domiani two families were wiped out. Thanasis Oikonomou lost his father, his communist brother, his wife, and his two small sons, and Takis Papageorgiou, a Democratic Army major, lost his parents, his two sisters, and his little daughter. Takis himself was killed in action in March 1949.

One of the lasting consequences of the civil war was that the Greek citizens were politically and ideologically dichotomized into two broad categories, the victors and the defeated. Those who were on the winning side, the loyal, "healthy," *ethnikophrones*, formulated and imposed upon Greek society an organized oppressive anticommunist sociopolitical system that seriously affected all state-citizen relations of domination until well into the 1970s. Those who were on the losing side or associated with it, an amalgam of communists, socialists, and progressives of various shades and colors, were not only silent and silenced, but were virtually written out of history, except in the role of the "enemy" in the moral Greek drama of Good versus Evil. Characteristic is Skartsiounis's personal adventure. He joined ELAS in 1942, at the age of seventeen, having already been a member of EAM's youth organization, EPON; the following year he became a member of the Communist Party. At the early stage of the civil war he lost his father and two brothers, also ELAS partisans.[34] He fought with the Democratic Army in the battle of Karpenisi and was one of the few in Diamantis's Second Division who managed to overcome the physical and psychological exhaustion—he even thought of committing suicide—and survive. He was arrested during his wanderings in the forests of Evrytania and transferred first to a hospital after having been seriously wounded, and then to a densely packed camp of political detainees, the so-called Dachau of Lamia, where he was subjected to torture. He was tried and imprisoned first in Crete (1949–1955) and subsequently in Corfu (1955–1961) and Aegina (1961–1964). But his sufferings did not end with his release:

> When I returned home in 1964 I was greeted by only five or six people. Most fellow villagers avoided talking to me not because they thought me a bad man but because they ran the risk of being stigmatized and losing their job. . . . Until recently there was an orchestrated campaign for my isolation. Even my closest relatives were advised not to talk to me. I usually sat in the *kafenia* in the company of shoppers and visitors from Karpenisi or Athens. . . . The authorities did not allow me to get a government grant after the disastrous earthquakes of 1966; and they repeatedly warned my fiancée and her parents about the dangers they ran if she married me. . . . Since 1974 things have changed for the better but the memory of the civil war haunts me even today [1986].

There is no doubt that there have been important changes in Greece since the restoration of democracy in 1974. The KKE has been legalized, the majority of political refugees have been allowed to return from eastern Europe to their homeland, the police files used in the persecution of EAM/ELAS members have been burned, and the EAM/ELAS organizations are no longer officially discredited. Memorable achievements of the resistance are now officially commemorated in a new spirit, and the dead and missing of the Left are remembered together with the others. In 1985 Evrytania elected its first leftist Member of Parliament (PASOK) for fifty years; and a few years later the local authorities in the villages of Fourna and Domiani built memorials of white marble and inscribed on them the names of the fallen from each side of the civil war. The villagers themselves show today a greater willingness to reassess the period. In the new political atmosphere that prevails in Greece, especially since the coming of PASOK to power in 1981, they feel confident in telling their story or in expressing sincere opinions and judgments, without fear of being stigmatized as not being nationally-minded or *miasma*, a label previously applied not just to communists, leftists, and sympathizers, but also to anyone who was "disloyal." Like all his co-villagers, Skartsiounis can read whatever newspaper he likes, go to whatever *kafenio* he wants, and join the men of his preference in the *kafenion* table. More importantly, the villagers appraise the events in the 1940s in a more balanced way, instead of merely casting them in black-and-white terms. This does not mean that there is either a consensus of opinion or a uniform political interpretation of the civil war. Even today, whenever the villagers discuss these events — and they are now rarely discussed — the intense memories of the period still haunt them. Most villagers see their recent past with less emotion and with more disposition to understand and know the exact truth about it. On my last visit in the municipality of Ktimenion (April 1997), I sat outdoors in a *kafenio* in Fourna with a teacher, the son of a former member of ELAS, who expressed to me the great desire of the current younger generation to heal the wounds of fratricide and face the challenges of the new post — Cold War era: "We have seen some terrible things here, we and our parents. Let's hope that it will never be like that again."[35]

NOTES

1. In 1940 the populations in Evrytania and Karpenisi were 53,471 and 3,510 respectively. In 1991 the figures were 24,307 and 5,868 respectively. I. Zoubos, *To dimografiko provlima stin Ellada kai eidikotera stin Evrytania* (The demographic problem in Greece and especially in Evrytania) (Athens, 1996), 33, 82, 88.

2. In the village of Karpofora in the southern Peloponnese, for example, the divisions were along lines of kinship, reinforced by prewar political alignment. The village of Imera in western Macedonia was divided along religious lines. L. Baerentzen, J. O. Iatrides, and O. L. Smith, eds., *Studies in the History of the Greek Civil War, 1945–49* (Copenhagen, 1987), 105–25; H. Fleischer and N. Svoronos, eds., *Praktika tou Diethnous Istorikou Synedriou. I Ellada, 1936–44. Diktatoria, katochi, antistasi* (Minutes of the International Historical Conference, Greece, 1936–44: Dictatorship, occupation, and resistance) (Athens, 1989), 508.

3. From 1910 until 1936 the Greek political world was polarized by the bitter conflict (national schism) between Venizelism-republicanism and anti-Venizelism-monarchism. In Evrytania, only Karpenisi had a distinctive social elite, small in size and strongly nationalist and monarchist.

4. There is as yet no historical study about Evrytania in the 1940s. This is

due not only to the scarcity of primary source material, but also to the "centralist" mentality of most Greek historians and their traditional emphasis on political and national history.

5. Omospondia Roumelioton Ellados, *Tris Omilies. Timitiko afieroma ston Pano Vasileiou* (Three speeches: A honorary tribute to Panos Vasileiou) (Athens, 1978), 41–43.

6. C. M. Woodhouse, *The Apple of Discord: A Survey of Recent Greek Politics in Their International Setting* (London, 1948), 146–47.

7. One of the few Italian reprisals in Evrytania was that of 24 December 1942. The guerrillas had killed some Italians near the village of Micro Xorio two days before, with the consequence that thirteen villagers from Micro and Megalo Xorio, ignorant of their fate, were arrested, forced to dig their graves, and shot. In the municipality of Ktimenion, the Italians appeared for the first time in the summer of 1941.

8. *Foni tis Evrytanias*, 20 Aug. 1939; G. Beikos, *I laiki exousia stin Eleftheri Ellada* (People's power in Free Greece) (Athens, 1979), vol. 2; and idem, *EAM kai laiki afto-dioikisi* (EAM and people's self-government) (Thessaloniki, 1976). Beikos passes over in silence his activities in EON in his two books, while it is not at all certain that he joined the Communist Party at the age of seventeen.

9. *Foni tis Evrytanias* circulated from 1936 until 1944. Up to its 243th issue it supported the Metaxas regime. It changed political line only when Greece was occupied by the Germans in May 1941.

10. The large number of tuberculosis cases in the immediate postwar period is an indicator of the degree of malnutrition suffered during the occupation. In the autumn of 1945 a society was founded in Karpenisi, a town well known before the war for its healthy climate, to take care of the infected people.

11. *Rizospastis*, 13 May 1977.

12. Beikos, *EAM kai laiki afto-dioikisi*, 14–44, 68–69. A crucial aspect of EAM's centralization was the voting procedure. There was a kind of "elective dictatorship" in the mountains. Noncommunist voters sometimes had their views suppressed in dubious "majorities" that resulted from the fact that they often could choose no one other than the usually sole candidate selected by EAM.

13. Woodhouse, *Apple of Discord*, 65.

14. See, for example, the inhuman torture and death of an Italian prisoner named Giovanni by ELAS guerrillas after the blowing up of the Gorgopotamos bridge on the night of 25 November 1942, in H. F. Meyer, *Vermisst in Griechenland. Schicksale im Griechischen Freiheitskampf, 1941–44* (Berlin, 1992), 122. The killing of rival band-leader Colonel Psarros in Roumeli in the spring of 1944 is a characteristic example of ELAS's determination to monopolize the armed resistance.

15. The violence of the Greek resistance is another issue that historians have yet to research. In his recent superb study on the morality of the Italian resistance, Claudio Pavone examines the antifascist violence not as a simple *response* ("Violenza antifascista contrapposta alla violenza fascista" [416], but as a problem of (political) culture. *Una guerra civile. Saggio storico sulla moralita nellà Resistenza* (Turin, 1991).

16. Beikos, *I laiki exousia*, 1: 305–9.

17. For the phenomenon of brigandage in nineteenth-century Greece, see J. Koliopoulos, *Brigands with a Cause: Brigandage and Irredentism in Modern Greece, 1821–1912* (Oxford, 1987).

18. *Rizospastis*, 12 Dec. 1942.

19. Beikos, *EAM kai laiki afto-dioikisi*, 73.

20. The choice before the KKE during the occupation was never between moderation and caution on the one hand and a revolutionary program on the other, although it has been presented in these ways by those who argue for the "missed" revolutionary opportunities. It has now been proved from documented research that the KKE had no intention of seizing power by force. See P. Grambas, "The Greek Communist Party, 1941–45: Internal Debate on Seizing Power," in M. Sarafis and M. Eve, eds., *Background to Contemporary Greece*, (London, 1990), 2: 181–99. Given the fact that Greece was traditionally under British influence, the KKE, led by the conciliatory and pragmatic George Siantos, avoided any extremist temptations and tried to foster national unity. Therefore, the charge that the party capitulated in a series of accords (Plaka, Lebanon, Kaserta, and Varkiza) seems unjustified. By contrast, the dogmatism and opportunism of the next communist leader, Nikos Zachariadis, decimated a much-promising generation, afforded the Right the opportunity to determine the nation's course for three decades, put the left-wing movement back by many years, and led his party to a new dark age of illegality.

21. The government's obligations consisted in the restoration of civil and trade union liberties, as well as the purging from the state machinery of fascist and quisling elements. EAM demobilized ELAS and was itself reconstituted into a new coalition of parties, of which the Communist Party was the strongest (400,000 members at the beginning of 1945). The other major left-wing party, the ELD (*Enosis Laikis Kimokratias*, Union of Popular Democracy), left EAM in April 1945 and merged with the small Socialist Party of Greece (SKE) into a united party. See H. Fleischer, "The Third Factor," in Baerentzen, Iatrides, and Smith, eds., *Studies*, 189–212.

22. *Lefki vivlos: Paravaseis tis Varkizas Flevaris-Iounis 1945* (Athens, 1945), reissued by Ellinika Themata (Athens, 1975); H. Richter, *British Intervention in Greece: From Varkiza to Civil War* (London, 1985), 163.

23. There are two valuable primary sources for the white terror in Evrytania. The first is the local republican weekly *Ta psila vouna*. Its first issue appeared in April 1945 under the editorship of Nikos Thanos, a former assistant editor of *Foni tis Evrytanias*. It was closed down by the monarchists at the end of the year. The second source is the remarkable series of letters from G. Bourdaras, a progressive politician and future minister of Posts and Telegraphs in the government of Sofoulis (November 1945–March 1946), published in *To Vima*: 7 July, 29 Aug., 30 Oct., 16 Nov. 1946; 16 Jan., 5 June, 23 Aug. 1947; 13 June 1948. Bourdaras consistently regretted and sharply criticized the persecution of leftists in Evrytania. See also V. Apostolopoulos, *To chroniko mias epopoiias. O Dimokratikos Stratos Ellados sti Roumeli* (The chronicle of an epopee: The Democratic Army of Greece in Roumeli) (Athens, 1995); and Kosmas Souflas, *Apo to diogmo ston emfylio* (From persecution to civil war) (Athens, 1986).

24. It is estimated that by the beginning of winter 1945 there were more than 600 rightist bandits in Evrytania. *To Vima*, 30 Oct. 1945.

25. For Sourlas, see A. Sevastakis, *Kapetanios Boukouvalas: To andartiko ippiko stin Thessalia* (Kapetan Boukouvalas: The guerrilla cavalry in Thessaly) (Athens, 1978), 92. Zervas wanted Sourlas to succeed him when he died: *To Vima*, 18 Sept. 1945 and 25 Mar. 1947. Georgios Papadopoulos, the leader of the colonels' junta, rewarded Sourlas by pensioning him off for his services against communism. For Vourlakis and his activities, see *To Vima*, 12 June 1948; and *Eleftheri Ellada*, 22 Mar. 1946. Comments about the cooperation of Sourlas and Vourlakis with the state authorities can be found in *To Vima*, 13 Oct. and 15 Oct. 1946; and in *Eleftheria*, 29 Sept. 1946.

26. ELAS had given up its arms in numbers exceeding those laid down by the Varkiza Agreement.

27. Greece was the only liberated country where collaborators not only were left unpunished but also were allowed to form their own illegal bands. In his two recent and well-documented studies (*The Greek Civil War, 1943–1950* [London, 1993]; *The Origins of the Greek Civil War* [London, 1995], David Close clearly shows that the real origins of the civil war lie in the period immediately following Liberation. Yet John Iatrides, the doyen of historians of the Greek civil war, continues to maintain in his recent volume that "the Greek crisis of 1946–49 has to be viewed as a result of a Communist-inspired revolution domestically conceived." J. O. Iatrides and L. Wrigley, eds., *Greece at the Crossroads: The Civil War and Its Legacy* (State College, Pa., 1995), 5.

28. In his recent letter to a local paper in Evrytania (*Evrytos*, May 1997), Priovolos describes Aris as "a popular, unique leader, the first *kapetan* — proto-kapetanios — of ELAS."

29. *To Vima*, 15 Jan., 12 Dec., and 13 Dec. 1946. Later the guerrilla seat was transferred to Fourna by Diamantis (Giannis Alexandrou), one of the most able and popular leaders in the Democratic Army.

30. *Eleftheria*, 22 May 1947; A. Papadopoulos, *Stefos Thanos. Agones sti Thessalia kai Evrytania* (Stefos Thanos: Struggles in Thessaly and Evrytania) (Athens, 1986), 140. The battle of Karpenisi was described in detail by most national newspapers. See also Apostolopoulos, *To chroniko mias epopoiias*, 176–93; D. Zafeiropoulos, *O antisymmoriakos agon, 1945–49* (The antibandit struggle, 1945–49), vol. 2 (Athens, 1956), 548–58; and F. Grigoriadis, *Istoria tou emfyliou polemou. To deftero antartiko* (History of the civil war: The second guerrilla movement), vol. 4 (Athens, 1964), 1253–57. After their withdrawal from the town, the remnants of Giotis's division proceeded to the north, but were encircled by government troops and decimated. The remnants of Diamantis's division turned to the south and in April occupied the town of Lidoriki. Diamantis was killed on 21 June 1949, and his body was displayed in the main square of Lamia. *Akropolis*, 31 Mar., 18–19 Apr., 19 May, and 22 June 1949.

31. For the battle inside Fourna, see the monarchist national paper *Vradyni*, 24 Apr., 1948.

32. A. Nachmani, "Civil War and Foreign Intervention in Greece: 1946–49," *Journal of Contemporary History*, 25 (1990): 491.

33. "The bit of truth behind all this—one so eagerly denied—is that men are not gentle, friendly creatures wishing for love, who simply defend themselves if they are attacked, but that a powerful measure of desire for aggression has to be reckoned as part of their instinctual endowment. . . . Homo homini lupus; who has the courage to dispute it in the face of all the evidence in his own life and in history? . . . Civilised society is perpetually menaced with disintegration through this primary hostility of men towards one another. Their interests in their common work would not hold them together; the passions of instinct are stronger than reasoned interests." S. Freud, *Civilisation and Its Discontents* (London, 1930), 85–86.

34. Indicative of the atrocities committed in the civil war is the following incident related to the author by Skartsiounis. The then-governor of Karpenisi, D. Karapiperis, ordered his followers to arrest Skartsiounis's father and bring to him his ears. But, instead of killing only the father, they also killed one of his sons, and took with them four ears. When Karapiperis saw the ears, he asked sarcastically, "Does Skartsiounis have four ears?"

35. W. Churchill, *The Closing of the Ring* (Boston, 1951), 532–33.

TEN

The Policing of Deskati, 1942–1946

Lee Sarafis

DESKATI IS a village in central Greece that lies on a small fertile plateau some 700 meters above sea level on the Hasia Mountains, west of Mount Olympus and east of the mountain range of Pindos. On the eve of the Second World War, it was a substantial upland community with a population of nearly 4,000 inhabitants. The villagers cultivated the plateau, growing wheat and corn, and raising large herds of sheep and goats (roughly 30–40,000 in the 1930s). Three years after the region was wrested from Ottoman rule in 1912, Deskati became the capital of a synonymous municipality, including another five small villages within a radius of fifteen kilometers, and falling under the prefecture of Kozani.

The mountainous surroundings and the neglect by the state authorities in Athens resulted in the isolation of Deskati from the large urban centers of the area. Today the village lies on the road that connects Grevena with Elassona, but this road was constructed only in the late 1950s. Before the Second World War, when someone from Deskati wished to go to Kozani or Larisa, he had to rely on his own transport and faced a journey of several hours at least. The assignment of delivering the post went into auction because only someone with a pair of strong horses or mules could get the job. The postman would travel to Larisa once a week (only under normal weather conditions), taking and bringing back the village's correspondence. This arrangement may be taken to symbolize the rather tenuous links that joined Deskati with Larisa, Athens, and the new Greek state. "The villagers of Hasia are very mistrustful towards anything that comes from the urban centres or represents the state authority," writes Lazaros Arseniou of this crucial relationship. "On the one hand their demands were always neglected by the authorities while on the other they were persecuted by the appointed bodies if they expanded their small land by one inch, or cut a single tree for wood."[1] Before the Second World War there were—at least so far as villagers later recalled—no significant class divisions. It was an egalitarian society (the words of the interviewees are suggestive: "We were all in the soup," "We lived a good life, we did not have the luxuries of today, but we did not starve either") that had not been marked by the political upheavals of modern Greek politics. In the memory of the villagers, life before the war was somehow difficult but happy, at any rate in comparison with what was to follow. As elsewhere in the central Greek mountains, all members of the family contributed to the daily work (children leaving school as soon as they had learned to read and write), and the everyday diet was provided by each family's garden and livestock.

Before the war, the Greek state chiefly impinged on the daily life of the village through its armed representatives. In the 1930s Deskati housed a police station with fifteen gendarmes and one commander. It was the only village in the region with a gendarmerie station. The other villages in the area were policed by detachments that were under the authority of Deskati's commander. On the whole, the commander of Deskati, who reported to Kozani, had the fifteen gendarmes of Deskati's station and twenty-five who were consigned to the nearby villages under his command. Although between the wars there was an effort in Greece to professionalize policing, and considerable expansion in the number of both gendarmes and locally appointed constables took place, in fact the tight control exercised over the police by the Ministry of the Interior meant that the force as a whole was highly politicized: by the late 1930s, it was largely anti-Venizelist and associated with a repressive mode of policing that alienated the local people.[2]

In the Hasia Mountains, there were special reasons for local mistrust. Cattle-thieving was still common in the 1930s. Isolated as it was, the area of Hasia gave shelter to small groups of men who had gone into hiding because of a vendetta or police persecution, or for personal reasons. Each group had a leader and lived by terrorizing the local rich shepherds (the bandits demanded food and clothing, providing "protection" in return). The last important bandit in the region of Deskati was active until 1937–1938. After that there were bandits of lesser importance, engaged in small-scale cattle-thieving. A relatively effective measure against cattle-thieving was the state proclamation that if a bandit would surrender himself and give out names and information about his colleagues' whereabouts, he would be let free. This measure helped more toward the elimination of banditry than did the work of the gendarmerie.

A woman who belonged to one of the few somewhat better-off families of Deskati in the 1930s told me that her father was kidnapped and held hostage for a month by a group of bandits. He was released when his family provided the ransom asked for by the kidnappers, who threatened the family that "if one member talks to the police about what we have done we shall not leave one single person by your family name alive! Nor any relative close or distant!" After a few days, someone from the nearby village of Krania gave away the position of the group, and the police arrested five of its members in an ambush and killed two. When the police were informed by the captured man about the kidnapping, they arrested him and his father and beat them up for not reporting the incident. His effort to explain was in vain. In the interviewees' words: "We did not trust the police. They would not give us protection from the thieves and then they would punish us for being victims of banditry."[3]

From the moment that a quisling government was established in Athens in 1941, a new status quo was imposed. The Greek gendarmerie continued to function in Deskati as part of the civil service, though now of course it was acting on behalf of the occupying forces. For over a year it went on with its usual duties, but until the end of 1942, according to oral testimony, the only time that it saw action was when it arrested two petty cattle-thieves, the Koufonikas brothers, who were forced to parade through the village's square, carrying their prey on their shoulders.

The Italians, however, did not rely on the gendarmerie alone to preserve "law and order." An Italian army garrison was positioned in Elassona, aiming to control the area of Hasia, while a network of collaborators was organized to work for the benefit of the occupying forces. The result was that while the gendarmerie carried out its official duties (i.e., protecting Greek citizens from any law-breaking—in this area, cattle-thieving), the other two groups introduced a new kind of policing that regarded Greek citizens as enemies.

The occupiers' first two tasks were collecting all guns in the villagers' possession and obtaining provisions for their armies. Both tasks necessitated the assistance of collaborators from the village itself, who provided information as to the whereabouts of the guns and plundered provisions. Deskati had always been a self-supporting village, relying on its own cultivation and cattle, so it was not really affected by the famine that was killing thousands elsewhere in Greece. Plundering and requisitioning themselves were not a danger to the village's sustenance, and interviewees remember the situation as disturbing rather than really threatening. But the confiscation of guns did affect both their security and their honor heavily, and they remember this in the grimmest of terms. Extreme violence came suddenly to the village when a small number of villagers were hanged in the central square—where the Italians had run up the Italian flag—after having denied they possessed guns. This sight scarred the memory of onlookers; talking to me decades later, the number of victims rose to dozens and even hundreds in their minds. Other men were summoned to the elementary school where the Italian garrison was stationed and were beaten so as to give away the hiding places of their guns. "Collaborators started indicating those villagers who were suspected of hiding a gun," recalled Konstantinos T. "One of these suspects was my father. . . . You see, my father loved hunting, he was the best hunter and had the best carbine in the region. The Italians hit him hard in the face; they wore a special kind of ring which hurt very much. My brother and I scaled up the school wall and looked inside. My father's face was bleeding heavily. When he saw us, he told us to run to our house and tell our mother to bring the hidden gun to the Italians. And so we did." Actually, a number of villagers who had fought in Albania or who used to go hunting before the war had kept and hidden their guns, not least for fear of cattle-thieving, as a gun always provided protection.[4]

There were no more than ten or so collaborators in the village. In general these were men who either were opportunists or felt an ideological affinity with fascism. In the mountains of Hasia, relations with the authorities were always minimal, so very few villagers willingly supplied the occupation forces with their services. As a rule they gave the necessary information to the Italians and later the Germans and practiced plunder only to a small extent. Two of Deskati's collaborators who did more substantial harm were punished for their actions, as we shall see later.

In 1942 the resistance movement in the area of Hasia suddenly expanded. The gradual organization of armed resistance groups started in the summer months, while by the autumn a committee heading a proper EAM organization was established in Deskati. This committee was approached by a couple of guerrilla groups from Olympus who planned to visit Deskati and spread the word of resistance to the villagers. At the same time, the idea of armed resistance had already spread among Deskati's gendarmerie, increasingly cut off from the disintegrating state apparatus in Athens. Kostas Zografos, a sergeant gendarme, was particularly influential with his colleagues.

On the evening of 20 December 1942, a guerrilla group secretly entered Deskati. It was composed of men from the area of Olympus; some came from the village of Tsaritsani. Their first act early the next morning was the punishment of two collaborators. Papakostas, originally from a nearby village, was the first to go. He was sitting at a *kafenio* near the central square and was shot by a member of the guerrilla group who happened to know him personally and could identify him. The other was Feretos, a gendarme who had served the Italians with enthusiasm. He had tortured many villagers in the quest for guns and was especially hated as a result. When he was arrested by the guerrillas and was brought to the central square, the people present shouted: "Death!"

These two killings were unprecedented and aroused mixed feelings in Deskati itself. The news of the executions spread very quickly, and as a result a great number of villagers gathered in the square to see them in person. Seizing the opportunity, the leader of the guerrillas addressed the bystanders and talked about armed resistance. His words — "Words we were hearing for the first time; and they were very appealing words, too," remembered one listener — led several people to volunteer to join the struggle; for a few teenagers this was the major turning point in their lives.

When the guerrillas entered Deskati, there was no foreign army guarding the place; Italian troops had been withdrawn from such outlying areas. "Protection" of the village was left to the gendarmerie, who might have been expected to fight the guerrillas and push them out of the village. If nothing like that happened, the reason was Kostas Zografos. This gendarme had already joined EAM and had prepared the force for the visit of the guerrillas with the help of another gendarme, Andreas Kapsopoulos. Their chief aim was to avoid any bloodshed. When the guerrillas surrounded the gendarmerie station at 7:30 on the morning of 21 December, Zografos's preparation proved successful: the gendarmes not only did not fire a single shot against the guerrillas, but they took their guns and joined them. They gathered all the gendarmerie's provisions (blankets, arms, ammunition, and food) and put them at the guerrillas' disposal.

The only one who did not take part in this enthusiastic volunteering was the station commander, Stayias. Realizing his men's attitude toward the guerrillas, he surrendered his arms but refused to join. According to one version, he said he was not prepared to join the resistance and preferred to think it over, having been defended by his men against charges of collaboration. According to another source, he claimed that he could not join without direct orders from his superiors. In any event, he was given an escort and a couple of horses to carry his things, and he left for Kozani. Meanwhile, news of the guerrillas' visit reached the nearby villages. During discussion with Stayias, the gendarmerie detachment from Karpero (having received word from Zografos) arrived and joined the gendarmes of Deskati. In fact, nearly all the gendarmerie stations in Hasia had a similar reaction when the villages were visited by guerrilla groups. In L. Arseniou's book *I Thessalia stin Antistasi*, there is a photo of the "Boukouvalas" guerrilla group taken in Deskati at the beginning of January 1943. Of the sixteen guerrillas in the group, seven are ex-gendarmes. Anticommunists and communists thus found themselves working side by side for national liberation: seen from the local perspective, in a village increasingly cut off from Kozani, let alone Thessaloniki or Athens, the old divisions of national politics faded against the more immediate tasks imposed by the struggle against enemy occupation.[5]

With the guerrillas' visit, Deskati became part of EAM-controlled Free Greece, and the everyday life of the village changed dramatically.[6] Both the administrative and the policing systems were organized on a new basis. Policing was carried out by the guard marshal (*frourarhos*) as head of Deskati's reserve ELAS unit, by the so-called People's Court, and through the local EAM organization itself. The *frourarhos* was responsible for the overall security of the village against any outside threat. He had the ELAS reserve under his command and was also responsible for guarding prisoners who had to be detained in the village for security reasons. The first guard marshal of Deskati was an ELAS officer named Vouros, who was not from Hasia. Later, there was someone else from the nearby village of Krania, but his name is not remembered. In the ELAS reserve were young men who could not join ELAS, either because of their age or because they were supporting a poor family or had an invalid father or very young siblings who needed to be looked after. They were not armed but had received some training to protect the village in an emergency.

The People's Court was presided over by notables of Deskati who had been in the civil service before the war (they had received a higher education than the average Deskati villager). One was Hristos Keramidas, a secretary of the village council; another was Giannis Zarbalis, an army officer. One would expect the People's Court to have been busy trying cases of cattle-thieving. On the contrary, the interviewees do not remember a single such case being brought to court. In their narrative they linked this phenomenon with the criticism of cattle-thieving made by the leader of the guerrilla group when he addressed the public. It went more or less like this: "From now on you must have solidarity and respect for each other. The stealing and cattle-thieving that is so popular around here must stop! We have no prisons or exiles to detain thieves. If one of you is caught stealing, he will just tell us what he prefers that we cut, his head or his feet. The decision is yours." Whether or not as a result of this warning, cattle-thieving stopped (at least in the area of Deskati).

The notion of solidarity found fertile ground in the village. One interviewee, Thanasis Akrivos, said to me:

> We took all our possessions from our houses and hid them in the area around the village. They told us this was the best way to protect the dowries and valuables from the Italians and Germans. Every one of us knew that whole fortunes were hidden in the bushes but not one ever thought of stealing any-

thing. On the contrary, if someone passed by and saw that something was not properly hidden he would cover and secure it.

If someone brought a complaint, the court would issue a summons and then both parties would appear before the *laikos epitropos* (a member of the People's Committee). Usually, when the matter reached this stage, the *epitropos* made an effort to reconcile the opposing parties. I heard accounts that referred to the exemplary efforts of both *epitropoi* (Hristos Keramidas and Giannis Zarbalis), who, in the majority of cases, managed to find solutions that satisfied both the accuser and the accused. Usually the *epitropoi* were dealing with complaints and misunderstandings of everyday life. In the summer of 1943 though, one case got out of hand.

A young man from Deskati had been flirting with a girl for quite a long time, and when he confessed his love to her, both their families thought that one day soon he would propose marriage. Time passed, and all of a sudden he got engaged to another girl. The first girl's family sued the man and, as no solution was found, the case was brought into the People's Court. The court's verdict was that the man was to be executed unless he changed his mind and married the girl. Hearing the verdict, everybody, even the father of the second girl, tried to persuade the man to change his mind. He was unshakable. A group of reserve ELAS fighters took him out of the village to carry out the sentence. Among the group were friends of the convicted, who tried to talk him into changing his mind, but he repeatedly said that he preferred to be shot. After a couple of hours and with the persistence of his friends, he eventually agreed to marry the girl, and his life was spared. The wedding took place the next day, and a week later he joined ELAS.

In the winter of 1943–1944, the Germans attacked Deskati during antiguerrilla operations. The ELAS reserve received word that the enemy was approaching the area in three detachments, one coming from Kozani, another from Elassona, and a third from Trikala. Realizing their inability to defend the village against such a large operation, Deskati's EAM ordered all the villagers to evacuate. The idea was that the Germans would not find anybody to arrest and torture to get information about where everybody was. The order was disobeyed by about ten men, who received the Germans and told them that there was no ELAS in the area and that the villagers had gone into hiding. After a thorough search in the surrounding area, the Germans found eighteen people from the village, whom they shot on the spot. Among them were eminent members of EAM and ELAS. The execution is commemorated by a monument that stands in the village square.

The Germans stayed a whole week in Deskati and burned eight or nine houses. When the villagers started coming back, they did so cautiously (first the men and later the women and children), fearing that a group of Germans might have stayed behind. As soon as the village had settled down, the people who had disobeyed EAM's order were brought before the People's Court. Because of the nature of the offense, the People's Court sat together with the Guerrillas' Court (*Andartodikeio*) of the ELAS Tenth Division.

I read and heard a lot about this case from both the rank-and-file and two EAM officials. It looks as if the majority of the people who stayed in the village were pro-German. The two men, who were basically accused of collaboration (their *germanophilia* was beyond question), were sentenced to four month's exile in a village above Grevena. The members of the court that I interviewed believe that the accused were guilty, but as they could not prove this, they think the decision was fair. The rank-and-file, on the other hand, told me that in retrospect they find the sentence outrageously lenient and that the families of those who had been executed struggled to get through the 1940s and 1950s. All the interviewees, though, share pride in the fact that in Deskati, no one was killed by the resistance movement.

Although Athens and the other urban centers entered a new political phase immediately after liberation from the Germans, things went on much as usual in the rural areas of central Greece. EAM's administration continued until March 1945, when the Varkiza Agreement led ELAS to surrender its arms and its members to return home. In this new period, the first body that undertook the policing of Deskati was the National Guard, intended to form the kernel of the new gendarmerie of the country. Men who had fought in the 1940–1941 war were called up to serve in it. Not locals, however: men from Deskati were posted elsewhere, and guardsmen from other places came to serve in Deskati. The majority of them had fought in the ranks of ELAS and were greeted with joy by the villagers. A second policing force was an Indian unit of the British empire forces that was established nearby. This battalion became the talk of the village, and its dark-skinned men impressed the villagers, many of whom felt, moreover, that both Deskati and the Indian soldiers were victims of British imperialism. Today they remember the Indians as very quiet and reconciliatory during the incidents between the pro-EAM villagers and the right-wing elements that had gradually begun to organize themselves in the area. The Indian unit remained in Deskati for about two and a half months. After its departure, the police were once again installed, and a new era began for the village.

A group of twelve gendarmes with a lieutenant in command was established in the summer of 1945. In addition to this, the central government introduced a novelty that held a more important position in the policing business: a "squad leader" (Papadakis) who had a paramilitary group of about twenty men under his command and the region of Deskati, Aghia Paraskevi, Dasohori, Tsiouka, Trikokia, and Paliouria under his authority. Papadakis did not report to the gendarmerie, but acted separately. And in the fall of 1945 he launched a new kind of aggressively anticommunist policing. As an interviewee remembers:

> We did not have a lot of clothes then, we were so poor. My mother sheared a couple of sheep that we had, she went to a neighbor who had just bought a knitting machine and she had a jumper made for me. She put it into sour cherry juice to dye it and it was dark red. I was very proud of this jumper! One day they got me, they were from the police, two big guys.
> "Come here! Why are you wearing this?"
> "'Cause I am cold."
> "Wasn't there any other color to dye the jumper?"
> And they started beating me. I remember the first blows, I don't remember anything else, I was unconscious. Then they threw me out in the street. My folks took me home, they managed to save my life.[7]

Incidents like the above were happening more often. Men and women who had served in the resistance movement — or were associated with it in some way — were caught, threatened, beaten up, persecuted one way or another. They had not violated the law in any normal sense, they could not defend themselves, they were not properly detained or tried. Policing now had strong elements of terror and unpredictability and consequently changed the everyday life of the village. Men worked all day away from their houses and then preferred to stay indoors. People avoided visiting the cafeterias and the square as only their home environment was relatively safe. There seemed to be no way out, because the persecution was conducted by the state's authorities.

In March 1946 the first national elections after the war took place, despite the abstention of the Left: "Only 149 men went to vote in the elections. . . . The number did not reach 150! . . . But those who did not vote were destined to be hanged. . . . This is what happened. Those who had abstained were automatically considered sympathetic to EAM. The police conducted further persecution and tightened their grip around the suspects. In such a situation many ELAS fighters left their villages and formed the OEK groups (*Omades Enoplon Katadiokomenon*, Persecuted Armed Groups). One such group of the Olympus and Tsaritsani area approached Deskati in the spring of 1946. It made contact with Deskati's EAM, which supplied it with food and clothing. The gendarmerie were informed of its whereabouts and set off to find and hit it, but in the skirmish one gendarme was killed. The incident triggered a mass wave of persecutions, and many villagers were arrested as suspects for the killing of the gendarme. One man remembers:

> The next day, after the gendarme's funeral, the squad of Deskati together with a group of civilians and a squad from Grevena went and swept the spot where the gendarme had been killed. They started from the east, they descended to the road from Elassona, down to the area of Loutro where we have our vineyards. Whoever they found they arrested, all the shepherds, the men who were working in the fields. I was one of them, they took us all to the police station. . . . When I arrived there must have been about 150 [people there]. Men, women and children. When making the arrests they were not taking just the men but gathered all the family.

And a woman recalls: "They arrested all our neighborhood. Every neighbor I had went through the police lockup. They were beating up everybody."

In the summer of 1946, on various dates, Papadakis's squad killed a number of people from Deskati and the nearby villages. The killings took place in a remote spot, always during the night. In a significant case, four people were dragged out of their houses in the night and went missing for two weeks. Someone happened to walk near the location where they had been killed, found the corpses, and informed their families. One corpse was terribly disfigured by brutal beating. The families were so terrorized that they gave very quick and quiet funerals to their dead.

But in the face of right-wing violence, the Left gradually reorganized itself. Another guerrilla group approached Deskati in September 1946, and this time it was larger, well-organized, and better equipped. It attacked the village, won the battle with the gendarmerie (one gendarme and two guerrillas were killed), and stayed in Deskati for three days. It was a very small interval for the majority of the villagers, who celebrated the victory of the guerrillas. As soon as the group left, though, a new, much worse wave of persecutions started. More than 700 people were detained at the police station at various times:

> The room was packed, there was no place to sleep. We tried to save some space for the mothers who were carrying their babies but even for them it was very difficult. There was so much noise at night with all the beating up and torturing. And it was happening in the next room, how could we sleep? It was so terrible.

From that point on, the civil war was to develop fast, with worsening effects for the villagers. Early in 1947 Papadakis was transferred to Kozani, while the persecution of the resistance became much more organized and systematic, supported by provisional laws and the establishment of martial courts. Policing itself gave way to the presence of the army, in the region and in the country as a whole, until the civil war was over.

NOTES

1. Thanasis Akrivos, interview no. 2, p. 1; L. Arseniou, *I Thessalia stin antistasi*, vol. 1 (Larisa, 1977), 218.

2. See D. H. Close, "I astinomia tis tetartis avgoustou," in H. Fleischer and N. Svoronos, eds., *Praktika tou Diethnous Istorikou Sinedriou. I Ellada, 1936–44. Diktatoria, katochi, antistasi* (Athens, 1989), 77–89; H. Richter, *Dio epanastaseis kai antepanastaseis stin Ellada, 1936–46*, vol. 1 (Athens, 1975), 58–73; S. Linardatos, *I tetarti avgoustou* (Athens, 1966), 69–71

3. Interview with Koula Akrivou-Papatsani (her father was the victim of kidnapping described here), pp. 18–19; and Th. Akrivos, interview, no. 2, p. 3.

4. Konstantinos Trikalides, interview, p. 2.

5. Arseniou, *I Thessalia stin antistasi*, 123.

6. For EAM's administration in Free Greece: M. Mazower, *Inside Hitler's Greece: The Experience of Occupation, 1941–1944* (New Haven and London, 1993), 265–96; Thanasis Tsouparopoulos, *Oi laokratikoi thesmoi tis ethnikis antistasis* (Athens, 1989); Georgoulas Beikos, *I laiki exousia stin Eleftheri Ellada* (Athens, 1979); Richter, *Dio epanastaseis kai antepanastaseis*.

7. Interview with Koula Papatsani-Akrivou.

ELEVEN

Protocol and Pageantry: Celebrating the Nation in Northern Greece

Anastasia Karakasidou

ON THE MORNING of 25 October 1945, a four-day sailing competition got under way in the northern Greek city of Thessaloniki, in conjunction with numerous other festivities commemorating two heroic moments in Greek history: the "liberation" of Salonika from the Ottomans by the Greek army in 1912, and Greece's refusal to allow an Italian invasion in 1940.[1] The city had already been decorated with national flags, which would remain in place for the entire four-day celebration. In fact, the police made rounds to assure that every home and shop was properly adorned with the national bunting, regarded by authorities as a general expression of loyalty to the nation-state and its government. Those who failed to respond in a timely manner were fined and noted in the secret police dossiers. The municipal government saw to it that the downtown squares and main streets of the city (such as Agia Sofia, Egnatia, Aristotelous, and the *Lefkos Pirghos* [White Tower]) were also decked out with flags and that public office buildings and the White Tower were bathed in lights.

Later in the morning of the 25 October schoolchildren and older youths, together with scouting units and associations and organizations, assembled at monuments throughout the city to lay commemorative wreaths as part of the national holiday, marking what might be considered two "life crisis events" in the history of the Greek nation. In the afternoon of this first day's festivities, the Thessaloniki Municipal Band began to perform outside the church of Agios Dimitrios, the patron saint of Thessaloniki, and a procession of St. Dimitrios's icon through the downtown area followed. Later that evening, the state theater held a concert in honor of the National Rights Commission (*Epitropi Ethnikon Dhikeon*), an irredentist group lobbying for a Greater Greece, which had been meeting in Thessaloniki at the time.[2]

If this had been a festive day, the next day was even more so, it being the main day of festivities. At 7:00 a.m., the municipal and military marching bands set off on a circuit of downtown Thessaloniki, accompanied by the gay ringing of church bells throughout the city. An official doxology was held, not at the church of Agios Dimitrios, whose name-day was being celebrated, but rather at Agia Sophia, the most famous Byzantine church in the city, Following the religious ceremonies, the army paraded in Aristotelous Square to the sound of music from the municipal band. Later that afternoon, the scouts and the army jointly held a torch parade, complete with fireworks. Fencing competitions were held in the National Theater, where a (dance) performance was also staged by the Lyceum of Greek Girls. The indefatigable municipal band paid an afternoon visit to the ongoing sailing competitions, and then at 7:00 p.m. set off on a circuit of the two major thoroughfares in the city's central waterfront district, Nikis and Tsimiski, marching and playing throughout the downtown area all through the night and well past dawn the next day.

On the morning of the 27 October, a "celebration of the flag" was held in all schools. Teachers and visiting dignitaries made patriotic speeches to the assembled students, who recited poems, performed theatrical sketches, and sang songs. In the harbor, the sailing competitions entered their third day. Meanwhile, the municipal band, refreshed with a few hours' rest, began to play again at 10:00 a.m., this time in front of the luxurious and famous Mediteranee Hotel on the city's harborfront street, where they remained until noon. Later, they moved to the White Tower; at 9:30 that evening, the National Theater hosted a performance by "Markos Botsaris," a theater company named after a hero of the 1821 Greek War of Independence.

City residents were feted by music again at 7:00 the next morning, 28 October, as the municipal band and the military bands made circuits through the city, playing to the accompaniment of "merry" church bells. At 10:00 a.m., the municipal band encamped near Agia Sophia, where yet another doxology was given, along with a proper speech from the Metropolitan of Thessaloniki. The ceremonies at the Byzantine church were followed by yet another army parade, and that afternoon the sailing competitions concluded with an awards ceremony. Around 4:00, the municipal band returned to play again in front of the Mediteranee Hotel, and three hours later they made one final round throughout the downtown area of the city, along its two major thoroughfares. That evening, fireworks fired from warships stationed in the harbor crowned the sky above the festive city, and the four-day celebration concluded with a scout ceremony of songs, poems, theatrical performances, and the like at the National Theater. During the four-day celebration, people throughout Greece were encouraged to tune into Radio Athens at specific times and follow along with the ritual extravaganza in Athens, the capital of the nation-state. In fact, loudspeakers were posted in many public places to transmit broadcasts of this sort during the long holiday.[3]

PROTOCOL AND ORDERING

> The purpose of the celebration mainly will be the creation of an atmosphere that will present to the people, in a lively manner, that glorious era, and which will make [them] relive, in the soul (*psihika*), those big days, and also [continuing on the celebration's official purpose] to pay tribute to the anniversary [of the "Ochi Day"], which is one of the greatest [events] in the 3,000-year-long Greek history.[4]

So began the very first national celebrations of the Twenty-Eighth of October, or "*Ochi*" [No] Day, which became an official national holiday in Greece just a year earlier, by Royal Order on 24 October 1944.[5] Just a few years earlier, the war had begun with Mussolini's invasion; now Greece had been liberated from foreign occupation but remained bitterly divided. *The Ochi* Day celebrations were a new national holiday invented to commemorate and perhaps smooth the nation-state's recent traumatic rite of passage. Inaugurated during a period of tension and crisis, when deep schisms permeated state and society, it was a ritual celebration of national unity introduced just a few years before those rifts would turn to open and widespread violence in a bloody civil war (1947–1949). The Second World War had shattered the previously established order, and it had also offered a challenge to the legitimacy of the nation-state, which had failed to defend its citizens or protect their lives. Postwar leaders, therefore, made a conscious effort to nationalize the war experience and to create an official memory of the conflict. Remembering the national trauma through festivals aided the process of nation-building. But these events were also important from the point of view of the participants. A great desire to celebrate, to have fun, and to take part in the revival of the national community were a widespread popular response to the end of the war. To that extent, the project of national revival described in this chapter, should be viewed not only as a manipulative program set from above, but also as a project that incorporated popular attitudes and desires

As mentioned above, 26 October is St. Dimitrios Day; it was also on this day in 1912 that Greek forces marched into the "liberated" city. In this sense, for many in northern Greece, the Twenty-Sixth of October commemorates the date of Macedonia's incorporation into the Greek nation-state. As a local national holiday, the program for the Twenty-Sixth of October celebration was prepared by city authorities. In contrast, the celebration of the Twenty-Eighth of October was, and still is, a nationwide observance, commemorating a critical national "moment": namely, the first time that Macedonia, as part of the modern Greek nation-state, shared the fate of Greece at a moment of foreign aggression and occupation. The program for the celebration on the Twenty-Eighth of October, therefore, was decreed by the national government and distributed to all state-appointed administrative personnel, who assumed responsibility for the protocol and pageantry of the national rituals.[6]

By way of contrast, the other important nationwide holiday, the Twenty-Fifth of March, commemorating the start of the Greek War of Independence, has a more important national celebratory presence in southern Greece, the region in which the revolution of national emancipation actually began in 1821. The commemoration has been celebrated since its establishment, by Royal Order, on 16 March 1838. In the words of the Minister of the Interior of 1947, the Twenty-Fifth of March is a "populist, demotic" celebration. That is to say, by 1947, the Twenty-Fifth of March celebration had become enshrined in Greek popular culture. It was a "custom in common" shared by the inhabitants of "Old Greece," but it had not yet attained the same degree of popularity in Macedonia. As a state-sponsored holiday, it was to be organized by local mayors. In Macedonia, however, the Twenty-Fifth of March celebrations were under the purview of prefects, suggesting the holiday had not yet attained "demotic" status.[7]

National celebrations such as this were carefully planned and executed across the breadth of the Greek state. Greece in 1945 was, in a way, a nation-state with a new face and recently redrawn borders. In the case of the *Ochi* Day celebrations, the Ministry of the Interior had drafted a set of general guidelines that were sent first to the General Directorates throughout the country, such as that of Northern Greece, and to all prefectures and districts, the principle administrative levels of state-appointed personnel.[8] These officials then forwarded the ministry's directives to their subordinates in municipality and township offices, individuals who were largely elected local representatives.[9] By Royal Order of the Metaxas era (20 March 1939), prefects were empowered to advise mayors and township presidents, since the goal of the celebrations was the "enforcement (*tonosi*) of patriotic sentiment."[10] Even in the decades following the liberation of Greece from German occupation, the national government continued to use laws dating to the dictatorship period in order to preserve tight control over the metaphoric imagery of national rituals and celebrations.

In this manner, a relatively uniform ritual protocol was passed down from central state administration to local communities.[11] This first 1945 protocol set the mood for commemorations in subsequent years. It became a programmatic statement on how the ceremonies should be properly orchestrated and officiated with the right combination of pomp and majesty. The original directives (1945–1955) examined here, which like all official documents were written in *katharevousa* (the classical Atticized Greek), included a great variety of detail, ranging from the purpose of celebration, who was responsible for what, who should attend and in what form of attire, what decorations were considered appropriate, and what ought to be included in the content of public speeches and special talks and activities for schools and youths, to how civil servants should behave, how the church would participate, how music and parades would be conducted, and how heroes should be venerated.

In fact, throughout the next decade, ministerial directives regarding this and other holidays diverged markedly little from these original protocols and the explicit purpose(s) set forth in those early directives. A new tradition was invented and eventually established as these national celebrations became a target for what Corrigan and Sayer have termed "state regulation of cultural forms."[12] The subsequent ritual celebrations included in their work detail other innovative elements that became traditionalized in years following. Beginning in 1946, for example, military planes passed over Thessaloniki and many other towns in Macedonia. This "tradition" still occurs today. The participation of the royal couple in these national celebrations begs an in-depth study. But, for the present purposes, suffice it to say that the annual presence of the king and queen in Thessaloniki for the 26 October St. Dimitrios Day celebration had deep symbolic significance as well as mass popularity. It was what might be called a localized national celebration, commemorating the day that Thessaloniki and Macedonia became an inalienable part of the Greek nation. The presence of the royal couple, as the symbolic heads of the Greek nation, accorded national recognition to the commemoration of this local moment in Greece's national history.

This chapter, then, traces the invention, propagation, transformation, and endurance of these "traditional" national celebrations, devised by state administrators as mechanisms for creating solidarity among and for the culturally diverse population residing within the territorial boundaries of the Greek nation-state. There is no doubt that the Greek state constructed and traditionalized the nation of the Hellenes through these repetitive ritualized activities. Greek authorities created the membership of the nation by maintaining the borders of the state and by propagating ideological notions of collective identity, unity, and solidarity. In addressing this programmatic effort, I hope to illuminate one of the fault lines that marks the Greek national consciousness: where popular culture (as expressed, for example, in folk songs and tales) encounters the great traditions of the nation's glorious history in the performance of national holidays. By addressing the protocols of these pageantries of nation-state identity, I hope to reveal the iconography of the nation and the reproduction of its "traditions." I follow this process of transformation through distinct time periods since the incorporation of Macedonia into Greece in 1913. Briefly, the years leading up to the Metaxas dictatorship in 1936 were marked by ambiguity in state attention to national celebrations; during the Metaxas era, direct state involvement in such ritual ceremonies intensified dramatically, a trend that continued in the post–World War II years. During the junta of the 1970s, the nation came to be celebrated virtually every day, whereas in the post-junta era, there is a marked tendency for the state and the public to celebrate the nation when it is perceived to be endangered.

HANGING OUT THE FLAG

As Hobsbawm might have anticipated, few in Greece appreciate either the novelty or the significance of these celebrations of the nation.[13] By the time the life of General Metaxas came to an end in 1941, several important changes had been introduced in the repertoire of public celebrations and ritual festivities of the Greek kingdom. By no later than 1937, Metaxas and his cohort had come to appreciate that some of the nation's symbols had come under severe and sustained challenge by communists and socialists who stressed class affiliation, rather than national affiliation, as a moral praxis and a cornerstone of ideological belief. In response, they formulated an Obligatory Law (*Anangastikos Nomos*, no. 4471/1938) explicitly aimed at creating a feeling of respect (*sevasmos*) to the country through worship of or deference to the flag.

It was apparently for group-identification purposes that the official flag of the Hellenes had been inaugurated by the First National Assembly of 1822 in Epidaurus. On 15 March 1822, a year after the outbreak of the revolution against the Ottomans, the provisional government of Greece decreed (by Order no. 540) the creation of a national flag with two colors: light blue, representing the sea and sky, and white, symbolizing the purity of the nation. Their blending in the form of a cross was a dual symbolism, entwining national sentiments with religious convictions.

The Metaxas-era state elites, however, cultivated a disciplined respect for the national flag through an "ethical law" (*ithikos*), as they described it, that would strengthen all the "norms" (*aksies*) that have guided Hellenism throughout the historical development of the "race" (*genos*) of the Hellenes. The national flag, in this sense, became a symbol that could lead the people and the nation. The flag is, in the words of this 1937 law, "the outmost tangible symbol of the unity and substance itself of the nation as a delineated unit." The national flag was also regarded as a "tradition" handed down by the Byzantine forefathers of the modern Greek nation, for the Byzantine emperors had used flags and passed the custom on to their heirs.[14]

The idealization of the nation is evident here. The incorporation of the "New Lands" (i.e., Macedonia and Thrace) in the second decade of the twentieth century brought Greece face to face with new problems, particularly those relating to the non-Greek population of Macedonia and Thrace. The arrival in 1922 of the Asia Minor refugees and their settlement in the Macedonian countryside caused a great polarization among the rural population, whereas the refugees themselves added new strata of cultural diversity in the territorial nation-state. The government had been unstable, and the bureaucracy seemed to serve no one efficiently except the well-connected clients of powerful patrons. With republicans and royalists at odds, there emerged General Ioannis Metaxas, who had been a member of previous governments, and who had the vision to create a ritual around a national symbol that would (re)unite the populace of Greece and heal the "national schism."

The national flag, as an identification banner, came to be venerated and acquired its sacredness through such mandatory ritual. Metaxas apparently knew what he was doing, for even in the late 1930s many townships and municipalities had yet to acquire complete familiarity with the national symbol. Government directives were circulated, describing the specific measurements of the flag and ordering that it should never be flown with old and faded colors, but rather only with new cloth and bright blue and white colors; shops and houses should raise the Greek flag from sunrise to sunset during days of celebration or sorrow as well as during religious ceremonies.[15] Metaxas and his government took this new symbol of the nation of the Hellenes and legally installed it and its colors as fundamental symbols of the Greek nation. They also began the "tradition" of institutionalized national celebrations. Their executive protocols ordered and structured the activities, while their pageantry contributed to the evocation of a glorious aura. At the same time, the era of the Metaxas dictatorship established the original protocol and pageantry for the 25 March celebration. For example, Royal Order no. 791 (6 March 1939) set out clearly the protocol of the ceremonies: students were to attend mass, flags were to decorate schools, patriotic speeches were to be given, parades were to be held, national dances were to be performed, torch processions were to be organized, and local administrators were required to report back to superiors on the success of the celebrations.[16]

After the German occupation, when patriotic sentiments were at a high point but were also filled with anxiety and the memory of trauma and war suffering, the Greek state invoked the Metaxas-era directives and law to reinitiate celebrations of the nation. In 1947, for example, state authorities recirculated the 1938 Metaxas law regarding venera- tion of the national flag.[17] In fact, a royal decree of 9 May 1947, entitled "Concerning the Definition of Public Ceremonies," was issued, stipulat- ing that there were to be three official national holidays to be celebrated each year: 25 March, 29 June (King Paul's nameday), and 28 October.[18] In 1948, the list of official national holidays was expanded to include three more national holidays: 1 January, 18 April (Queen Frederika's birthday), and 21 May (the nameday of Crown Prince Constantine).[19] On all national holidays, flags were ordered flown on the shops and homes of the Hellenes. All these national celebrations were meticulously planned and highly scripted, with program and protocol guidelines set by the national government in Athens. Yet, local communities were given the freedom to add items of local importance to the program to make it more emotionally or spiritually in tune with the local populace.

LOYALTY AND ROYALTY

It was after the enthronement of King Paul II in 1946 that the Greek royalty became directly involved in the construction and cultivation of national loyalty among the citizens of Greece.[20] In so doing, of course, they were promoting their own legitimacy as well as the legitimacy of their presence and active involvement in the Greek political arena. The royal family was, in effect, attempting to endear itself to the Greek peo- ple again, after its absence during the occupation had helped intensify republican sentiment at large. While elsewhere in Europe monarchies were abolished or political powers were taken away from them, the Greek royals promoted themselves as heads of the Greek national fam- ily through social welfare programs. In fact, the monarchy picked up an old southern Greek "tradition" of baptizing the children of their sub- jects (much like politicians baptized the children of their clients): after obtaining permission from the families involved, local prefects would baptize infants in their name, covering the expenses of the ritual, and occasionally even giving them the name of the king or queen.[21] Books were published about their activities, such as Andreas Skandamis's *Kings on the Battlements* (1952), which included the texts of speeches delivered by the royal couple at towns throughout Greece. While her predecessor, by contrast, had been more actively involved in such asso- ciations as "Friends of the Forests," Queen Frederika became deeply involved with the Greek nation and its people.[22]

The royal palace staff included a grand-ritual performer, whose re-

sponsibilities were to devise rules concerning the royal couple's participation in rituals of state and nation. Given the fact that European royalty had followed a ritual protocol for centuries, it comes as no surprise
that when the king and queen began to participate in these national
celebrations, the level of necessary protocol was raised incrementally.
Maps and diagrams were devised to indicate seating arrangements on
parade review stands, with the royal couple seated at center, flanked by
the military and civil administrators to their left and right, respectively.[23]

For example, the royal couple made a formal visit to Thessaloniki in
January 1947 in order to "be in touch" with the ethnically diverse inhabitants of Macedonia. The visit, which included a tour of the countryside, lasted one week, during which time Queen Frederika presented
gifts to the children of men who had been drafted into the Greek army.[24]
Royal participation in the celebrations of national holidays began with
the Twenty-Sixth of October commemorations of that same year. By
that time, civil war had already broken out, and in the midst of the
fighting the governor general of Macedonia and his staff had to turn
their attention to preparations for the arrival of the royal couple in
Thessaloniki. Accompanied by General Papagos, the king and queen
flew into the city and were driven to their palace in an entourage of four
cars and a light truck for their luggage. Four rooms had been prepared
for their use. They spent a half hour changing and dressing for the
ceremonies, which included the doxology, a military parade, and a lun-
cheon banquet, and returned to Athens immediately afterward.[25]

Likewise, when the Church of St. Dimitrios in Thessaloniki was rebuilt in 1948, the royal couple traveled to Thessaloniki by ship to inau-
gurate the new cathedral. Protocol was followed to the letter, and the
royal couple was received with all the honor and pageantry requisite for
a visit by the monarchy.[26] Politicians assembled in jackets and tall hats,
while the military turned out in full dress uniform to greet the royal
couple at their boat. Although the visit lasted only one day,[27] there was
a formal dinner that evening. Men were instructed to dress in dark-
colored suits, while the ladies were to wear long dresses covering their
shoulders but no hats or head apparel.[28]

RITUALS AND PERFORMANCE

Anthropologists have argued that one effect of ritual action is an ele-
vated psychological or emotion identification with the social collectivity
symbolized by the ceremonies. I will not attempt here to propose standards of measurement by which we might assess the degree to which
national celebrations effected such responses. I do assume, however,
that some degree of consciousness, emotional pride, and sense of secu-

rity is generated during such ceremonies, especially when the nation (as focus of these ritual activities) faces a moment of crisis: danger and opportunity. These national celebrations, I suggest, represent a moment of juncture, a point at which *communitas* through ritual is not only existential and spontaneous, but also normative and ideological. I also assume that these festive ritual occasions played an important role in gradually establishing (and reproducing) a "consensus" on national identity by manipulating popularly held emotional and spiritual associations with Greece. This was made possible for such a diverse participating audience because of the ambiguity or multiplicity of meaning behind the symbols employed in these ritual celebrations. There was—and is—a rhetoric to these rituals, so to speak, a symbolic and psychological subtext that generates feelings regarding these national celebrations.

Yet these ritual commemorations did not have the power of rituals of conversion, at least not in and of themselves. They did not, for example, convert Slavic-speakers into nationally conscious Greeks merely by virtue of their participation in or observation of such ceremonies. They did not prompt people to alter states of consciousness, such as the speaking in tongues that occurs in some conversion rituals. Undoubtedly, national celebrations did influence solidarity and facilitated the conversion of Slavic-speakers in Macedonia to Greek conscious nationals, but such conversions were not effected through the transformative powers of these ritual celebrations alone.

The hellenization of Slavic-speakers in northern Greece had been a major concern of Greek authorities during the interwar period. In the 1920s, for example, Greek administrators were pursuing a campaign to erect heroes' monuments in the public squares of towns and villages throughout northern Greece, hoping to foster a sense of common belonging to the Greek national collectivity, as well as to its historical traditions and its ranks of martyrs.[29] Local authorities in Greek Macedonia, however, repeatedly complained to the governor general of Macedonia that they were failing to generate any enthusiasms from the "foreign speakers" (*allofoni*) in the countryside in these rituals of adoration.[30] Yet, it is noteworthy that, when festive ritual celebrations of national commemoration were inaugurated, the same local authorities reported a much more enthusiastic response from their "foreign-speaking" subjects. Clearly, these festive, local national celebrations fostered a far more positive response from the Slavic-speakers of northern Greece than did more solemn occasions of tribute or homage to national martyrs.

Following the inaugural "*Ochi* Day" celebrations of 1945, however, the prefect of Florina, the northwestern prefecture of the country bordering with Yugoslavia and Albania, reported that all the population had paid tribute to their local heroes' monuments. The state-mandated protocol or program of the celebration had been followed to the letter; civil servants had held their own separate festivities; the town's high officials had delivered speeches concerning the importance of the anniversary; Greek and British military vehicles had taken part in the town's parade; the doxology had been well attended; folk dances were performed in the afternoon at the town's stadium, followed by a "panoramic" torch procession through the town; and order had been maintained throughout the celebrations. The prefect's report contained a degree of sentimentality; he noted that the local population had felt such elation "heretofore unheard of in the chronicles of Florina."[31]

Such rhetoric contains an evident degree of hyperbole, for within a few short years the area around Florina and the town itself was embroiled in a vicious civil war in which pro-Greek and pro-Macedonian forces were battling each other for control of the land they both called Macedonia. Yet these national celebrations were implemented once again after the civil war, following the original scripts of 1945 with remarkable consistency. It was the gradual repetition of these commemorative performances, with the ideological "subterranean themes" and the symbolic manipulation of their metaphoric imagery in festivities, speeches, broadcasts, pageants, theatrical productions, parades, and the like, that eventually contributed to the successful development of Greek national consciousness in the region.

The gradual transformation of national consciousness among Slavic-speakers in northern Greece had been brought about through the *repetitive* ritual action of national celebrations *in conjunction with* other policies and practices over the years, issues that I have addressed elsewhere. Yet the power of these events in particular lay not in their direct and obvious appeal to patriotic sentiment, which in many instances had to be aggressively cultivated in some parts of northern Greece, but in the subtle symbolic manipulation of the metaphoric images embedded in their principal subtexts. In what follows, I shall attempt to explore some of the subtexts of these national celebrations, in the hope of better understanding their efficacious role in the transformation of national consciousness.[32]

All these performances contained or even centered on themes of nation and nationhood: imagination, continuity, sacredness, and danger. As a whole, these subtexts attempted to reproduce a moment in the long history of this young nation. This may help to explain why the school-taught version of the history of the 1821 Greek War of Independence is written in such a manner that it takes students an entire school year to cover. Details of every single battle are covered, chronicling the day-by-day activities of the heroes and martyrs of the national cause.

The authors and speakers of such (national) history offer young minds a myriad of details that feed imaginations. At the same time, the extraordinary amount of time devoted to rather short events fosters an elongated perception of the modern nation-state's relatively short history. Indeed, one might even argue that it supports the aura of timeless continuity in the history of the nation.

In the casting and performance of an authentic historical event, its reproduction, however inauthentic, nevertheless invokes the "aura" of that original event. Regardless of how inauthentic the reproduction of the aura surrounding such "moments" may seem to the critical observer, it was the (re)creation of such an aura surrounding these crisis events rather than the authenticity of the method of recreation that was critical to the success of such efforts. There are, for instance, plenty of examples of people attending a parade and coming away with little or no sense of solidarity with its theme, or of others who might openly criticize, mock, or joke about the spectacle. Attention to detail is a critical part of such efforts, for thick description enlivens an account and provokes historical imaginings among those who participate in, witness, read about, or hear of such momentous events. To such a script is added the moral narratives of the nation, as seen in officially promoted rhetoric surrounding the personal and bodily sacrifices made by heroes at critical moments of danger when the nation was threatened, actions taken under the spiritual guidance of Orthodox Christianity, as inherited from the Byzantines. As noted above, the reproduction need not be historically "authentic": facts may be in error, dates and sequence of events may be confused; objects and symbols may appear irrespective of their historical context. A (national) spiritual illumination is fostered not necessarily through authenticity, but rather through rhythmic and repetitive, uniformed and detailed spectacles of ritualized performance commemorating the nation.

The theme of Greece as a young country with a long history is repeated frequently, with a profound impact on the consciousness of lay citizens. National celebrations were inclusive, if not universal, observances, in that they entitled a meshing rather than a bifurcation of elite and popular cultures. Indeed, their effectiveness in raising national consciousness was arguably predicated upon the manner in which they played down differences of class, culture, or ethnicity. For all but a few, the nation (rather than class, ethnic, regional, or other difference) remains sacred, subtly reported and psychologically recorded in the reproduced aura of the commemorative crisis event.

Consider how in 1946, the General Military Command of the Third Army Corps (headquartered in Thessaloniki) wrote a letter of concern to the Minister of the Interior.[33] In it, an evidently annoyed military

King Paul and Marshal Tito at the railway station, Thessaloniki, 6 June 1954.

officer brought to the civilian government's attention the excessive use being made of the national anthem. The sacred song, they insisted in tones evocative of the Metaxas adoration of the flag, was being played far too often, and in unofficial popular contexts, to the extent that it stood in danger of losing the respect it requires and its power to evoke patriotic sentiments. The national anthem, the military insisted, should be reserved only for occasions at which state representatives were present. Deference and reverence were demanded by the guardians of the state's security, who warned against popularizing the music officially symbolizing Greece. They sought, in effect, a monopoly of the privilege to reproduce the aura of the nation through its rhythmic march-like anthem. From their perspective, the military was defending the state's authority to determine where, when, and in what context the aura of the nation might be evoked through its music.

METAPHORIC IMAGES AND POPULAR THEMES:
SUBTEXTS IN NATIONAL CELEBRATIONS

Though the nation has a timeless, eternal, and historical quality, there are also specific events from its History (an orthodox version of history, often crafted in terms of state) that mark "moments" in the nation's unending epic of liberation, freedom, and enlightenment. A celebration such as *Ochi* Day commemorated a recent event within the context of a 3,000-year national history. The citizenry honor and pay "tribute" to the heroes of 1940 to "bring back alive the glorious era" of the ancient. Government directives of national celebrations and ritual commemorations sought to evoke a state of mind conducive to popular imaginings of the glorious era of the nation's ancestors and critical junctures of its sacred history. Nations are, indeed, states of mind.

One key subtext to these ritualist national celebrations was the *imaginative reality* they fostered. By constructing an atmosphere of pageantry and glory, participants and observers alike were encouraged to imagine, in personally meaningful ways, the heroic events that gave rise to the modern Greek nation. The 1945 directive regarding the inaugural *Ochi* Day celebration, for example, stipulated that on the day preceding the official celebrations (i.e., on 27 October), schools should organize commemorations for youths to "worship" and make pilgrimages to local heroes' monuments, where the young people would lay wreaths to the martyrs who had sacrificed themselves in defense of the sovereignty of the nation. Scouts were to participate, presumably in uniform or in another marked manner, alongside other students in these rituals, together with reserve troops and representatives of injured and crippled victims. The entire assemblage was always directed to line up in an honor guard formation so that "children will feel that their presence there is something formal and which the country considers of greatest importance." Impressionable young minds are brought in ritual procession before the names or faces of heroic ancestors so that they are almost obliged to engage in their own imaginings of national history as well as of their place within it. Commemorative prayers were offered, and after wreaths were laid, a moment of silence was observed.[34]

National celebrations also emphasized the *continuity* of the national collectivity, stretching back some 3,000 years, a very long history indeed for a relatively young nation-state. The links contemporary state elites claim to the heritage of glorious personages of ages past are affirmed in these ceremonies. Unaltered rituals, as Cannadine put it, "give an impression of continuity, community and comfort." These commemorations also invoked (to various degrees) the *shadow of threat* or danger to the national collectivity and its continuity, and the presence of the military in these rituals was intended as an expression of security to the populace. Finally, all these marked observances included a strong religious element or sacredness, as Orthodox Christianity presented as a steadfast symbol of the great arch of unity of the Hellenic "race" (*genos*) throughout its imaginative national history.[35]

It is important to note the dual character of the two major national celebrations: that is, their strong secular national as well as religious themes. Both the Twenty-Fifth of March and Twenty-Eighth of October are "dual holidays" (*diples eortes*), embodying both secular and sacred ritual action. The theme of Hellenism rooted in Orthodox Christianity was a motif that found strong expression during periods of military dictatorship in Greece, both under Metaxas and during the junta years. Similarly, the ringing of church bells, and the doxology and mass in churches and cathedrals, contributed to both the detail of protocol and the aura of pageantry. Through the Church, the heroic martyrs of the nation receive their proper religious rite: *epimnimosines deisis*. On such occasions, one could view the high clergy in all their ornate costume, their dense incense and Byzantine chants contributing to the aura of age-old continuity of the Hellenes.

I can recall, as a young girl, leaving church on those days and being stopped on the way out by a doorwoman, a woman who was active in local church affairs, who pinned miniature Greek flags on everyone's blouse or lapel. Sometimes this was done on Sundays or on major saint's day celebrations. Usually, one was handed a small piece of bread as *andidoron* ("in place of gift") when departing a Greek church after mass. On national commemorative occasions, however, one might receive both bread and flag; the latter might be thought of as an *andidoron* itself, something one receives "in place of gift" from the nation.

These subtexts found their clearest expression in the focus and content of speeches delivered by dignitaries and officials as part of the commemorative activities. In schools, most addresses were made by teachers to impressionable young minds. Consider the following text, which educators were required to consult before writing their own speeches. National celebrations, it read, are a "re-baptism in the national waters [that] secure the maintenance and promotion of the nation," and eventually history will "show us how we should celebrate, how we should worship great national holidays like [the Twenty-Eighth of October]."[36] Though it may be possible now to assess the degree to which student participants in such celebrations absorbed the content of these talks as requisite knowledge of the nation, such speeches bear evidence of the key subtexts of ritual commemorations of national identity and solidarity. As "re-baptisms" of nationhood, these festivities had a strong ideological character, promoting the legitimacy of the Greek nation in young minds. "Oh, Children of the Greek people," declared a speaker from the Thessaloniki prefect's office on 24 March 1949, "descendants more than worthy of the Marathon Fighters, of the Bulgarian Killers, of the Warriors of 1821 and the Albanian Epic . . . Children of Greece . . . the country is thankful to you. Religion blesses you. The people admire you. Long live the Nation. Long live the Greek army. Long live the King."[37]

Local administrators were directed to prepare programs that included talks or homilies to be delivered "by [those] who handle speech skillfully." The directive concerning the inaugural *Ochi* Day celebrations in 1945, for example, stipulated that speakers should directly address the historical event of 28 October 1940, and include in their remarks characteristic descriptions of what happened that day, such as developments at the "front," comments and reactions of leading world figures regarding Greece's action, and the contribution the Greeks made to the victory of the United Nations.[38] It was in this context that the formal celebratory speech, delivered by a professor in the Aristotelian University of Thessaloniki, was inaugurated in 1946 and became what is now a well-established tradition in national celebrations in northern Greece. Even to this day, the panegyric speech on national holidays continues to be delivered by a professor in the university's Ceremony Room.

Some of these enlightened "skilled at handling speech" men believed that the general public (*laos*) had a poor appreciation of their ancient Greek heritage. Consider the speech of Panayiotis Christou, delivered to a crowd gathered in the university's Ceremony Room on 26 October 1972.[39] Christou contended that contemporary Greeks not only lack an obsession for their ancient ancestors but also lack appreciation for the great men of classical antiquity. He complained, for example, that there were no statues of Philip and Alexander in Thessaloniki, and that there was not a single bust of Aristotle the Philosopher on the grounds of the university that bore his name. Yet, what is most interesting (for present purposes) about this speech is the manner in which its author used the occasion of the Twenty-sixth of October to talk about the ancient Greeks. The history of Greece, he argued, began not in 1821; such short-sightedness would lower the status of the Greeks, who deserve distinction among those (Third World) countries that attained independence after the collapse of colonialism. No one seems to care, Christou argued, that Alexander the Great began his great campaign to conquer and hellenize the populations of Asia and the Middle East some 2,300 years ago. He concluded that this unfortunate state of affairs exists because tradition is too heavy for the average people to bear. Modern Greeks of the early 1970s, he lamented, do not dare to compare themselves with the ancients; contemporaries believe they are better off than their ancestors. "Communism," he contended, "has got rid of tradition."

It is noteworthy that in the context of national celebrations, civil servants had special obligations to their employer, the state. Most civil servants attained their posts through clientelistic ties, and most who served in Macedonia were originally from southern Greece. It was their duty to pay tribute to the nation's ancestors and its history. Civil servants were instructed to gather at their places of work on the morning of the celebration. State buildings were to be decorated with pictures of national heroes as well as with flags, and were to be lighted all through the evening for the duration of the festivities.[40]

The protocol and pageantry of national holiday celebrations also helped "to bring light to" ("to illuminate," or "to enlighten," *fotagigisis*) the new nation of the modern Hellenes. This was symbolized graphically in illuminated public buildings with lighted windows and flood-lit facades bunted with national flags, as well as in torch processions, the decoration of shop windows with national colors, and fireworks displays. National enlightenment was also aided by state directives instructing authorities to place loudspeakers in public areas so that people could hear and follow along with the ceremonies as celebrated in Athens. Cinemas were instructed to put on a particularly festive tone prior to showing a film on such holidays. The omnipresence of music is apparent in many early accounts of these celebrations. In Thessaloniki, both the military and municipality bands went around the city playing war songs (*thouria*) and military marches. Kertzer noted that the rhythm of martial music or chanting at demonstrations has far more effect on the psyche of participants and observers than do lyrics, melody, or harmony. Many a child attending a parade wanted to have a little Greek flag to hold and wave, and the commercialization underlying these national celebrations was another force that warrants further exploration.

POMP, CIRCUMSTANCE, AND DICTATORSHIP

By the time the colonels seized power in the military coup of 21 April 1967, the national commemorations had become part of the annual ritual cycle for all Greeks. The new military regime, however, intensified its efforts to cultivate patriotic feelings through national celebratory rituals. The military junta (1967–1974) saw itself in much the same way as the Metaxas dictatorship had thirty years earlier: as saviors of the Greek nation and its modern state. Their decrees and directives were quite explicit about what should be done to save the country from "Slavo-Communism" (*Slavokommounismos*), a phrase that symbolized their reevaluation of the perennial threats the country seemed to face since its inception — Slavs endangering the existence of the Greek nation and communism threatening the Greek state. This duality of danger, in which doubts were cast on the abilities of both nation and state to continue their existences, focused on neighboring countries to the north. Indeed, the continuing viability of the new nation of the Hellenes came to be likened to the defeat of this dual threat.

The propaganda slogans promoted by the junta in primary schools during the 1970 commemoration of the colonels' coup d'état were indicative. These slogans, which were required to be transmitted to young schoolchildren, stressed the theme of Greece as an extraordinary country, a locale or place (topos) of martyrs and heroes. The Christian Hellenes were promoted as the sole hope for the country, the only ones who could legitimately reside in such a topos. The folk were regarded as grand, faithfully following the traditions of Hellenism. At the same time, the junta emphasized that the future of Greece was guaranteed by the heroes of Greece, who had the courage to say "No" (*Ochi*) to the nation's enemies. The Helleno-Christian humanity of the population, the colonels declared, leads the development of Greek civilization, which is "respected by friends and awesome to enemies."[41]

Through their own, more militaristic pageantry and protocol, the junta thus sought to "inspire again . . . the way of thinking and acting [that was] solely Greek and solely Christian."[42] Each month the colonels sent schoolchildren a list of day-to-day historical events that had occurred during that month. Teachers were required to relate these events, embellished with accompanying stories to provoke imaginings of the young, each day. These events were drawn principally from three major

eras: classical antiquity, the Byzantine empire, and the wars of liberation, state formation, and consolidation.[43] During the years of the "Reconstruction of Democracy" following the fall of the junta in 1974, the
rhetoric and subtexts of national celebrations continued, although their
militaristic elements were deleted. Yet, it is noteworthy that the children
of the junta years, the young adults of today, adopted a hard-line and
militaristic position during the recent Macedonian controversy, for
example.

PRESENT-DAY CELEBRATIONS

> If today Athens symbolizes the center of the state mechanism,
> [then] Thessaloniki, the capital of Macedonia, is the heart of
> Greece.
>
> — Christos Kar.

Today, shops offer not only small Greek flags, but also (and often in
combination with) small blue-gold banners adorned with the Star of
Vergina. The new group-identification banner attempts to evoke the
aura of the ancient Macedonians of Greek national tradition: the spiritual glory of those who claimed to be the forefathers of the modern
Greeks. Having shared a territory with us, however discontinuous in
time, we are linked to them, in the timeless domain of national myth-
making. Few in Greece today tolerate the notion that the territory of the
nation-state (or at least a part thereof) was once inhabited by non-
Greek people.

In this sense, the recent controversy over Macedonia and the rightful
use of the name represented a moment of ethnogenesis for all the Greek
people. While the debate was led by a few elite ideologues, it was also
fueled by the political opportunism of party and government leaders
who seized an opportunity to convert public perception of themselves as
corrupt and boring bureaucrats to one as champions of the nation's
martyred heroes. Consider the Twenty-Sixth of October celebrations in
1992, staged in Thessaloniki for the defense of national history during
this period of intense ethnogenesis. Shortly after the unprecedented
large "Macedonia is Greek" demonstration of over one million people,
held in the city on 14 February 1992, the minister of northern Greece
urged the public to celebrate the Twenty-Sixth of October because it is a
day of national memory, a day that proves the "uncontrollable (para-
fori) love of the Greek toward his country."[44] The Metropolitan of
Thessaloniki told the public that "Greece never dies," while the mayor
said he was convinced that "the population of Thessaloniki had a solid
national and religious consciousness through the centuries."[45] Thus, by

1992, at the height of the crisis, the symbols (both old and new), the slogans, the myths, the heroic events, the ideology, and the recurrent themes of imagination ("Macedonia is Greek"), continuity, danger, and sacredness had fostered the creation of a new existential or spontaneous *communitas* for the population of Greece.

When the students paraded in front of the Academy of Athens during the commemoration of the Twenty-Fifth of March in 1993, they did so to the music of "Renown Macedonia" played by the Gendarmerie Philharmonic. The song, although not originally written as a military march, was rescored as such in recent years. As one man in Florina remarked in reference to the tune, "This is not a military march song. What have they done to it?" We had been sitting together in the town's square early one evening, where he had been explaining to me why Macedonia has always been Greek. A group of soldiers had marched into the town's square, en route to lowering the national flag flying in front of the Metropolitan church, singing aloud the verses of "Renown Macedonia." Even my companion, an ardent supporter of the Greek cause in Macedonia and a schoolteacher himself, was obliged to acknowledge the awkwardness of the situation. In Athens, meanwhile, at the heart of the Greek state, young people paraded in the presence of the Minister of Education and Religion, dressed in traditional clothes.[46] Greece, according to the minister, "is a country destined to guard the Thermopylae," to be alert and prepared in the face of present danger to fulfill the need for national unity.[47]

The Twenty-Fifth of March 1993 parade in Thessaloniki was led by what were heralded as the last remaining acknowledged Macedonian Fighters,[48] along with the war cripples and the Red Cross. The duality of the holiday, both its national and religious aspects, was stressed throughout the celebrations. Doxology and wreaths, parades and music, the celebrations followed what is now a well-rehearsed structure. A professor of law from the Aristotelian University spoke about national consciousness,[49] and the *Galanolefki* (Blue and White Flag) flew proudly.

The Twenty-Fifth of March celebrations the following year took place in a significantly different context. By then, Greece's unilateral economic embargo of the Former Yugoslav Republic of Macedonia was in effect, and the local authorities in Thessaloniki decided that the time was right to offer a demonstration of national unity on the Macedonian issue. The mayor urged the public to raise flags every day through 31 March, a date designated for yet another public demonstration for Macedonia.[50] An announcement from the municipality read: "The Twenty-Fifth of March reminds us of [the nation] and 31 March [will be a] demonstration for Macedonia."[51] Historical films and documentaries depicting important moments in Greek national history were broadcast by major television stations, both public and private. Most noteworthy, however, was that although newspaper reports on 24 March 1994 noted the death of the "last Macedonian Fighter,"[52] the media nevertheless reported a few days later that the parade on the Twenty-Sixth had been led by the last living Macedonian Fighter.

The Minister of the Interior, who attended the ceremonies in Thessaloniki, emphasized (like his predecessors) the duality of the celebration: it was a day for Hellenism as well as a day for Orthodoxy.[53] The Twenty-Fifth of March is also the Day of Annunciation, commemorating the conception of Christ within the virgin womb of Mary. Strikingly, the state of Greece was conceived by the nation of the Hellenes on the same date, roughly 1,821 years later. As comprehension of the Annunciation requires either the conviction of faith or creative imagination, so, too, does one need to "imagine" the genesis of a nation or a national community. Embedded here is the notion of the Savior coming to tell the public that Greece will never die (the message of the Metropolitan) and that Hellenism and Orthodoxy will always go hand in hand. Greece, like Christ, is immortal, and will be resurrected even in the face of defeat by enemies.

The invented traditions and royal rituals of the British monarchy would one day appear as little more than "primitive magic" to an educated citizenry, or at least so argued one nineteenth-century contemporary. The ritual celebrations of nationhood in northern Greece, twentieth-century traditions of even more recent invention, continue to exercise profound influence over the public. The ritualized repetition of the theme "nation in danger" has neither tired the Greeks nor prompted them to reflect critically on how much "primitive magic" goes into the perpetuation of the traditions of modern Hellenism. Nation-state and national citizen alike need myth and ritual, and the national ceremonies that provide such nourishment are both elastic and dynamic. National celebrations stretch the imagination across time. Ceremonial music and marches, as "venerated patriotic hymns," framed the evocation of the aura of heroic moments. The language of the symbols was understood by both participants and observers. A period of unprecedented change, the second half of the twentieth century has provoked expressions of continuity and comfort that are perceived in the nation's celebrations. At moments when the nation is defined "in terms of its enemies," the "aura" of past confrontations with enemies adds to the degree both of anxiety and of comfort. Yet as rituals, national celebrations in northern Greece do not have a liminal character of the sort that often arises at times of radical social upheaval. Rather, they exhibit a more spontaneous or existential *communitas* that goes to the root of social experiences and evokes subtexts "profoundly communal and shared." But the purpose of the celebrations was apparent to their architects. By 1950, the state had decided to schedule the inauguration of public works during periods of national celebration.[54]

Connecting the national and religious elements in these public celebrations is thus the thread of national imagination. The 1994 parade in Athens had been led by the military, while in Thessaloniki the Macedonian Fighters had been scheduled to lead the procession, which was to be reviewed by the Minister of the Interior. Elementary-school students, following what is now a well-established tradition, took to their stages with patriotic plays and songs, poems and speeches. One schoolteacher who produced such a production maintained that students should be taught to communicate the ideals of the nation "in the name of the history of the nation."[55] The panegyric speech was delivered, as usual, at the Aristotelian University, this time by a professor of pharmacology. At the peak of the Macedonian controversy, when the embargo of the Former Yugoslav Republic of Macedonia was intensifying and emotions were high, this professor of pharmacology chose to speak about "the health care [system] of the 1821 revolutionary Fighters."[56] One would be hard pressed to think of a more appropriately noncontroversial topic.

NOTES

1. The Greek Army entered Salonika on 26 October 1912. On 28 October 1940, the war between Greece and Italy began.

2. Irredentist fervor throughout the country was high, and the National Rights Commission was meeting to plan a course of action by which to lobby the victorious Allies for the (re)acquisition of what they considered "unliberated" Greek lands. Much attention was focused on the Dodecanese Islands, which were later acquired from Italy, and on the disputed area of northern Epirus. For more on the "northern Epirus" dispute between Greece and Albania, see Janet Hart, *New Voices in the Nation* (Cornell, 1995).

3. The fireworks show was among the most popular aspects of this four-day celebration. The only other time of the year when city residents saw fireworks was at the opening of the Thessaloniki International Trade Fair. This description of events is based on the Historical Archive of Macedonia, Archives of the General Directorate of Northern Greece (AGDNG), file no. B9/1, Program for the celebration of the 28th of October, 1945. See also AGDNG, file no. B9/1, Directive from the Deputy Minister of the Press, Mr. B. Dendramis, to Governors, Prefects, and Eparkhs, 12 Oct. 1945.

4. AGDNG, file no. B9/1, Directive from the Deputy Minister of the Press, Mr. B. Dendramis, to Governors, Prefects, and Eparkhs, 12 Oct. 1945.

5. AGDNG, file no. B9/1, Program for the celebration of the Twenty-Eighth of October, 1945. The Twenty-Fifth of March, commemorating the start of the Greek War of Independence in 1821, was also celebrated the year after libera-

tion from the Germans. It was not, however, well organized, and the Minister of the Interior had merely suggested that religious, military, educational, and other authorities should consult each other to plan a celebratory program. AGDNG, file no. B9/1, Directive from the Minister of the Interior, Mr. Athanasiadis-Novas, to all Governors, Prefects, and Eparkhs, 12 Mar. 1945.

6. AGDNG, file no. B9/3, "Regarding Formal Ritual and Celebrations," Circular no. 24991/91, from the Ministry of the Interior, 21 Apr., 1947.

7. Ibid.

8. AGDNG, file no. B9/1, from Mr. Athanasiadis-Novas, to all Governors, Prefects, and Eparkhs, 12 Mar. 1945; Archive of the General Directorate of Western Macedonia (AGDWM), file no. 20/3, Letter from the Deputy Minister of the Press to Governors General, Prefects, and Eparkhs, 27 Oct. 1945

9. AGDNG, file no. B9/1, From the Prefect of Thessaloniki, Mr. G. Georgiadis, to Eparkhs, Mayors, and Township Presidents, 20 Oct. 1945. Funds for such celebrations were for the main part provided by local municipal and township governments (AGDNG, file no. B9/2, Telegram from the Prefecture of Thessaloniki to Mayors and Township Presidents, 18 Oct. 1949).

10. AGDNG, file no. B9/3, "Regarding Formal Ritual and Celebrations," Circular no. 24991/91, from the Ministry of the Interior, 12 Apr. 1947.

11. In contrast, the efforts of Greek state elites and local administrators in the 1920s to promote national commemorations that focused on newly erected heroes' monuments (iroa) in Slavic-speaking towns and villages in northern Greece were dramatically unsuccessful (see below).

12. P. Corrigan and D. Sayer, *The Great Arch: English State Formation as a Cultural Revolution* (Oxford, 1985).

13. E. Hobsbawm, *Nations and Nationalism since 1789* (Londong, 1990).

14. From the Directorate of the Gendarmerie, Office of Public Security, 17 Feb. 1937, no. 25/28/1, which was published in the government newspaper *FEK* (*Fylla Efimendas tis Kyverniseos, Government Gazette*) 23–25 Jan. 1937; AGDNG, file no. B9/4, From the Union of Discharged Army Officers of Thessaloniki, to the Ministry of Defense, 2 Apr. 1948.

15. AGDWM, file no. 4/3, Letter from the Prefect of Kozani to the Mayor of Kozani City, 20 Feb. 1937.

16. AGDWM, file no. 6/2, From the Superintendent of the School District to all Schools, 10 Mar. 1940.

17. AGDNG, file no. B9/3, From the Ministry of the Interior to All Prefects, 22 Aug. 1947.

18. The decree was published in *FEK* 98 (ta'), 15 May 1947.

19. AGDNG, file no. B9/4, From the Ministry of the Interior to Governors, Prefects and Eparkhs, 16 Oct. 1948. Additional minor holidays were also added to the official list, including the United Nations Day of Freedom (8 June), New National Army Day (15 May), as well as World War I Armistice Day (11 November) and Victory Day (16 August). Yet these new minor holidays did not survive; only the major national and local commemorations continued.

20. At the first *Ochi* Day celebrations in 1945, however, the postwar monarchy was not yet well organized enough to present themselves. In October 1945, the highest attending officials at the celebrations in Thessaloniki were the

Minister General Governor of Macedonia, the highest military commanders of Central Macedonia and of Thessaloniki, the prefect of Thessaloniki, former ministers, the mayor and the municipal council, the director and senate of the university, and former government ministers living in Salonika (AGDND, file no. B9/1, Program for the celebration of the Twenty-Eighth of October, 1945.

21. AGDWM, file no. 13/9, Letter from the Ministry of the Interior to all Prefects, 27 Dec. 1946. Also, AGDNG, file no. B9/7. The queen also opened bank accounts for female babies to be used, in due time, as their dowry (*prika*). In order to qualify for such honor, however, the family had to show loyalty to the country and be free of communist ideological influences. It came as no surprise to my mother that I was declined such an account when I was born, and my mother remembers, to this day, the secret police man walking up and down the neighborhood checking on my family's behavior.

22. AGDWM, file no. 4/10, Letter from the President of the Association, Princess Irene, entitled "General Orders for the organization of the National Youth," 5 Jan. 1939.

23. AGDNG, file no. B9/5, 26 Oct. 1949.

24. AGDWM, file no. 3/3, Telegram from the Sub-Ministry of the Press to the General Directorate of Western Macedonia [based in Kozani], 7 Jan. 1947.

25. AGDNG, file no. B9/3, From the Minister of Northern Greece, 23 Oct. 1947.

26. AGDNG, file no. B9/4, General Program of St. Dimitrios Church Inauguration and the celebrations of the Twenty-Sixth and Twenty-Eighth of October Anniversaries, 1948.

27. In other instances in later years, they arrived by plane and flew out again immediately following the ceremonies. See, for example, AGDNG, files no. B9/5 and B9/7.

28. AGDWM, file no. 3/3, telegram from the Sub-Ministry of the Press to the General Directorate of Western Macedonia, 7 Jan. 1947.

29. See A. Karakasidou, "Cultural Illegitimacy in Modern Greece: The Slavo-Macedonian 'Non-Minority,' " paper presented at a workshop on "Minorities in Greece," St. Anthony's College, Oxford University, 5–8 January 1994.

30. Archive of the General Directorate of Macedonia, file no. 19, From the Prefect of Florina to the Ministry of the Interior, 29 Jan. 1929.

31. AGDWM, file no. 20/3, Report entitled "Celebration of 28 October in Florina," by the Prefect of Florina, Mr. Xirotiris, sent to the Ministry of the Interior, 6 Nov. 1945.

32. A. Karakasidou, "Cultural Illegitimacy"; idem, "Women of the Family, Women of the Nation," *Women's Studies International Forum* 19, 1–2 (Jan.–Apr. 1996): 99–110; idem, *Fields of Wheat, Hills of Blood: Passages to Nationhood in Greek Macedonia, 1870–1990* (Chicago, 1997).

33. AGDNG, file no. B9/2, From the General Military Command of the Third Army Battalion to the Ministry of the Interior, 2 Dec. 1946.

34. Through their own associations, war cripples assured their inclusion in such ceremonies. When, for example, in 1945, an association of war cripples in Iannina (Epirus) was not invited to that city's local holiday commemorating its

liberation from the Turks, they complained to the Ministry of Defense. The Ministry issued directives that war cripples should be invited to all official celebrations of this sort, because they "represent the immortal history of our nation, [and] are living symbols" (AGDNG, file no. B9/2, From the Ministry of Defense to military commands, 1945).

35. D. Cannadine, in E. J. Hobsbawm and T. Ranger, eds., *The Invention of Tradition* (Cambridge, 1983), 105.

36. Archives of the Mavrorahi Village School, "Example Speech" to be followed and delivered for the Twenty-Eighth of October celebrations, 1970.

37. AGDNG, file no. B9/5, From a Speech by Mr. Men. Tsiakiris entitled, "His Salutation to the Nation's Fighters," 24 Mar. 1949.

38. AGDND, file no. B9/1, Directive from the Deputy Minister of the Press of Governors, Prefects, and Eparkhs, 12 Oct. 1945.

39. The text of this speech was published by the "King Paul" National Foundation, as *The Duty to National Heritage: Panegyric Speech Delivered on 26 October 1972* (Athens, 1973).

40. AGDNG, file no. B9/1, Directive from the Deputy Minister of the Press to Governors, Prefects, and Eparkhs, 12 Oct. 1945.

41. Archives of the Mavrorahi Village School, Circular to all area elementary schools from the Third Army Battalion of Greece, entitled "The Bells of 21 April," 1970.

42. Ibid.

43. Ibid.

44. *Thessaloniki*, 26 Oct. 1992.

45. "Unity and Vigilance," *Thessaloniki*, 26 Oct. 1992.

46. The significance of the dress lay in the fact that generally speaking, urban culture in Greece regards "traditional clothes" or costumes, like most other rural or "traditional" elements, as rather banal.

47. "Students Parade in Athens," *Thessaloniki*, 26 Mar. 1993, p. 41.

48. Macedonian Fighters" are the men who fought for the Greek side during the Macedonian Struggle of 1901–1903, a ethnico-religious war between Greece and Bulgaria.

49. "The Message of National Unity Came from the Youth," *Thessaloniki*, 26 Mar. 1993, pp. 8–9.

50. Extended periods of repetitive festivities have been used in national celebrations of the past to mobilize public opinion. In 1949, for example, nationwide six-day festivities marked the Twenty-Fifth of March celebrations, running 20–25 March of that year. These festivities were under the formal protection of the crown (AGDNG, file no. B9/5, From the Deputy Minister of the Press and Communication regarding the "For Work and Victory" national celebration, 1949), and each day of the celebration was devoted to a particular commemorative theme: the Church, the farmer, work, youth, international solidarity, and (on the Twenty-Fifth) the nation (AGDNG, file no. B9/5, Celebration of the National Week, "For Work and Victory," 1949). At the time, Greece was still embroiled in civil war, and the government keenly sought to assure the United States and other key allies that it was worthy of their support. A few months later, the Greek national army achieved a strategic victory in the civil war, and

the country soon raced ahead into the Cold War era with economic development through a reconstruction and rehabilitation program generously funded by
the West.

51. *Thessaloniki*, 24 Mar. 1994, p. 13.

52. "The Last Macedonian Fighter Died," *Thessaloniki*, 24 Mar. 1994, p.
11.

53. "Glorious Day," *Thessaloniki*, 26 Mar. 1994, p. 9.

54. AGDNG, file no. B9/6, From the Ministry of the Interior to the General
Directorate of Macedonia, 20 Mar. 1950.

55. "Students on Stage," *Thessaloniki*, 26 Mar. 1994, p. 40.

56. "The Anniversary of the National Awakening in the Aristotelian University," *Thessaloniki*, 26 Mar. 1994, p. 40.

TWELVE

"After the War We Were All Together": Jewish Memories of Postwar Thessaloniki

Bea Lewkowicz

THE SECOND WORLD WAR brought dramatic demographic changes to Thessaloniki, a city in which nearly a quarter of the prewar population had been Jewish. In 1943, two years after the German army had entered it, about 48,000 Jews[1] were deported to Auschwitz and Bergen-Belsen. By 1945 the Jewish community had shrunk to 2,000 people, of whom some had survived the concentration camps, some in hiding (in Athens or in smaller villages or islands in the rest of Greece), and some fighting with the *andartes* (resistance fighters) in the mountains. These survivors had to adapt their lives to a totally changed environment. Upon their return from the mountains, from other parts of Greece, and from the concentration camps, they found themselves in a different city, a Thessaloniki without Jewish schools, without Jewish shops, without synagogues, without Jewish neighborhoods, and most importantly, without Jewish families.

Statistics published in December 1945 illustrate that the vast majority of the 1,908 people who were registered in the community in that year were young and single. Among the 679 women, 362 were unmarried and 103 were widows. Among the 1,229 men, 735 were unmarried and 260 were widowers. If we also consider the membership numbers by age group, it clearly emerges that not only was the vast majority of the Jewish population not married, but many were left without parents, grandparents, uncles, and aunts. 1,465 people were between the ages of twenty and fifty, 124 were aged between fifty and seventy, and only 17 over seventy. The number of children was also very small: 116 children registered in the community were under the age of fourteen.[2]

The survivors returned to a city where their homes and their shops had been taken over by Orthodox Greeks, and all Jewish synagogues (except one) and other educational and cultural establishments had been destroyed by the Germans. The reconstruction of Jewish life in Thessaloniki and throughout Greece was particularly difficult due to the unstable political climate and the severe economic crisis Greece was undergoing. Immediate help was given by the American Joint Distribution

Photo of Mrs. Hella Kounio holding a photo of her old house, Thessaloniki, 1994. Reproduced by kind permission of Bea Lewkowicz.

Committee (AJDC, known colloquially as the "Joint"), the Conference for Jewish Material Claims against Germany (CJMCAG), and the Jewish Agency. These organizations supplied general financial, medical, and welfare assistance and helped with the setting up of community offices. The rehabilitation program of the AJDC proceeded in two phases: from 1945 until 1951, the emphasis was on emergency relief care; from 1951 onward the focus shifted to the revival of Jewish communal organizations.[3]

Records show that 4,000 Greek Jews received financial help from the AJDC. Very practical help was given by the "Joint" to young couples. By setting up a dowry fund, the "Joint" provided wedding rings, kitchenware, and kerosene stoves. A census prepared by the AJDC in 1946 estimated the number of Jews in Greece to be around 10,000, most of whom lived in Athens, to which they had fled during the war. Athens thus became the new Jewish center in Greece after the war, and Thessaloniki declined in importance.

Several waves of Jewish emigration occurred after the war. Immediately after the war, many young Jews who were the only survivors of their families headed to Palestine, or to North or South America. The second wave of emigration took place in 1949, after the civil war.

About 2,000 Jews (from the whole of Greece) moved to Israel between 1945 and 1951. Among them were also a number of Communist Jews (sentenced to exile on some remote Greek islands), who were allowed to emigrate to Israel on the condition that they renounced their Greek citizenship. The third wave of emigration took place between 1951 and 1956, triggered by the amendment of the Displaced Person Act, which allowed Greek Jews to go to the United States. By the end of 1956, about 6,000 Jews remained in Greece.

The postwar years were characterized by the painful process of reclaiming personal and communal property. In places with less than twenty families, the communal property was transferred to the Central Board of Jewish Communities in Athens. Unused synagogues and schools were sold in order to create income. In Thessaloniki the most important transaction of this sort was the sale of the Baron Hirsch Hospital to the Greek government in 1951. The 1950s were characterized by the attempt to revive the community's educational activities. In Thessaloniki, all Jewish children went to two private primary schools, which had made a special agreement with the community. In these schools, the Jewish children were taught Hebrew and religion. The community also purchased a piece of land and started to run a yearly summer camp (which now takes place in Litohoro).

There is no clear periodization for communal Jewish history in postwar Greece. The immediate war years were characterized by the process of individual health recovery; the reclamation of property; many weddings, some of them group weddings; a subsequent baby boom (between 1945 and 1951, 402 births were registered in the Jewish community of Thessaloniki); and the above-mentioned emigration. From the early 1950s onward, the focus shifted from individual to communal reconstruction; after 1956, the year in which the last wave of emigration took place, the demographic and economic situation of the community started to stabilize. The AJDC ended most of its activities by the mid 1960s.

When the junta came to power in 1967, the colonels dismissed the community assembly and council and appointed a new council, a process that all organizations that functioned as a "legal entity under public law" had to undergo. The new council undertook significant changes: the size of the assembly was reduced from fifty members to twenty (this measure was put into effect in 1975, following the first elections after the dictatorship), the rabbinical council was abolished, the official language of the council (in which the minutes were taken) was changed from Ladino to Greek, and most importantly, the new council reevaluated the communal properties, which led to a drastic increase in communal revenues. In the decades to follow, the by-now financially independent community opened a Jewish school and an Old People's Home, and provided welfare, social, and religious services to its members.[4]

Until 1992, the Jewish community maintained a relatively low public profile in the city of Thessaloniki. Since the celebrations of "Sepharad 92," the anniversary of the expulsion of the Jews from Spain in 1492, a gradual development toward a more public profile has taken place, marked by other official commemoration ceremonies (such as the fiftieth anniversary of the deportations in 1993 and the honoration ceremony for non-Jewish Greeks who helped Jews during the Second World War in 1994) and by the opening of a Jewish museum in the city.[5] The low public profile of the community went hand in hand with a general silence (or, more precisely, silences) about the Jewish presence in Thessaloniki. The history of the Jews has not formed a part of the public memory of the city of Thessaloniki, and there is hardly any mention of Jews or the fate of the community during the Second World War in Greek guidebooks or schoolbooks. With the exception of the newly unveiled Holocaust memorial in a suburb of the city, there is no monument or plaque that reminds visitors of the Jewish presence in Thessaloniki. There are no "Jewish sites" that are part of the urban consciousness of its inhabitants. Most community buildings are not recognized by noncommunity members as "Jewish buildings."[6]

The following episode demonstrates very clearly what the word "silence" means in this context. After long negotiations between the community and the municipality of Thessaloniki, the municipality decided to name a square in Harilao *Platia Evreon Martyron* (Jewish Martyrs' Square). The square is located in an area that was known as the Jewish quarter of Ekato Peninda Ena (151) before the war. During my fieldwork in 1994, I set out to visit the square, which is located about fifteen minutes from the center of Thessaloniki. When I told the taxi driver where to take me, he insisted that such a square did not exist. He assured me that he had never heard of it in all the thirty years he has been driving a taxi in the city, and he became offended when I, being a *xeni* (foreigner), insisted on the existence of the square. After ten minutes of intense arguing he agreed to let me direct him.[7] When we finally managed to find the square, it turned out that we were both proven right. The two signposts with the name of the square were covered with black graffiti. The only legible thing on the signposts was *Platia* (Square). During my visits to Thessaloniki in the last couple of years, I have returned to the *Platia Evreon Martyron* to find that the signposts were sometimes legible and other times sprayed over with graffiti. This is the square where a Holocaust memorial was recently unveiled.

METHODOLOGY

The interviews upon which this chapter is based were conducted during two periods of fieldwork in Thessaloniki in 1989 and 1994.[8] I collected life histories and conducted semistructured interviews with Salonikan Jews of different age groups on a wide range of topics. In total there are forty-five interviews, which I divided into four groups: Jewish subjects born before the war (group A); those born during the war and in the postwar years (group B); those born after 1956 (group C); and those who are currently not members of the Jewish community (group D), either because they had converted to Christianity or because they had been born as Christians. Among the twenty interviewees in group A are eight women and twelve men; among the eleven in group B are six women and five men; among the ten in group C are eight women and two men; among the five in group D are one woman and four men. Since this chapter is about the postwar period, I mainly concentrate on groups A and B, who experienced this time themselves, either as adults or children.

The interviews varied in length and themes. Some people I interviewed several times, some only once. Consequently, I had different relationships with the different interviewees. The interviews with the older generation tended to be much longer than the ones with the other age groups. While the average interview length with the older group was about three and a half hours, the average interview length with the other interviewees was about one and a half to two hours. Because of the semistructured/conversational interview approach, topics like the experience of the German occupation, the Holocaust, the reconstruction of the community in the postwar years, and the general impact of the war on families and individuals are topics that were discussed in most interviews, but to very different extents. Not only did the content vary, but also my style of questioning. My aim was to ask questions in an open manner to enable the interviewee to offer his or her own "analytical framework;" but in instances where I felt it was necessary, I did conduct more directive interviews, in which I asked specific questions. However, if I had the impression that someone was uncomfortable or did not want to discuss a specific topic, I did not follow it up. This is a relevant methodological remark because it sometimes meant that I shifted the focus of the interview if the evoked memories were too painful. The task of the interviewer in this process is quite difficult, because many times one gets contradicting messages from the interviewee. For example, the first thing Mrs. M. (Af14)[9] tells me after I ask a very open question about her memories of the Jewish community of Thessaloniki is: "Don't ask me that. Don't make me go back. I can't." However, she then proceeds to give me a detailed account of her whole life in which she talks openly about the prewar time, her experiences during the war, and her return to Thessaloniki. The point I would like to underline here is that the interview might have taken a very different direction if I had reacted to her initial remark by shifting the conversation to "easier" topics.

THE FIRST TO RETURN: MEMORIES OF ESCAPE AND RETURN

The first people to return to Thessaloniki had been either with the partisans in the mountains or hidden in other parts of Greece. Among my interviewees, three fought with the partisans in the mountains, five survived under various circumstances in Athens, and one woman and her daughter had escaped to the island of Skopelos. The two men and the one woman who were with EAM/ELAS were in all in their early twenties and were not married. Moreover, they all had some kind of a personal connection to a communist acquaintance or friend, or to somebody who had some connection to these circles, who convinced them that they should leave Thessaloniki and go to the mountains. Mr. B. remembers that the night he was supposed to leave the ghetto with a group of ten other young Jews, only five showed up because the others had changed their mind (Am7). Many were reluctant to leave the other family members, particularly elderly parents, behind. Young men without other male siblings felt a strong sense of responsibility toward the other family members, whom they did not want to abandon (Am13). Some left with the approval of their families, some without it. Mrs. P., whose father and brother had died before the German occupation, was pushed by her mother to leave and to stay with acquaintances in the Italian-occupied zone (Af15). Mr. B., on the other hand, did not inform his family about his imminent departure. Before he left, he wrote a good-bye note and put it under a pillow. When he returned home after a couple of days because the escape from the ghetto had failed, his family was very upset because they believed that he had endangered the whole family. The second time his escape was successful. One night in March 1943, his communist acquaintance took him to a house near the ghetto, where he met some other Jewish men; from there they were taken to the area of Veria.

In all the interviews with people who left Thessaloniki to go to the mountains or other parts of Greece, the leaving behind of family members is often a very traumatic moment in the narrative: "This is one sin that will remain always in my head, when I left my parents. My father was in bed, he could not get up, he was young. My mother when they took her was fifty, she was sitting by the bed and father got up and blessed me" (Af14). Mrs. M., who made this statement, escaped from the ghetto on 20 March 1943 with her husband and two friends through the help of an Armenian friend who had paid a German soldier to drive them to Athens with a German truck. The German soldier dropped them off in Katerini, and they made their way through the mountains to the Italian-occupied zone. When talking about her escape, she immediately adds that two days later, four people who tried to leave the ghetto were betrayed and shot, and she expresses her anger about how few people were really willing to help and how impossible it was to find somebody to help the parents escape.

Some families managed to escape the ghetto by splitting into smaller groups. Mrs. S., a divorced woman who lived with her daughter at her parents' house, recounts in her memoir how they were advised to escape separately (Af18). "With a painful heart," they followed the advice. She and her daughter made their way to the island of Skopelos, with the help of a communist friend. Her parents and three brothers managed to get to Athens, and from there, via Turkey, to Palestine.

When Italy fell in September 1943 and the Germans occupied the whole of Greece, Jewish families or couples who had gone into hiding together had to split up again. In some cases the women stayed behind in Athens with the children while their husbands went to fight in the mountains or with the Greek exile army in Egypt. In other cases the mothers were also separated from their children. Mrs. M. recounts how she tried to find a hiding place for her two-year-old child. When she left Thessaloniki with her husband, the child had stayed behind with a Christian couple, but after a month they had became scared and the child was sent to Athens. Because the child was a boy (and he was circumcised), most monasteries had refused to take him in, but finally she did find one.

> Then I went to the last monastery. . . . It was September, it was hot, the whole day we walked, from Omonia to Agiou Loukas, where the "Divine Providence" monastery was and there the angel of God was there. She was a tall and beautiful nun, with big blue eyes. Sister Elaine, she was Belgian. She told me not to cry. We will take him and what God protects is well protected. Then she called Mrs. Kalkou, a widow with eight children who lived with the nuns and told her: You have seven children and now you will have eight. That was it. Two children slept on the top and two at the bottom of the bed. They ate whatever Sister Elaine would send" (Af14)

Other mothers with children, who had been able to obtain false papers or who had converted to Christianity, claimed to be widows or deserted wives. One interviewee was left behind in Athens when her mother was arrested by a Greek policeman who told her that it would be better not to take the child with her. She survived the war in the care of a Christian couple (Bf22).

After the German troops withdrew from Athens in December 1944, fighting between EAM/ELAS and the Greek government supported by British forces broke out, which meant that there was no communication or transport to other parts of Greece. This therefore delayed the return of many to Salonika. There were also other delays. One interviewee who was eager to return to Salonika to be reunited with his father and sister who had survived in villages in the mountains was drafted on the street in Athens into the Greek army for two years.

The first Jews to return to Thessaloniki were the ones who were with the partisans in the mountains. Mr. B. found himself near Florina when he heard that the German had left Salonika: "We went on a truck on all kinds of dangerous roads. It took us about a week for eighty or ninety kilometers" (Am6). The first thing he did was to go to his old house:

> I started hitting the door of my house but nobody was there. The door was locked. I am glad nobody was there because I was enraged, I was out of my mind. A neighbour across the street whom I knew before the war, saw me and said: "you come to my home." . . . Well, I did not know if he was from the Right or the Left and I did not care." (Am16)

After a couple of days the people who were staying in his house agreed to give Mr. B. a room. The reclaiming of apartments and shops was of course an experience that many returnees had to face. Experiences of betrayal and friendship are often linked to this process.

Mrs. M.'s husband also came to Thessaloniki quite soon after the Germans had left. He went to see his shop and it was entirely empty, there were "only the walls." His wife joined him a couple of months later.

> On the very first opportunity (after the revolution in Athens) . . . I came with my child on a ship from Piraeus overnight. We were the first refugees who came from Athens. There was a terrific storm that night, everybody was sick. The next day we landed on the quay and my husband was there and we met him. That's how we started all over. It was a terrible time. We were those who had survived either in the mountains, or in the city, or like me in Athens and it was a crazy time. People got in touch with the community." (Af14)

The community, which had reestablished itself with the return of the first Jews from hiding and from the mountains, became an important point of orientation and support for the returnees. Through a certificate provided by the community, for example, Mrs. M. was able to claim a room in her mother's apartment, which had been occupied.

During this time the early returnees waited of course for the return of the deportees, still in hope that their families might return. The first deportees were met with shock and disbelief:

> We were eagerly waiting for the people to come back. We heard that a group was coming from the Vardar. They were saying that everyone had been burnt and that they had exterminated them all. We, the people who were here, were thinking that the people were insane, saying crazy things. It was a very hard time. People started coming between May and July. When I heard that my brother-in-law had come without my sister Marcella and with another wife I went crazy. I did not want to meet him. My people were betrayed. It was a very difficult time. I did not want to live. I did not feel that it was worth being in a city which was like a ghost." (Af14)

The above quotation illustrates the complete sense of betrayal and isolation the speaker felt and still feels. She feels betrayed by the people who denounced the hiding place of her parents and her sister; betrayed by the Jewish leadership, especially by Rabbi Koretz, who convinced the Jews to follow the deportation orders to Poland; and betrayed by Christian friends, or even family members, who were given property or belongings that they did not return.

These feelings of betrayal and shock must have been common to all the Jews who came back to Thessaloniki in 1945. They not only returned to a "ghost city," an image frequently used in the interviews to describe a city empty of Jews and Judaism, but they also returned to a city in which houses and shops were taken over by Christian-Orthodox Greeks, who did not know and did not want to know anything about the previous owners.

Though the group of people who survived in hiding or in the mountains might have experienced betrayal, they also had experienced Christian help and support. For example, one woman who had been with EAM/ELAS underlines how helpful the Christians had been to the Jews, either by bringing them to villages or by buying food for them while they were in hiding in Athens. In this context, she also tells me the story of the beautiful chandelier in the synagogue. The only remaining synagogue during the German occupation was the *Monastirioton* synagogue, which was used as a warehouse (some interviewees say it was used as a stable). Before leaving Thessaloniki, the Germans wanted to destroy whatever had remained in the synagogue. When one priest realized what was about to happen, he asked the Germans if he could have the chandelier for his church. The Germans gave it to him, and after the war, he returned it to the Jews, who put it back in its place, where it is still today (Af15). In the narrative of my interviewee, this is an important story because it proves that Greeks and Jews were "like brothers and sisters." As in other interviews, the wartime experience (i.e., the perception of one's own and other experiences) almost becomes a measure stone for general questions, about the relationship between Greeks and Jews in particular. To have survived in hiding or with the partisans would not have been possible without the help of non-Jews, and therefore the issue of Greek help, expressed by the attitude of the Church, the partisans, and the ordinary public, is a central theme in all the interviews.

The experience of the deportees returning from the concentration camps was very different from that of the Jews who had been in the mountains or in hiding. Because of their different experiences, they formed two distinct groups in postwar Thessaloniki, whose mutual mistrust is expressed in the following quotation: "They thought they were heroes just because they could stay alive after what the Germans did but they were not heroes. They were begging for a place to sleep when they came back" (Am6). Both groups, the partisans and the camp survivors, formed their own political parties in the first elections of the community, which took place in the early 1950s. The more Socialist party of the partisans was called *Partida Renaisainssia* (which translates from Ladino as the "Renewal Party"), and the party of the displaced persons was called *Partida Los Omiros* (literally, the "Party of the Hostages") (Am4).[10] Each party thought that it could better represent the Jewish community, the partisans because they had fought against the enemy, the camp survivors because they had suffered most (Bm25).

The self-perception of the partisans was certainly different from that of the camp survivors. Like the camp survivors, the partisans had been expelled from their homes and separated from their families, but they had also fought for the "real Greece." Their participation in the "heroic struggle" and the bonds that they had formed with fellow Greek partisans during the war helped them to cope with the extreme sense of uprooting that all the returning Jews experienced. The efforts of all partisans, including the Jewish ones, were officially acknowledged by the PASOK government in 1981. Interviewees who had received the medals and a formal certificate by the Greek state took a great deal of pride in showing them to me.

In many interviews with concentration-camp survivors, the interviewees mention their camp experience and the death of their family members very early in the interview, which points to the traumatic nature of their wartime experiences and to the importance attributed to this part of their life history. When asked a general question about his family background, Mr. B. answered one minute into the interview:

The whole family was from Saloniki, everybody was born here. I had two sisters, one older, one younger. Unfortunately, they went to the concentration camp. They died there. I also lost my aunt with her three children. A young girl my age, a younger girl, and a younger boy. They all died in the concentration camp. I was there for two years. Since I was in Auschwitz I knew that my mother, my father, and my older sister went straight away to the Crematorium. My younger sister worked as a secretary (Schreiber), but later got dysentery and died. I was liberated in 1945 by the Americans. Although I knew that nobody had survived I came back. (Am4)

In contrast to the Jews who spent the entire war in Greece, the concentration-camp survivors who returned on their own knew that they were not likely to find any other surviving family members. Many young men came back without their parents and wives, as the number of widowers indicated above: "I have lost everybody, my wife and everyone else. I came back alone. I was all alone. The situation was very difficult" (Am13). Others had hoped that at least one family member had survived and therefore returned: "After seven days we came to Salonika. We were liberated the 5th of May and we came here 25 September. I came back for my brother, but nobody had survived, nobody. 55,000 people had left and 900 came back from the camp. If I had known that I was alone I would not have come back" (Af1). Mrs. A., who made the preceding statement, had participated in the "death march" from Auschwitz to Ravensbruck and Malchow, near where she was liberated by the Russians. Where the survivors found themselves at the time of the liberation, who liberated them, and their state of health (many suffered from typhus) determined how and when they could return to Greece. Some came from Munich by plane to Athens, some came by bus from Bulgaria, some came through Yugoslavia. Because Mrs. A. had been liberated by the Russians, she came through Bulgaria. With twenty-five other Greek Jews, she was taken to Thessaloniki by bus. She recalls the first moment when they crossed the border: "We all fell to the ground and kissed the Greek soil. That was the first thing we did" (Af1). Once they had arrived in Thessaloniki, the returnees were taken to a Greek army base on the outskirts of town, where they were registered and examined by the Red Cross. Only after the Greek authorities realized that they were not *kataskopoi* (spies) was the group allowed to leave.

Since most concentration-camps survivors did not have anything or anyone to go back to, the first place they went for housing, help, and support was the Jewish community. In many cases the survivors who had come back together stayed together. Many were settled temporarily in the building of the former Jewish orphanage in Faliro. People also received some money (one woman tells me that she received 5,000 drachmas, another one that she received 2,000 drachmas), clothing, and food (for some time free lunches were provided). Because of the bad economic situation of the community, their support was limited. Other help was provided by the AJDC.

After the experience of the concentration camps and the return to a "ghost" city, void of many familiar references, the Jewish community appeared to many survivors as a shelter and connection to the old world. One man tells me: "Since our return from the concentration camp we are protected by the Jewish community of Salonika" (Am13). The notion of the community as a "protector" reveals the high degree of insecurity that many of the survivors felt (as a result of their uprooting), a feeling that has most likely been passed on to their children. The Jewish community was also transformed after the war into a community of people who have suffered together, as the following quotation shows: "We, the Jews of 1945 Saloniki, came back to a city empty of Jews and Judaism. Our only joy was to encounter another Jew in the streets of Saloniki. A surprise, an embrace with Jews we have never met before and an eagerness to inquire and weep together" (Af18).

However, the experience of protection and closeness went sometimes hand in hand with the experience of conflict. Mr. B., who immediately after his return from the camp worked in the welfare commission of the community, speaks about these difficulties: "The community did not have much money. All the people who returned needed support and asked for help. It was very difficult. How could I say to somebody: I have no money for you. It was very difficult. Sometimes people got very angry. But all we wanted was to help each other" (Am4). Not all concentration-camp survivors spent their first months in Thessaloniki in communal housing. One of my interviewees shared a room with his cousin, and one was able to return to her old house, which had been requisitioned by her husband. Mrs. K., her husband, and their two children constitute a very rare case because they had all survived the concentration camp. While her husband and son came back through France, she and her daughter went to Yugoslavia, from where they crossed the border with difficulties to Greece (due to the beginning of the civil war). Erika Kounio-Amariglio describes in her book how happy she was to return to her old house.

Father found our old house on Koromila Street empty and in a bad state. But our old house, empty as it was, was waiting for us. . . . It was our house with its veranda, its garden with white pebbles in front of the beautiful blue and crystal clear sea, the sea I dreamt about in Auschwitz. . . . It did not bother us that we had nothing: we were alive and again all together in our house, only that was important."[11]

This quotation underlines the importance of two aspects of "return": the return to "being all together again," to meeting other family members, and the return to "our house," to the place where one had lived before the deportations. Most survivors' returns though, were characterized by not finding other family members and by not being able to go back their prewar accommodation. This caused a sense of total uprootedness and discontinuity among most returnees.

Mrs. A. did not have anywhere else to go but to the housing provided by the community. She recalls that she was given 2,000 drachmas, one bed, and one blanket. She also recalls that she could not bear to be with the other camp survivors because they were going out a lot, they were singing and dancing, wanting "to live their freedom." She contrasts her own mood to that of her friends: "I had suffered a lot, also from the Russians [she means Russian soldiers]. I did not want anything. My friends were going out and came back at 2 or 3 o'clock in the morning. I did not want to see this" (Af1). She subsequently found a job as a live-in nanny with a Christian family.

WELCOME HOME

The memory of returning home is not only associated with the absence of family members and friends and the help of the community but also with the reaction of the Greek Orthodox population toward the returnees. All the interviewees who discuss this topic do so in the context of reclaiming their belongings. People who did not get back what they had left behind with their Christian friends talk about this issue more extensively. In most of these cases, where shop merchandise, furniture, and other valuables were left in the care of somebody else, those entrusted with it that it had been taken by the Germans, or by robbers, or that it had to be sold in order to survive. Mrs. M. received a letter from the Christian brother of her sister-in-law just two weeks after they had left Thessaloniki for the mountains, saying that robbers had taken the entire contents of her husband's shop (material for clothing), which had been left under his care. After her return to Thessaloniki, the mother of her sister-in-law also did not return her piano and the other things she had left with her. Mrs. M. has no doubt that her Christian family members took advantage of the situation. "They became millionaires. This happened within our family. Who knows from how many they have taken?" (Af14). Other memories of an unfriendly welcome by the Greek

Orthodox population refer to remarks made by "surprised" acquaintances and neighbors, such as, "Ah, you survived?" or "What a pity you were not made into soap."[12] When talking about these incidents, the interviewees stress that people who made remarks like that had "taken things from the Jews" (Af18).

Other people were luckier and received some or all of the goods back that had been under the protection of a Christian friend or neighbor. Such people found it easier to reestablish themselves. Although the high number of people who were registered as unemployed in the community — 808, according to *Israelitikon Vima* in November 1945 — indicates how dire the economic circumstances for most returnees must have been, most interviewees do not talk extensively about their economic situations. Often they summarize this topic by saying: "Slowly, slowly everyone managed to get his home and his shop" (Af15). It is not clear to what time frame "slowly, slowly" refers.

"A New Life Is Beginning"

The topic that clearly dominates the discourse about the period after the war is marriage — for many of the interviewees, their second one — and the birth of children. Indeed, while the themes discussed above have illustrated that personal experiences shape the perception of treason and help during and after the war and explain therefore why narratives may vary considerably, this is not the case when it comes to the topic of postwar weddings and childbirths. There seems to be a consensus among all my interviewees that there "was a special feeling common to all survivors, to get married and make a family" (Am4), or in other words, "to make a family after the catastrophe and to replace all the people who were lost" (Am4).

"They came back and they were all alone and did not find anybody, so they were saying: '*ade, ela, ela* [come on]' and people started marrying quickly. They wanted to be together" (Af3). In the personal narratives of the interviewees, getting married and having children marks "the new beginning" of their lives, a new beginning associated with the day-to-day problems of the postwar years.

> It was not an easy time, but at the same time it was a kind of "a new life is beginning." Everyone started having babies. There were many weddings and births. I could not have babies, I lost two. I stayed nine months in bed to have my daughter. It was like the heart cracking. Every day you did not know, would you have some news, would you not have some news. Would you have some fights with the court for the problems with the store that you have to get back, the house that you have to have back. (Af14)

Photo of Mrs. Palomba Alalluf holding a photo of her
wedding in 1946, Thessaloniki, 1994. Reproduced by
kind permission of Bea Lewkowicz

It is important to point out that marriages were both a psychological
and an economic necessity in the postwar years. In particular, women
who were left without any other family members to support them were
under pressure to marry. In many instances they married older men
whose wives and children had been killed in the camps. Mrs. A. describes how she got married as follows: "His first wife was taken to the
Lager. When he came back he did not find her and he took me. What
could I do? I did not have anyone. I did not love him" (Af1). After
having left the Christian family she worked for because they had accused her of stealing, marriage seemed to be the only option. She moved
in with her future husband, who was twelve years older, and became
pregnant. Since her husband had been married before the war, they had

to wait until they could get married. The Jewish community had decided to let a year pass after the return of the camp survivors before widowers and widows could remarry. Eventually Mrs. A. got married on 2 June 1946 in a group wedding ceremony with nine other couples. Between 1945 and 1947, thirty-nine such group weddings took place (twenty-two in 1946 alone).[13] These weddings took place in the building of *Matanot le Vionim*, which houses the Jewish school today and was a charity organization giving meals to poor pupils until the war.

> We were very poor. I did not have money to buy a wedding dress. All the girls wanted to get married and make a family, to go to Israel and to America. Therefore they married us all together. I got married with three of my friends. Five couple on one side, five on the other side, the rabbi [Michael Molho] and some men from the community in the middle. (Af1)

These group weddings embody the postwar situation of many Jews in Thessaloniki. The couples married together because they had no relatives with whom to celebrate; they had only each other to help and support. The weddings are seen both as a means to cope with the feelings of loss and loneliness and as a sign for a new beginning. Mr. B., for example, who was the president of the community for many years, recalls that these weddings were something very special to the Jewish community of Thessaloniki. After getting married, many couples shared their accommodations with two or three other couples until each one was able to move to their own flat or decided to emigrate. Of the ten couples who got married in the above-mentioned ceremony, three emigrated to America, four to Israel, and the others stayed in Thessaloniki (Af1).

Marriage was viewed both by individuals and the community (which encouraged marriages) as a step forward, either to facilitate emigration or to facilitate reestablishment in Thessaloniki. I was told that the community in some instances gave some dowry to the newly wed couples, in the form of sewing machines (Af10). Since most group weddings took place in 1946, we can assume that most people who performed these weddings were camp survivors. If we look at the marriage statistics, we can also notice that the average marriage age for males in 1945, when forty-five weddings were registered, was twenty-six (for females, twenty-three), whereas in 1946, when 151 weddings were registered, it was thirty-six (for females, twenty-six). These figures indicate that most men who married in 1945 were young and had come back from the mountains or from hiding, whereas men who married in 1946 were older, had mostly come back from the camps, and often were marrying for the second time. The wedding statistics reveal another interesting point: twenty-three of the brides who were married in 1946 and 1947 had converted to Judaism. Due to the much smaller number of conversions in the following year and various references to this fact in the interviews, this number suggests that a number of Jewish men married Christian women who had helped them hide during the war.

Following the many weddings in the postwar years, there was a baby boom. Between 1945 and 1951, 402 children were born, compared to 234 between 1951 and 1971 and 205 between 1971 and 1994. The number of new births was so high that the AJDC funded a special gynecological clinic in order to accommodate the medical needs of all the pregnant Jewish women. The doctor in charge was Dr. Menashe, a concentration-camp survivor who was the first president of the community after the war until he emigrated to the United States in 1952 (Am4).

EMIGRATION

The decision whether to stay in Thessaloniki or to leave was probably one of the most pertinent issues for Jewish couples and individuals in the postwar period. When talking about emigration, one should also bear in mind that not all camp survivors returned to Thessaloniki; many instead found their way to France, Israel, or America (Am4). Some families were already split up during the war.

The push factors that made people move to Israel, the United States, or other parts of Greece (mostly Athens) were again both psychological and economical. The most common answer people gave me when asked about postwar emigration was: "The ones who had nobody and nothing here, they went to Israel and the United States" (Af5). It certainly seems to have been the case that people who had managed to reopen a family business and reclaim family property were less likely to leave than others. For those who had reclaimed their own or their family businesses, the prospect of "being an employee" somewhere else seems to have been among the strongest reasons to stay. (Am4).

However, one should not underestimate other factors. Mrs. M., for example, tells me why she did not want to stay in Thessaloniki: "I wanted very much to go to America. I was sick from the problems with my parents [who had been deported and killed]. I got very melancholic, I could not help it. I started saying, we should go. What are we going to do? To raise our children here?"(Af14). The concern for the children was also voiced by another interviewee who emigrated to the United States in 1956: "I was well off here. I was well paid. I built my own house. But I asked myself: What kind of a future will my children have in Greece? That's what pushed me" (Am6). Another factor driving emigration in the 1940s that should not be overlooked is the outbreak of the civil war. The prospect of being drafted into a war in which one "did not know whether you are an enemy or a friend" (Am3) after having survived the camps must have also contributed to the decision to emigrate.

TRAITORS

For a handful of people, emigration from Thessaloniki was a way out of a community in which they were no longer accepted. I hereby refer to Jews who were perceived as traitors and collaborators. This is a topic not widely discussed in the interviews. One person who is commonly perceived as a traitor and held responsible for the fact that so many Jews were deported to Poland is Rabbi Koretz. One interviewee tells me that "when his wife and son came back to Thessaloniki nobody talked to them" (Af15). They both emigrated to Israel. The only other references to traitors in the interviews concern the trial in Thessaloniki in which one Jew was hanged for collaboration with the Germans (Af15) and the treatment of children whose father was believed to have been a traitor. The following episode, recounted by a teacher who worked in the community, highlights some of the dilemmas the Jewish community faced after the war.

> After school, every afternoon we used to meet. I used to play little piano pieces and small songs for the children and we used to have chocolate and beverages given to us by the "Joint." One day a mother comes and tells me: "Madame S., please send away these two children because their father was a traitor, a real traitor, send them away." I said: "No Madame, the children have nothing to do with that. The children are children, beautiful children. Why should I send them away?" The woman replied: "Do you think so? I had four children and they killed them, why they should live?" She was right. He was a traitor and he saved his children, she wasn't a traitor and she lost four children. "You are right," I said, "but I am not going to kill these children. They live here." (Afg18)

Mrs. M., who is very involved with the women's organization of the community, remembers that immediately after the war, some women were not accepted in the club. These were women who were associated with the community leadership during the war who had been deported in the last transport to Bergen-Belsen, where they stayed in a separate camp, called the *Albala Lager* or *Lager del Los Privilegiados* (The Camp of the Privileged). She adds that "memories fade when the years pass" (Af12), and therefore the issue was resolved over the years.

"WE WERE ALL TOGETHER"

Analyzing all the interviews, there is much more emphasis on unity and the breakdown of social distance within the community than on divisions and conflict, though this does not mean that the postwar community was not riven by conflicts, disputes, and suspicion. One of the interviewees who emigrated to the United States very clearly remembers a lot of polemics and fighting between community members and that "every Jew was a headache for the community" (Am6). We need to bear in mind that memory can be affected by the position of the speaker (was and is he or she politically active in the community?), by present (at the time of the interview) experience and perception (of "community," for example), and by the wish to focus on the "positive" aspects of reconstruction rather than on the "negative" ones.

Undoubtedly, the community played a central role in helping individuals to reestablish themselves. Most community members were involved in the life of the community in one way or the other, either in leadership functions, as members of a committee, or as visitors to and participants in social and religious communal gatherings. Very soon after the return of the camp survivors, the community held elections to constitute the Community Assembly (fifty people) and to form a community council (nine people). The fact that there were different parties (Zionist, Partisan/Socialist, and Displaced Persons parties) is not seen as a sign of division but as a sign of vitality and survival: "This small community which had just escaped death showed its vitality. All the parties worked for the same aim, the reestablishment of the Jews. They were all concerned with the return of property and education" (Am4). The "reconstruction" of the reconstruction years, for example with regard to the different parties, does not necessarily reflect the experience of party politics at the time, in which many people probably would have liked a more unified community.

The stress of community unity on the political level is mirrored by the stress of unity on the social level: "Here after the war, we were all one. We did not have different classes. How many were we? When we had a wedding, for example, everybody was invited. . . . To the synagogue everybody is invited, when you have child, when you have a Brit Milah or a Bar Mitzwah everybody is invited" (Af3).[14] The unity or the breakdown of social boundaries among the few Jews in postwar Thessaloniki is certainly an important topic in all narratives about the postwar years, although it is presented in a different light in the different interviews. Some people see it as a positive phenomenon, some view it with a high degree of embitterment. Mr. B. talks about this issue as follows: "At that time, nobody thought about being rich or poor. The main thing was to be alive, and to enjoy this life. That was the most important thing. At that time we enjoyed life more than today. Today one is rich, one is poor, one is this or that, but at the time we were all together" (Am4). In contrast to this positive memory, Mrs. M. says: "We are nobody now. We don't belong to any class. You cannot classify among 800 people" (Af14). These kinds of statement are clearly linked to personal biographies and personal coping strategies. Mr. B. was actively involved in the reconstruction of the community, while Mrs. M. emigrated with her husband and two children to the United States.

It seems that people who were actively involved in the reconstruction of the community tend to stress more the notion of social unity in postwar Thessaloniki. This notion not only is viewed differently by some interviewees but also is not shared by everyone. Mrs. A. tells me: "The rich don't speak with the poor. We are not united. The rich are rich, the middle class are middle class. They never spoke to each other" (Af1). This view was certainly not the majority view, but it might indicate that there is a different social perception of class difference. Class difference, mainly defined in terms of income and family background, looks different from the perspective of Mrs. A., who remained relatively poor after the war. For her it is clear that the "rich marry the rich and the middle class the middle class" (Af1); she includes herself in the latter. In this statement she refers clearly to the more recent situation, but it is interesting that she extends the time period "after the war" (which I had used in my question) to today.

Class differences among community members after the war were thus not totally eradicated, but social boundaries were definitely blurred and social distance certainly reduced. As one interviewee puts it: "People belong to different classes, but since the Holocaust was very, very recent everything else came second. Jews felt first as Jews and then as belonging to different classes" (Bm25). The stress on cohesion and unity expressed itself clearly when it came to the education of the children. The community had decided to send all Jewish children to two private Greek primary schools. Arrangements were made with the schools to allow external teachers to come to the schools and teach Jewish religion and Hebrew to the children. The community had also created a special club and a summer camp for the children in order to "prevent assimilation and give them a good Jewish education" (Am4). What is perceived among the older generation as the breakdown of class boundaries and the feeling of togetherness as a result of the catastrophic decimation of the community is perceived in a much more positive light in terms of closeness by the generation that grew up after the war.

GROWING UP AFTER THE WAR

The children who grew up in Thessaloniki after the war were raised as members of a small minority. In contrast to their parents, they did not know what it was like before the war: "For my father Salonika and the community is something else, a mixture of before the war and after the war. For me it is only what I saw after the war. . . . I know we are only a very small minority. My father did not grow up in a city in which there was a Jewish minority. This is a very big difference" (Bf29). The children who grew up after the war can be divided in two groups: the very few children who had survived the war, and those who were born in the postwar baby boom. Although these groups differ considerably in size, they describe their socialization in very similar ways, emphasizing the close bond that existed between the children.

Among my interviewees, two were born during the war, both in Athens. Mr. A. survived in hiding with his mother while his father was with the partisans in the mountains. Mrs. B. survived with a Christian couple who pretended to be her parents. Mr. A. came back to Thessaloniki with his parents in 1954. Like Mrs. B., whose mother had survived Auschwitz and settled in Thessaloniki in 1947, he regularly went to the club in the community center and to the *Kataskinosi* (sometimes also referred to in Hebrew as the *Keitana*), the yearly summer camp for the children. Both remember the activities related to the club and the summer camp in a very positive way. They stress that they felt "like brothers and sisters," that the club and the *Kataskinosi* was "like a family" and like a "second home." "I was very happy when I stayed there with all the children. There were about twelve children in my age who had survived. We were like brothers and sisters" (Bf22). The feeling of family is associated with notions of closeness and similarity: "I really feel nostalgic about the friends I met in the *Kataskinosi* because of one thing. It was like family to me. My name was not strange to them. I was among people that were called Florentin or Coen, names which were similar to mine" (Bm21). The club and the *Kataskinosi* provided the children with a kind of family framework that many did not have because of the Holocaust. For the children, the communal atmosphere was perceived in contrast to the atmosphere at home. Mr. A. describes how things were at his home: "I remember my mother crying a lot. I remember very much the feeling of loss we had in the house and I remember my feeling of not being able to compete with the other children because I did not have a grandmother, a grandfather, an uncle, an aunt, a nephew, a niece, a cousin" (Bm21). For Mrs. B., who did not attend the same school as the other Jewish children, the small room in the community center and the summer camp were an escape not only from the melancholic atmosphere at home but also from the antisemitic atmosphere at school, where the other girls used to call her *Evrea* ("Jewess").

Apart from the relationship with the other children, most interviewees also remember vividly the Israeli teachers (*morim*) who were brought from Israel (with the help of the Jewish Agency) to work with the children. The learning of Hebrew songs and Israeli dances enhanced the feeling of togetherness among the children (Bm21). Because of this socialization and the personal ties to Salonikans who had emigrated to Israel, Israel became an important source of identification for the post-war generation. The community also encouraged young people to study in Israel, which many (especially the boys) did.

In contrast to the small group of children who survived the war, the baby boom generation constituted "a rather strong group of Jewish boys and girls, who did not feel as a minority at all" (Bm25). As a consequence of the community's policy to send the Jewish children to two schools, there were classes in which 50 percent of the children were Jewish. This changed when the children went to high school: "It was like a very nice family at elementary school, you felt secure. When I went to high school I was very shocked at the beginning. I had lost many of the privileges I had as a protected child in the elementary school" (Bf29). This statement illustrates the sense of insecurity some of the second-generation children must have felt, which went hand-in-hand with the notion of safety and protection among Jews and a community that was there to protect its members. The link to the historical experience of their parents is obvious. Mrs. V. recalls what she felt like as a young girl: "I felt different. If we are Greeks, why did Greece not protect the Jews during the Holocaust? Why did nobody protect them?" (Bf30). Based on the sample of my interviews, it seems that gender needs to be looked at in this context. There is clearly more stress on vulnerability and insecurity among the women I interviewed than among the men. Although the men stress the closeness and lifelong importance of the friendships among the Jewish children, they also recall that they rebelled against the "low-profile mentality" of their parents. They did not want to "keep quiet" about their Jewishness, they did not identify with "the Jews from the camps, who thought that we cannot sing very loud or dance very openly." Instead, they wanted to be "proud Jews" who "fight back" (Bm21). This element of rebellion is completely missing in the interviews with the women of that generation, and one gets the impression that the girls developed a more distinct sense of responsibility toward their survivor parents, taking them into account, for example, when considering a move or a choice of spouse. "A lot of my friends went to Israel [to study]. I also wanted to go but my father would not let me because he had lost already one girl in the concentration camp. He did not want to lose me as well. When he said something like this, there was no more question about going" (Bf30). The sense of duty to their parents as Holocaust survivors is very striking in the next quotation. When asked about mixed marriages, Mrs. S. replies: "I felt that I did not have the right to marry a Christian guy because my father went through the Holocaust. It was my feeling that I could not do this to my father, who was a believing Jew and has been in a concentration camp" (Bf29). The most plausible explanation for the development of this kind of gendered postwar Jewish identities is that the girls on the whole grew up more protected than the boys and that there was more pressure on them to marry at a young age within the community. Most women whom I interviewed in this generation talk about the effect of the Holocaust on their upbringing. They relate the fact that their parents sent them to good schools and wanted to give them a good education in their parents' experience: "They prepared us to survive, as if there would be another Holocaust. My father always said: I survived because I knew some languages. That's why he wanted to teach us foreign languages" (Bf30). Some people of the second generation describe their parents' feeling of insecurity; others express it themselves. Mr. M. remembers that his parents, who belong to an old Salonikan family, did not take it for granted after the war "that they as Jews will be here tomorrow" (Bm27). Feelings of contingency or lack of durability do not relate only to place but also to people. Mrs. V.'s way of describing her relationship with her Christian friends (in 1994) illustrates this notion.

> Yes, I live here, I like to live here, I have many friends here, but I don't know, if there will be another Holocaust, if these friends will be friends then. We are friends now, yes of course, because we have our position, our prestige, and all these things, they have to learn from me, I have to learn from them, we exchange ideas and all these things, but I don't know if they will be friends in a difficult-hard time." (Bf30)

SURVIVAL STRATEGIES

In the previous pages I have tried to illuminate the process of return and reconstruction in the light of the most profound effect of the war on the surviving Jews: the experience of uprooting and dislocation. The war had taken away "home" from most Jews, in both a narrow and a broad sense. Their "home" was not there anymore because of the postwar presence in which families were absent and houses often occupied by strangers; their "hometown" was also no longer there because of the destruction of most Jewish references to the past, the biggest of which was the destruction of the old Jewish cemetery. After the Jewish cemetery had been destroyed in 1942, Jewish tombstones were scattered all over the city, used as building material for houses, walls, stairs, courtyards, and churches. One interviewee talks about visiting a house in which the whole staircase was built of Jewish tombstones; on each stair you could read another Jewish name (Af15). After the war, the new university was built on the site of the former cemetery.

These radical changes in the lives of individual Jews and in the landscape of the city brought about a new meaning for Jewish community and Jewish identity in postwar Thessaloniki. The war transformed a heterogeneous and settled population group (who had developed a very strong notion of their Salonikan identity) into a homogeneous, vulnerable, and uprooted minority group. Bereft of a real home, the community became a substitute home, in which relationships between its members were perceived in terms of an extended family framework providing support, help, friendship, and a link to the past. Because of the traumatic experience of the Holocaust and the subsequent experience of dislocation, the community and contact with other Jews provided a "secure safe haven" for the older generation and an "intimate place to socialize" for the younger generation. The concepts of "being together" and *Enter Mosotros* (which means "among ourselves" in Ladino) are distinct expressions of the newly formed postwar minority identity.

Ethnic and religious identities are often formulated in terms of symbolic kinship because kinship provides a model of relatedness based on a "natural connection" and a "shared essence." In the case of the Jewish community in postwar Thessaloniki, the "natural connection" between the Jews was the shared historical experience, the shared memory of a very different prewar Thessaloniki, and the shared absence of family. But the family metaphor of community expresses more than the function of a substitute family of community; it also describes the "privatization" and marginalization of the postwar Jewish community. The community became marginal in terms of numbers, but more importantly, in terms of the public memory of the city. Formulated in the discourse of the Greek nation-state, history was viewed through the looking-glass of historical continuity and homogeneity, not through one of multiculturalism and heterogeneity. This meant that the history of the Jews in Thessaloniki was largely ignored.

In terms of a communal survival strategy, this "privatization" was reflected in the maintenance of a very low public profile. I suggest that this "low-profile identity" is an expression of powerlessness and a response to the war and postwar experience, as illustrated in the following quotation: "We were not like the prewar [Jewish] Salonikans who had their own deputies and who could influence the local mayor. We knew there was very little we could do. We will always run the risk of provoking, without wanting it" (Bm25). We can state, therefore, that the two most important Jewish adaptation strategies in postwar Thessaloniki were, on the individual level, the re-creation of families, and on the communal level, the creation of a community with a low public profile and a high private profile, providing protection, support, help, and a family framework for its members in the changed, non-Jewish environment.

The notion of the Jewish community as family is still relevant today. A young woman describes the relationship to other Jews of the same generation by saying: "We had no choice. So we were always together as a family" (Cf41). In contrast to their parents or grandparents, many of the younger generation talk about this aspect of community in the context of constraint and pressure. They want a more open community, and they are able to voice their discomfort about the omission of Jews from the public memory more easily: "We cannot accept the memory loss of our countrymen, and we cannot accept that the Jewish presence in our town is ignored, just like that" (Bm25). The process of the reconstruction of the community started immediately after the war. The process of the reconstruction of Jewish memory, though, has just recently begun.

NOTES

1. The number of deportees varies according to different sources. During 1943 and 1944, between 54,533 (M. Mazower, *Inside Hitler's Greece: The Experience of Occupation, 1941–1944* [New Haven and London, 1993], 256) and 62,573 (M. Molho, *In Memoriam: Hommage aux Victimes Juives des Nazisen Grece* [Salonika, 1988]) Jews from all over Greece were deported to Auschwitz and Bergen-Belsen, between 46,061 (based on records of the Greek Railway) and 48,774 (based on the remaining records of Auschwitz-Birkenau) from Thessaloniki alone (H. Fleischer, "Greichenland," in W. Benz, ed., *Dimensionen des Völkermords* [Munich, 1991], 241–73).

2. *Evraiko Vima* 5, 21 Dec. 1945.

3. J. Plaut, *Greek Jewry in the Twentieth Century, 1913–1983: Patterns of Jewish Survival in the Greek Provinces before and after the Holocaust* (London, 1996), 74.

4. The legal status of the community dates back to Law no. 2456 from 1920, which gave all Jewish communities in Greece this special status; Jewish Community of Thessaloniki, *A Short History of the Jewish Community* (Thessaloniki, 1978), 40.

5. B. Lewkowicz, "Greece Is My Home, But . . . Ethnic Identity of Greek Jews in Thessaloniki," *Journal of Mediterranean Studies* 4.2 (1994): 237.

6. S. Marketos, "Ethnos choris Evreos: Apopseis tis Historiographikis Kataskevis tou Ellinismou," in *Synchrona Themata*, vols. 52–53, no. 17 (1994): 52–69. That is not to say that no research has been published elsewhere. The growing volume of material on this subject may most conveniently be followed in the bibliographic surveys of the *Bulletin of Judaeo-Greek Studies*.

7. I had a very similar experience in Athens. I was invited to a wedding that took place in the synagogue of Athens. The airplane was delayed and I was in an extreme hurry to get there in time. After jumping into a taxi and explaining where I wanted to go, the taxi driver started arguing with me. He had never heard of a Jewish synagogue. I told him to drive to Melidoni Street. He had never heard of the street either. He made it quite clear that he thought I was a confused foreigner, and even when we got there he still looked very doubtful. One thing was clear, this was not a language problem. He simply had not heard of such a thing as a Jewish synagogue before.

8. I would like to thank the Jewish Community of Thessaloniki and all my interviewees for their generous help and cooperation throughout my research. I would also like to express my deepest gratitude to all the people who welcomed me with open arms and made me feel at home in Thessaloniki.

9. This label indicates the number of the interview, and to which group (A, B, C, D) and which gender (m, f) the interviewee belonged. In order to protect the identities of the interviewees I use abbreviated names.

10. The concentration-camp survivors refer to themselves as *omiros* ("hostages") who were in *omoria* ("taken hostage") in the *stratopedo* ("concentration camp").

11. E. Counio-Amarigilio, *Peninta chronia meta: Anamniseis mias Salonikiotissas Evraias* (Thessaloniki, 1995), 131.

12. Kokot writes that the Asia Minor refugees in Thessaloniki whom she researched still sometimes jokingly refer to Jews "who were made into soap" (*tous kanane sapounaki*) when they speak about the war. W. Kokot, "Kulturelle Modelle und Soziale Identitaet in einem Fluechtlingsviertel in Thessaloniki," dissertation, University of Cologne (1995), 197.

13. All the figures concerning marriages are based on my own research of the community archives.

14. *Brit Milah* is the Jewish circumcision ceremony, *Bar Mitzwah* the ceremony that marks the initiation of a thirteen-year-old boy into the Jewish religious community.

THIRTEEN

Memories of the Bulgarian Occupation of Eastern Macedonia: Three Generations

Xanthippi Kotzageorgi-Zymari
with Tassos Hadjianastassiou

THE FIRST INTERVIEW I conducted on the Bulgarian occupation of the Second World War occurred when I was sixteen. It was on 29 September, the occasion of the annual memorial service for my grandfather, who was executed on that day in the year 1941 in Drama. My grandmother played the role of informant in this amateur interview. This endeavor was my attempt to justify that annual family ritual and to satisfy my curiosity regarding a tragic event that, although it had little direct effect on me, obviously had exercised a catalytic effect on my mother and grandmother. This was evident not only in the days immediately prior and subsequent to the date of the memorial but sporadically in different phases of our common life — especially in times of misfortune. Later, when I applied myself to the study of the Bulgarian language and visited Bulgaria, I accepted as natural and expected my mother's disappointed surprise regarding my dealings with the "coarse and barbarian" Bulgarian language as well as my visits there. I thought back then that this did not daunt me in the least. In the end, though, the existential power of those memorial services and of that amateur "interview" proved to work in their own unique way toward the formation of my own personal memory. The result was that some years later I applied myself to the historical study of the Bulgarian occupation in eastern Macedonia and Thrace (1941–1944) and chose to have three main themes as my objects of study: the function of personal memories from the occupation for the formation of the personal and collective memory of all those who experienced the occupation to a greater (first generation) or lesser (second generation) degree, and of all those who merely "knew of it" (third generation) through the memories of those preceding them; the degree to which these memories influenced the personal and social lives of the subjects in question; and the role of memory in the formation of a personal or collective image regarding an entire people and in the creation or enforcement of ethnic-cultural stereotypes.

METHODOLOGICAL FRAMEWORK

The exceedingly personal introduction to this article, within which I hinted beyond the shadow of a doubt that I also constitute a "specimen" from the third generation, is an absolutely conscious choice.[1] It constitutes in and of itself an indication of the function and power of personal memory regarding the occupation, which, of course, by no means possesses a generalized character. This personal web, as well as the use in general of oral witnesses, often tends to raise hesitation regarding the "objectivity" of such studies amongst those who dispute the value of oral history because it uses an absolutely subjective source of knowledge. However, besides the fact that history constitutes in any case a subjective interpretation of the past and present, oral history is "objective" exactly in that it comprises a transliteration of the experienced reality of the historical subjects themselves. These historical subjects are members of many intricately intertwined smaller and larger units — a fact that makes them also collective subjects, that is, bearers of the local historical view on history.[2] In this chapter I have endeavored with the utmost respect to synthesize these two aspects of our historical subjects. Furthermore, I have attempted to employ in a positive way the fact that, although a researcher, I have also participated in the collective memory of a certain portion of the informants. This I see as a factor that minimizes the distance that could separate my emotional reality from those of the informants, and reinforces that reality for the best possible comprehension of and sympathy for their personal and collective memory. Even so, as a safeguard against emotional involvement, which could harm the formulation of the questions as well as the final drafting of the conclusions, a valuable safety-valve in this project was my close cooperation with Tassos Hadjianastassiou, who conducted the greater part of the fieldwork.[3] I personally bear responsibility for the formulation of the working hypothesis and the principles that govern the research as well as the creation of the questionnaires that were used, with the agreement of my colleague, in the research field. The interviews and the completed questionnaires that evolved from this were the result of common elaboration, as was the formulation of the observations that guided the drafting of this chapter.

This work is actually an indicative case study. Since the region occupied by the Bulgarians covered more than 16,000 square kilometers and concerned thousands of settlements, we had to focus our research on a specific area in order to render the research both effective and meaningful. Thus, our mixed questionnaire-guide was applied to, and biographical interviews were taken from, inhabitants from two villages within the prefecture of Drama, Doxato and Choristi.[4] The prefecture of Drama

(eastern Macedonia) was the one that suffered most from the consequences of the Bulgarian occupation in northern Greece. As for the two
aforementioned villages, they suffered not only from the "administrative" measures taken by the Bulgarian authorities throughout the occupation, but also from the consequences of the suppression of the Drama
revolt, in which these two villages played a significant role. Moreover,
this specific population has suffered famine, deportations, and atrocities
three times in the twentieth century (1912–1913, 1916–1918, 1941–
1944) by the same aggressors.[5]

About sixty individuals from the two villages, men and women from
three generations, participated in this research project. People presently
seventy to ninety years of age who experienced the occupational reality
firsthand as adults were chosen as the first-generation informants. The
second generation consisted of individuals who were children during the
occupational era (who are presently in the sixth decade of their life) and
who preserve some memories from that period. Finally, the third generation is made up of today's generation of people who are in their thir-
ties, people who, save for the indirect contact with the personal, familial, or social memory of their intimate as well as their wider
environment, have no experience of the occupation. Regarding gender,
occupation, education, and political alignment, the choice of informants
was intentionally random and was governed mainly by the accessibility
to the informers and their desire to participate in the research project.
The only presupposition regarding the people of the first generation,
and to a lesser degree those of the second, was that the informers had
remained in the area for the total duration of the occupation, or at least
that they had traveled to and fro, circumstantially compelled by reasons
directly related to the occupation (workers in the Bulgarian labor battalions, migrants to Germany for economic reasons, insurgents in armed
bands of the opposition, etc.). Our intention regarding the locality of
the informers and their having remained in the region even to this day
was satisfied to the utmost only in the case of the informers of the first
generation. In the cases of the second and third generations, the informers are today either inhabitants of the same villages or are internal
immigrants to the capital of the prefecture (Drama) or to the capital of
the administrative region of Macedonia (Thessaloniki).[6]

HISTORICAL BACKGROUND

The Bulgarian occupation of eastern Macedonia and Thrace during the
Second World War commenced on 20 April 1941 with the invasion of
the Bulgarian armed forces into Greek Macedonia, and concluded in
September to October 1944 with the retreat of the Bulgarian forces and

the political authorities involved in the occupation. For the German military forces, this occupation was temporary and was to be policed by their Bulgarian allies. For Bulgaria, however, this occupation was a golden opportunity to finally annex these much-coveted fertile regions to its own territory, in this way securing definitively an outlet to the Aegean Sea. Thus, on 14 May 1941, the official annexation by Bulgaria of the "newly liberated land" was triumphantly announced. From that moment until the end of the occupation, the Bulgarian policy was one of the political annexation-assimilation of these regions into the main Bulgarian national body, and it was expressed in ways that touched upon all aspects of social, political, and economic life.

On the administrative level, Greek political, military, police, and other authorities were disbanded and replaced by Bulgarian counterparts. The Greek schools were closed and replaced with Bulgarian ones. Along with the Greek intellectuals (doctors, lawyers, teachers, notary publics, etc.), who were deported by the Bulgarian authorities because they "could influence the population," Greek Metropolitans and a great number of Greek priests were also expelled from the territory, many of them having been maltreated. The positions of the expelled priests were filled by Bulgarian clergymen, who conducted services only in the Bulgarian language. The compulsory use of the Bulgarian language, in both written and spoken forms of speech, was imposed throughout the occupied area, and the use of the Greek language was forbidden. The possession and use of Greek historical books and printed material was also forbidden, and Greek printing-houses were not allowed to operate. Measures were also taken that aimed at the economic impoverishment of the Greek population, as well as at its oppression and physical extermination — labor battalions, forced labor. Last but not least, the Bulgarian government tried to alter the ethnic composition of the area, both by the compelling or forcing migration of inhabitants of non-Bulgarian descent from the region, for the most part Greeks and to a smaller degree Muslims and Jews, and by settling colonists from Bulgaria. Directly connected to the Bulgarian policy toward the Greek population was the harsh reaction of the Bulgarian authorities to the Greek national resistance in the region. This resistance, in an unorganized initial phase, led to the Drama revolt of 28–29 September 1941.[7] Due to this revolt and the violent suppression that followed, the Bulgarians advanced to mass executions of the civilian population.

In the beginning of our research the following questions were dominant: What does a foreign occupation leave behind in the memory of the people who lived through it? Which experiences are recorded and survive in their conscious and subconscious? How vivid are these memories after fifty years? In which ways do people believe that the occupation influenced their lives, and to what extent? Which of the experiences are passed on as personal or collective memory to later generations? How do later generations filter through these experiences, and to what extent do they assimilate them? Especially, when the foreign conqueror is a neighboring army, known from the past for similar actions, how does the new occupation influence the individual and collective image of that neighboring people in the consciousness of the people who lived through the occupation, as well as in that of following generations?

THE PRINCIPAL AND SECONDARY ACTORS: THE FIRST AND SECOND GENERATIONS

Like all typical "grandparents," the informants of the first generation of both villages were more than eager to be the narrators and our guides to their past. All had stories to relate from the occupation era, and all had established opinions. Their feelings toward the occupation and the occupants remained more or less the same as they were immediately subsequent to its termination, albeit less vivid now. The representatives of the second generation were just as eager as the first to provide us with information. Informants from both generations gave extended interviews within which they not only eloquently rendered isolated events of the occupation that made up the flesh of their present memory, but also successfully communicated the intensity of these memories and the emotions connected with them. It is particularly noteworthy that the collective and individual memories of both the first and second generations were found to be intense and rich.

Undoubtedly for all, the most painful of memories from the period of the occupation were of the events following the ill-fated Drama revolt. These are the prevalent memories from the occupation, memories that are deeply rooted within the collective subconscious, regardless of whether the specific individuals lost loved ones due to the executions that followed. In a society where all knew each other and family relations were close and extended, two whole villages were suddenly plunged into a permanent state of mourning: one informant, for example, declared that she had lost thirty-five relatives. Despite this, however, the existence of a collective subject in this case was particularly intense. All informants, even those who hadn't lost people from their immediate family, always spoke of the executions in the first-person plural: "They slaughtered us." All the informants repeatedly lingered over the events and descriptions of the executions—the "slaughter," as they called it— each contributing different aspects. This was also the first subject they referred to when queried on the occupation, which, for all practical purposes, seems to be totally identified with the events of 28–29 September 1941. The executions left an especially intense scar on the collective memory of the Choristians as the "slaughter of *Giola*" (*Giola* means "ditch" in Turkish), especially since all inhabitants of the village were potential victims, including women, children, and the aged. In the case of Doxatians, however, because the executions occurred without eyewitnesses, the main point of reference for their memory was the imprisonment by the Bulgarians of the women, children, and elderly within the village school for two days without food and water. Of course, the most intense and emotionally loaded was the memory of those who were among the potential victims and of those who lost relatives and friends. Many of those who lost their fathers or young siblings in the executions seemed to have been traumatized for life psychologically, socially, and economically. Some couldn't manage to continue their education, others were compelled to emigrate to German-occupied Greece, many had suffered starvation, most felt that they were socially marginalized: "Ever since then I have a lot of complexes . . . anywhere you went they called you 'the orphan' . . . my mother as a widow did not fit anywhere." They saw the executions as being responsible for all the hardships suffered after the occupation, that is, during the recuperation period (the mid-1940s to the mid-1950s): "The men who were the pillars of our house are gone"; "Our family has four dead. Only we women and children have remained."

Regarding the period after the executions, most of the informants of both the first and the second generation maintain indelible memories of the intense fear they felt ("You were afraid to go outside because of the chance of being seen by a Bulgarian"). This is especially true for the second generation, which was comprised then of children of about eight to ten years of age. One of the informants recalled the following incident: After the revolt, he was playing with other children when they suddenly saw a Bulgarian gendarme approaching. Some of them bolted away, and others literally peed in their pants. Besides this, memories regarding the lack of freedom and the limitation of movement, the strict control and house searches, as well as the physical violence of the authorities, were especially unpleasant. Such memories were particularly evident in informants of the first generation who were the main targets of such actions; abuses were dealt out at the drop of a pin ("*Bulgarian* beatings, we called it"): "If the Bulgarian mayor was passing and you did not notice him and salute he'd come up to you and give you two slaps on the face"; "If you were caught speaking Greek, they'd beat you." Each informant recalled the ill treatment or public disgrace that they themselves, relatives, or co-villagers suffered. Many informants emphasize the psychological consequences of the oppression, connected with fear and the deprivation of their freedom. The memories of the

various forms of forced labor imposed by the Bulgarian authorities—
especially as reiterated by the informants from the first generation—
also fell under this category of psychological oppression. "Bulgaria?
Forced Laboria!" was a common expression used by the informants
with an air of irony or ridicule, but also with a feeling of outraged
frustration: "They made us hunt grasshoppers in the fields with sheets!"
They also had unpleasant memories of those fellow inhabitants who
were "Bulgarized" or "were written up as Bulgarians" during the occupation. Such Greeks were in fact represented in a worse light than
the worst of the "bad" Bulgarians ("They are the ones who committed
the worst ignominies"). Informants would often come back to this subject and would describe the "Bulgarized" in the darkest of colors, calling them "spies," "traitors," "janissaries," "tattle tales," "terrible
fascists."[8]

Finally, those aspects during and immediately after the occupation
having to do with everyday economic life—notably hunger, deprivation,
and illness—had a major impact on the memory of our informants:
"Hunger, hunger, lice and psora"; "We would go out to graze! (We ate
weeds)"; "Within a year we were skeletons." The Bulgarians comman-
deered all beasts of burden and wagons; there was no work left, unemployment ravaged the population; the harvests of cereals were withheld
almost exclusively by the Bulgarians ("That which the Bulgarians left us
wasn't even enough for a month"); and the price paid by the authorities
for the tobacco they bought at a yearly rate had no economic value.
Most products were obtainable only through the black market and
from certain stores at which only those who declared themselves as Bulgarians could shop. Most informants, and especially those who had personal experiences from the period, would describe the economic situation in the following melodramatic way: "It was a catastrophe . . .
everyone gave up everything they had. A suit for five kilos of corn"; "A
Singer sewing machine for eighteen kilos of corn." Their diet also
changed radically; most informants remembered with loathing the plain
boiled potatoes and legumes, the oil made from sunflower and sesame
seed, the corn bread, the millet and wild herbs they gathered in the
fields. The latter especially influenced the representatives of the second
generation, for they, as children, had gathered the herbs that comprised
the basis for their families' diet as well as the wood from the mountains
for heating, cooking, and bartering. This was invariably done bare-
footed ("with sacks wrapped around our feet instead of shoes, walking
in the ice of the mountains for hours with bloody feet"). Others remember illicitly gathering wheat from the fields, which they would hide in
jugs or coffee jars in order to escape the control of the Bulgarians ("We
would steal our very livelihood"). If perchance they were suspected by

the Bulgarians, their houses would be searched. In these circumstances, many fell ill due to hunger or hunger-related diseases, died, or fled to the German zone.

The Bulgarian occupation determined the life situation that all experienced for the next ten or fifteen years: "Within four years we had pined away. All was dead." All, without exception, described the conditions as "miserable" and "deplorable." The occupation ruined some, stifled the progress of others. Some had to work extremely hard for many years to reestablish themselves — those who managed to: "Mere survival was a battle. All was lost. Clothing, food, shoes." Most remark that they needed more than six or seven years to reestablish themselves personally and as a family, while many needed as much as fifteen years: "I got reestablished after '55 . . . and that slowly." Many remark that this difficult situation led to the departure of family members, relatives, friends, and co-villagers to other parts of Greece (Athens, Thessaloniki) and to Germany in order to survive and maintain those who remained. For example, 400 people from Choristi alone went as workers to Germany in 1957 and 1958.

One subject to which both the first and second generations seemed to be more or less indifferent was the ecclesiastical and educational situation in the village during the occupation. Recollections are vague, few, and rarely negatively charged. It seems that the informants' lives were not affected essentially by the banishment of the Greek priests, by the establishment of Bulgarian clergymen in their place, or by the imposition of Bulgarian, which no one understood, as the language of worship. Most attended the services either simply because both Bulgarian and Greek Churches have the same dogma (Eastern Orthodox, "They are Christians and we are Christians") or because they were drawn by habit and the need for a religious life: "I went because I needed the Church . . . it doesn't matter, I would say to myself, I'm going to Church anyway"; "You would go to light your candle, to plead with St. Athanasius: St. Athanasius, save us from the Bulgarians." The same emotional indifference was also observed to be the rule for most in the case of education. The first generation did not have any direct interest in the subject. It seems that there were some among the second generation who, even if the occupation had not intervened, would not have attended the Greek schools for many years anyway, either because of their economic situation or because of the social conditions that prevailed then. However, many refer with bitterness to the fact that the lack of Greek education during the occupation meant the termination of all education for many children because they had grown older after the occupation, or they had already started to work, or they had to work. Most note that very few Greek children attended Bulgarian schools (among them were two of our informants from the second generation), which were essentially only for those who wrote themselves up as Bulgarians. Those two informants, who each attended two years of Bulgarian elementary school, are the only ones who perceived the connection between these schools and the official Bulgarian propaganda, which was clear in the fact that the main orientation of these schools was the teaching of the Bulgarian language.

Another subject to which few references were made, strangely enough, was the national resistance. The only exceptions were three representatives of the first generation who had taken an active part in that resistance movement. This is remarkable when one considers that many inhabitants of those villages were active members in the KKE previous to the occupation and had organized the first revolutionary movement in Greece, while quite a few others supported, as they themselves admit, the rebels during the occupation. The explanation, however, is simple: most of the rebels had fled during the group executions in the two villages, and thus those who were innocent and uninvolved with the resistance fell victim to the vengeance of the authorities. The social power that the strong feeling of this injustice exercises (an injustice that has kept all families of both villages in a permanent state of mourning) is still very evident and leads many to openly accuse the resistance of being responsible for the loss of their loved ones.

At this juncture it must be noted that the order that we imposed in the course of our analysis of our informants' memories was somewhat artificial and scarcely corresponds to the shape or reality of the interviews themselves. For many of our informants, especially those from the first generation, who experienced the spectre of the occupation in all of its aspects, there were few variations in their memories: "What to remember? . . . We were starving, afraid, oppressed. Anything that you could conceive of as being bad, we had it." The total effect of the occupation on the lives of the informants of the second generation was recapitulated spontaneously by one of them as follows: "The deprivation of education in a Greek school, the lack of a proper diet and cultural life, as well as the fear I felt during my childhood years, had an irreversible effect on my life afterwards."

Memories and emotions regarding the era immediately after the termination of the occupation remain especially intense. All declared that "these are experiences which will never leave us." Most even declared that all that had occurred "cannot be overcome." They declared this despite the fact that today they do not often reflect on the specific events of the occupation, especially since the occasions that could lead to such reflections and discussions are now few and far between. Perhaps the only remaining opportunities are whenever relatives, friends, or co-villagers of the same age happen to gather together; for rare indeed are the cases where the younger generation—children or grandchildren—ask about the occupation. These discussions and the memories they bring to the fore evince pain, sorrow, grievance, bitterness, and indignation in our informants—in rare cases, even vindictiveness: "I have no hatred but I have bitterness in me. . . . Why did they behave with such barbarism to us?" "Outrage against the enemy: 100%. Not 99%, 100%." Some identify their feelings on the occupation with their feelings from the first Bulgarian occupation (1916–1918) and thus "strengthen" these memories. Others condense all their feelings subconsciously in their own special way: "May God grant that such a thing never happen again. May our children, our grandchildren, never live through such times." Even those who for "didactic" reasons state theoretically that their children or grandchildren need a "Bulgaria" to straighten them out (from a wasteful and lavish lifestyle) immediately qualify: "For two days only, maybe three or four. No more."

The bitterness, grievances, and trauma of many still have not yet healed, especially for those who lost loved ones due to the executions. A few (10 percent) did not want to discuss the occupation (although they finally did) and would not even attend the yearly memorial service that was fixed as an official institution for the remembrance and honor of those who died then.[9] Most, however, do attend, not merely because these two older generations are seen in any case to participate more in such religious ceremonies on a nationwide basis, but also because they perceive such events to be a family obligation—"I've got victims there, how can I not go?"—as well as an obligation to the community: "Those who were killed were our brothers, friends, our children; we played with them." At the memorial services, when the names of their loved ones or friends are mentioned, they are often deeply moved, and vivid and intense memories are recalled: "When we go, the memorial and all the rest take place, and we naturally become very worked up. After all we see, feel, and remember on such days, we end up like zombies." Not one of our informants tried to forget, either because they couldn't or because they believed that it was their duty to remember; and this not only in honor of the past (the dead), but also as a positive heritage for the future (children and grandchildren). Most even emphasize that memories must be maintained and transmitted as paragons of ethnic continuity and as restraining factors for such events in the future: "Let's not forget history. . . . If you forget history, that's it, you're finished"; "That which we suffered should be taught to the following generations in order that such events are not repeated by the Bulgarians or the Greeks."

The views and stories of parents and relatives naturally influenced the

opinions of all informants regarding the Bulgarians, even before the occupation, in a negative way. They felt "hatred," "antipathy," and/or
"fear" toward them. The Bulgarians were portrayed by the former to
later generations as "coarse," "vulgar," as a "bloodthirsty people,"
"maleficent," "Greece's worst enemy": "We always considered them to
be barbarians, slaughterers"; "We used to say: can a Bulgarian and
goodness be found together? That's what we heard for so many years."
This impression was later reinforced rather than refuted by all that occurred during the occupation. The first generation as a whole attributes
the behavior of the Bulgarians to "hatred from time immemorial" that
they harbor against the Greeks, or simply to "hatred," "spite," and
"jealousy." However, among the second generation only one or two
viewed the events in an emotionally loaded way. Most from this group,
attribute the behavior of the occupational authorities strictly to politics,
and they consider it as absolutely "natural" for conquerors to act in
such a way. They rationalize the behavior of the Bulgarian authorities
when they, almost unanimously, accept the view that the Bulgarians
made inroads into the region in order to satisfy an "age-old" ambition:
"The dream of the Bulgarians is to annex eastern Macedonia into Bulgaria. They therefore wanted to erase all traces of Hellenism here";
"They wanted an outlet into the Aegean. Their gaze was always riveted
here." Most, of course, do not spare the opportunity to emphasize that
the Bulgarians were allies with the Germans and that they therefore
were able to enter the region "holding onto the coattails of the Germans," as they say with all the negative connotations that expression
may contain. They even add that the Germans gave them Greek Macedonia because the Bulgarians "helped them pass through" (thus distin-
guishing this from the "heroic behavior of Greece"): "The Germans
brought them. How could the Bulgarians possibly handle it by themselves?" In this way, their final retreat was seen as disgraceful and immediately correlated with that of the Germans: "Germany collapsed,
and they left too."

Despite the generally negative impression regarding the effects of the
occupation on their family, their wider social environment, and their
own personal lives, most of our informants nevertheless were in a position to discern variations in the behavior of the Bulgarian authorities
who were established in their villages. Their behavior was almost invariably characterized by them as depending on ideology, culture, and
personal idiosyncracies. Of course, the general impression was that the
"good" Bulgarians were exceptions to the "enemy-conqueror" rule.
Among the "good," some were noted for their "philanthropy," which
was attributed to their leftist tendencies or their education. The impression of many informants that the "good" Bulgarians were autoch-

thonous to "old" Bulgaria (north Bulgaria) was also characteristic ("The Bulgarians from up there were gentlemen"), whereas their correspondents in the south were seen as robbers, misfits, and hangmen. This difference may allude to "recollections" from the intense Greek-Bulgarian competition during the Macedonian Struggle (1904–1908) and the Balkan Wars (1912–1913), within which the Bulgarians of today's southern Bulgaria were most active. They may also allude to the bigotry surrounding the population exchange between the Greek minority of Bulgaria and the Bulgarian minority in Greece (from 1919 on). The latter settled mainly in southern Bulgaria. These, of course, were quick to resettle Greek Macedonia during the occupation. Also, despite the fact that many relate that during the occupation medical care was very limited, or that Greeks were not allowed to have medicine, many comment very positively on the traveling Bulgarian doctors who visited their village; and they stressed that those doctors would care unconditionally for both Greeks and Bulgarians. Informants who complained that it was not in the doctors' interest to care for Greeks seemed to have been influenced by the generally negative feelings that memories of the occupation gave them. The same goes for those (only about two or three from the first generation) who group all Bulgarians into one big category: "For us they were all the same. All Bulgarians . . . Bulgarians!" Informants who sometimes use the same illustrations to describe both Bulgarian occupations (1916–1918, 1941–1944) also attribute some of the more intense memories from the first occupation to the second, despite the fact that the second was clearly milder. It should be noted here regarding both occupations that the regimes and the aims guiding them were similar and were made very clear to the inhabitants of the region. The fact that Bulgaria not only repeatedly undertook military occupations but also imposed a forced annexation determined the way in which the inhabitants experienced that given reality, which they all expressed accurately with one word: when they referred to the two occupations, they didn't speak of the "Bulgarian occupation," but rather of "Bulgaria I" and "Bulgaria II."

What do the informants believe about the Bulgarians today? Most do not trust the Bulgarians, either as a country or as a people: "They have no honor"; "The Bulgarians change friends at the drop of a pin." They do not believe the Bulgarians can change: "The Bulgarians cannot cease to be Bulgarians." On the contrary, they believe that "at the first opportunity and with proper support they'll be here again" — "Harmony with the Bulgarians is impossible. Some day they'll do the same thing to us." Even those who believe that "only a select group of Bulgarians, not all of them, . . . have their eyes pinpointed here," are categorically of the same opinion. Those who try to distinguish between the people and the government (35 percent) think that most of the simple citizens have a friendly attitude toward the Greeks and that the official nation is the one that invariably has designs on Greece. Also noteworthy, however, is the fact that the same percentage of the representatives of the first and the second generations correlate the Bulgarians with other "enemies" of Greece, either the Turks initially or the "Skopjians" later on. The correlation with the former is made as a verification of the barbarity of the Bulgarians as a people, whereas the correlation with the latter is made as a verification of the "conspiracy" against Greek Macedonia. Half of the representatives from the first generation still feel threatened and afraid. On the other hand, from the second generation, no one felt obviously threatened, some because of their faith in the beneficial economic relations between the two countries that are evolving, others because of the view that in both countries political propaganda is supposedly not being applied any more; most, however, suggest that the present anomalous political and economic situation of that neighboring country is the reason why they pose no threat.

The issue of vengeance was not put forward even by those who consider that "they did me damage that has affected my whole life." Rather, they continue, "I am not interested in vengeance or anything like that. To do them harm? No, I feel sorry for them." Nevertheless, the vast majority of informants do not forgive the Bulgarians for their actions; only one from each generation declared forgiveness for them. The reaction for most was, "How can we forgive them? They slaughtered us," and, "Are you kidding? Forgive them? No way!" Indeed, many believe that the issue of compensation for those who suffered and had victims in their families is still valid and timely and that the agreements between the two countries should be reassessed. Among those who profess forgiveness it is observed that this is not a natural inner desire but rather a logical and realistic dictum: "For the sake of having a friendly neighbor"; "Mainly for the reinforcement of peace in the Balkans." It is characteristic that none of our informants had established, or desired to establish, friendly relations with Bulgarians. Only three informants from the first generation and half from the second remark that this was by chance, despite the fact that they had visited the neighboring country for tourism, or for professional or health reasons, while two or three from the second generation had female relatives who married Bulgarians during the occupation (an extremely small percentage). All others are categorical on this issue. They neither want to visit the country, nor do they want any contact with Bulgarians; therefore, to establish friendship would be unthinkable: "Bulgarians? As friends? What on earth are you talking about?"; "I don't even want to see them. A more barbaric people is not to be found under the sun." Some are deliberately more vague; they try to avoid taking a set position on the issue: "When all is said and done, what are the Bulgarians anyway, friends or enemies?" Their own words, however, while attempting to dodge the issue, attest to the fact that the Bulgarians are "enemies," a "different, lower other" worthy of an impersonal and indifferent pitying, a neighbor who fulfills the role of a "necessary evil" and with whom it is preferable not to have too many relations, and by no means, of course, personal relations:

> With the passage of time, we don't keep the hatred we had back then, but of course we continue to consider the Bulgarians as our enemies. We might say today that we are friends, but honestly deep down inside I can't see them in a good light. He's a Bulgarian, he's my enemy. . . . I know very well that they are always thinking about how to take Macedonia from us.

> They hate us Greeks, they are jealous of us because we live better, we are smarter. They can't stand us. Because we are better.

> Now that I see them coming here I feel sorry for them. I don't say "Good, they deserve it." No, I feel sorry for them. I could send them clothes and stuff like that, but if my son told me he was in love with a Bulgarian woman I wouldn't be able to hack it. No, I would suffer very much.

THE LEAST INVOLVED, THE MOST IGNORANT: THE THIRD GENERATION

The third generation consists of people who were born from 1955 on. In general, they were reluctant to converse with us and to answer questions. Most, as if wanting to escape a boring chore, would declare abruptly, "Just write that we know nothing," and would immediately resume their work or their assiduous backgammon playing. Even those who in the end agreed to speak with us stressed beforehand that they knew little, as if begging our pardon. This fact led us to employ in their case a written questionnaire that they could fill out in our absence if they preferred.

It must be remarked from the beginning that the third generation has been raised in a totally different environment from that of all previous generations. The trend toward new occupational possibilities—that is, not exclusively agriculture—and the frequent infusion of internal and external immigrants from 1950 on has created a climate of economic security and prosperity in both villages. The poverty and deprivations of the initial years after the occupation are unknown to the younger generation, which was brought up in an environment replete with consumer goods and comforts. Coupled with the above is the significant factor that this generation grew up during an era of broad exposure to television and cinema. On the one hand, these factors nullified the traditional function of family assemblies and the oral tradition of the village; on the other hand, they trained the young to relegate wars and catastrophes to the level of myth-history and not real history — whether this has to do with true images on the news or television series and movies. This stance of the younger generation is not unrelated to the characteristic complaint of those of the first and second generation that "it all seems to be an American-style movie to them!" This generation, strangers existentially to the struggles and persecution suffered by their parents and grandparents, and only cognizant of the relatively calm period after the fall of the junta in Greece (1974 on), is marked by a political indifference. The third generation regards with condescension or even irony the zeal of their grandparents, their idealism toward the resistance, and their seemingly fanatical patriotism.

Indifference to ideals is interwoven with an indifference to and ignorance of historical events. This generation's knowledge of the occupation, especially regarding its historical origins, is generally limited. Most of them (66 percent of our informants) do not know that the Bulgarian occupation was connected with the Bulgarian alliance with the Axis. Regarding the regime, its administration, its economic, educational, and ecclesiastical organization, and the measures taken by the occupation authorities, half of those questioned knew nothing and the remainder knew little. All, of course, were cognizant of the well-known massacres at Doxato and Choristi, without, however, being able to describe how or why these events actually occurred. But they were observed to possess more knowledge at least on the history of their own families during the occupation, since the information source was to be found in their immediate environment. The vast majority (75 percent) knew of the fate of their family during and after the years of the occupation. The remainder neither knew nor were interested in the fate of their family during that period. Many, indeed, did not even know if some members of their family were among the victims in "Bulgaria I" (1916–1918). The source of their conscious or unconscious knowledge, without exception, was the accounts of their relatives, and only one informant stated that he learned of the occupation at school, while another happened to read something about the Bulgarian occupation. Therefore, one may well conclude that the collective and personal memory, even if fragmented and circumstantial, definitely did leave some mark on the consciousness of this generation as well.

However, at first sight, the occupation not only seems to have had no influence whatsoever on the life of the third generation, but also seems not even to problematize this generation at all existentially. For those of this generation, the events of the occupation belong to a long-lost epoch that has no relevance for contemporary society. It is noteworthy to remark in this context that only two of the informants answered that they often reflect on what it would be like if another occupation were to occur. Nevertheless, the general stance we observed justifies the alienation of the younger generation from the memorial service that is held every year on 29 September. It turns out that none of those who moved to other cities in the years following the occupation participated in these annual memorials any more, and of those who still live in the two villages, only half attend.

The attitude of this generation toward today's Bulgaria is strictly ideological and not emotional. Of course, ideology involves emotion, and the two are often interwoven, but the way in which this third generation regards the Bulgarians is clearly more on the ideological side of the scale. Most informants (80 percent) declare that they do not harbor any prejudice against the Bulgarians, despite the fact that their elders always refer to them as "evil and barbaric." Even the behavior of the authorities during the occupation and the harsh reprisals employed against the Greeks were rationalized, and indeed, the same percentage of those interviewed from this generation declared that "all conquerors do the same anyway." In this case, they suggested the fact that Bulgarians wanted to take over eastern Macedonia and western Thrace as a key to a proper interpretation because "they always wanted an outlet into the Aegean Sea" and because "they always considered Macedonia to be a Bulgarian region." It seems, therefore, that they themselves do not perpetuate the hatred that separated the two peoples for decades. Rather, they are seen to forgive the Bulgarians for the crimes committed by the occupational authorities, regarding rationally the fact that neighboring peoples should have good relations if they are to live peacefully. One of those interviewed even went so far as to declare that the issue of forgiving the Bulgarians is nonexistent; she felt that she was not harmed in any way by them. Another, representing the typical attitude of that generation, stated that the younger generation "has nothing to do with those events," implying that Bulgarians of corresponding age probably share the same view. This positive attitude vis à vis the Bulgarian people is rather typical of the third generation; indeed, it is quite characteristic that, while 50 percent believed that Bulgaria as a state will always harbor designs for the acquisition of Greek Macedonia and Thrace, they also believe that this concerns only official Bulgarian policy and is not representative of the Bulgarian people themselves. Even those who do not forgive the crimes committed by the authorities of the occupation (20 percent) emphasize that this does not imply a vindictive attitude toward the Bulgarians.

Has the younger generation completely rid itself of the stereotypical representations passed down by older generations regarding the neighboring people? This has not occurred to the degree that this generation would like to believe. Twenty percent of those interviewed do not forgive the Bulgarians for the crimes committed during the occupation;

about half of them consider that Bulgaria perpetuates the same designs on Greek territory, and continue to see the Bulgarians as potential conquerors and as "natural enemies." Even in cases where Bulgaria is not considered an "enemy," it continues to be an underrated "Other." Thus, it was not at all uncommon that cases regarding issues of identity and ideology were expressed in the following manner: "I have nothing against the Bulgarians, but it bugs me when the Athenians call us who live up here 'Bulgarians,' " exclaimed one youth from Doxato, referring to the rivalry between the fans of soccer teams from Athens and Macedonia respectively. Regarding friendship and the cultivation of friendly relations with the neighboring people, this is not a spontaneous natural movement as much as it is a practical and realistic demand and a necessity for securing friendly relations between neighboring countries.

From the above, one can certainly conclude that the younger generation finds itself in a perplexing position. It is groping to comprehend the issues surrounding Bulgarian occupation rationally and realistically, it is trying to transcend the scars of the past, but, deep inside, the past is present and leaves its mark here and now. Within the memory of this generation, despite its sparsity, there exist recollections of accounts of the occupation. The stronger and clearer of these are the recollections from the personal trials of their families during the occupation. The official ritual for the expression of this collective memory is annually present, regardless of the fact that half do not attend any more. Most try to combine the need to preserve the past in honor of those who were lost or suffered with the need to live a different kind of present and future with the same neighboring people. Characteristic of all this is the following declaration of a representative member of that generation:

> I do not forgive them [referring to the Bulgarians] for all that has occurred. This fact, however, should not become an obstacle for cooperation in cases where they have good intentions. The past cannot be erased and we would be guilty of grave ingratitude to do such a thing, at least towards those who were lost, suffered or suffer to this day. For, regarding those who lost their loved ones, I believe that the occupation has not terminated yet because their memory is very alive. Despite all this, however, practical needs demand that we cultivate friendly relations and that we separate the aggressors of the past from today's Bulgarians. Let me put it this way: if nothing else, when we act in this way at least we are serving our national interest.

CONCLUDING REMARKS

Our work traces the scars that even a brief occupation leaves behind, as well as the consequences these experiences have on the socioeconomic life of the individuals involved and on the community to which they belong. It also sheds light on the way in which the individual and the community recuperate from or simply cope with the scars of occupation.

The subjective memories of the informants of the first and second generation led to the formation of a collective memory and remembrance of the occupation that produced the following dominant opinion of this occupation: it was harsh and unjust, it was brought to bear by barbarian enemies, its goal — which was achieved — was to destroy them biologically, economically, and socially. Along with this, the collective memory of successive Bulgarian occupations has contributed to the creation and cultivation of a particular local ethnic ideology. This ideology is seen to be characterized mainly by an emphasis on the purity and genuineness of the Greek identity of the inhabitants as well as the glorification and martyrization of the locality and the people themselves. For some, the locality in question was only their own village, either Choristi or Doxato; for others, it was the prefecture of Drama; for still others, it was the whole of eastern Macedonia. In any case, regardless of the specific interpretation of the "locality," that "locality" is invariably identified with the "promised land" coveted by the Bulgarian enemies. Within this view, the traditional, native inhabitants of this land, the Greeks, are those who must be exterminated, they are the object of enmity, hatred, and the physical manifestations of these attitudes: persecutions and executions. Onto this is added the collective consciousness of the wronged, the concept of the innocent victim, which was seen to be widely conceptualized in the interviews as the "slaughter" of 1941. This is clearly seen to parallel the greatest symbol of innocence and sacrifice in the Greek folk tradition: the "lamb-sheep," Jesus Christ ("They gathered us like sheep to *Giola*"; "In herds and flocks, like sheep they gathered the men and slaughtered them"). Within this collective consciousness, the negative ethno-cultural stereotypes that have already been formed regarding the neighboring people and nation — which are perceived as being absolutely "fitting" for them — are strengthened. These stereotypes, however, exist mainly as a kind of gut instinct for personal and ethnic survival. Because of this, it is not surprising that they can coexist with a humanism that neutralizes any feelings of hatred or vengeance against that neighboring people.

The third generation, unacquainted with personal and collective experiences of the occupation, for all practical purposes has no part in the memories that come from the occupation. Indeed, they even maintain a rather supercilious attitude regarding the emotions evoked in the previous generations by experiences and memories of the occupation. Despite this, they preserve many of the same ethno-cultural stereotypes regarding the Bulgarians. These attitudes, cut off from their context of origin, have the potential to constitute the basis and background for the cultivation of naive, generalized prejudices that could evolve, under the proper circumstances, into an irrational fanaticism, the more so because this generation is unprepared for such circumstances.

The annual religious memorials, the visits to the graveyards, the ceremonial placing of wreaths in honor of the victims of the occupation, the public recitation of their names, the giving of commemorative speeches with a heroic-martyrological air on the events of the occupation, all constitute an institutionalized form of collective memory on the national and religious level. They also constitute a tangible public manifestation of collective memory that increases its power and guarantees its maintenance and duration to a greater or lesser degree within the individual and collective subconscious of all generations. This is so despite the fact that the bearers of this experience — the representatives of the first and second generations — will ultimately depart the scene, for these memories will still remain, albeit in the form of trite official national observances.

These factors concerning a population that has suffered three times in this century due to the policies of the same neighbor can explain in part why history still plays such a crucial role in the volatile region of the Balkans, which in the twentieth century evolved and continues to evolve as an amalgam of ethnic and national competitions among the various peoples of the peninsula.

NOTES

1. Useful from among the vast scholarly literature on this subject were R. Hirschon-Filippaki, "Mnimi kai tautotita: Oi Mikrasiates prosphyges tis Kokkinias," in A. Papataxiarchis, ed., *Anthropologia kai Parelthon: Symvoles stin koinoniki istoria tis neoteris Elladas* (Athens, 1993), 327–56; Anna Collard, "Dierevnontas tin koinoniki mnimi ston elladiko choro," in ibid., 357–89; D. Nugent, "Anthropology: Hand-Maiden of History?" *Critique of Anthropology* 15.2 (Sept. 1985): 71–86; A. Bravo, "Myth, Impotence and Survival in the Concentration Camps," in R. Samuel and P. Thompson, eds., *The Myths We Live By* (London, 1990), 95–110; Popular Memory Group, "Popular Memory: Theory, Politics, Method," in *Making Histories — Studies in History-Making and Politics* (London, 1982), 205–52; N. Wachtel, "Introduction: Memory and History," *History and Anthropology* 2 (1986): 207–26.

2. For the relation between individual and collective memories, see Wachtel, "Introduction," 215, 220.

3. Tassos Hadjianastassiou is preparing his doctoral thesis on the Greek resistance movement against the Bulgarians in the area during the occupation.

4. Choristi and Doxato, two large villages that, during the period of our study, were rather well-developed economically and culturally, are 5 and 10 kilometers southeast respectively from the capital of the prefecture of Drama.

5. Doxato was fired upon by the Bulgarian army, which was retreating in the face of the advance of the Greek army, during the Second Balkan War on 13 July 1913, and many inhabitants, including women and children, were slaughtered. During World War I, from 1916 to 1918, when the region was put under Bulgarian occupation, most men from Doxato and Choristi were held hostage in Bulgaria, where most were wiped out by abuse, hunger, or illness. Some Doxatians returned, although of the 525 hostages of Choristi, fewer than fifty returned; thus one or more member from each family was lost. Characteristic of the scars upon personal and collective consciousness provoked by these events are the renderings in various demotic songs written during that era, mainly by women (wives, mothers, and sisters) who were left behind. For more on this, see *Bulgarian Cruelty in Eastern Macedonia and Thrace, 1912–1913* (Athens 1914) (in Greek); American Red Cross Commission to Greece, *The Typhus Epidemic in Eastern Macedonia by Major Samuel J. Walker* (Athens, 1919); *Rapports et enquêtes de la commission interalliée sur les violations du droit des gens commises en Macédoine Orientale par les armées bulgares* (Nancy-Paris and Strasburg, 1919); Ministère des Affaires Etrangères et des Cultes, *La vérité sur les accusations contre la Bulgarie*, vol. 2, (Sofia, 1913).

6. At this juncture, the support of Dimitrios Paschalides must be especially emphasized. This leading historian of the region has personal and familial ties in both villages. He treated this research project as if it were his own personal issue and thus graciously put at our disposal his knowledge, connections, and homes in Doxato and Choristi.

7. I.e., the insurrection provoked by the local branch of the KKE (Communist Party of Greece) of Drama that occurred there and in the vicinity on 28–29 September 1941. The revolt broke out initially in Doxato, where Greeks from there and from neighboring Choristi attacked and fired upon the police station, killing six or seven Bulgarian policemen. In Choristi, other rebels recruited men and set off toward the mountains. This insurrection was bloodily suppressed. All its leaders were killed either in battle or in their attempt to escape by passing through German-occupied Greece. Bulgarian retaliations were especially harsh and were borne by those who had nothing to do with the insurrection, since the instigators had fled to the mountains. In Doxato, 350 men, divided into tens, were executed on the night of 29 September; in Choristi on 30 September, 135 men were executed in a ditch outside the village. After the revolt, a period of terrorism and asphyxiating control began in both villages: arrests, house searches, physical violence against the citizens.

8. Janissaries were members of the Ottoman soldier corps who were seized from the local Christian population when they were between eight and fourteen years old and brought up as Muslims loyal to the Sultan.

9. This is similar to what Anna Bravo describes as "the personal urge to remember and also to forget," or "the recounting self still confronting the suffering self" (Bravo, "Myth, Impotence and Survival," 98).

FOURTEEN

"An Affair of Politics, Not Justice": The Merten Trial (1957–1959) and Greek-German Relations

Susanne-Sophia Spiliotis

"AN AFFAIR of politics, not justice" was how the West German Foreign Ministry in the summer of 1957 characterized the impending prosecution in Greece of a German citizen, Maximilian Merten.[1] Why did the prosecution of Merten produce a contradiction between justice and politics? This question lies at the heart of my analysis. I should clarify at the outset that I do not propose once again to rehearse the question of Merten's personal responsibility and guilt, to undertake, in other words, a theoretical recapitulation of the trial. Rather, I wish to analyze the significance of the Merten affair and, more generally, the question of war crimes in the context of Greco-German relations after the war.[2]

During the occupation, Merten, then a lawyer, had served as military administrator for Thessaloniki, chiefly responsible for the provisioning and administration of the city. He carried out his duties in a high-handed and arbitrary manner, and seemed to the city's inhabitants to sit at the summit of the German hierarchy, or at least somewhere high up. He was nicknamed the "King of Thessaloniki" and "Ruler of the City," though in fact this exaggerated his real position.[3]

In the spring of 1943, collaborating with Adolf Eichmann's special envoys Dieter Wisliceny and Alois Brunner, Merten prepared the deportation of the Jews of Thessaloniki, within the framework of the so-called final solution of the Jewish question. He signed orders for the confiscation of Jewish property, for the marking of Greek Jews, and for their confinement in ghettoes. There is evidence that he benefited illegally from the wealth that the deportees left behind.[4] This aside, he was firm in his anticommunist beliefs, and from 1943 supported right-wing organizations such as the PAO (Panhellenic Liberation Organisation).

After the end of the war, Merten was arrested by the Americans in occupied Germany. In 1946, the U.S. authorities proposed to surrender him to the Greek government in accordance with a 1943 agreement among the Allies that provided for the handing over of war criminals to those countries where they had committed their crimes.[5] Yet even though the legal authorities were already enquiring after Merten, especially among German and Bulgarian war criminals, the Greek government did not want to receive him.

The Greek military envoy in Berlin (and later ambassador to Bonn), General Andreas Ypsilantis, actually intervened with the U.S. occupation authorities in Germany to suggest that Merten be set free, emphasizing his "blameless conduct" and the "valuable services" that he had provided to Greece during the German occupation![6] It is obvious that the contacts that Merten had made during the occupation in Thessaloniki with leading Greek circles, contacts to which he himself would later allude repeatedly, now became useful. And as these contacts concerned the future Greek Prime Minister Konstantine Karamanlis, Minister of Defense Themelis, and Interior Minister Makris, they were potentially explosive for Greek political life, carrying the suspicion and even accusations of widespread collaboration. Let us note here that Merten would also hint at his knowledge of the activities of German political leaders during the war, accusing, for example, Hans Globke, Konrad Adenauer's close collaborator, of active involvement in the persecution of the Jews.[7]

Without being further inconvenienced by what he had done during the war, Merten managed — like many of his compatriots — to begin a new career in postwar Germany. He worked for a time in the German Ministry of Justice and dabbled in politics. Together with the future president of West Germany, Gustav Heinemann, in 1952 he founded a political party that opposed Adenauer's policy of accepting the permanence of the division of Germany in the interest of West Germany's links with the West.[8]

A desire not to touch its sensitive Nazi past constituted one of the foundations of the politico-social ideology of postwar Germany. For the sake of domestic tranquility, Adenauer urged his compatriots to avoid polarizing or categorizing society into those who were politically blameless and those who were tainted. He sought to restrict the prosecution to "those who were genuinely guilty."[9] On the basis of such criteria, Merten was evidently *not* regarded as "genuinely guilty."

But in Greece, too, the so-called pacification of society was a basic concern of liberal governments. The bloody decade of the war, occupation, and civil war had deepened political divisions. War and civil war had destroyed the economy to such a degree that without foreign support, the country faced a problem of subsistence. In order to stabilize the situation, therefore, and secure social peace, two preconditions needed to be satisfied. First, the political schism had to be bridged, by bringing the forces of the Left back into the mainstream of politics. The Cold War, however, limited the room for maneuver in domestic policy.[10] Indeed, the official anticommunism of postwar Greek governments blocked efforts to overcome the impact of extremism, as was illustrated by the well-known conservative slogan, "Karamanlis or Communism." Second, economic reconstruction had to take place. After the Marshall Plan ended in 1951, the importance of West Germany as a dynamic economic factor for the Greek policy of stabilization became ever more evident. On this point, postwar circles in Greece were agreed. According to their logic, social peace in Greece depended upon economic stabilization — and indirectly, therefore, upon good relations with Germany as well.

So we should not be astonished to find that the important 1952 law "On Measures of Pacification," which aimed at the social reincorporation of left-wing forces — understood, naturally, to be those which complied with strict criteria of "national-mindedness" — also encompassed the regulation of the question of war criminals.[11]

From the first moment of the resumption of diplomatic relations between Greece and Germany in December 1950, the war-crimes issue required special handling. German diplomacy expressed the opinion that "the harmonious opening up of relations between the two countries requires a general, swift, and so far as possible noiseless settlement of the war crimes question."[12]

Already, however, the Greek War Crimes Office, headed by the director of public prosecutions, Andreas Toussis, had prepared roughly 900 cases against Germans on charges of war crimes committed in Greece. The Greek "pacification" law provided as a possible remedy, and "to facilitate prosecution," that the prosecution of war crimes in Greece could be suspended on the condition that the appropriate legal authorities in Germany undertook their own prosecution of the accused.[13] It should be emphasized that the final decision to suspend prosecution in Greece, even though linked to the initiation of a German prosecution, remained a matter for Greek justice. Upon this legal basis, Greek war crimes files on German suspects were handed over in 1952 and 1956 to the German Justice Ministry.

But the German authorities did not make much headway, and failed to live up to their obligation with regard to Greek justice: they simply left the files closed, so that the suspension of prosecution in Greece lost its justification, as the Greek director of public prosecutions, Toussis, emphasized more than once. However, the Bonn authorities believed that unofficially the Greek government had indicated in April 1952 that the question of war criminals had been definitively settled with the handing over of the files to Germany, hoping thereby to "put an end to any possible outstanding impediments to the resumption of the old traditional friendship between the two countries." Greek policy, in other words, did not hesitate to violate the spirit of the law for the sake of good relations with Germany and for the economic benefits that might accrue. It appears that the Germans never bothered with the way they themselves had ignored their formal obligations to a small Mediterranean country.[14]

In 1955–1956 the whole problem of reconciling justice and political expediency came to a head. West Germany regained "full power of sovereignty" by the terms of the May 1955 peace treaties and, with renewed international prestige, believed it could persuade the Karamanlis government to settle the still-unresolved war-crimes issue with a general amnesty.[15] At just that time, however, the political scene in Greece had been transformed by the remergence of the Left as a substantial political force for the first time since the civil war. Karamanlis won the 1956 general elections but was forced to come to terms with the Left's new power. Under these conditions, acquiescing to the German request would have put the Karamanlis government in a difficult position. Declaring an amnesty would have presupposed a debate in Parliament, and this would have provided the opposition with an opportunity not merely for reviving memories of the occupation, but for bringing to the surface matters relating to the Right's collaborationist past, something that would, in the words of the German ambassador in Athens, Theodor Kordt, "from one side have been unpleasant for the Greek government and from the other have been negative for German interests."[16] It was, moreover, very likely that the opposition would exploit the situation to criticize the general political orientation of the government toward the West, a highly debated choice, which would thereupon come to seem responsible for, or at least closely connected to, the violation of legal obligations and the humiliation of national sentiment.[17]

By way of summary, then, one might say that neither the Greek nor the German side showed much interest in a judicial approach to the issue. Their chief concern was how to bring about a constitutional resolution — in other words, "clearing up" the matter politically — with as little fuss and as few repercussions as possible.

Toward the end of 1956, a "Greek solution" was found: if Germany provided compensation to the victims of war crimes, an amnesty might be more easily carried through.[18] Bonn, however, rejected this idea, referring to the 1953 Treaty of London, which stated that the fulfillment of material claims arising out of the war was to await a general peace treaty.[19] This presupposed Germany's reunification, which seemed unlikely to take place in the near future. Quite apart from that argument, the German government, relying upon its reading of unofficial assurances from Athens, held that Greece was bound anyway to suspend legal action against war criminals, irrespective of the question of compensation.[20]

In the spring of 1957 Toussis, the Greek director of public prosecutions, responded to German inaction by warning that he would be forced to resume the investigation of German war criminals.[21] Just then, in April, Maximilian Merten traveled to Athens, where he planned to appear as witness in a civil case involving an old acquaintance, his wartime interpreter Arthur Meissner. Before appearing in front of the Greek examining magistrate, Merten visited the legal section of the German embassy to confirm that his appearance would not have unforeseen consequences for himself. Reassured, he presented himself before the magistrate, gave his statement, and was arrested on the spot. Toussis confirmed that his arrest was amply warranted.

Strong protests from Germany, both at Merten's arrest and at Toussis's decision to activate the prosecution of Germans charged of crimes in Greece, did not bear the desired results. The exiguous data that the German Ministry of Justice provided to demonstrate the considerable efforts of German justice to prosecute German war criminals failed to help. The German embassy in Athens actually refused to convey the results to the Greek judicial authorities, commenting that these initiatives "reveal the lack of seriousness of German justice in prosecuting war criminals and damage its credibility."[22] The flow of events could no longer be stopped. Hopes of a "silent clean-up" were receding fast as the Merten affair became more publicly discussed and the list of charges Merten faced lengthened. He was now accused not only of participation in the extermination of the Jewish community of Thessaloniki but also of reprisals against the civilian population, a charge that at that time weighed more heavily in the public consciousness than any other. Despite the strenuous efforts of Germans in the diplomatic arena, Merten remained incarcerated for nearly two years in the Averoff prison in Athens, and only at the end of 1958 did there appear once more the possibility of a political and legislative resolution of the issue.[23]

In the context of Greco-German economic negotiations, Bonn linked its desire to support Greece economically with a benevolent outcome of the whole war-crimes issue, including specifically the Merten case.[24] In a confidential annex to the economic agreement of 13 November 1958, Karamanlis promised German Chancellor Adenauer that Greece would suspend all prosecutions and hand Merten over to Germany.[25]

So far as Merten was concerned, however, this promise could not be immediately realized, as public opinion in Greece had become very sensitive.[26] Lawyers for Jewish civil plaintiffs were prominent in the political opposition; the case against Merten had assumed the form of an attack on the character of the Karamanlis government itself. The compliant attitude of the Right toward the Germans could easily be presented as a continuation of wartime collaborationism. In this explosive climate, at the beginning of 1959, the silent surrender of Merten to

Germany would have amounted to a silent admission of guilt by leading members of the Greek government. Thus Merten's trial in Greece could no longer be avoided. By way of consolation, Karamanlis promised the Germans that he would at least influence the composition of the special military court. He also promised — and this was even more important — to grant amnesty to Merten and to hand him over to Germany, as soon after the trial as conditions permitted.[27]

At last, on 11 February 1959, Merten's trial opened in Athens with substantial international interest. From the very first day, the president of the special military court, Colonel Kokretsas, decreed the exclusion of civil plaintiffs in an effort to avoid the further politicization of the matter. The main object of the trial became Merten's contribution to the extermination of the Jewish community of Thessaloniki.

His defense was organized by the German Foreign Ministry, which had a legal office largely devoted to such tasks. Minimizing his own role, Merten planted responsibility for the so-called final solution of the Jewish question in Europe exclusively upon the Nazi leadership, in particular upon the chain of command Hitler-Himmler-Heydrich-Eichmann. According to this interpretation, Merten was only a functionary, without the power of initiative and consequently without responsibility.[28] On 5 March 1959, nearly two years after his arrival in Athens, Merten was sentenced to twenty-five years — five years more than the prosecution had suggested.

Merten was acquitted of the charge of having ordered reprisals against the civilian population, but found guilty and heavily sentenced for the killing of five Jews, including three small children; for the terror he had imposed; and for the ghettoization of Thessaloniki's Jews and their deportation to Poland. Among other charges, he was also found guilty of the forced labor imposed on the Jews and for the destruction of the Jewish cemetery.[29] Merten's punishment was intended to assuage public opinion by showing the willingness of the Greek state to punish war criminals severely. This was the image that the Karamanlis government wished to project. We know, however, that at the very same moment, Merten's amnesty had been decided. Karamanlis had never planned to hold Merten in a Greek jail. He was simply awaiting the appropriate, favorable circumstances for his release.[30] The start of negotiations in May 1959 between West Germany and Greece on the question of compensation to the latter finally gave the government the opportunity to solve the Merten affair.

Greek and German negotiators differed, naturally, on how to define the beneficiaries of any reparation payments. The former wished to include civilian victims of reprisals. It was commonly felt that the compensation of this category of victims would redound to the credit of the government and counterbalance the unfortunate impression created by its desire to put an end to the punishment of war criminals. Bonn, on the other hand, referred solely to the victims of the so-called persecution for racial, religious, or ideological reasons, thus—in the Greek context—signifying chiefly the Jews. The compensation of this category of victims had been already agreed to by West Germany with sixteen European states, whose citizens had been the victims of racial persecution.[31] At first sight, these agreements constituted an exception to the rule according to which German compensation for material claims arising out of the war would only be handled after a peace treaty had been signed. However, Germany accepted that these victims had suffered from the ideology of National Socialism rather than from the war itself, and should thus be compensated in advance of a peace treaty.

At the same time, following a visit by a group of opposition Greek MPs, East Germany proposed offering reparations to Greece that, unlike those offered by West Germany, would chiefly concern the victims of reprisals.[32] East Berlin was, of course, actuated by its own interests. According to international law, the payment of compensation constituted a deed between two states. At that time, East Germany was not internationally recognized in the West, while for its part West Germany threatened to cut off diplomatic relations with any state that extended recognition to its eastern neighbor.[33] For Greece to accept East German reparations would thus threaten a breach of relations with Bonn and pose problems for the NATO alliance as a whole. Athens and Bonn had to react fast to forestall the political and psychological benefits that would otherwise accrue to the Greek opposition on the one hand, and to East Germany on the other. In March 1960, the two nations signed a reparations agreement.[34]

By this time Merten was at large in Germany. A few months earlier, on 3 November 1959, a decree had come into force with the euphemistic title "On the Modification of the Legislation on War Crimes."[35] This allowed the government to wrap up the Merten affair without having to term this an amnesty, and on 5 November, Merten left unnoticed from the Athens airport for Germany. Legal action against him in Germany was at once suspended, and formally terminated in 1968, partly because of a lack of evidence but also because of a statute of limitations.[36] He received compensation from the German government for time spent in Greek prisons; he died in 1976.

Hannah Arendt characterized the Merten trial in 1961 as "unique because trials of war crimes ended in all countries except in Greece in very heavy sentences."[37] In her view, one reason for this exceptionalism was the indifference of the Greeks to the fate of their Jewish compatriots.

Arendt could hardly at that time have been aware of the political background to the Merten affair. The relevant archives were only opened in 1990. From these it appears that the contradictions between justice and politics that characterized the development of the Merten affair cannot solely be explained in terms of Greek "indifference." These contradictions were, on the contrary, the product of conscious policy. It is obvious that political and economic interests, both Greek and German, defined the manner in which the Merten case was handled, and more generally, the question of war crimes in postwar Greek-German relations.

NOTES

1. BA/ZWA B 141/966, s142, Aufzeichnung (Kanter) vom 25.7 1957.
2. Despite its political significance, the Merten affair has been neglected by scholarly research. The broader subject of the punishment of German war crimes in Greece has apparently been dealt with only superficially and on the basis of secondary sources. See A. Rückerl, *NS-Verbrechen vor Gericht. Versuch einer Vergangenheitsbewältigung* (Heidelberg, 1984), 296ff. Only since 1990 has it been possible for scholars to gain access to the relevant German archives of the *Zentrale Rechtsschutzstelle*. This study is based on extensive research in Greek and German archives: Archeion Efeteiou Athinon: Dikografia tou Merten; Bundesarchiv Koblenz BA, Zentrale Rechtsschutzstelle: Rechtsschutzsache Dr. Merten (b305–1041ff); Bundesarchiv-Zwischenarchiv Hengelar (BA/ZWA); Bundesjustizministerium, Kriegsverbrecherprozesse Griechenland (b141/9563–9573); Bundesfinanzministerium/Altablage; Wiedergutmachungsvertrag Griechenland (VB/4-01470 D-grie, Heft 1); Politisches Archiv des Auswärtigen Amtes, Bonn (PAAA), Institut für Zeitgeschichte, München; Zentrale Stelle der Landesjustizverwaltungen, Ludwigsburg: Dr. Max Merten (V 508 AR-z 139/9, I–III).
3. Archeio Efeteiou Athinon, Dikografia tou Merten, pp. xii–2, deposition of the witness Nikolaou Hassid, Thessaloniki, 20 May 1957. See also depositions of witnesses in German translation in BA/B 305-1102f, Handakte Matsoukas.
4. See BA/B 305-1041, Schmoller (German Embassy, Athens) to Foreign Ministry, 16 May 1957.
5. This refers to the *Declaration of German Atrocities* in the context of the foreign ministers' meeting (United States, Great Britain, and the Soviet Union) in Moscow, 29 Oct. 1943. See Department of State, *Foreign Relations of the United States* (Washington, D.C., 1943), 1:768ff.
6. See BA/B 305-1041, Ypsilantis — Spruchkammer Bad Aibling, 11 Nov. 1947; BA/B 305-1048, Merten-Dr.Vogel, 25 May 1958; Archeio Efeteiou Athinon, Dikografia tou Merten, 5a, 7a, 8a, 9a, 10a; Institut für Zeitgeschichte, München, Eichmann Vernehmung, bl.36, Interrogation Merten, 8 June 1961.
7. *Der Speigel* 40 (1960): 5ff.; 12 (1962): 9.

8. The party was the *Gesamtdeutsche Volkspartei* (All-German People's Party).

9. See the statement by Chancellor Adenauer, 20 Sept. 1949, in *Regierungserklärungen, 1949–1973* (Berlin and New York, 1973), 21.

10. I refer here above all to the Truman Doctrine of March 1947.

11. Law 2058, 18 April 1952, "On Measures of Pacification," *Government Gazette* (1952), Chapter E, "On War Crimes," paras. 20–24.

12. PAAA, Abteilung 3, Band I 515-10/23, Trützschler (Auswärtiges Amt)-Bundesminister für den Marshall-Plan, 16 Aug. 1951. Grundherr (West German ambassador in Greece)-Auswärtiges Amt, Bonn, n.d.

13. Law 208/1952, para. 21.1.

14. See the Greco-German exchange of memoranda, 28 Apr.–3 May 1952, in BA/ZWA: B 141/9573, Denkschrift der Zentralen Rechtsschutzstelle vom 2 March 1959, Anlagen 10 and 11, pp. 181ff.

15. See I. von München, ed., *Dokumente des geteilten Deutschland* (Stuttgart, 1968), 230.

16. BA/ZWA, B 141/9564, p. 17, Auswärtiges Amt (Bonn)-Botschaft der BRD, Athens, 22 July 1955; ibid., Kordt (Athens)-Bonn, 14 Nov. 1955; ibid., BMJ-Vermerk (Grützner), 30 Sept. 1955.

17. BA/ZWA B 141/9564, pp. 34ff., Kordt (Athens)-Bonn, 14 Nov. 1955.

18. BA/ZWA B 141/9566, pp. 10ff, Aide-Memoire of the Greek Foreign Ministry, 27 Nov. 1956; ibid., Kanter note, 7 Aug. 1957, on conversations in Athens with, among others, Public Prosecutor Toussis on the Merten case, 22–31 Mar. 1957.

19. Law 3480/7 Jan. 1956. On the 1953 London Agreement on German foreign debts, see Greek *Government Gazette*, A'6 (1953): 196; and C. Buchheim, "Das Londoner Schuldenabkommen," in L. Herbst, ed., *Westdeutschland, 1945–55* (Munich, 1986), 219–29

20. See note 14 above.

21. BA/ZWA B 141/9566, pp. 19ff.; Kanter (Federal Justice Ministry)-Athens, 23 May 1957; also ibid., pp. 132ff., Justice Ministry memorandum to Cabinet, 2 July 1956.

22. BA/ZWA B 141/9566, pp. 30ff; Kordt-Bonn, 6 Apr. 1957.

23. BA/ZWA B 141/9568, p. 135, Schmoller (Athens)-Bonn, 8 Nov. 1958.

24. PAAA Referat 206, Band 134, Memorandum, Zentrale Rechtsschutzstelle, 25 Sept. 1958.

25. BA/ZWA B 141/9568, pp. 137–44, Justice Ministry notes, 18 Nov. 1958; BA/ZWA B 141/9573, pp. 26ff., Seelos (Athens)-Bonn, 11 Dec. 1958.

26. BA/ZWA B 141/9573, p. 33, German Ambassador (Athens)-Bonn, 4 Jan. 1959.

27. PAAA Referat 206, Band 134, Seelos (Athens)-Bonn, 5 Jan. 1959.

28. PAAA Referat 206, Band 134, Walters an Zentrale Rechtsschutzstelle, 31 Jan. 1959.

29. PAAA Referat 206, Band 134, Schmoller (Athens)-Bonn, 6 Mar. 1959.

30. PAAA Referat 206, Band 134, Observations of the Foreign Ministry on Comments by the Greek Ambassador in Bonn, Ypsilantis, 23 Apr. 1959.

31. See chiefly BMF VB/4-01470 D Griechenland Wiedergutmachungsvertrag, vol. 1.

32. These were the Liberal MP E. Korthis and the Progressive E. Savvopoulos. See *Kathimerini*, 3 March 1959.

33. The so-called Hallstein Doctrine.

34. See Law 4178/14 Aug. 1961.

35. Law 4016/3 Nov. 1959.

36. See *Der Spiegel*, no. 32 (1961).

37. H. Arendt, *Eichmann in Jerusalem* (Munich and Zurich, 1987), 231.

Contributors

RIKI VAN BOESCHOTEN is a historical researcher who works for the Council of Ministers of the European Union. She has published *From Armatolik to People's Rule: Investigation into the Collective Memory of Rural Greece, 1750–1949* (Amsterdam: Adolf Hakkert, 1991) and a full-length study of the village of Ziakas between 1900 and 1950, *Anapoda chronia: Syllogiki mnimi kai istoria sto Ziaka Grevenon (1900–1950)* (Athens: Plethron, 1997).

MANDO DALIANIS was a child psychiatrist with the Child and Adolescent Psychiatric Unit of the Karolinska Institute, Stockholm. She published *Children in Turmoil during the Greek Civil War, 1946–49: Today's Adults* (Stockholm: Karolinska Institutet, 1994). In 1949–50 she was imprisoned in the Averoff Women's Prison, Athens, where she began the work that culminated more than four decades later in the above publication.

ELENI HAIDIA is a researcher at the Institute for Balkan Studies in Thessaloniki. She has published several articles on problems of justice after the war and completed a thesis on the special collaborators' courts set up in Thessaloniki in 1945.

STATHIS N. KALYVAS is Assistant Professor of Politics at New York University. He is the author of *The Rise of Christian Democracy in Europe* (Ithaca, N.Y.: Cornell University Press, 1996). His current research explores the dynamics and logic of violence in civil wars. His most recent publication on this topic is "Wanton and Senseless? The Logic of Massacres in Algeria," *Rationality and Society* (1999).

ANASTASIA KARAKASIDOU is Assistant Professor of Anthropology at Wellesley College. She is the author of *Fields of Wheat, Hills of Blood: Passages to Nationhood in Greek Macedonia, 1870–1990* (Chicago: University of Chicago Press, 1997).

XANTHIPPI KOTZAGEORGI-ZYMARI is a researcher at the Institute of Balkan Studies in Thessaloniki, where she has been supervising a research project on collective memory and the history of the Bulgarian occupation of eastern Macedonia, with the assistance of Tassos Hadjianastassiou.

BEA LEWKOWICZ is an anthropologist completing her doctorate at the London School of Economics on the ethnography of Jewish life in postwar Thessaloniki.

MARK MAZOWER is Anniversary Professor of History, Birkbeck College, London. He has written *Greece and the Interwar Economic Crisis* (Oxford: Oxford University Press, 1991), *Inside Hitler's Greece: The Experience of Occupation, 1941–1944* (New Haven and London: Yale University Press, 1993), and *Dark Continent: Europe's Twentieth Century* (London: Penguin, 1998).

PROCOPIS PAPASTRATIS is Professor of History at Panteion University, Athens. He is the author of *British Policy towards Greece during the Second World War, 1941–1944* (Cambridge: Cambridge University Press, 1984).

JOHN SAKKAS received his Ph.D. degree from the Department of Economic and Social History at Hull University in Hull in 1993. He is the author of *I EAMiki Antistasi, 1941–1944* (Athens: Papazisi, 1998. He is currently teaching history and politics in the Department of Mediterranean Studies at the University of the Aegean in Rhodes.

LEE SARAFIS is completing a doctorate at the University of Sussex on oral history and the civil war in the village of Deskati, where she has been carrying out fieldwork for some years.

SUSANNE-SOPHIA SPILIOTIS wrote her master's thesis on the Merten affair and is the author of *Transterritorialitaet und Nationale Abgrenzung: Konstitutionsprozesse der griechischen Gesellschaft und Ansaetze ihrer faschistoiden Transformation, 1922/24–1941* (Munich: Oldenbourg, 1998).

TASSOULA VERVENIOTI is the author of *I gynaika tis Antistasi: I eisodos ton gynaikon stin politiki* (Athens: Odysseas, 1994), a study of women in the wartime resistance. She is currently researching questions of women's history in the period 1944–1955.

POLYMERIS VOGLIS wrote his doctoral dissertation at the European University Institute on political prisoners in Greece in the late 1940s. He is Postdoctoral Fellow in Hellenic Studies at Princeton University.

Index